Decentralised Governance
Crafting Effective Democracies
Around the World

Edited by
Jean-Paul Faguet and Sarmistha Pal

 Press

Published by
LSE Press
10 Portugal Street
London WC2A 2HD
press.lse.ac.uk

First published 2023

Cover design by Diana Jarvis

Print and digital versions typeset by Siliconchips Services Ltd.

ISBN (Paperback): 978-1-909890-84-8
ISBN (PDF): 978-1-909890-85-5
ISBN (EPUB): 978-1-909890-86-2
ISBN (Mobi): 978-1-909890-87-9

DOI: https://doi.org/10.31389/lsepress.dlg

The full text of this book has been peer-reviewed to ensure high academic standards. For our full publishing ethics policies, see https://press.lse.ac.uk

Suggested citation:
Faguet, Jean-Paul and Pal, Sarmistha (eds) (2023) *Decentralised Governance: Crafting Effective Democracies Around the World*, London: LSE Press. https://doi.org/10.31389/lsepress.dlg License: CC BY 4.0

To read the free, open access version of this book online, visit https://doi.org/10.31389/lsepress.dlg or scan this QR code with your mobile device:

Contents

Extended contents

PART 2: POLITICS

4. Realising the promise of partial decentralisation

5. Devolution under autocracy: evidence from Pakistan

6. Social fragmentation, public goods, and local elections: evidence from China

List of figures and tables

Figures

Tables

Further figures are published in the book's supplementary materials for chapters 5, 6, 8, 10, and 11, published on LSE Press's Zenodo community site. See https://zenodo.org/communities/decentralised_governance/

About the editors

Jean-Paul Faguet is professor of the political economy of development, Department of International Development, London School of Economics and Political Science. He is the co-programme director of the MSc in Development Management. He is also chair of the Decentralization Task Force at Columbia University's Initiative for Policy Dialogue. He works at the frontier between economics and political science, using quantitative and qualitative methods to investigate the institutions and organisational forms that underpin development transformations. He has published in the economics, political science, and development literatures, including *Is Decentralization Good for Development? Perspectives from Academics and Policymakers* (Oxford, 2015) and *Governance from Below: Decentralization and Popular Democracy in Bolivia* (Michigan), which won the W.J.M. Mackenzie Prize for best political science book of 2012.

Sarmistha Pal is professor of financial economics at the University of Surrey. In the past, she served as a research fellow at the Department of Applied Economics, University of Cambridge, research affiliate at the Centre for the Study of African Economies, University of Oxford, and also a Leverhulme research fellow in the United Kingdom. Currently, she works as a research fellow at the IZA- Institute of Labour Economics in Bonn (Germany), and is also an academic member of the European Corporate Governance Institute. Additionally, she serves as an editorial board member for the *Journal of Development Studies*. Pal's research primarily focuses on public finance, public policy, institutions, and political economy, with a particular emphasis on emerging economies. As an applied economist, she conducts empirical analysis to examine the impact of various laws, social policies, corporate practices, as well as public policies on economic outcomes for different entities such as individuals, households, firms, banks, and communities. She employs various quasi-experimental methods in her research.

About the authors

Farzana Afridi is an associate professor of economics at the Indian Statistical Institute in Delhi. Her main area of research is in development and labour economics. Her current research interests include female labour force participation, the design of public programmes in developing countries, and the effects of social identities on labour productivity.

Daniel Chachu is currently a PhD student at the Department of Economics, University of Ghana. He has visited UNU-WIDER and also the Department of Economics, University of Zurich. Daniel's research focuses on development economics and public economics.

Valentina Chegwin is an economist and graduate research assistant at the Columbia Population Research Center. Valentina conducts research on early childhood development, education, health, and economic inequality in relation to social policy design, with a focus on developing countries. Before joining Columbia, Valentina worked as a research assistant and policy consultant in the Social Protection and Health Division at the Inter-American Development Bank. She also worked as a research assistant at the Center for Studies in Economic Development at the School of Economics at Los Andes University in Bogota, Colombia. Valentina is currently a social policy and policy analysis PhD candidate at Columbia University and holds an MS and BA in economics from Los Andes University.

Michael Danquah is a development economist and research fellow at UNU-WIDER, currently serving as co-focal point for the project 'Transforming Informal Work and Livelihoods' within UNU-WIDER's 2019–23 work programme. He is also a research fellow at the International Growth Centre in Ghana and previously worked at the Department of Economics, University of Ghana, Legon. His research interests concern the economic development of sub-Saharan Africa, primarily focusing on issues such as informality, inequality and poverty reduction, and productivity growth.

Shantayanan Devarajan is professor of the practice of development at Georgetown University's Edmund A. Walsh School of Foreign Service. He was previously the senior director for development economics (DEC) and a former acting chief economist of the World Bank Group. His research covers public economics, trade policy, natural resources, and the environment.

Amrita Dhillon is a professor of political economy in the Department of Political Economy at King's College London. She is also research group leader for quantitative political economy. Her training is in theoretical modelling including political economy, public economics, game theory, and development. Her main field of research is political economy.

Rachel M. Gisselquist, a political scientist, is a senior research fellow with the United Nations University, World Institute for Development Economics Research (UNU-WIDER) and a member of the institute's senior management team. She works on the politics of the developing world, with particular attention to ethnic politics and inequality between groups, state fragility, governance, and democratisation in sub-Saharan Africa.

Dashleen Kaur is a PhD candidate at the University of British Columbia. Her research interests are political economy and development economics, with a focus on gender.

Stuti Khemani is a senior economist in the Development Research Group of the World Bank. She joined through the Young Professionals Program after obtaining a PhD in economics from the Massachusetts Institute of Technology. Her area of research is the political economy of public policy choices, and institutional reforms for development.

Adeel Malik is a development macroeconomist at the Department of International Development of the University of Oxford with a strong multi-disciplinary orientation. His research engages with questions of long-run development, political economy, and economic history, with a special focus on Muslim societies. Apart from engaging with cross-country empirics on development, he is trying to develop a broader research lens on the political economy of the Middle East, as well as the interplay between religion, land, and politics in Pakistan. His work combines quantitative and qualitative research methods.

Monica Martinez-Bravo completed her doctoral studies from MIT in 2010 and is an associate professor at CEMFI. Her research interests are in the fields of political economy and economic development. She is a research affiliate of CEPR, BREAD, and IGC and an editorial board member of *Review of Economic Studies*.

Michael Mbate is a senior research officer at ODI's Development and Public Finance programme. Michael specialises in public finance and governance, with a focus on public spending, fiscal decentralisation, service delivery, and accountability in developing countries. His work relies heavily on the use of causal inference econometric analysis. He holds a PhD from the London School of Economics (including visiting fellowships at Columbia University and the University of California Berkeley). He has previously been with different institutions such as the United Nations Economic Commission for Africa, the United Nations Industrial Development Organization and the African Union.

Rinchan Mirza is an assistant professor in economics at the University of Kent. He holds a DPhil in economic and social history from the University of Oxford, an MPhil in economics from the University of Oxford, and a BSc (Honours) in mathematics and management from King's College London. His fields of interest are the economic history of South Asia, development economics, applied econometrics, migration studies, health economics, the political economy of religion, institutions, and development.

Anirban Mitra is a senior lecturer in economics at the University of Kent, where he is a member of the Microeconomics Research Group. His research focuses on development economics and political economy – often in their overlap. He is interested in the role of economic factors behind ethnic and civil conflicts, particularly in the context of South Asia. His other works relate to institutional design and its ramifications on elements of public expenditure and income distribution. Anirban has been a member of the CESifo Research Network (Munich) since 2014. He is currently a Leverhulme research fellow. Prior to joining Kent, he was employed at the University of Oslo.

Dilip Mookherjee is professor of economics and director of the Institute for Economic Development at Boston University. Educated at Presidency College Calcutta, Delhi School of Economics, and the London School of Economics, he has taught previously at Stanford University and the Indian Statistical Institute, New Delhi. He works on a combination of theoretical and empirical topics related to inequality, development, political economy, and organisations. Current empirical projects include local governments, political clientelism, financial development, community networks, entrepreneurship, and marketing supply chains in Asia. Theoretical topics include corruption, automation, and globalisation. He is a fellow of BREAD, NBER, CEPR, a member of the Economic Development and Institutions Network, on the executive committee of the Econometric Society, and lead academic for the India programme of the International Growth Centre. He has written many books and also some edited volumes; the latter include his 2006 edited volume *Decentralization and Local Governance in Developing Countries: A Comparative Perspective* (jointly with Pranab Bardhan), published by the MIT Press.

Isabela Munevar is a doctoral student in economics and education at Teachers College, Columbia University. She also holds both an MS and a BA in economics from Los Andes University. Before joining CCRC, Munevar was a research assistant and policy consultant in the Social Protection and Health (SPH) and Education divisions at the Interamerican Development Bank (IDB). At the IDB, she actively participated in several impact evaluations and policy design interventions for the Colombian, Ecuadorian, and Brazilian governments, on topics related to early childhood development, education, and economic inequality.

Gerard Padró i Miquel is a professor of economics and political science at Yale University, where he is also the director of the Leitner Program of International and Comparative Political Economy. He is interested in the interplay between politics and economics as a barrier for development with a focus on civil conflict and on the politics of non-democratic regimes. His previous work has been published in the *Quarterly Journal of Economics, American Economic Review, Review of Economic Studies* and *Quarterly Journal of Political Science*, among others.

Jean-Philippe Platteau is emeritus professor of economics at the University of Namur, in Belgium. He has devoted his research career to studying the role of institutions in economic development and the processes of institutional change. He is the author of numerous journal articles and several books, including *Islam Instrumentalized: Religion and Politics in Historical Perspective* (CUP, 2017), *Institutions, Social Norms, and Economic Development* (Routledge, 2000), and (with J.M. Baland) *Halting Degradation of Natural Resources: Is There a Role for Rural Communities?* (OUP, 1996).

Nancy Qian is the James J. O'Connor Professor at Kellogg MEDS of Northwestern University and the founding director of China Lab, a part of Northwestern's Global Poverty Research Lab. She is a native of Shanghai, China, and holds a PhD in economics from MIT. Prior to Kellogg, Professor Qian taught at Yale University and Brown University, and was a postdoctoral fellow on the prestigious Harvard Academy Scholars programme. Her research provides empirical evidence for a set of core questions in development economics that broadly fall into four subcategories: demography and development, geography and development, institutions and development, and culture and development.

Arka Roy Chaudhuri is an assistant professor in the Economics Department of Shiv Nadar University. He researches in the fields of political economy, development economics, and experimental and behavioural economics.

Fabio Sánchez is professor of economics at the University of Los Andes. He has an extensive career working for institutions such as FEDESARROLLO, the main think tank on economic issues in Colombia, where he worked as a researcher. He has also worked as the head of the macroeconomic unit at the National Planning Department of Colombia, and as the director of the Center for Economic Development Studies (CEDE). He has done extensive research on the links between equity and macroeconomic issues, social policy and violence, and economic history, including his PhD thesis on the effects of the Great Depression in Colombia.

Abu S. Shonchoy is currently an assistant professor in economics at the Florida International University. His current research interests centre around financial inclusion, skills training, infrastructure, and education. He is a J-PAL affiliate professor and a fellow of IZA and GLO.

Zaki Wahhaj is a professor in economics at the University of Kent. Following his PhD in economics from MIT, he spent two years as a postdoctoral fellow at the Centre for Research in Economic Development (CRED) at the University of Namur, Belgium, and three years as lecturer in development economics at the Department of International Development (ODID), University of Oxford. His current research deals, broadly, with the themes of social norms and household decision-making in developing countries.

Yang Yao is a Chinese economist, academic, and author. He is a professor, director of the China Center for Economic Research, and dean of National School of Development at Peking University. He is the executive director of the Institute of South-South Cooperation and Development and is an editor of *China Economic Quarterly*.

Editors' acknowledgements

We would like to express gratitude to several colleagues and organisations who have contributed to the success of this project. Firstly, we extend our sincere thanks to Patrick Dunleavy and the editorial and production team at LSE Press for working so closely with us to bring this book to fruition. In everything from thematic content to the look and feel of the book, their professionalism and dedication have been exemplary. Open access is, of course, not free, and so we are especially grateful to the Press for making it possible here. We also thank Vijayendra Rao for originally steering us towards the open access option.

We thank Helen Ghodbane and Bi Yifei for their help organising our book workshop in December 2021. Their contributions were essential in ensuring that the workshop was a success.

Sarmistha Pal would like to express her gratitude to Surrey Business School, particularly Dean Professor Steve Wood and Research Director Maia Laura di Domenico, for their financial and organisational support towards this book project. Jean-Paul Faguet thanks LSE's Department of International Development for intellectual and financial support. The generosity of both our universities has been invaluable in making this book possible.

Sarmistha Pal would like to acknowledge her co-authors Indraneel Dasgupta, Sugata Ghosh, Anirban Mitra, and Zaki Wahhaj, with whom she has been collaborating on various political economy research projects. These earlier and ongoing works have paved the way towards this book project, and she is very grateful for their contributions.

Both editors thank the colleagues who wrote the chapters that follow. It was a privilege and a pleasure to work with all of you.

Last but not the least, both editors would like to give heartfelt thanks to their spouses and daughters for unwavering support over the past three years.

—*Jean-Paul Faguet and Sarmistha Pal*

1. Decentralised governance: crafting effective democracies around the world

Jean-Paul Faguet and Sarmistha Pal

For over 60 years, decentralisation has been one of the most powerful reform movements in the world, affecting all of its regions and most of its countries. This marks a major inversion of the much-longer-term global pattern, which featured centralised public administrations and the gradual march of the bureaucratic instruments of centralisation across large parts of the world over centuries (Faguet 2012). And then, unexpectedly, around the middle of the 20th century, decentralisation began sprouting everywhere. Take, for example, countries across Africa and Asia. Decolonisation bequeathed highly centralised governments to most of them, usually mirroring their previous colonial administrations. Here the backlash was especially quick, with the first decentralisations launched within a decade of independence.

What did these decentralisations achieve? The literature and policy consensus of the 1970s and 1980s were full of hope about decentralisation's potential to make government more effective and responsive to citizens. But a wave of empirical studies in the 1980s and 1990s cast doubt on its ability to meet these lofty goals. At the turn of the new millennium, evidence on the effects of four decades of decentralisation remained mixed, unclear, and for many analysts deeply frustrating.

Since then, a growing body of research has shown that decentralisation can indeed improve public sector efficiency by, in effect, bringing government closer to the people. While decentralised governments may be captured by elites or undermined by the clientelistic distribution of public resources, a broad consensus holds that – under the right conditions – decentralised systems produce more effective public services and are more democratic. But what these conditions are, and where they hold, have until now remained insufficiently understood. This volume seeks to answer those questions, identifying specific ways in which decentralisation can improve governance, and exploring also how it can go wrong.

How to cite this book chapter:

Faguet, Jean-Paul and Pal, Sarmistha (2023) 'Decentralised governance: crafting effective democracies around the world', in: Faguet, Jean-Paul and Pal, Sarmistha (eds) *Decentralised Governance: Crafting Effective Democracies Around the World*, London: LSE Press, pp. 1–18. https://doi.org/10.31389/lsepress.dlg.a
License: CC BY 4.0

In this volume we bring together a new generation of studies that blend theoretical nuance with empirical innovation. We begin by taking stock of 50 years of decentralisation studies, arguing that – done correctly – decentralisation can improve the democratic accountability and responsiveness of governments by changing the incentives local officials face. We examine how reforms have fallen short of initial expectations due to problems of corruption, elite capture, and political clientelism that can severely distort decentralised governance. We provide fresh evidence from around the world, including Bangladesh, China, Colombia, Ghana, India, Indonesia, Kenya, and Pakistan, highlighting the pros and cons of decentralisation under both democratic and autocratic regimes, providing examples of good and bad practice in both, and drawing lessons for future reforms. Throughout, our goal is to understand in detail, with strong micro foundations, how decentralisation operates differently under different regimes and across a variety of institutional and social contexts.

We document evidence of declining barriers to entry for local political leaders and rising political contestation and improving quality of candidates. We show the emerging role of local entrepreneurship in resolving collective action problems in ethnically diverse societies, leading to greater democratisation and higher local development. These changes are being aided by broader changes in local polities, such as norms governing local public service delivery and improving public transparency and monitoring, aided by complementary reforms such as birth registration cards, citizen-based data systems, and decentralised administration and funding arrangements that create checks and balances for local government officials and limit the scope of corruption. And we explore how some 21st-century reforms to decentralised government use advances in information technology to dramatically reduce costs and enhance welfare provision by tackling corruption, elite capture, and clientelism.

The book's chapters consist of some thematic, critical surveys of recent advances in the decentralisation literature, combined with a larger number of cutting-edge studies of decentralisation in action. The authors are a combination of some of the most influential thinkers in the field with early-career scholars, many themselves from developing countries, employing the latest evidence and methods to explore these complex issues analytically with a blend of qualitative and quantitative data.

We hope the resulting book will prove a worthy update of Bardhan and Mookherjee's influential 2006 volume, which set down an important marker for the field at the turn of the new millennium. Much has happened since then in the world of decentralisation. A great deal of high-quality, fine-grained data has become available during the last two decades, along with more sophisticated empirical methods, that previous generations of researchers did not have access to. And there have, of course, been many additional experiments in reform.

The confluence of these factors implies: (i) a need for a new core reference in this field, and (ii) a significant opportunity to evaluate where and why decentralisation has worked better, and where worse, with better evidence. The current climate of increasing geopolitical conflict and democratic failure in the post-globalisation years also makes the volume a timely venture. As citizens, not just academics, we need to find ways to make the politics of decentralised governance function better. Our hope is that this volume can help generate positive externalities that nurture federalism and deepen democracy.

The remainder of this chapter is developed as follows. Section 1.1 provides an overview of 50 years of decentralisation studies, highlighting both the positive and negative potentials of reform. Section 1.2 discusses the interactions between decentralisation reform and politics at both local and national levels, including the ramifications of decentralisation for political transition that have until now been poorly understood. Section 1.3 discusses decentralisation as 'mechanism design', focusing on non-political aspects of service provision in a decentralised context, such as tax and transfer systems, anti-corruption monitoring, and big data approaches to targeting, as well as how to measure local government performance. Section 1.4 looks to the future of the field.

1.1 Fifty years of decentralisation studies

In Chapter 2, Jean-Paul Faguet provides a broad survey of 50 years of decentralisation studies. In the aggregate, the results of these studies are contradictory, confusing, and indeed sometimes confused. Faguet employs three tools to bring order to the evidence:

- A clear, restrictive definition of decentralisation that excludes many parallel reforms that are often clumped under the same rubric but which are analytically distinct in incentive terms; he suggests 'democratic devolution' but the larger point is that research should specify a clear definition and employ it consistently.
- Weighting empirical evidence in terms of its quality (empirical identification) and comparing results that are like-for-like.
- Admitting that any sincere decentralisation will generate a heterogeneity of responses that, in any particular dimension, differ from one another as much as the underlying socio-geographic units (districts, provinces) do. Accepting this from the outset allows us to exploit that heterogeneity to ask better questions that probe why some decentralised units perform better than others. This, in turn, sheds light on how entire decentralised systems may be pulled up towards better outcomes.

This last point, in particular, is tied to a wealth of conceptual and methodological insights that we are only beginning to fully comprehend. The questions that we have asked over five decades have very often taken the form 'Is decentralisation good or bad for X?', where X is a diverse array of important policy outputs or outcomes, such as primary school enrolment rates, the unit costs of infrastructure provision, or corruption. Studies have, in effect, approached decentralisation as if it were a technocratic issue. They have treated the specifics of reform design, the many, many decisions about how to unpick centralised public services and decentralise which components to what levels – in other words, where expenditure, taxation, and rule-making powers should ultimately lie – as if they were given, choosing instead to compare across countries to identify 'the effects of decentralisation'.

This approach was always more of a methodological convenience than a theoretical precept – something researchers fell into rather than asserted on principle. But it coloured the results of the empirical literature all the same, affecting what questions were asked and how studies were structured. It is only more recently that researchers have begun to internalise the idea that both the decision to decentralise and also the many decisions that follow about *how* to decentralise precisely *which* state functions are not fundamentally technocratic issues. They are, rather, political issues everywhere and all the time. As Faguet (2019) and Faguet and Shami (2021) have shown, decisions to decentralise are taken by leaders in service to the political advantages they seek, and implemented – or not – by officials whose power and status will be directly affected by the outcome of reforms. Even if such a decision were taken on technocratic grounds, it would have powerful political effects, as Devarajan and Khemani argue in Chapter 4, providing politicians with high-power incentives to try to steer reform in directions beneficial to them.

1.2 Politics

'Done correctly,' Faguet points out, 'decentralisation can improve the democratic accountability and responsiveness of governments by changing the incentives that local officials face' (Chapter 2). Reform reorients officials' incentives from upward-pointing, towards the central administration, to downwards-pointing, towards local voters. This is one of the simplest but most powerful features of a sincere democratic devolution, which will ultimately affect not only local but also national public goods, as well as the responsiveness and accountability of the state writ large.

Done correctly, decentralisation should also lead to local governments better attuned to local economic conditions (Khan et al. 2014; Khan, Faguet, and Ambel 2017). The policies they implement should spur public sector efficiency in ways that boost economic growth. Perhaps less obviously, Faguet argues, the creation of multiple levels of government can be leveraged by different social groups and minorities to defend their interests against an encroaching majority. This can help stitch a country together more tightly from the bottom up, draining wind from the sails of leaders who preach secession, and decreasing the risks of conflict and civil war in diverse developing countries. Indeed, the simple fact of creating multiple layers of government helps end the winner-takes-all problem inherent in centralisation that can, by itself, destabilise a country.

But this 'done correctly' hides far more than it reveals. Countries have chosen to decentralise in very different ways, devolving, for example, different sets of powers over different public services to different levels of subnational government, with different revenue-raising powers and different degrees of subnational democracy. Consider, just as an illustration, three neighbouring South American countries between the 1970s and 1990s. In the 1980s, Chile's military regime decentralised to unelected regions, provinces, and municipalities, all headed by appointed officials who responded to the military government and, ultimately, to General Pinochet himself. Essential services were extensively privatised, and municipal governments in particular became much more 'service delivery agents' than sites of governance where citizens were represented and public priorities were debated and agreed.

A decade later, Bolivia decentralised a range of primary public services to elected municipal governments, largely bypassing departments. The reform prioritised participation and citizens responded enthusiastically, voting in far greater numbers than ever and even defending decentralisation in pitched street battles when a subsequent government tried to reverse it. By contrast, 20 years earlier, Brazil's de facto regime had decentralised significant resources and authority to states, largely ignoring municipalities. But it permitted subnational elections, and so national authoritarianism coexisted with significant subnational democracy. These examples are only three of many that we might choose. They underline that decentralisation is not 'a reform' but rather a highly heterogeneous class of reforms. The ways in which we study decentralisation should seek not to iron out such differences but rather exploit them in the interest of greater understanding.

Devarajan and Khemani take this on frontally in their chapter (Chapter 4). They begin their analysis with the original Musgrave (1959) and Oates (1972) arguments in favour of decentralisation based on the economic efficiency of the subsidiarity principle, and the superior matching between local policies and preferences that decentralisation permits. But, as noted above, empirical tests of these ideas over the decades have proved mixed and disappointing. This is where their contribution begins. They argue that empirical disappointment stems from the failure of the Musgrave–Oates principles to incorporate the essentially political nature of decentralisation into its analysis. (The same failure lies at the heart of the methodological issues that Faguet seeks to correct with his three tools.)

This leads Devarajan and Khemani to the striking assertion that most decentralisations are partial. Not only are they not full expressions of some similar underlying, common blueprint; they are not even full expressions of the diverse blueprints that national reformers publicly declare or write into law. It is common, for example, for political decentralisation to advance much faster and further than fiscal decentralisation. The reasons for this are that the prevailing political incentives that govern the behaviour of bureaucrats and public sector officials vary enormously across countries and time periods. As the design of decentralisation is an inherently political act, different national reforms will tend to deviate from economic efficiency in very different ways. Hence, most decentralisations are incomplete in the sense that economic theory would predict, and often feature large mismatches between devolved responsibilities and accountability. These partial decentralisations nonetheless represent equilibria that balance competing political forces, making it difficult to tinker at the margins with a decentralisation that is settled – for example with the allocation of powers or resources.

But, if politics is problematic for empirical studies of decentralisation, it also provides strong grounds for hope in our real-world experiments. Devarajan and Khemani argue that increased contestation in local elections, alongside other characteristics of local democracy, could well lead to improved service delivery. This is because political decentralisation has often led to more, and better, people becoming involved in local politics. It has shone a brighter light on issues of local governance, focusing citizens' attention there and bringing more information into the public realm. As a result, citizens are more aware of local corruption and better able and willing to judge officials' performance more generally. This has the potential to shift social norms about public service so that bureaucracies improve their performance and strengthen the legitimacy of government as a whole. They describe a mechanism for achieving precisely such outcomes, illustrated with the Brazilian state of Ceará, and conclude with a positive view of decentralisation's prospects for realising its original promise. They close with a recommendation to approach decentralisation as a mechanism design problem geared towards improving public services and strengthening state legitimacy.

Mookherjee probes further into the political distortions that often attend decentralised service provision. His wide-ranging chapter (Chapter 3) reviews a wealth of recent studies of transfer programmes in developing countries, reassessing the effectiveness of decentralised mechanisms in improving public sector accountability, programme effectiveness, and helping to meet a number of programme-specific goals. Three key problems of decentralised governance that he focuses on are elite capture, corruption, and clientelism. 'Elites' can be tribal chiefs, large landowners or businessmen, or religious leaders, to name only a few classic examples. Recent literature shows widespread capture of local governments by elites in developing countries, especially where elites are powerful. It is underpinned, at least in part, by the high levels of trust that villagers place in their patrons. The latter may be a survival strategy among poor people who intermittently face times of need that are both unpredictable and potentially severe.

Another distortion widespread in developing countries is clientelism. Although often grouped alongside elite capture, Mookherjee shows that this is an analytically distinct phenomenon with interestingly different implications for development. First, and unlike capture or corruption, clientelism is often consistent with pro-poor targeting. This is because politicians focus clientelistic benefits on the poor, who value them more highly than better-off voters and hence are cheaper to 'buy off'. Second, clientelism may not require high levels of social or economic inequality within the community but it does operate better where there are high levels of poverty. The studies Mookherjee reviews identify two big empirical effects: (i) clientelism undermines accountability, as voters are tied to patrons regardless of their public policy performance; and (ii) clientelism biases politicians towards private benefits, which are more susceptible to its logic, over public benefits, which, being non-excludable, are not. In addition to such intra-community distortions, Mookherjee also examines *inter*-community targeting distortions, resulting from the opportunistic manipulations of programme budgets across local governments by high-level officials. Most studies show evidence of bias towards co-partisans, such as Azulai (2017), who shows central government favouritism in grant allocation towards own-party controlled local governments in Brazil.

Probing deeper into how decentralisation interacts with political systems, our colleagues turn to detailed country studies of Pakistan, China, Indonesia, and Kenya. In Chapter 5, Malik, Mirza, and Platteau argue that institutional changes under General Zia's regime stimulated the return of family politics in Pakistan. Zia's aim was to stabilise his de facto regime by co-opting powerful families and the religious elite, and to undermine his most powerful political opponents. The family- and clan-based politics he nurtured grew in importance until it displaced the programmatic politics that had begun to develop in the late 1960s around the Pakistan's People's Party. As a result, powerful political dynasties became consolidated, effectively killing off party-based politics in Pakistan. The authors use a unique and extensive database on political genealogies in the Punjab province to provide evidence for the emergence and persistence of political dynasties over time. They also show increasing political competition via the splitting of political dynasties over generations. Malik, Mirza, and Platteau argue that the increasing importance of political dynasties at the subnational level has contributed to the capture of local bureaucracy by elected politicians, thus entrenching clientelism for the long term. More broadly, the Pakistan case richly illustrates how authoritarian regimes often direct the course of electoral politics in ways that allow them to concentrate and consolidate power. Indeed, doing so may be a primary motive for decentralising in the first place.

Martinez-Bravo, Padró i Miquel, Qian, and Yao examine the impact of voters' religious heterogeneity on public spending and public goods provision in China in Chapter 6. By creating millions of elected subnational governments over the past 50 years, decentralisation has dramatically increased the number of electoral polities across the world. Perhaps the single most dramatic increase is China's, where the introduction of village elections created nearly 700,000 new electoral democracies within an otherwise authoritarian system. The chapter exploits variation in this huge experiment to explore the thorny question of the social preconditions required for democracy to prosper. They do this by examining how the introduction of village elections in China interacts with voter fragmentation in determining the allocation of government-provided public goods. One of the chapter's most provocative points is to document the return of religion as an important dimension of social identity and group clustering in post-Mao China, overtaking other divisions such as kinship groups.

Faced with corruption, unresponsive local officials, and the severe under-provision of public goods across large areas of rural China, the Communist Party introduced village elections in the 1980s and 1990s as a structural remedy to the previous system of central appointment of village leadership. Prior to the introduction of elections, local expenditures on public goods were similar across villages with very different levels of social fragmentation. Elections increased public expenditure, and increases were largest in the most homogeneous villages. But, in the 8 per cent of highly heterogeneous villages, public goods expenditure decreased. The authors further show that changes in public expenditures occurred exclusively for village-raised funds; public goods funded by transfers from higher levels of government were unaffected by the introduction of elections. These results imply that the factors causing heterogeneous villages to experience lower (or even negative) gains from elections are locally specific. Martinez-Bravo, Padró i Miquel, Qian, and Yao infer two possible, non-mutually-exclusive mechanisms: (i) heterogeneous villages have a lower preference for public goods, and elected village leaders better reflect these underlying preferences; and (ii) homogeneous villages are better able to hold elected leaders to account, perhaps through more effective monitoring.

If decentralisation can change a country's national political dynamics so comprehensively, surely it will have significant effects at the local level too. What might these be? The rich literature on fiscal decentralisation is surprisingly silent about its ramifications on the organisation of local governance. Mitra and Pal provide a way in, focusing their Chapter 7 on the impact of fiscal decentralisation on local-level leadership selection. The authors exploit exogenous variation in local polities after Indonesia's fiscal decentralisation in 2001, which offered enhanced autonomy to local communities (which sit within districts). Using fine-grained survey data on methods of leader selection in local communities, Mitra and Pal observe three distinct methods of leader selection in Indonesian localities: majority voting (that is, electoral democracy), consensus-building (that is, deliberative, participatory democracy), and oligarchy (that is, leaders selected by the local elite).

Surely the method of leader selection is important in terms of policy implementation and the provision of local public goods and services at the local level, especially in a fiscally decentralised setting. Whether the leader of a community reflects the preferences of the entire populace or is only sensitive to the needs of a select few (that is, the local elite) will determine the pattern of local public spending, and thereby social welfare in the community. This underlines the need for a fuller understanding of the factors that affect the method of a community's leader selection.

Mitra and Pal document that different governance types are associated with different patterns of budget allocations, as well as significant differences in local income and spending following fiscal decentralisation. More interestingly, the authors show that community homogeneity is a key driver of leader selection by consensus-building. By contrast, ethnically diverse communities have increasingly selected their leaders via voting.

Furthermore, voting (relative to consensus-building) communities registered significantly higher income and higher development spending after decentralisation, which Mitra and Pal attribute to higher levels of local entrepreneurship. The issue of elite capture is likely to be particularly problematic in ethnically diverse communities (Mitra and Pal 2021), highlighting a trade-off between gains from decentralisation and losses from elite capture. Local social norms may, however, help promote community reciprocity that can help align policy to community preferences (Pal and Wahhaj 2017). The chapter departs from this literature to show that local political entrepreneurs use voting to align economic interests in ethnically diverse communities, helping them overcome some of the collective action problems otherwise natural to heterogeneous polities. This mechanism, they show, works better when income inequality is modest.

Lastly, and in the spirit of 'complexifying' the state, Mbate's Chapter 8 links local-level corruption in Kenya back up to national-level dynamics to show how their interaction can sometimes strengthen, and other times weaken, local governance. He begins with Kenya's accountability deficit, examining how parliamentary oversight mechanisms meant to hold local executives to account often fail. A critical factor contributing to weak oversight is poor coordination between parliament and subnational government institutions. Mbate uses administrative data that directly match parliamentary sanctions with incidences of subnational corruption to demonstrate how party politics can impede the legislative oversight of local politicians. His results show that co-partisanship and the need to preserve party credibility encourage collusive behaviour between parliamentarians serving in oversight committees and subnational politicians in ways that weaken parliamentary oversight. But this effect declines substantially when committee members face an electoral threat or similar long-term career concern. These findings suggest that the accountability of local-level officials far from the capital is strongly influenced by the structure and composition of legislative committees, as well as the nature of political incentives that legislators face. This points to the importance of micro design of a decentralised system. To work effectively, accountability and anti-corruption mechanisms must fit not just the legislative institutions that oversee and implement them but also a nation's political party system. The larger lesson is that local governments in a decentralised system cannot be viewed in isolation. Even in a highly decentralised country, they remain part of a larger system whose workings can powerfully affect even far-flung localities.

1.3 Mechanism design

The second overarching theme of this book concerns more technocratic, non-political aspects of effective service provision in a decentralised context. There is a great deal involved in successful governance beyond elections and politicians' incentives. Creating an effective decentralised system implies adapting structures, rules, norms, and behaviours to new actors and dynamics that a centralised system may not have contemplated. Using Devarajan and Khemani's terms, we might think of this as mechanism design.

Again, Chapter 2 by Faguet lays out the basics, summarising the insights of five decades of research on this aspect. The fiscal federalist literature teaches us that efficiency can be improved when we devolve to lower levels of government services that are heterogeneous in demand, geographically specific, have low economies of scale, and are reliant on local information. How low should the services go? Each level of government should be responsible for all services and expenditures that do not impose externalities on other jurisdictions. Devolved services can then be tailored to the preferences of local citizens.

How should such services be funded? Local taxes and other charges should be neutral and should not distort economic activity, and their costs and benefits should be transparent to citizens. Tax incidence should be equitable across taxpayers. Local taxes should focus on immobile tax bases. And the administration and compliance costs of such systems should be low. These guidelines imply that property taxes and specific user charges are best suited to local governments, whereas taxes that are complex or levied on mobile tax bases, such as income and capital taxes, should be assigned to higher-level authorities.

The combination of large expenditure needs with limited taxation possibilities means that locally generated revenues will typically fall far short of requirements. Intergovernmental transfer systems arise to fill these (large) gaps, and also to pursue other policy goals. Revenue is shared among different levels of government in two broad ways: (i) by formula (for example, per capita) or according to origin (for example, natural resource royalties); and (ii) targeted to specific priorities (for example, primary education), or untargeted (for example, block grants). The precise mix of revenue-sharing mechanisms will vary greatly across countries as according to their economies, geographies, histories, and other major characteristics. But, in the real world, a great deal of such variation is not easily explained. The share of intergovernmental transfers in local government revenues varies remarkably among countries in the same region, or at similar levels of development.

The second half of Mookherjee's Chapter 3 takes up the baton with extensive evidence from a series of recent innovative policy experiments to improve monitoring and supervision, and devise institutional alternatives to political decentralisation that achieve some of the same outcomes, such as formula-bound programmes that reduce the authority of locally elected officials. In India, for example, the use of biometric identification cards to verify employment beneficiaries reduced programme leakages from 'ghost' beneficiaries by

41 per cent. Beneficiaries were paid more quickly and reported earnings rose 24 per cent while programme costs did not change. And, in many countries, community-driven development (CDD) programmes have been supported by the World Bank and other donors. These seek to involve beneficiaries, including the poor, in the definition of priorities and administration of programme benefits. But such programmes also tend to suffer from elite capture, as local elites frequently gain effective control over funds and decision-making. In a number of cases, non-elite citizens have been hired as monitors to help screen potential beneficiaries, and programme management has been contracted out to NGOs or private firms as remedies. But both sets of measures are understudied, and so their empirical effects on CDD programmes are poorly understood. Mookherjee notes that more research is needed.

Lastly, Mookherjee infers from a suite of studies a feasible set of 21st-century reforms to decentralised government that would use advances in information technology to drastically alter welfare provision. We might call these reforms 'anti-political' as they would replace elected local officials' discretion in the making of policy and administration of public resources with a formula-based system of private benefits. A big data approach would predict the level of poverty of each household or individual in a country on the basis of administrative surveys. The benefits programme would be implemented using a nationwide household or individual-level ID system with biometric identification, combined with electronic transfers to low-cost bank accounts or mobile phones. Mookherjee predicts that such a system has the potential to improve pro-poor targeting significantly at relatively low cost, and suggests it might greatly reduce losses and distortions due to capture, corruption, and inefficiency. But any such programme would first have to solve important economic, administrative, and informational problems. It would also, in effect, recentralise public expenditures, something that must be taken into account before a reform is embarked upon.

Over the past few decades, corruption has taken centre stage as a core problem of development. But how anti-corruption efforts, which have also become commonplace, interact with decentralised governance is little studied and little understood. The positive role of decentralisation in draining the swamp of corruption is largely assumed from first-order theorising about politicians' incentives, along the lines laid out in Chapter 2. Put simply, it is unlikely that decentralised monitoring of corruption is universally superior to the centralised sort. Rather, decentralised efforts are likely better for certain kinds of services, or under certain conditions. What are they?

Afridi, Dhillon, Roy Chaudhuri, and Kaur seek to bring deeper understanding to this debate in Chapter 9 by linking the effectiveness of centralised versus decentralised anti-corruption monitoring to the activities being monitored. They first develop a theoretical model, and then use it as a lens through which to survey the rather diverse empirical literature. The model shows that centralised audits are more effective in certain types of activities, for example procurement, where detailed documentation exists and corruption can be more clearly defined as distinct from mismanagement. Decentralised or community monitoring has higher efficacy when collective action problems can be solved, when monitoring teams have a sense of agency, and when the composition of teams is more homogeneous.

Community monitoring has the advantage of agents' deeper knowledge of local conditions, making it less costly for the government to target monitoring resources better, but may suffer from problems of elite capture. Afridi et al. use their model to identify conditions of relative efficacy of centralised versus decentralised monitoring strategies. The empirical literature that they then survey examines heterogeneous countries, heterogeneous institutions (formal and informal), and heterogeneous political systems. The evidence implies that both centralised and decentralised anti-corruption interventions are success-ful in some instances but fail in others. Programmatic and institutional details appear to matter a great deal. Failure is likely to reflect the composition of local institutions as well as the nature of political competition.

An ideal tool for combating corruption and enhancing accountability would require analysts to measure local government performance across a develop-ing country. In Chapter 10, Chachu, Danquah, and Gisselquist develop such a tool and then test it on the case of Ghana. Basing their work on Putnam, Leonardi, and Nanetti's (1994) good governance framework, they sketch out an idealised tool that captures three key dimensions of good governance: policy pronouncement, political processes and internal operations, and pol-icy implementation. But a lack of available information leaves them unable to implement this tool for Ghana. So they resort to a second-best approach that combines a weighted quality-of-reporting measure with data on political processes and internal operations, and policy implementation to construct a composite index for local government performance. Implementing the tool reveals large variations in both the nature of local governance across regions of Ghana, and the quality of information reported. The authors conclude that some local governments, especially urban ones, tend to perform better than rural ones. More importantly, they find an inverse relationship between poverty and the quality of reporting across regions. The latter underlines the importance of transparency and disclosure rules for generating the informa-tion that supports effective local governance.

Local information is surely key to the success of local monitoring, gov-ernance, and accountability. The question of how to produce and manage high-quality information on developing-country citizens lies at the heart of Shonchoy and Wahhaj's Chapter 11. They focus on recent initiatives to create digital birth records and increase registrations in Bangladesh. The absence of systematic birth records can be a serious impediment for implementing public policies related to children, such as monitoring truancy or restricting the minimum age of marriage. The authors document how the Bangladeshi government has instituted local, government-run digital centres linked to a national database, and promoted registrations by making birth certificates a requirement for receiving key public services, for example school enrolment and marriage registration.

Using first-hand data collected from a rural district in Bangladesh, Shonchoy and Wahhaj document the problem of birth certificate validity among a very poor population. Discrepancies in local governments' ability to produce valid birth certificates range from 39 per cent to 67 per cent across five local authorities within a single district in Bangladesh. The authors provide suggestive evidence that this is due to limited local administrative capacity to register births. This pertains, among others, to lack of education and awareness within the union parishad leadership, lack of experience registering births among union digital centre (UDC) staff, corruption and nepotism leading to inappropriate equipment for registering births in the UDC and unqualified persons being assigned to UDCs, and unrealistic targets set by the Bangladesh government to process birth registrations within a set time frame without sufficient investment in capacity-building.

The last chapter (Chapter 12) brings together our two overarching themes in a single case, Colombia, in an empirically rich study of a decentralisation reform that granted almost complete autonomy over education to some municipalities while placing others under the authority of higher-level administrations. Chegwin, Munevar, and Sánchez explore the natural experiment created by Colombia's 2001 law, which 'certified' municipalities above the arbitrary threshold of 100,000 inhabitants and granted them significant additional resources and authority over policy and expenditures, while removing resources and authority from non-certified municipalities and allowing departmental administrations to direct their policies and expenditure priorities. This permits a direct comparison of decentralised (treated) versus centralised (control) municipalities. The authors find that autonomy in the delivery of public education increased student enrolment, teacher quality, and student performance in certified municipalities after 2001.

By what mechanisms did these changes come about? Chegwin et al.'s evidence suggests that better student outcomes were due less to the quantity of education resources that decentralised municipalities managed and more to the superior ways in which resources were used, which generated significant efficiency gains in certified municipalities. Such gains may flow from their lower transaction costs of matching local preferences with educational interventions. In the intellectual battle between local politics and centralising technocracy, the Colombian case supports empowering local democracy over higher-level priorities and administrative control.

Finally, readers may find it helpful to consider how the remaining chapters across Parts 1 and 2 vary in their coverage of regions and governing regime types. Figure 1.1 summarises the chapters' main analytical themes, whether they focus on liberal democracies, authoritarian systems, or both, and their country and regional coverage. They sum to a book that covers a wide variety of developing countries, ranging from open democracies to closed dictatorships,

Figure 1.1: A synoptic overview of the book

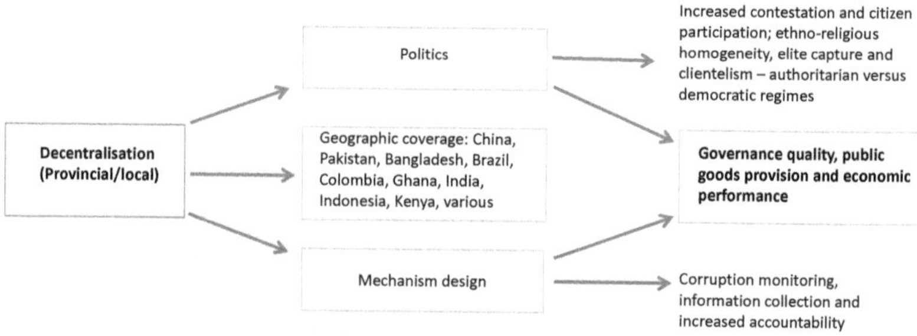

across Africa, Asia and Latin America, with deep, rich analyses of some of the most challenging country cases in the developing world.

1.4 Scope for future research

While we believe that the chapters included in the volume make substantial contributions to the success/failure of decentralised governance, these studies also raise further questions still to be answered. Here we list some of these issues.

Devarajan and Khemani observe that we know little about whether decentralisation has strengthened the legitimacy of government as a whole and shifted social norms so that bureaucracies perform better. Can local-level politics shape incentives and norms in a community? Such changes are not guaranteed and more research is needed in this respect. While Malik et al. establish an intriguing descriptive association between local decentralisation, the rise of family dynasty, and capture of local bureaucracy under military rule in Pakistan, further research is needed to establish the underlying causality. Mitra and Pal have shown how fiscal decentralisation in Indonesia may give rise to local entrepreneurship in ethnically diverse voting communities in a bid to align the economic interests of diverse populations. The observed empirical associations, while robust, are not strictly causal. While showing that religious heterogeneity could constrain the potential benefits of local election reforms for public goods provision (after a period of severe under-provision of public goods) in authoritarian China, Padro et al. do not take account of the demand for local public goods provision. The latter is, however, essential for welfare assessments of public goods provision. These results are taken as a springboard for further careful exploration of these associations, which are at the heart of such transitions after varying decentralisation reforms in democratic and authoritarian regimes.

Mookherjee (Chapter 3) analyses a set of 21st-century reforms to decentralised government that use advances in information technology to drastically alter welfare provision. While these reforms, using a household-/individual-level ID system with biometric identification along with electronic transfers to low-cost bank accounts, have shown potential to significantly improve pro-poor targeting at relatively low cost (reduced corruption and inefficiencies), concerns remain about the likelihood of recentralisation changing the balance of power between central, regional, and local governments. The trade-off between successful technology-driven welfare provision and recentralisation needs to be understood better.

There is a general consensus that corruption is a persistent problem in decentralised systems. Reviewing the existing literature, Afridi et al. note that decentralised monitoring of corruption is unlikely to be universally superior to centralised monitoring. Our knowledge remains quite limited in this respect. Understanding the conditions and processes by which top-down audits work well and those under which social audits (ensuring representation, voice and impact) work well is thus a first-order question. The literature on the efficacy of audits in relation to punishments is sparse; we also know little as to which types of processes are more suitable for top-down audits. To a large extent the state of this literature is a reflection of the lack of available information about the monitoring process.

The essential role of information in securing transparency and accountability is further highlighted in a number of subsequent chapters. While parliamentary scrutiny can discipline lower-level governance despite having scope for political opportunism (Mbate's Chapter 8), public information on the functioning of the oversight committee that can provide insights into their effectiveness and capacity remains limited. Chachu et al. highlight the role of social capital for promoting public sector efficiency in a decentralised set-up that has roots in Putnam's work (Putnam, Leonardi, and Nanetti 1994), which, however, could not be implemented because of lack of information in this respect. Shonchoy and Wahhaj further highlight the limitations in local capacity in registering births and also the reliability of existing birth records, which is an essential ingredient for improving state capacity to deliver a range of public services to citizens. At a minimum, decentralised governments should be encouraged and supported to provide disaggregated local data and timely reports on various monitoring processes to ensure transparency and accountability of decentralised local governments. Access to such information is integral for ensuring the effectiveness of public service provision; this could also provide voters with critical information to hold local politicians accountable, thus securing the health of local democracies.

Conclusions

Decentralisation, both fiscal and political, has long been advocated as a powerful tool of good governance that devolves political and/or fiscal powers to local governing bodies. But a long list of arguments invites caution and suggests that, even if reform increases the accountability of local governments and strengthens the voices of the poor and marginalised, it may also enhance the influence of local elites, breed clientelism, and increase corruption, thus distorting governance and development. What knowledge can we distil from such contradiction? How do we untie this conceptual knot?

One of the overarching themes of this book is that for too long, too much of the decentralisation debate has been cast in the wrong terms. Correct questions do not take the form 'Is decentralisation good or bad for X?' where X is some policy output or outcome of interest. This is because decentralisation is not a simple change, like flipping a policy switch, with results that are linear, discrete, and predictable. It is, rather, a complicated process by which the centre lets go of power and resources in favour of autonomous subnational governments that are as diverse as the underlying societies they represent. For this reason, decentralisation does not 'do' any particular thing; it does a great many things. It does a great many different things in the same policy space, with often strikingly different outcomes in different municipalities and regions – in the same country, under the same decentralisation programme. That should surprise no one. In a powerful sense, this is what decentralisation is for. We decentralise to get more heterogeneity. Those hoping for a step change in homogeneous outcomes have picked the wrong reform.

It follows that the right way to think about a complex, multi-layered reform like decentralisation is not via first-order theorising. Decentralisation is a complicated set of changes in a country's governance arrangements. It can be implemented in many different ways. Reformers face a daunting set of choices as they design and execute real decentralisation programmes. These 'details' are not only not trivial; they are crucial if a decentralisation programme is to fit a country's needs and challenges. Getting decentralisation right is difficult, but also immensely valuable because it can improve the quality of a country's governance.

How do we 'get decentralisation right'? Not via simple decision rules or dramatic measures. The way to get it right, rather, is through a combination of political and technocratic measures that work with the grain of national and subnational political incentives, and combine old and new technologies to bring relevant information before citizens and public servants in support of high-quality public decisions and more public accountability to citizens. The chapters in this book shine a number of lights on how to do this. They answer questions about when and why decentralisation works across the globe under very different circumstances, what it can achieve when it works, and when and why it does not, with a particular focus on recent policy reforms.

Two key features are noteworthy. First, interactions between decentralisation and politics were acknowledged from the start in the 1960s, but until recently mostly ignored. This is a vastly under-researched area that several of our chapters attempt to bring light to. Contributors document evidence of declining barriers to entry for local political leadership and rising political contestation. An increasing importance of political dynasties at the subnational level may lead to the capture of local bureaucracy by elected politicians, thus entrenching clientelism over the long term. Successful decentralisation programmes are accompanied by transparent democratic mandates, local accountability, and community reciprocity that help align policy to community preferences. Ethnic homogeneity can facilitate successful decentralisation, though decentralisation may work under ethnic diversity too if political entrepreneurs can align the economic interests of diverse populations. It is notable that dysfunctional regional and local politics are often at the heart of growing discontent around the globe today. These chapters show ways to make decentralised politics work better.

Second, the volume identifies several potential non-political mechanisms through which the promise of reform can be realised. We document that decentralisation may generate improvements in the delivery of public services and faster local development when aided by enhanced public transparency and disclosure, centralised or decentralised monitoring (depending on the type of activity being monitored), parliamentary sanctions, and democratic accountability supported by citizen-based information systems, as well as democratic norms governing local public service delivery. In so doing, we highlight the challenge of tackling recentralisation as information technology takes a more central role. We also focus on institutional capacity constraints, for example poor physical and digital infrastructure, the lack of qualified and trained personnel, and setting unrealistic targets for political reasons, all of which create barriers to the effective implementation of decentralisation. But our evidence shows that, with a strong will and clear leadership, such problems can be overcome.

Decentralisation is not in itself a good or bad thing. Designed and implemented strategically in ways that take advantage of the political and mechanism design insights offered here, it can promote democracy, efficiency, and accountability. We can make such claims with confidence because we document the same in a number of the chapters that follow. Decentralisation for subnational development assumes additional significance in the current climate of geopolitical discontent and unrest in the aftermath of spectacular globalisation and technological progress since the 1990s. Dysfunctional decentralisation systems likely explain some of the crisis of democracy in the world today. Making them operational and effective has never been more important.

References

Azulai, Michel (2017) 'Public Good Allocation and the Welfare Costs of Political Connections: Evidence from Brazilian Matching Grants'. London School of Economics Working Paper. https://www.sv.uio.no/econ and-events/events/guest-lectures-seminars /job-market/dokumenter/azulai-public-good-allocation-and-the-welfare -costs-of-political-connections.pdf

Bardhan, Pranab and Mookherjee, Dilip (eds) (2006) *Decentralization and Local Governance in Developing Countries: A Comparative Perspective,*

Cambridge, MA: MIT Press.
https://doi.org/10.7551/mitpress/2297.001.0001

Faguet, Jean-Paul (2012) *Decentralization and Popular Democracy: Governance from Below in Bolivia*, Ann Arbor: University of Michigan Press. https://doi.org/10.3998/mpub.175269

Faguet, Jean-Paul (2019) 'Revolution from Below: Cleavage Displacement and the Collapse of Elite Politics in Bolivia', *Politics & Society*, vol.47, no.2, pp.205–50. https://doi.org/10.1177/0032329219845944

Faguet, Jean-Paul and Shami, Mahvish (2021) 'The Incoherence of Institutional Reform: Decentralization as a Structural Solution to Immediate Political Needs', *Studies in Comparative International Development*, vol.57, pp.82–109. https://doi.org/10.1007/s12116-021-09347-4

Khan, Qaiser; Faguet, Jean-Paul; and Ambel, Alemayehu (2017) 'Blending Top-Down Federalism with Bottom-Up Engagement to Reduce Inequality in Ethiopia', *World Development*, vol.96, pp.326–42. https://documents1.worldbank.org/curated/en/971991468180852923/pdf/WPS7511.pdf

Khan, Qaiser; Faguet, Jean-Paul; Gaukler, Christopher; and Mekasha, Wendmsyamregne (2014) 'Improving Basic Services for the Bottom Forty Percent: Lessons from Ethiopia', Washington, DC: World Bank. http://hdl.handle.net/10986/20001

Mitra, Anirban and Pal, Sarmistha (2021) 'Ethnic Diversity, Social Norms and Elite Capture: Theory and Evidence from Indonesia', *Economica*, vol.89, no.356, pp.947–96. https://doi.org/10.1111/ecca.12423

Musgrave, Richard A. (1959) *The Theory of Public Finance*, New York: McGraw Hill.

Oates, Wallace (1972) *Fiscal Federalism*, New York: Harcourt Brace Jovanovich.

Pal, Sarmistha and Wahhaj, Zaki (2017) 'Fiscal Decentralisation, Local Institutions and Public Goods Provision: Evidence from Indonesia', *Journal of Comparative Economics*, vol.45, no.2, pp.383–409. https://doi.org/10.1016/j.jce.2016.07.004

Putnam, Robert D.; Leonardi, Robert; and Nanetti, Raffaella (1994) *Making Democracy Work: Civic Traditions in Modern Italy*, Princeton, NJ: Princeton University Press. https://doi.org/10.1017/CBO9781107415324.004

PART 1

Taking stock of six decades of decentralisation

2. Understanding decentralisation: theory, evidence, and practice

Jean-Paul Faguet

Summary

What is decentralisation, what is its underpinning rationale, and why might it matter for development? This chapter reviews five decades of research on decentralisation and has three overarching objectives:

a. to understand what decentralisation is, what it is not, and connect conceptual ambiguities in the literature to the mixed and inconclusive results that for so long plagued it;

b. to distil an enormous literature on international experiences of decentralisation into clear empirical conclusions; and

c. to derive policy lessons for countries considering decentralisation on how best to assign power over expenditures and responsibility for service provision, and also authority over taxation, among different levels of government.

I propose a concise definition of decentralisation that is both conceptually clear and empirically tractable, and review empirical evidence on decentralisation's ability to overcome some of the key obstacles holding back development.

Beginning slowly in the 1960s, and with gathering speed in the decades that followed, decentralisation has become one of the broadest movements and most contentious policy issues in development. Around the late 1970s it seized the imaginations of policy reformers, and has never really let go (Bardhan and Mookherjee 2006; Faguet 2004a; Manor 1999; Rondinelli 1981;

How to cite this book chapter:

Faguet, Jean-Paul (2023) 'Understanding decentralisation: theory, evidence, and practice', in: Faguet, Jean-Paul and Pal, Sarmistha (eds) *Decentralised Governance: Crafting Effective Democracies Around the World*, London: LSE Press, pp. 21–48. https://doi.org/10.31389/lsepress.dlg.b License: CC BY 4.0

Rondinelli, Cheema, and Nellis 1983; Ter-Minassian 1997). Many of us who began studying the phenomenon three decades ago assumed that the decentralisation wave was then cresting. To our surprise, the wave has continued to build across the world and shows little sign of subsiding.

A 1999 study by the World Bank estimated that between 80 and 100 per cent of the world's countries were implementing decentralisation in one form or another. This includes not only well-known reforms in developing countries such as Bolivia, India, and South Africa but also – under the guises of subsidiarity, devolution, and federalism – deep reforms in some of the world's most developed countries and regions, such as the EU, UK, and US. Since then, new or deepening reforms have been announced in more than 35 countries as diverse as South Korea, France, Cambodia, Turkey, Japan, and Kenya. It is not just the breadth of reforms across countries that impresses but also their depth. Campbell (2001) shows that, across Latin America, between 10 and 50 per cent of all central government revenues are now spent by subnational governments. Hence, we can summarise that decentralisation is happening, or has recently happened, in the vast majority of countries across the globe, with significant effects on these countries' fiscal accounts and (as we shall see below) on how they are governed.

Worldwide policy experimentation has been accompanied by a huge outpouring of research attempting to ascertain the effects of decentralisation on different aspects of economic, political, and social development. These studies often find contradictory outcomes across different countries, and even within countries. From the late 1980s onwards, study after study bemoaned the decentralisation literature as indeterminate, confusing, and of limited use to policy reformers. Policymakers were left little wiser about whether they should pursue reforms, or how they should proceed if they did. But recently, more sophisticated empirical approaches have combined with fundamental methodological insights to find a way through this tangle of apparently contradictory evidence.

What relevance does decentralisation have for developing countries with comparatively poor infrastructure and weak state capacity? Many such countries have made tentative steps towards decentralising that are partial and still incomplete. What role, if any, should further decentralisation play in their attempts to improve public sector effectiveness and the provision of local goods and services? The question is particularly important because so much of the decentralisation literature focuses on high-income countries. This is for understandable reasons: many of the earliest decentralisations happened there, where data are comparatively high-quality and abundant, facilitating empirical study further.

But, at a minimum, policy lessons from this literature need translation before being applied to developing countries. The reasons for that are similarly straightforward. High-income countries tend to enjoy stronger tax revenues and higher levels of human capital. These combine to produce governments that are more capable, with more policy options and greater policy flexibility, than less well-off countries. But, interestingly, many developing countries have stronger traditions of self-government at the local level, especially in rural areas, than more urbanised high-income countries. This may give them certain countervailing advantages that well-designed decentralisation programmes can take advantage of.

In sum, decentralisation is not the same for developing and developed countries. The purpose of this chapter is to provide some 'translation' by reviewing theory and international evidence on the ability of decentralisation to address state weaknesses in ways that promote human and economic development in middle- and low-income countries. In the sections that follow we first review the various definitions of decentralisation that researchers have put forward and examine the key theoretical arguments in favour of decentralisation that are most relevant for developing countries. We then outline the methodological advances that have allowed researchers to put order into this previously confused literature. We use these insights as a lens through which to review international evidence on decentralisation's ability to overcome some of the key obstacles holding back a country's development. And we draw lessons from the fiscal federalism literature on how best to assign powers and responsibilities over expenditure and taxation among different levels of government, and how to structure intergovernmental transfer systems to solve the problems that inevitably result.

2.1 Understanding decentralisation

What is decentralisation? What is its underpinning rationale? Why might it matter for a low- or middle-income country? This section briefly reviews the most important definitions of decentralisation in the academic literature, along with the underlying logic of each, in order to arrive at the most relevant definition. We then briefly outline the principal arguments in favour of this kind of reform, which have to do with deepening democracy and improving accountability of public officials to the governed.

The huge scale of policy experimentation with decentralisation has provoked an equally huge research literature examining its effects. This includes literally hundreds of published academic papers in peer-reviewed journals; if to this we add rigorous 'grey literature' studies conducted by multilateral organisations such as the World Bank, IMF, and IDB, as well as reputable think tanks, NGOs, and government agencies, the number ascends into the many thousands. But attempts to summarise the lessons of this research have left many scholars frustrated. The empirical literature appears to be broadly inconclusive, with many contradictory findings on any specific question of importance, regardless of region or countries' level of development.

As examples, consider three prominent surveys that sought to summarise the state of knowledge on decentralisation. Litvack, Ahmad, and Bird (1998) found that 'one can prove, or disprove, almost any proposition about decentralization by throwing together some set of cases or data'. A follow-on study by Shah, Thompson, and Zou (2004), which reviewed 56 newer, more quantitative studies, found that decentralisation sometimes improved, but other times worsened, service delivery, corruption, macroeconomic stability, and growth across a large range of countries. Most pessimistically of all, Treisman (2007) found that the empirical literature's results are inconclusive, weak and contradictory. 'To date,' he concludes, 'there are almost no solidly established, general empirical findings about the consequences of decentralization.' This leaves us in a bizarre paradox: after 50 years of policy experimentation and hundreds or even thousands of studies, we appeared to know very little about whether decentralisation is good or bad for any policy outcome that we care about. And yet enthusiasm for policy reform not only persists but continues to grow.

More recent research has found a way through the empirical and conceptual thicket that has characterised the decentralisation literature (Faguet 2014). The solution contains three components: (i) definitional, (ii) empirical, and (iii) conceptual. On the definitional side, much of the literature's indeterminacy arises from the word's very different meanings. Slater (1989), Faguet (2012), and others have pointed out that 'decentralisation' is polysemic, meaning very different things to different people and in different countries where it has been implemented. A number of studies, particularly from the 1980s, begin by delineating different kinds of decentralisation, as if they were variants of the same underlying product. The typical taxonomy would include: deconcentration, delegation, devolution, and privatisation.

As we shall see below, the distinctions between these 'decentralisation variants' are crucial on both theoretical and empirical grounds, and hence it is important to consider them in more detail. *Deconcentration* is when central government shifts personnel, equipment, and offices from the capital city to cities and towns elsewhere in the country. Chains of command, reporting, and accountability, as well as fiscal flows in terms of expenditure and taxation, remain largely unchanged. The main point is to get public officials out of the centre and into the periphery. This can be beneficial when it brings more accurate and detailed information on local needs and conditions to bear on government decision-making. By spreading central government salaries and expenditures more evenly around the country, it can also be politically popular, and may contribute to reducing centre–periphery inequalities.

Delegation is when central government shifts managerial responsibilities for certain expenditures or service provision to organisations outside the regular bureaucratic structure, such as quasi-autonomous public agencies. Chains of command, reporting, and accountability are somewhat altered for the services in question, but public officials' incentives continue to point upwards, and the central government monolith may not be overly disturbed.

By contrast, *devolution* (or sometimes 'democratic devolution'; see Manor 1999) is a much more fundamental reform. It shifts power and resources from central government officials to local government officials with independent mandates whom the centre cannot control. Its effect is to fundamentally change authority over, and accountability for, those resources and responsibilities that are decentralised. Instead of the central Ministry of Education being responsible for the operation of a particular primary school, for example, authority over that school passes to an elected local government. Rather than petitioning distant central bureaucrats, parents and other local citizens seeking to improve the school's operation can take their demands to local officials, whose electoral prospects they hold in their hands. The incentives of education-providing officials are thus shifted from upward-pointing, towards senior officials in the ministry, to downward-pointing, to voters.

Lastly, *privatisation* is the divestiture of public functions to the private sector via the sale or transfer of related assets. It is justified on the basis of improved innovation and managerial efficiency, which should result from the reorganisation of public services on a for-profit basis. Public goods and services that are privatised are typically subjected to careful regulation, as they may constitute essential services (for example, health, water) or natural monopolies (for example, water, electricity). Privatisation is the most radical of these four 'types of decentralisation'. Without elaborating further for lack of space, I will simply assert that privatisation – while an interesting and important phenomenon in its own right, and certainly worthy of study – is sufficiently different from the other three types that it should not, in my view, be classed as a form of decentralisation. It is better understood as one of a menu of additional measures often undertaken alongside decentralisation by reformers eager to reduce the size of the central state or radically alter organisational incentives, rather than as a reform that is analytically comparable to deconcentration or devolution.

The deeper problem with this definitional dissonance is that the literature has often treated these measures as if they were minor variants of the same underlying reform, akin to different flavours of ice cream. But, in fact, deconcentration, delegation, and devolution differ fundamentally in organisational terms. They establish incentives that are fundamentally different from one another, which public officials – being rational – respond to in fundamentally different ways. We should not expect their effects to be similar, and indeed they are not. Studies that compare countries that deconcentrated with others that devolved or delegated are committing a basic methodological error. It is no wonder that their empirical findings are indeterminate – the studies themselves are confused. Happily, the solution to this problem is straightforward: pick one form of reform and compare only examples of that. This is the first key to making sense of the cacophony of decentralisation results.

Henceforth we define decentralisation in a restrictive way that is clear and conceptually discrete, so as to facilitate analytical precision. *Decentralisation is the devolution by central (that is, national) government of specific functions, with all of the administrative, political and economic attributes that these entail, to democratic local (that is, municipal) governments that are independent of the centre within a legally delimited geographic and functional domain.*

With respect to *empirical evidence*, Channa and Faguet (2016) point out that not all empirical evidence is created equal. Studies differ significantly in terms of the sectors they examine, the questions they ask, and the strength of their empirical identification. By classifying empirical results according to these three criteria, the authors show that the evidence does indeed speak with a more unified, less confused voice. Higher-quality evidence indicates that decentralisation increases technical efficiency across a variety of public services, from student test scores to infant mortality rates. Decentralisation also improves preference matching in education, and can do so in health under certain conditions, although the evidence for the latter two is somewhat weaker at this stage.

The third key to making sense of our evidence is *conceptual*. For too long, we have asked the wrong questions of our evidence, along the lines of 'Is decentralisation good or bad for X?' where X may be any policy output or outcome of interest, such as primary education provision or PISA scores. The problem with this approach is that it assumes decentralisation is a relatively simple reform with symmetric effects across different subnational units. This misunderstands the nature of decentralisation, which involves the transfer of power and resources to subnational jurisdictions that differ from each other in important ways. We should expect such jurisdictions to behave in ways that are as different to one another as are their underlying characteristics.

Put another way, the correct answer to the question 'Is decentralisation good for primary education?' is 'Yes, of course it is'. And the correct answer to the question 'Is decentralisation *bad* for primary education?', in the same country at the same time, under the same decentralisation reform, is 'Yes, of course it is'. In the presence of decentralisation, some municipalities will behave in ways that improve primary education outcomes. But other municipalities will behave in ways that worsen it, and many other municipalities will muddle along without great improvement or decay compared to centralised provision. Such heterogeneity is in the very nature of decentralisation; it is built into the reform.

A better class of decentralisation research question admits heterogeneity from the start, and asks 'Why are the good cases good and the bad ones bad?' And, more importantly, 'How can we shift the balance of outcomes away from bad realisations, towards good ones?' To do so is to acknowledge that the outcomes of decentralisation are simply the aggregation of hundreds or thousands of local dynamics across a country. Hence, to understand the effects of decentralisation at the national level, we must first understand how local government works. Faguet (2009; 2012) provides a theoretical model of local government, with quantitative and qualitative empirical tests.

2.2 The benefits of decentralisation

Why might decentralisation be a good idea? What are the key opportunities and constraints around which it should be designed to best suit a developing country? How might it help a country overcome some of its biggest development challenges? This section examines key arguments in favour of decentralisation through the lens of some of the social and political-economic characteristics typical of many developing countries. We then review empirical evidence on the extent to which reform has helped overcome key development obstacles.

Enthusiasm for decentralisation has an enviable pedigree. Arguments about the benefits of devolving authority to subnational units of government stretch at least as far back as Montesquieu (1748) and *The Federalist Papers* (Madison, Hamilton, and Jay 1788). The belief that the natural or most advantageous organisation of society involves multiple hierarchical tiers goes back much further. Aristotle (350s–340s BC) deconstructed the Greek city state 'into a three-tier hierarchy of households, villages, and the polis, each of which aims at a different good' (Treisman 2007, pp.7–8). Building on classical reasoning, Dante (c.1314–20) argued that 'Only in a pyramid of different-sized, nested communities could the full multiplicity of human potential be realized all at once' (Treisman 2007, p.8).

Modern claims about the advantages (and disadvantages) of decentralisation follow this gist but are far more numerous, typically framed in terms of economic and political variables (Figure 2.1). Although they span a number of disciplines, and use distinct terminologies and catchphrases, we can summarise them as follows. We divide them into arguments for versus arguments against decentralisation. We list arguments against for clarity and fairness, but focus the discussion that follows on the conditions associated with positive decentralisation outcomes.

Figure 2.1: Arguments for and against decentralisation

Arguments for. Decentralisation can
- improve information re: local wants and needs   ⎫
- increase citizen voice and participation   ⎪ 'Closer
- improve government accountability and responsiveness ⎬ to the
- deepen democracy   ⎭ people'
- improve the efficiency of government and public services
- improve economic performance
- strengthen the liberties of individuals and groups
- reduce the risk of civil conflicts

Arguments against. Decentralisation can
- decrease efficiency in public goods production
- decrease the quality of policymaking
- increase graft and corruption
- facilitate elite capture of government
- increase fiscal deficits and hence macroeconomic instability.

Improving democratic accountability and responsiveness

The first four arguments listed in Figure 2.1 are tightly intertwined, and can be bundled together as 'improving democratic accountability and responsiveness' by bringing governance and decisions 'closer to the people'. These are, in my view, the most important and powerful of all the arguments concerning decentralisation. In various forms and with different language, Mill (1895–61), Montesquieu (1748), Rousseau (1762), and Tocqueville (1835–40) all debated these points. This is what policy advocates refer to when they claim decentralisation will take government 'closer to the people'. The latter is more slogan than argument, although there is an unfortunate tendency in that literature to present it as an argument. The more serious version of Wallis and Oates (1988), widely cited, holds that decentralisation makes government more responsive to local needs by 'tailoring levels of consumption to the preferences of smaller, more homogeneous groups' (p.5). While this account is descriptively correct, it is analytically insufficient. Why does homogeneity imply responsiveness? Is the fundamental problem one of scale? It is my view that the principal sources of responsiveness lie deeper, in the incentives that officials face in decentralised versus centralised government regimes.[1]

The fundamental logic is as follows: by devolving power and authority from upper (usually central) to lower (regional or local) levels of government elected by their respective constituencies, decentralisation fundamentally changes the incentives that local authorities face, and thus – not surprisingly – their behaviour. (For ease of exposition, all subnational levels of government are henceforth referred to as 'local' government.) Under centralisation, those who hold authority over local matters are not elected by local citizens but rather *selected* by higher-level authorities, regardless of whether they are physically located locally or in the capital. Immediate accountability for their performance is thus upwards to the central government officials who have power over their salaries, careers and broader professional prospects (Riker 1964). Accountability does not run downwards to the citizens who consume the public goods and services they are meant to produce except at one or more removes, in the sense that central government officials are ultimately beholden to national electorates. 'Local' officials thus face clear, strong incentives to respond to central government priorities and concerns, and weak, muffled incentives to respond to local citizens' needs.

The most important effect of decentralisation is to reorient these incentives. 'Local' officials become local officials, whose tenure and career prospects are in the hands of the local citizens they serve, who elect them. The incentives that govern their performance are no longer received from on high but rather determined by those most directly affected by what they do. And accountability to local citizens is direct, no longer running through a national administration or various layers of bureaucracy.

This supply effect in the constitution of local authority generates a complementary demand effect. Citizens see the change in local officials' performance, understand the incentive change that has occurred, and become more involved in local politics (Faguet 2004b). They vote and exercise voice more because both tools are more powerful than before, and so more worth their while. This change will hold for both relatively homogeneous populations and those that are relatively heterogeneous, though the effect may differ in strength and type according to degree of homogeneity, as Mitra and Pal's results in this volume suggest. Elected officials, being largely rational, respond better to citizens' demands – not just because they 'should' but because it is in their interests to do so. The net effect is to shorten and tighten the loop of accountability between those who produce public goods and services and those who consume them.[2]

One of the main points of this chapter is that decentralisation works – if and when it works – through a fundamental effect on officials' incentives, and thence on government accountability to the governed. Surprisingly often, both enthusiasts and critics of reform omit this basic point in favour of second- and third-order arguments about whether decentralisation can increase growth or reduce ethnic conflicts, points to which we return below. Many of these things, such as inflation, the fiscal deficit, and ethnic conflicts and political stability in a nation more broadly, are important, and decentralisation may indeed affect them. But it does so via incentives and accountability; there is no direct effect. In the best cases, the new equilibrium that emerges after reform features greater citizen voice and participation and greater government responsiveness. It is one in which democracy has been both deepened and strengthened.

Boosting public sector efficiency and achieving faster economic growth

The fifth and sixth arguments in Figure 2.1 are also closely related. The case for decentralisation improving public sector efficiency follows directly from greater accountability and responsiveness. A public sector that is more responsive to citizens will tend to produce public goods and services better suited to local conditions and to citizens' needs (Khan et al. 2014). Such services will tend to be more effective in terms of solving real problems. More effective public services in areas such as education, transportation, and water and sanitation will, in turn, better support private sector activity. Private firms will find it easier to operate in such environments, and hence will be more likely to invest. This will lead to better economic performance and higher economic growth.

A separate logical chain posits that by increasing local governments' share of tax revenues, decentralisation gives them a larger stake in the performance of the local economy. This motivates local officials to implement policies that support businesses and promote growth for two reasons: (i) economic growth increases local tax receipts and hence officials' freedom of action, and (ii) growth increases officials' popularity. The effect is to make local governments compete for mobile capital by reducing public sector waste, inefficiency and corruption, and by providing infrastructure. When this happens nationwide, efficiency rises and the economy grows faster (Brennan and Buchanan 1980; Hayek 1948; Jin, Qian, and Weingast 2005; Roland 2000).

Strengthening individual and group liberties

Scholars from Hamilton (1769–1804) to Tocqueville (1835–40) to Weingast (2014) have argued that, in a decentralised or federal system of government, strong, legitimate local governments can protect individual freedoms by checking central government abuses. They can use their resources to resist or counteract specific government actions (for example, by suing central government, or implementing a countervailing tax or credit), and can threaten the centre financially by withholding tax receipts, in defence of their citizens. Diaz-Cayeros (2006) related how, in late 19th- and early 20th-century Brazil, repeated attempts by the centre to encroach on state power and independence were resisted using such means plus the credible threat of violence. In Brazil, state-level police forces, especially of Minas Gerais and Sao Paolo, 'constituted true armies that could effectively challenge the federal government' (p.211).

As for individuals, so too for ethnic, religious, and other identitarian groups (Faguet 2019). Many developing states were born out of international agreements, often with arbitrarily defined borders based on colonial partition more than internal political factors, with little to hold them together beyond guarantees by the international system (for example, Englebert 2000; Herbst 2001; Jackson and Rosberg 1986). They exist de jure but perhaps not de facto. Unlike European states in which power over a territory and its population generally came first and sovereignty and international recognition followed, many developing countries have not been able to consolidate power in order to achieve the internal consent or territorial reach necessary to exert authority over the entire state (Jackson and Rosberg 1986). This is a fundamental problem facing many African leaders (Englebert 2000; Herbst 2001).

The state may instead be made up of different ethnic groups spread over sometimes vast geographic areas, each with its own customs, language, and culture. A consciousness of common nationality is often lacking. Citizens do not feel represented by the government and perceive that leaders cater mainly to people of their own tribe or region, rather than to all citizens equally. In addition, parallel or rival forms of authority (for example, traditional chiefs, religious leaders, or drug lords) may supersede the authority of the state (Myrdal 1968).

How might decentralisation affect these challenges? First, bringing locally elected subnational leaders from different segments of the country into government, and thus giving representation to people of different groups, may incite parts of the population that formerly felt excluded from the state to feel represented and included (Faguet 2019). Indeed, federal, decentralised institutions have long been recommended as a mechanism to hold together fractured, 'multi-national states' (Brancati 2004; Horowitz 2003; Lijphart 1977; Stepan 2001; Zuazo, Faguet, and Bonifaz 2012). Where divisions are defined territorially, decentralisation is said to promote the formation of multiple but complementary identities where citizens can simultaneously carry both an ethnic identity and a national identity (Stepan 2001). Decentralisation can thereby act as a pressure valve for nationalist aspirations. In Canada and Spain, for example, decentralisation has been deemed a success in keeping fractious provinces like Quebec and Catalunya from seceding. In the UK, the devolution of regional powers to the Northern Ireland Assembly was the critical element that made successful peace talks with the Irish Republican Army possible.

But there are also many opposing arguments. Some claim that decentralisation will build a federalist mentality, undermining efforts to build national unity and identity. It may even deepen divides between groups and intensify conflict by reinforcing cultural or ethnic identities. Second, decentralisation may lead fractious groups to want ever more autonomy. In this vein, former British Prime Minister John Major argued against devolving powers to Scotland, claiming it was 'the Trojan horse to independence' that would lead to friction and eventually demands for full independence (Brancati 2009). With more power and independence, decentralised areas may realise they can manage their affairs better on their own. Decentralisation may give subnational leaders experience in governing. Several decentralised regions have seceded after first setting up their own decentralised institutions. South Sudan is one recent example.

The key theoretical issue is whether decentralisation will stoke centripetal or centrifugal forces. Opponents of decentralisation claim devolving power and resources will empower those who seek secession, and – if they prove reasonably competent – assuage citizens' ill-formed fear of the unknown by showing them local authorities who provide services and manage public budgets adequately. Proponents claim that the same stimulus – the devolution of power and resources to even secessionist politicians – will generate the opposite response. Like an onion, it will peel away the outer layers of support from such leaders and parties, stripping them of constituents whose demands can be satisfied by more limited measures of autonomy, such as local control over public services, minority language rights, and symbolic goods such as public art and celebration, so isolating the hard secessionist core that seeks full independence from the mass of citizens (Faguet, Fox, and Pöschl 2015a).

Which side of this argument is correct is not an issue of decentralisation per se but rather depends on the nature of the secessionist impulse and the source of such parties' and leaders' appeal. Where groups are distinct, geographically concentrated, and highly mobilised against one another through violence, it may be difficult to imagine continuing cohabitation within a single nation, barring the comprehensive defeat of one group. But where groups are harder to distinguish, or where they comingle, or where mobilisations are only partial, decentralisation may offer the 'steam valve' required to satisfy those who actually demand autonomy, not full secession, and help to ultimately hold a nation together.

In practice, the more important factor is likely to be the regional specificity of elite interests. If coherent regional elites have more to gain from secession (greater control over resources at the cost of lost markets and lost influence) than autonomy (partial control over resources, continued access to national markets and policymaking), then national integrity is in much greater peril. Regional elites will have an incentive to invest in creating conditions propitious to national schism. Beyond funding political parties and campaigns, this may well extend to supporting armed insurgencies and investing in the sorts of violence against civilians that peace talks cannot later reconcile. The recent history of the Balkans richly and sadly illustrates this dynamic.

On the other hand, the evident success of both developed and developing federations that have strong regional identities but much stronger national identities, such as Brazil, Germany, India, and the United States, demonstrates that decentralised government can stitch together diverse countries in ways that lead to neither subnational tyranny nor secession. One of the keys is regionally diverse elite interests. There are undoubtedly powerful elites in Sao Paolo, North Rhine-Westphalia, Uttar Pradesh, and California. Any of these would rank as a medium-sized to large independent country in both population and GDP. It would be a perfectly respectable country of important weight in the international system. And yet secession is not seriously debated in any of these places. Why don't these states' elites agitate for secession?

Because their political and economic interests span state boundaries. Business and political leaders in California and Uttar Pradesh have more to lose than to gain from splitting from the other 49 US or 27 Indian states, despite the fact that all of them are smaller. Pulling up the drawbridges would leave elites in North Rhine-Westphalia and Sao Paolo unambiguously in control of a non-trivial country instead of a state. But, from their leading positions in these states, elites in all four exert considerable influence over much larger and more important countries. And they have access to considerably larger internal markets, and can influence international treaties that give them better access to the world economy and a stronger voice in international affairs. They benefit from the unity of a nation they can expect to sway and perhaps even lead. They would lose from its break-up. So they invest in unity, not division.

Interestingly, Stepan (1999) argued that another deciding factor in the ability of federalist states to hold together fractious groups is the timing of elections. When elections are introduced in the subunits of a new federal polity prior to countrywide elections, and in the absence of countrywide parties, the potential for subsequent secession is high compared to when national elections are held first. National elections produce a sense of common identity and purpose whereas subnational elections can generate fractious local parties. Of the nine states that once comprised communist Europe, six were unitary and three were federal. Yugoslavia, the USSR, and Czechoslovakia are examples of countries that first held subnational elections prior to national elections, and subsequently broke up into 22 independent states.

Can decentralisation be designed in ways that hold fractious groups together rather than promoting secession? Yes – by decentralising power and authority to a level *below* that of major ethnic, linguistic, or other identity groups. In this way, empowered subnational units will tend not to be identified with group identity or privilege. Rather than stoking divisive tensions, local government will instead become identified with issues of efficiency and service provision (Faguet, Fox, and Pöschl 2015a). In a country where an ethnic minority is concentrated in one region, decentralising to the regional level is far more likely, all else being equal, to reinforce ethnic divisions, and place authority and resources in the hands of those with most to gain from national break-up. Decentralising to the local level, by contrast, will create many units of any given ethnicity, and most likely others that are mixed. No level of government will be associated with any particular ethnicity, and hence not with ethnicity per se. Comparisons across local governments will tend to focus more on issues of competence in service provision than identity, revindication, or pride.

This is not to say that decentralisation somehow neutralises the importance of ethnic or religious identity for governance. Indeed, in this volume, Martinez-Bravo et al. (Chapter 6) find that the accountability-enhancing effects of village elections in China were larger in more homogeneous villages, and ascribe this to a greater capacity of such electorates to monitor their leaders. The leaders of homogeneous villages then implemented policies that better reflected villagers' underlying preferences. Likewise, Mitra and Pal (Chapter 7; also 2022) show in this volume that ethnically more diverse communities in Indonesia tend to use voting to choose their leaders, whereas more homogeneous communities use non-electoral, consensus-building methods. The former, furthermore, were more successful than comparable consensus-building communities in raising local income and local development. And Martinez-Bravo (2014; Martinez-Bravo, Mukherjee, and Stegmann 2017) showed differential effects of social heterogeneity on local development depending on how community leaders are chosen (elected vs nominated). These results all underline the more general point that decentralising to a level beneath that of the main ethnic or religious cleavage in a society tends to associate that identity with public investment and service provision rather than with group privilege and pride. It is not that identity ceases to matter after decentralisation, as those studies have shown, but rather that decentralisation redirects it from some of the destructive ways in which it can be activated by separatist leaders.

Complementary reforms that promote a single internal market for goods and services nationwide can also help by preventing the development of elites with regionally specific economic interests who might gain from national schism. These would instead be substituted by elites whose assets or historical bases might be in a particular region but whose economic interests are multiregional, and who therefore have a strong interest in national integrity and growth (Faguet, Fox, and Pöschl 2015b). Specific measures such as improved infrastructure and transport links can help bring this about, in addition to facilitating the flow of people and ideas across an economy, so binding it together from the bottom up.

Reducing the risk of conflict and facilitating power-sharing

The relationship between decentralisation and conflict has long been a topic of debate (Green 2008). Arguments overlap significantly with those on self-determination and secession, since the failure to integrate regions and minorities into the state is a key source of conflict. As argued above, decentralisation can accommodate diversity by giving territorially concentrated groups the power to make their own decisions about issues that most interest them (Lijphart 1996; Tsebelis 1990). This may diffuse social and political tensions and prevent conflict (Bardhan 2002). Giving groups control may protect them against abuse or neglect from the centre or from one another, which can cause conflict. For instance, if a group is experiencing economic disadvantage, it could be given the power to control its own resources and decide how to allocate resources. If fear of social extinction is the cause of conflict, it could be granted control over issues such as education, religion or culture in order to protect its language and customs (Brancati 2009).

Others take the view that decentralisation will instead lead to increased conflict with fractious groups. Roeder and Rothchild (2005), for example, contended that decentralisation will give subnational leaders the resources and 'institutional weapons' they need to mobilise the local population and demand more political power from the centre, thereby elevating tensions. Subnational leaders may also gain prominence and followers, and subsequently threaten the power of national political elites, again causing conflict. Some note that decentralisation has produced local leaders who discriminate against minorities in their own regions (Horowitz 2003; Lijphart 1993). Brancati (2009), for example, pointed out that allowing parts of northern Nigeria to adopt their own (Sharia) law has aggravated rather than defused tensions between Christians and Muslims, when the Christian minority was forced to comply. This underlines the importance of protecting minority rights, which theorists going back at least as far as the *Federalist Papers* (Hamilton, Madison, and Jay 1788), and including most major contributions since (see for example, Dahl 1971; Dahl 1989), have considered critical to the stability and sustainability of democracy as a form of government.

How can decentralisation be implemented so as to dampen, and not promote, conflict? Decentralised governments that are responsive to national minorities will drain tensions from the polity. But local governments that become 'little tyrannies', ignoring or oppressing local minorities, will stoke tensions, threatening not just particular governments but the notion of democracy itself. Hence decentralisation should be designed with strong local accountability mechanisms that align local leaders' incentives with the will of local citizens and allow voters to hold politicians responsible for their decisions. And central government should enact strong safeguards of minority rights nationwide, to which individuals and groups can appeal in any locality.

How do we construct local political systems that promote responsiveness to voters and avoid little tyrannies? A well-developed political science literature on the trade-offs between descriptive vs substantive representation is relevant here. Descriptive and substantive representation are generally considered the two most important forms of electoral representation. Their main difference is that, in descriptive representation, representatives have similar backgrounds to the people they represent, whereas, in substantive representation, representatives focus on the issues most important to a particular group (Mansbridge 1999). But, beyond this distinction, lessons for policymakers are few. While some studies show that descriptive representation ensures substantive representation, others do not find a tight correspondence between the two, and so the literature is mixed in this respect (Bratton and Ray 2002; Mansbridge 2003).

In a post-conflict environment, or one where the risk of conflict is high, decentralisation can underpin power-sharing arrangements that settle power struggles and stave off violent conflict. This mechanism operates by creating or empowering subnational levels of government to which political power, responsibility, and resources, are devolved. In doing so it also creates new fora for political competition, and hence new prizes over which opposing parties can compete. This solves the winner-takes-all problem inherent to centralisation, where parties in government wield huge central government resources and reap huge rewards, and opposition parties are left to wither. In a federal system, by contrast, opposition parties can still win power over states and local governments (O'Neill 2003), and hence enhanced voice in national debates and opportunities to display competence in government. The penalty of losing national elections is much less steep, and so the temptation to win at any cost greatly lessened. This can help cement the peace in a post-conflict environment.

Decentralisation, for instance, has recently been advocated for Iraq and Afghanistan with exactly this in mind (Barfield 2011; Brinkerhoff and Johnson 2009). Green (2011) explained how Ethiopia's decentralisation process in the 1990s was part of a civil war settlement that successfully maintained the peace for three decades. The country was divided into 11 federal regions. This fragmented the political opposition, creating various new parties that competed against one another for power over the newly created regions, while preventing a return to conflict for power over central government. Peace was maintained and the government in power at the federal level remained free of coups (and electoral defeat) for three decades. Such shifts in power arrangements can be used to diffuse power struggles at the top. But, in other cases, decentralisation may merely shift conflict downward rather than eliminating it altogether. Uganda's government under President Yoweri Museveni implemented a decentralisation programme in 1986 in order to reduce national-level conflict.

While successful in this regard, Green (2008) argued that the ultimate effect was to replace conflict at the top with conflict at the local level.

Can decentralisation be designed so as to promote power-sharing? A properly operating decentralised system should naturally lead to the sharing of powers that have been devolved to different subnational levels of government. Few additional reforms are required other than the avoidance of electoral and fiscal distortions. In countries where politics is closed or captured, measures that promote open, competitive local politics will tend towards fairness and power-sharing, and away from capture and conflict. Electoral finance laws that support a level political playing field have particular importance in this regard, as one of the most powerful and prevalent ways in which democracy is distorted is through the flow of money into campaigns. Where political competition is open to new entrants and the playing field is level, elections will tend to be fought over issues of substance to local voters. In such places, political conflict and violence will tend to transform naturally into electoral contestation, which is by far the better outcome.

2.3 How to build decentralisation – a framework for development

Let us now turn to the specifics of policy design. How do we allocate powers and responsibilities across hierarchical levels of government? Which levels of government should we design in the first place? Which services and powers, and how many resources, do we devolve to which levels?

These questions are part of a different but closely related literature called fiscal federalism. Fiscal federalism focuses on two interrelated issues: who taxes and spends? That is, the division of taxing and spending responsibilities among levels of government (national, regional, local, and so on). And what is taxed and spent on? That is, the discretion given to regional and local governments to determine expenditures and revenues.

According to the fiscal federalism literature (Besley, Faguet, and Tomassi (2003) provide a useful overview), public services should be devolved to subnational levels of government when they have the following characteristics:

- Geographic specificity, meaning they are characterised by low externalities, or economic 'spillovers', to other regions or localities;
- Heterogeneous demand, meaning citizens across the country do not prefer the same public good or service – citizens in different locations have different preferences;
- Local information is important for their production, implying that such local information is comparatively expensive or difficult for central government to obtain; and,
- Low economies of scale, meaning it is not more efficient to produce a particular good or service in one, centralised way or location.

The broad principle of government design that fiscal federalism puts forward is the *encompassing principle*, which holds that powers and responsibilities should be assigned to levels of government such that all relevant externalities are encompassed by that level of government. Hence national externalities and public goods, such as national defence or a trunk highway system, are best dealt with by national governments, while local externalities and public goods, such as rubbish collection and street lighting, are best dealt with by local governments.

Building on this, one of the crowning achievements of fiscal federalism theory is the Oates decentralisation theorem (1972). This holds that local governments should be responsible for all forms of spending that do not inflict externalities on other jurisdictions. The level and type of such spending can be tailored to the desires of local residents. This is why services like rubbish collection, street lighting, and fire prevention are particularly well-suited to a high degree of decentralisation, that is, to local government. But it is important to note that actual political jurisdictions across most countries will rarely match the optimal scope of all the public goods and services that must be provided. Hence there will always be a need for intergovernmental cooperation among different hierarchical levels to provide a full suite of services.

How should decentralised tax systems be designed? Fiscal federalism puts forward five basic guidelines for designing revenue systems:

- local taxes should be as neutral as possible, such that they do not distort economic behaviour;
- the benefits and costs of local taxes should be clear to citizens;
- the incidence of local taxes should be equitable across taxpayers;
- administration and compliance costs should be kept low, implying that complex taxes should be retained by central tax authorities; and
- mobile tax bases should be taxed nationally, not locally.

Employing these criteria shows that the most appropriate local taxes for local governments in developing countries are property taxes and user charges. Property has the advantage of being easy to identify and assess, which is not the case for many other classes of assets or economic activity. Further, property values are linked to local prosperity and hence local policy. This provides local governments with an incentive to undertake policies that increase the size of the local economy. It also provides a channel by which local officials are encouraged to be accountable to local taxpayers. User charges include public transport fares, housing and business rents, market fees, and water and heating charges, to name a few. They help defray the costs of providing these services, and help make local officials directly accountable to the users of these services. Some highly developed countries also devolve income taxes and VAT to regional and local governments, although this is much less common in developing countries. The evidence shows that the lowest-income countries are unable to mobilise much local revenue through property taxes, partly because citizens are not used to paying them and partly because in most local-ities poverty levels are high and property valuations are low.

For countries at any level of development, local taxes are likely to be greatly exceeded by local expenditure needs; this is doubly true for developing coun-tries. How do we square this circle? The answer is intergovernmental transfers among different levels of government. In practice this tends to mean reve-nue-sharing by central authorities, who have significant advantages in raising taxes that are complicated or based on mobile assets, with regional and local authorities. Revenue-sharing can take one of two broad forms:

a. *by formula*, for example on a per capita basis; or
b. *by origin*, where tax revenues are returned to the localities where they originated, for example oil and mineral rents, or commercial taxes.

Additionally, central governments typically choose to make grants or subven-tions that are either:

c. *targeted* to support specific expenditures, such as primary education; or
d. *untargeted*, for discretionary use by local governments (for example, block grants).

Targeted grants are typically used to support priorities favoured by national government, while untargeted grants allow regions and localities to choose their own priorities. Targeted and block grants generally have two main pur-poses: vertical and horizontal equalisation. *Vertical equalisation* refers to attempts to close the gap between the costs of services devolved to subna-tional governments, and the revenues they are able to mobilise. *Horizontal equalisation* refers to the attempts to close the gap between richer and poorer districts' revenues. This is intended to ensure greater equality in public ser-vice provision, such that, for example, rich districts do not have much-better schools, roads, and water provision than poor districts, thus generating a vicious circle in which wealth begets wealth and poverty begets poverty.

How are these guidelines implemented in practice? Figure 2.2 shows the value of all intergovernmental transfers to local governments as a propor-tion of local government revenues for a selection of developing and developed countries. There is considerable variation among countries, from lows of 10 per cent in Iceland and Switzerland to more than 80 per cent in Indonesia and Lithuania and more than 90 per cent in Uganda. There do not seem to be any instantly obvious patterns by region or level of development. This non-pattern is broadly repeated for the larger set of countries for which data are available. It illustrates how considerably real-world practice differs from the principles of fiscal federalism outlined above, not least because many countries have implemented decentralisation only partially, a key point at the core of Deva-rajan and Khemani's chapter in this volume.

Figure 2.2: Intergovernmental transfers as a percentage share (%) of total local government revenues, in 2020

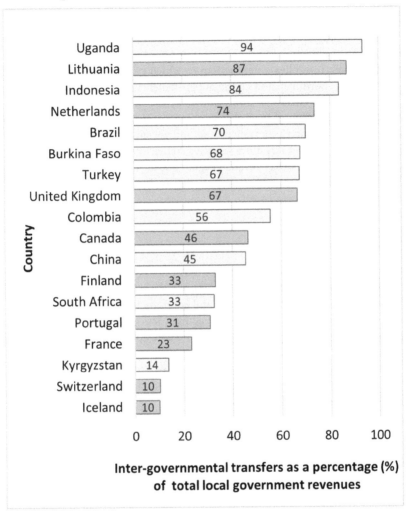

Inter-governmental transfers as a percentage (%) of total local government revenues

Source: IMF Global Financial Statistics; OECD Fiscal Decentralisation Database.
Notes: Blue bars show European (or European-influenced) liberal democracies.

One of the overarching conclusions of the fiscal federalism literature, which would appear to be obvious but is seldom acknowledged and perhaps insufficiently understood, is that decentralisation does not do away with the centre. The decentralisation literature often portrays key policy options as 'central versus local'. This is mainly a rhetorical device, and is very far from capturing what actually happens to fiscal flows and public authority in countries that decentralise. The reasons for this flow naturally from our discussion above. Decentralisation does not imply getting rid of one level of government in favour of another but rather an increasing 'complexification' of public service provision in the interest of greater responsiveness, higher quality, and greater economic efficiency (in addition to a number of potential second-order benefits discussed above).

Decentralising the provision of education, for example, does not imply that budgets and authority over schools are transferred wholesale to local governments. Rather, it implies a new system in which central, regional, and local governments coordinate and cooperate intimately to mobilise revenues, hire personnel, define curricula, build infrastructure, and supply and maintain schools for the benefit of local children. A decentralised education system is far more complex than a centralised one, and will always involve multiple levels of government. But it is more sensitive, better informed, and more robust, and should produce better results (Faguet 2004a; Faguet, Khan, and Kanth 2020; Faguet and Sánchez 2008; Faguet and Sánchez 2014; Khan, Faguet, and Ambel 2017).

Conclusions

This review of decentralisation theory and evidence has found a great deal of signal in the noise within this immense literature. The ambiguous empirical literature rife with mixed results and contradictory policy advice that so many authors bemoaned for so long is actually less confusing than it initially appears. The way through this empirical and conceptual thicket involves:

- Defining decentralisation in a clear, restrictive, discrete way. I suggest democratic devolution, but others may be chosen so long as they are clear and analysts stick to them.
- Realising that all evidence is not created equal. Higher-quality evidence shows that decentralisation increases technical efficiency in public services and can improve preference matching too.
- Asking better questions about decentralisation that, in the presence of any specific reform, admit heterogeneity of response. Rather than seeking uniform or average effects, exploit instead the variation that naturally results from any decentralisation reform to explore why some subnational units perform better than others, and how we can shift the balance of outcomes from worse to better ones.

Done correctly, decentralisation can improve the democratic accountability and responsiveness of governments by changing the incentives that local officials face. Incentives shift from upward-facing in a centralised regime, where officials seek to please superiors at higher levels of the administration, to downward-facing in a decentralised regime, where officials seek to please voters. Done correctly, decentralisation can also improve public sector efficiency in ways that lead to faster economic growth. Local governments more attuned to the needs of voters will also be more attuned to local economic conditions, and will tend to implement policies and investments that support growth in the local economy.

Perhaps less obviously, decentralisation can strengthen individual and group liberties by creating more levels of government that representatives of different social groups or minorities can use to promote their interests. In this way, decentralisation can stoke centripetal forces that help hold a diverse nation together, peeling layers of popular support away from the hard core of secessionist leaders who would split a country apart. Such dynamics are likely at play in countries like Brazil, Germany, and India, where powerful elites from important, coherent regions could invest in movements to divide their countries but choose not to. Decentralisation to a level below that of a nation's major social cleavage can help in this regard. Relatedly, decentralisation can decrease the risk of conflict and facilitate power-sharing if it is designed with accountability mechanisms that align leaders' incentives with voters', and strong safeguards for minority rights. The simple fact of creating subnational governments helps end the winner-takes-all problem inherent to centralisation that can destabilise a country by raising the cost of losing power to unacceptable levels.

How should decentralising countries allocate public powers and responsibilities across different levels of government? The fiscal federalism literature teaches us to devolve services with geographic specificity, heterogeneity in demand, low economies of scale, and where local information is important for their production to lower levels of government. Each level of government should be responsible for all forms of spending that do not inflict externalities on other jurisdictions. These services can then be tailored to the needs of local residents.

How should decentralised tax systems that pay for such services be designed? Local taxes should be neutral and non-distortionary. The benefits and costs of local taxes should be transparent to citizens. Tax incidence should be equitable across taxpayers. Administration and compliance costs of such systems should be low. And local taxes should focus on immobile tax bases. These guidelines imply that property taxes and user charges are most natural to local governments, whereas taxes on income and capital should be levied by higher-level authorities.

Subnational expenditure needs are likely to greatly exceed locally generated revenues. How do we square this circle? Revenue-sharing among levels of government by formula or according to origin, in ways that are targeted to specific priorities or untargeted, such as block grants, is the answer. But data shows that the real world diverges significantly from these ideal guidelines. The share of intergovernmental transfers in local government revenues varies remarkably among countries in the same region, or at similar levels of development.

Lastly, reformers should remember that decentralisation does not eliminate the centre, nor even debilitate it. Rather, it ushers in a new era of more complex service provision that demands coordination and cooperation among multiple tiers of government. When such a system achieves its potential, it describes a public sector that is more responsive, more efficient, and more robust, producing outputs of higher quality for its citizens.

Acknowledgements

I am grateful to the World Bank for supporting this research, and thank Neelam Nizar Verjee and Tiago Carneiro Peixoto for detailed and insightful suggestions. I also thank Catherine Boone, Patrick Dunleavy, Rachel Gisselquist, Adnan Khan, Stuti Khemani, Dilip Mookherjee, Michael Mbate, Sarmistha Pal, Mahvish Shami, and colleagues at the LSE's International Development Department, the World Bank, and the LSE–Surrey Workshop on Decentralized Governance for their thoughtful comments. All remaining errors are my own.

Endnotes

[1] The degree of homogeneity of a population – ethnic, religious, or otherwise – is nonetheless important as it may affect the manner and ease with which local vs. central officials are able to aggregate public goods preferences (Alesina, Baqir, and Easterly 1999). I return to this issue in more detail in the discussion of individual and group liberties.

[2] Martinez-Bravo (2014) explored the extent to which decentralisation promoted democratisation or elite capture among local governments in Indonesia.

References

Alesina, Alberto; Baqir, Reza; and Easterly, William (1999) 'Public Goods and Ethnic Divisions', *Quarterly Journal of Economics*, vol.114, no.4, pp.1243–84. https://doi.org/10.1162/003355399556269

Bardhan, Pranab (2002) 'Decentralization of Governance and Development.' *Journal of Economic Perspectives*, vol.16, no.4, pp.185–205. https://doi.org/10.1257/089533002320951037

Bardhan, Pranab and Mookherjee, Dilip (eds) (2006) *Decentralization and Local Governance in Developing Countries: A Comparative Perspective*, Cambridge, MA: MIT Press. https://mitpress.mit.edu/9780262524544/decentralization-and-local -governance-in-developing-countries

Barfield, Thomas (2011) 'Afghanistan's Ethnic Puzzle: Decentralizing Power before the US Withdrawal', *Foreign Affairs*, vol.90, no.5, pp.54–65. https://www.jstor.org/stable/23041776

Besley, Timothy; Faguet, Jean-Paul; and Tommasi, Mariano (2003) 'A Synoptic Guide to Decentralization', Initiative for Policy Dialogue, Columbia University. http://eprints.lse.ac.uk/49818

Brancati, Dawn (2004) 'Can Federalism Stabilize Iraq?' *The Washington Quarterly*, vol.27, no.2, pp.7–21. https://doi.org/10.1162/016366004773097687

Brancati, Dawn (2009) *Peace by Design: Managing Intrastate Conflict through Decentralization*, Oxford: Oxford University Press. https://doi.org/10.1093/acprof:oso/9780199549009.001.0001

Bratton, Kathleen A. and Ray, Leonard P. (2002) 'Descriptive Representation, Policy Outcomes, and Municipal Day-Care Coverage in Norway', *American Journal of Political Science*, vol.46, no.2, pp.428–37. https://doi.org/10.2307/3088386

Brennan, Geoffrey and Buchanan, James M. (1980) *The Power to Tax: Analytical Foundations of a Fiscal Constitution*, New York: Cambridge University Press. https://doi.org/10.1017/S0047279400011971

Brinkerhoff, Derick W. and Johnson, Ronald (2009) 'Decentralized Local Governance in Fragile States: Learning from Iraq', *International Review of Administrative Sciences*, vol.75, no.4, pp.585–607. https://doi.org/10.1177/0020852309349

Campbell, Tim (2001) *The Quiet Revolution: The Rise of Political Participation and Leading Cities with Decentralization in Latin America and the Caribbean*, Pittsburgh, PA: University of Pittsburgh Press. https://digital.library.pitt.edu/islandora/object/pitt:31735055592533

Channa, Anila and Faguet, Jean-Paul (2016) 'Decentralization of Health and Education in Developing Countries: A Quality-Adjusted Review of the Empirical Literature', *World Bank Research Observer*, vol.31, no.2, pp.199–241. https://doi.org/10.1093/wbro/lkw001

Dahl, Robert (1971) *Polyarchy: Participation and Opposition*, New Haven, CT: Yale University Press.

Dahl, Robert (1989) *Democracy and Its Critics*, New Haven, CT: Yale.

Diaz-Cayeros, Alberto (2006) *Federalism, Fiscal Authority and Centralization in Latin America*, Cambridge: Cambridge University Press. https://doi.org/10.1017/CBO9780511617928

Englebert, Pierre (2000) *State Legitimacy and Development in Africa*, Boulder, CO: Lynne Rienner.

Faguet, Jean-Paul (2004a) 'Why So Much Centralization? A Model of Primitive Centripetal Accumulation', LSE-STICERD Development Economics Discussion Paper No.43, London School of Economics and Political Science. http://eprints.lse.ac.uk/482/1/Centralization.pdf

Faguet, Jean-Paul (2004b) 'Building Democracy in Quicksand: Altruism, Empire and the United States', *Challenge: The Magazine of Economic Affairs*, vol.47, pp.73–93. http://www.jstor.org/stable/40722254

Faguet, Jean-Paul (2009) 'Governance from Below in Bolivia: A Theory of Local Government with Two Empirical Tests', *Latin American Politics and Society*, vol.51, no.4, pp.29–68. https://doi.org/10.1111/j.1548-2456.2009.00063.x

Faguet, Jean-Paul (2012) *Decentralization and Popular Democracy: Governance from Below in Bolivia*, Ann Arbor: University of Michigan Press. https://doi.org/10.3998/mpub.175269

Faguet, Jean-Paul (2014) 'Decentralization and Governance', *World Development*, vol.53, pp.2–13. http://dx.doi.org/10.1016/j.worlddev.2013.01.002

Faguet, Jean-Paul (2019) 'Revolution from Below: Cleavage Displacement and the Collapse of Elite Politics in Bolivia', *Politics & Society*, vol.47, no.2, pp.205–50. https://doi.org/10.1177/0032329219845944

Faguet, Jean-Paul; Fox, Ashley M.; and Pöschl, Caroline (2015a) 'Does Decentralization Strengthen or Weaken the State? Authority and Social Learning in a Supple State', in Faguet, Jean-Paul and Pöschl, Caroline (eds) *Is Decentralization Good for Development? Perspectives from Academics and Policy Makers*, Oxford: Oxford University Press.

Faguet, Jean-Paul; Fox, Ashley M.; and Pöschl, Caroline (2015b) 'Decentralizing for a Deeper, More Supple Democracy', *Journal of Democracy*, vol.26, no.4, pp.60–74. https://doi.org/10.1353/jod.2015.0059

Faguet, Jean-Paul; Khan, Qaiser; and Kanth, Devarakonda Priyanka (2020) 'Decentralization's Effects on Education and Health: Evidence from Ethiopia', *Publius: The Journal of Federalism*, vol.51, no.1, pp.79–103. https://doi.org/10.1093/publius/pjaa025

Faguet, Jean-Paul and Sánchez, Fabio (2008) 'Decentralization's Effects on Educational Outcomes in Bolivia and Colombia', *World Development*, vol.36, pp.1294–316. http://dx.doi.org/10.1016/j.worlddev.2007.06.021

Faguet, Jean-Paul and Sánchez, Fabio (2014) 'Decentralization and Access to Social Services in Colombia', *Public Choice*, vol.160, no.1–2, pp.227–49. https://doi.org/10.1007/s11127-013-0077-7

Green, Elliott D. (2008) 'Decentralization and Conflict in Uganda', *Conflict, Security and Development*, vol.8, no.4, pp.427–50. https://doi.org/10.1080/14678800802539317

Green, Elliott D. (2011) 'Decentralization and Political Opposition in Contemporary Africa: Evidence from Sudan and Ethiopia', *Democratization*, vol.18, no.5, 1087–105. https://doi.org/10.1080/13510347.2011.603476

Hayek, Friedrich A. (1948) *Individualism and Economic Order*, Chicago, IL: University of Chicago Press.

Herbst, Jeffrey (2001) 'States and Power in Africa: Comparative Lessons in Authority and Control', Princeton, NJ: Princeton University Press.

Horowitz, Donald L. (2003) 'The Cracked Foundations of the Right to Secede', *Journal of Democracy*, vol.14, no.2, pp.5–17. https://doi.org/10.1353/jod.2003.0033

Jackson, Robert and Rosberg, Carl (1986) 'Sovereignty and Underdevelopment: Juridical Statehood and the African Crisis', *Journal of Modern African Studies*, vol.24, no.1, pp.1–31. https://doi.org/10.1017/S0022278X0000673X

Jin, Hehui; Qian, Yingyi; and Weingast, Harry R. (2005) 'Regional Decentralization and Fiscal Incentives: Federalism, Chinese Style', *Journal of Public Economics*, vol.89, pp.1719–42. https://ideas.repec.org/a/eee/pubeco/v89y2005i9-10p1719-1742.html

Khan, Qaiser; Faguet, Jean-Paul; and Ambel, Alemayehu (2017) 'Blending Top-Down Federalism with Bottom-Up Engagement to Reduce Inequality in Ethiopia', *World Development*, vol.96, pp.326–42. https://documents1.worldbank.org/curated/en/971991468180852923/pdf/WPS7511.pdf

Khan, Qaiser; Faguet, Jean-Paul; Gaukler, Christopher; and Mekasha, Wendmsyamregne (2014) 'Improving Basic Services for the Bottom Forty Percent: Lessons from Ethiopia', Washington, DC: World Bank. http://issuu.com/world.bank.publications/docs/9781464803314

Lijphart, Arend (1977) *Democracy in Plural Societies*, New Haven, CT: Yale University Press. https://www.jstor.org/stable/j.ctt1dszvhq

Lijphart, Arend (1993) 'Power-Sharing, Ethnic Agnosticism, and Political Pragmatism', *Transformations*, vol.21, pp.94–99. http://transformationjournal.org.za/wp-content/uploads/2017/03/tran021007.pdf

Lijphart, Arend (1996) 'The Framework Document on Northern Ireland and the Theory of Power-Sharing', *Government and Opposition*, vol.31, no.3, pp.267–74. https://doi.org/10.1111/j.1477-7053.1996.tb01190.x

Litvack, Jennie Ilene; Ahmad, Junaid; and Bird, Richard Miller (1998) *Rethinking Decentralization in Developing Countries*, Washington, DC: World Bank.

Hamilton, Alexander; Madison, James; and Jay, John (1788/1961) *The Federalist Papers*, New York: Tudor.

Manor, James (1999) *The Political Economy of Democratic Decentralization*, Washington, DC: The World Bank. https://doi.org/10.1596/0-8213-4470-6

Mansbridge, Jane (1999) 'Should Blacks Represent Blacks and Women Represent Women? A Contingent "Yes"', *Journal of Politics*, vol.61, no.3, pp.628–57. https://doi.org/10.2307/2647821

Mansbridge, Jane (2003) 'Rethinking Representation', *American Political Science Review*, vol.97, no.4, pp.515–28. https://www.jstor.org/stable/3593021

Martinez-Bravo, Monica (2014) 'The Role of Local Officials in New Democracies: Evidence from Indonesia', *American Economic Review*, vol.104, no.4, pp.1–45. https://doi.org/10.1257/aer.104.4.1244

Martinez-Bravo, Monica; Mukherjee, Priya; and Stegmann, Andreas (2017) 'The Non-Democratic Roots of Elite Capture: Evidence from Soeharto Mayors in Indonesia', *Econometrica*, vol.85, no.6, pp.1991–2010. https://doi.org/10.3982/ECTA14125

Mill, John Stuart (1895–61/1993). *Utilitarianism; On Liberty; Considerations on Representative Government; Remarks on Bentham's Philosophy*, G. Williams (ed.), London: Everyman.

Mitra, Anirban and Pal, Sarmistha (2022) 'Ethnic Diversity, Social Norms and Elite Capture: Theory and Evidence from Indonesia', *Economica*, vol.89, no.356, pp.947–96. https://dx.doi.org/10.1111/ecca.12423

Montesquieu, Baron de (C de Secondat) (1989) [1748]. *The Spirit of the Laws*, trans. A.M. Cohler, B.C. Miller and H. Stone, Cambridge: Cambridge University Press.

Myrdal, Gunnar (1968) *Asian Drama: An Inquiry into the Poverty of Nations*, New York: Pantheon.

O'Neill, Kathleen (2003) 'Decentralization as an Electoral Strategy', *Comparative Political Studies*, vol.36, no.9, pp.1068–91. https://doi.org/10.1177/0010414003257098

Oates, Wallace E (1972) *Fiscal Federalism*, New York: Harcourt Brace Jovanovich.

Riker, William H. (1964) *Federalism: Origin, Operation, Significance*, Boston, MA: Little, Brown.

Roeder, Philip and Rothchild, Donald (eds) (2005) *Sustainable Peace: Power and Democracy after Civil Wars*, Ithaca, NY: Cornell University Press.

Roland, Gerard (2000) *Transition and Economics: Politics, Markets, and Firms*, Cambridge, MA: MIT Press.

Rondinelli, Dennis A. (1981) 'Government Decentralization in Comparative Perspective: Theory and Practice in Developing Countries', *International*

Review of Administrative Sciences, vol.47, pp.133–45.
https://doi.org/10.1177/002085238004700205

Rondinelli, Dennis A.; Cheema, Shabbir; and Nellis, John (1983) 'Decentralization in Developing Countries: A Review of Recent Experience', World Bank Staff Working Paper No.581. Washington, DC: World Bank.
https://documents1.worldbank.org/curated/en/868391468740679709/pdf/multi0page.pdf

Rousseau, Jean-Jacques (1978) [1762]. *On the Social Contract*, R.D. Masters (ed.), trans. J.R. Masters, New York: St. Martin's Press.

Shah, Anwar; Thompson, Theresa; and Zou, Heng-Fu (2004) 'The Impact of Decentralization on Service Delivery, Corruption, Fiscal Management and Growth in Developing and Emerging Market Economies: A Synthesis of Empirical Evidence', CESifo DICE Report, 1/2004, pp.10–14.
https://www.ifo.de/DocDL/dicereport104-forum2.pdf

Slater, David (1989) 'Territorial Power and the Peripheral State: The Issue of Decentralization', *Development and Change*, vol.20, pp.501–31.
https://doi.org/10.1111/j.1467-7660.1989.tb00356.x

Stepan, Alfred (1999) 'Federalism and Democracy: Beyond the U.S. Model', *Journal of Democracy*, vol.10, no.4, pp.19–34.
https://doi.org/%2010.1353/jod.1999.0072

Stepan, Alfred (2001) 'Toward a New Comparative Politics of Federalism, (Multi)Nationalism, and Democracy: Beyond Rikerian Federalism', in Stepan, Alfred (ed.) *Arguing Comparative Politics*, New York: Oxford University Press, pp.315–61.

Ter-Minassian, Teresa (ed.) (1997) *Fiscal Federalism in Theory and Practice*, Washington, DC: IMF.

Tocqueville, Alexis de (1994) [1835–40]. *Democracy in America*, P. Bradley (ed.), trans. H. Reeve, London: Everyman's Library.

Treisman, Daniel (2007) *The Architecture of Government: Rethinking Political Decentralization*, New York: Cambridge University Press.
https://doi.org/10.1017/CBO9780511619151

Tsebelis, George (1990) *Nested Games: Rational Choice in Comparative Politics*, Berkeley: University of California Press.
https://www.jstor.org/stable/10.1525/j.ctt1pnk3s

Wallis, John Joseph and Oates Wallace E. (1988) 'Decentralization in the Public Sector: An Empirical Study of State and Local Government', in Rosen, H.S. (ed.). *Fiscal Federalism: Quantitative Studies*, Chicago, IL: University of Chicago Press.
https://www.nber.org/system/files/chapters/c7882/c7882.pdf

Weingast, Barry R. (2014) 'Second Generation Fiscal Federalism: Political Aspects of Decentralization and Economic Development', *World Development*, vol.53, pp.14–25. http://dx.doi.org/10.1016/j.worlddev.2013.01.003

Zuazo, Moira; Faguet, Jean-Paul; and Bonifaz, Gustavo (eds) (2012) *Descentralización y democratización en Bolivia: La historia del Estado débil, la sociedad rebelde y el anhelo de democracia*. La Paz: Friedrich Ebert Stiftung. https://eprints.lse.ac.uk/45840/1/Binder1.pdf

3. Decentralised targeting of transfer programmes: a reassessment

Dilip Mookherjee

Summary

Decentralised governance has been widely adopted in developing countries in the hope of incorporating local information into policymaking, enhancing accountability and encouraging democratic participation in the delivery of public services to the poor and needy. However, evaluations of experience with this change have highlighted problems of corruption, elite capture, and clientelism that have undermined the success of decentralisation in improving targeting of transfer programmes. Given recent advances in information technology, this chapter suggests the need to consider suitable reforms, including enhanced monitoring and recentralisation initiatives that reduce local officials' scope for discretion. It provides an overview of recent research on these topics, and discusses key questions raised by their findings.

The period between 1950 and 1990 was characterised by centralised implementation of public benefit programmes in developing countries, whereby 'implementation' of a benefit programme refers to its management and allocation across potential recipients. A wide range of types of benefits were involved, including land, water, and subsidised farm inputs such as credit, fertiliser, and seeds; local infrastructures, such as roads, canals, sanitation, and public health; and workfare programmes and welfare services, such as low-income housing, food aid, pensions, education, and health benefits. Top-down, centralised implementation during this early phase involved the

How to cite this book chapter:

Mookherjee, Dilip (2023) 'Decentralised targeting of transfer programmes: a reassessment', in: Faguet, Jean-Paul and Pal, Sarmistha (eds) *Decentralised Governance: Crafting Effective Democracies Around the World*, London: LSE Press, pp. 49–71. https://doi.org/10.31389/lsepress.dlg.c License: CC BY 4.0

delegation of these tasks to a bureaucracy appointed by and accountable to a central government at either the federal or state level. This system gave rise to growing disenchantment owing to targeting failures, leakages, losses, corruption, and lack of responsiveness to local needs.

Subsequently, the past three decades have witnessed a shift from centralised towards decentralised implementation, with authority moving from state bureaucrats to local government officials elected by local citizens. The primary motivation was both to improve the information base of allocation decisions and to align the incentives of officials more with the interests of local citizens. As vividly described in a comparative case study of irrigation management systems in South Korea and the Indian state of Andhra Pradesh (Wade 1997), decentralisation was expected to achieve these objectives owing to the closer proximity and accountability of local delivery officials to the citizens that were meant to be served. The 2004 World Development Report accordingly chose decentralised delivery of public benefits as its theme and endorsed it with a sense of hope, noting that:

> Too often services fail poor people in access, in quality, and in affordability ... this year's World Development Report argues that services can be improved by putting poor people at the center of service. How? By enabling the poor to monitor and discipline service providers, by amplifying their voice in policymaking, and by strengthening the incentives for providers to serve the poor. (World Bank 2004)

However, the argument that decentralisation enhances accountability of service providers remains highly controversial. Historically influential counterarguments were made by designers of both the US and Indian constitutions that local governments are more prone than central governments to 'capture' by local elites, especially in areas of high inequality, poverty, and lack of popular participation in politics (Hamilton, Madison, and Jay 1787; Pal 2019). These objections are complemented by additional concerns that local democracy in developing countries tends to be characterised by higher levels of political clientelism, where local incumbents manipulate benefit allocations to benefit their loyal supporters or swing voters and so increase their chances of being re-elected. Such problems create non-trivial trade-offs between centralised and decentralised implementation, which have been the subject of extensive research in recent years. Theoretical analyses have argued that the overall outcomes are likely to be highly context-dependent (Bardhan and Mookherjee 2000, 2005, 2006a). This point appears to be borne out by a large body of empirical research (reviewed in Mansuri and Rao 2013 and Mookherjee 2015) evaluating the functioning of local governance in various developing countries.

A growing awareness of these problems has motivated some recent reform efforts, especially those involving enhanced monitoring or reducing the extent of discretion provided to local government officials. This form of 'recentralisation' has often drawn on emerging new technology and the 'big data' capabilities of central governments. The latter part of this chapter provides a perspective on the potential benefits, drawbacks, and wider implications of these recentralisation initiatives. Some qualifications are in order. First, 'recentralisation' initiatives are confined to the administration of transfer programmes delivering individually consumed or 'private good' benefits, rather than covering infrastructure programmes providing local public goods. They amount to a shift of government expenditure systems in developing countries closer to that of developed countries, where most transfer programmes (for example, social security) are centralised and formula-bound, while the role of local governments is limited to the provision of infrastructure and local public goods. Second, while the 'first-generation' literature focused on problems of inter-jurisdictional externalities, scale economies, and taste heterogeneity across jurisdictions, by contrast I focus here on the implications of recentralisation on problems of misallocation owing to governance and accountability defects that have been the topic of the 'second-generation' literature on fiscal federalism[1]. While the recent literature has focused mainly on intra-jurisdiction misallocation from capture and clientelism, it has also devoted some attention to related forms of inter-jurisdiction misallocation. But issues of inter-jurisdiction externalities have been largely ignored. However, on a first approximation this omission is not particularly glaring because recentralisation reforms chiefly concern the allocation of transfer benefit programmes that involve negligible externalities (beyond receiving individuals or households) or scale economies.

The first section of this chapter extends the earlier literature reviews mentioned above to include more recent literature on *intra-community* targeting distortions, that is, the extent to which local governments succeed in targeting public benefits to intended beneficiaries *within* their own jurisdictions. The key mechanisms that may prevent successful targeting are elite capture, corruption, and clientelism. Section 3.2 turns to *inter-community* targeting distortions, resulting from the opportunistic manipulations of programme budgets *across* different local governments by officials at higher levels. Section 3.3 describes the outcomes of various ('recentralisation') reforms intended to reduce these distortions, including attempts to improve monitoring and supervision, institutional alternatives to political decentralisation, and transitioning to formula-bound programmes that reduce the authority of locally elected officials. The evidence suggests that drastic reforms involving elimination of local control over cash and in-kind transfer programmes may be needed to achieve significant improvements in pro-poor targeting. Finally, Section 3.4 discusses other considerations that need to be included in evaluating these reforms, notably the implications for insurance, administrative challenges, and some wider implications for federalism and democracy.

3.1 Intra-community targeting distortions

Figure 3.1 depicts the allocation of transfers across different households by a local government within a given community – a 'private good' benefit programme targeted for 'deserving' households. 'Deservingness' refers to a household attribute that is not observed by the central government or in the public domain. In the case of a welfare programme, poor and needy households constitute deserving households. However, for an input subsidy programme intended to promote growth, those deserving are productive households. Local government officials can identify deserving households within the community and have delegated authority over intra-community allocation of a programme budget assigned to them by higher-level governments. Despite being well-informed, local officials may not be motivated to allocate benefits to the needy or otherwise 'deserving' households owing to problems of capture, corruption or (political) clientelism. Intra-community misallocation refers to the resulting deviation of actual allocations from those intended.

The hierarchy within local communities in developing countries is headed by traditional elites (landlords, influential families and notables, tribal or religious leaders, wealthy business interests) and political elites (local government officials). Traditional elites have long-standing social and economic relations with non-elite households, often resembling vertical patron–client ties. Political elites are of a more recent origin, either appointed or elected by local citizens, and subject to periodic turnover. *Elite capture* refers to symbiotic relationships between traditional and political elites within the community involving the exchange of government benefits or other privileges for financial contributions in the form of campaign contributions or bribes. *Corruption* consists of the self-diversion of benefits by political elites, or favourable treatment given to households paying bribes or those with personal social connections. *Political clientelism* refers to political patron–client ties between incumbent political elites and pro-incumbent non-elite households, involving voting for the former in exchange for benefits.

Figure 3.1: Intra-community misallocation

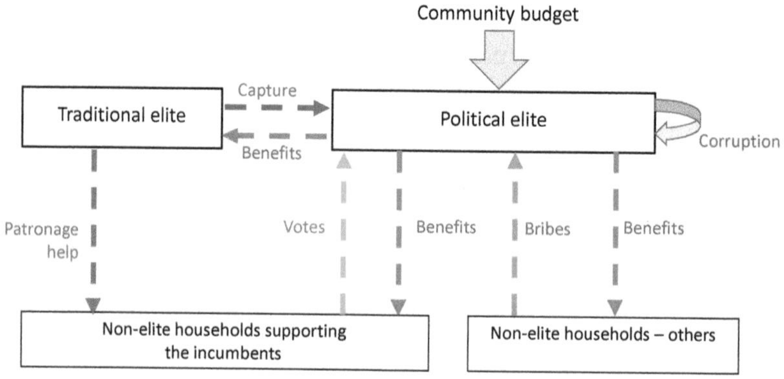

In some cases, traditional elites also constitute or overlap with the political elite or have close social connections with the latter (see Chapter 7). In that case, elite capture collapses into a form of corruption. More generally, the distinction between elite capture and corruption is not sharp. For this reason, we club the two phenomena together under a common 'elite capture' umbrella. On the other hand, there is a clear conceptual distinction between elite capture and political clientelism, in terms of both their underlying mechanisms and consequences. Elite capture biases benefit allocations in favour of traditional elites vis-a-vis non-elite households (a form of vertical inequity), owing to horizontal social ties or transactions (campaign contributions or bribes). Political clientelism biases allocations across non-elite households in favour of pro-incumbent households (a form of horizontal inequity) motivated by vertical political transactions (exchange of benefits for votes). The vertical equity consequences of clientelism are ambiguous, depending on how pro-incumbent partisanship is correlated with household economic status. For instance, it may enhance vertical equity if poorer households are more prone to support the incumbent in clientelist fashion. While elite capture adversely impacts all non-elite households, the impact of political clientelism is typically favourable for the incumbents' non-elite supporters (at least in the short run) and unfavourable for other non-elites.[2]

Elite capture

Most of the earlier (pre-2015) literature focused on elite capture. More recent literature has provided further vivid demonstrations of elite capture, drawing on fine-grained details of the institutional context, besides better data and creative identification strategies. The specific type of local elite varies with the context. In African countries such as Sierra Leone (Acemoglu, Reed, and Robinson 2014) and Malawi (Basurto, Dupas, and Robinson 2019), they are tribal chiefs. In the Indian state of Maharashtra the local elites are large landowners (Anderson, Francois, and Kotwal 2015). In Pakistan the elites are religious leaders (Mehmood and Seror 2021) or long-entrenched political dynastic families (Malik, Mirza, and Platteau 2021). They are political elites in Thailand's credit programme (Vera-Cossio 2022), and agents appointed by political elites in Uganda's agricultural extension programme (Bandiera et al. 2020).

The relation between traditional elites and non-elites resembles a patron–client relationship, in which clients have traditionally depended on their patrons for employment or insurance against idiosyncratic shocks. Elite capture is then driven by traditional forms of social or economic clientelism, to be contrasted with political clientelism. For instance, in the Maharashtra context (studied by Anderson, Francois, and Kotwal 2015), elite capture took the form of traditional landowning elites suppressing the take-up of a government employment guarantee programme by the poor, in order to keep market wages low and preserve traditional dependency patterns. The extent of elite capture (measured by adverse consequences for non-elites) has typically been higher in communities characterised by greater concentration of power among traditional elites: for example, more unequal land distribution in the case of Indian landed elites, or less political competition between tribal chiefs in Sierra Leone. In both these contexts, village surveys showed greater trust expressed by clients in their patrons in these communities, possibly explained by the greater extent to which people relied on patron support in times of need.

While these patterns recur across many different contexts, there are some notable exceptions. In Indonesia (Alatas et al. 2012) or the Indian state of West Bengal (Bardhan and Mookherjee 2006b; Mookherjee and Nath 2020), the extent of elite capture seems quite limited. In Pakistan, Malik, Mirza, and Platteau (2021) found more harmful impacts of election of entrenched dynasts in jurisdictions where they were exposed to greater political competition. The authors explain this via a clientelistic mechanism aggravated by greater political competition, rather than by elite capture (which competition tends to limit).

Political clientelism

The recent literature has presented growing evidence of political clientelism, where local government officials condition the distribution of private benefits to recipients voting for or expressing political support for their own party (Dunning et al. 2013; Hicken 2011). Citizens are then effectively coerced to vote for the incumbent, reducing the accountability pressure on incumbents and cementing their grip on political power. Benefits are targeted along partisan lines (to favour loyal supporters or swing voters).

The type of misallocation resulting from political clientelism differs in essential ways from those resulting from elite capture. Clientelism is often consistent with pro-poor targeting since the poor value government benefits more (at the margin) and are therefore more willing to 'sell' their vote in exchange for these benefits (Stokes 2005). So the associated misallocation is different: it need not consist of errors of inclusion, that is, diversion to recipients who are not entitled to receive them, or who are less deserving in terms of need. Within the set of intended beneficiaries, incumbents often discriminate on the basis of political partisanship: rewarding supporters and denying others (especially those that support their political rivals). This results in systematic exclusion errors (sections of the deserving poor that are systematically denied benefits on account of their lack of political support) and associated violations of horizontal equity (where selection among equally deserving groups is based on political partisanship). These forms of misallocation can be hard to detect when programme budget constraints prevent all deserving beneficiaries from receiving benefits, which is often the case in poor countries. Local officials then have discretion over who among the intended beneficiaries will actually receive benefits. Discrimination in favour of their political supporters is frequently difficult to establish by external researchers or auditors.

Another difference from elite capture is that clientelism may not require high levels of social or economic inequality within the community, though it usually thrives where poverty is widespread. Greater political competition can enlarge clientelistic distortions, by raising the incentives for insecure incumbents to engage in political favouritism that ends up holding back long-term development. Indeed, this is essentially the explanation provided by Malik Mirza, and Platteau (2021) for their finding in Pakistan that adverse developmental impacts resulted from closer election races that entrenched dynasts won.

Compared with capture, clientelism generates other distinct forms of misallocation. It creates a bias among officials in favour of 'private good' benefits programmes (especially those of a short-term recurring nature), relative to local public goods (since these are worthless as a clientelistic instrument owing to their non-exclusionary nature). Some authors argue that clientelism generates a broader lack of accountability of elected officials, insofar as residents may be compelled to vote for them despite glaring lapses of governance (for example, manifest mismanagement, neglect of urgent public interest causes, or immoral behaviour). Many recent empirical illustrations of clientelism rely on evidence of these kinds of distortions, associated with the supply of local public goods. For instance, Khemani (2015) found that reported levels of vote-buying in Philippine villages were negatively correlated with health service delivery. Using a regression discontinuity associated with the roll-out of the non-clientelistic programme Bolsa Familia in Brazil, Frey (2019) showed that it was associated with a marked rise in share of health and education shares of municipal government budgets. Using instrumental variable and difference-in-difference methods, Bardhan et al. (2020) provided evidence that voters in West Bengal in India responded to receiving 'private good' welfare benefits (employment in workfare programmes, or low-income housing benefits) but not of 'public good' benefits (such as local roads and irrigation projects). Consistent with these voting patterns, changes in political competition motivated upper-level officials to discriminate more in favour of local areas controlled by their political party, but this effect was observed only for private good benefits.

3.2 Inter-community misallocation: upper-level manipulation

Programme budgets flow down the administrative hierarchy of higher-tier and local governments, as shown in Figure 3.2. The central or provincial government decides on a budget for each district government, which then allocates it between different local community governments at the bottom tier. District government officials may be granted autonomy over the allocation across local governments under their jurisdiction, owing to their superior information concerning relative deservingness of different local communities

Figure 3.2: Inter-community allocation

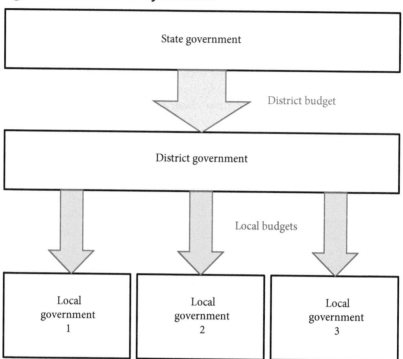

relative to the provincial administration. However, these officials may abuse their authority by biasing allocations in favour of certain local areas.

Upper-tier officials could be personally biased in favour of either their own home area or areas dominated by their own ethnic group. Alternatively, a partisan bias could be at work in favour of areas where larger programme allocations would help generate more votes (or more salient vote shifts) for their particular party. These distortions could and frequently do arise even in centralised or non-democratic systems. For instance, Burgess et al. (2015) demonstrated that, in periods when strong autocracy prevailed, strong ethnic favouritism was exhibited by successive presidents of Kenya between 1960 and 2013 in allocating road-building projects. This favouritism disappeared when the country transited into a democracy. Partisan distortions also arise in developed countries such as the United States in the form of 'pork barrel' politics, where the allocation of infrastructure projects has been influenced by the partisan bias of national legislators (Levitt and Snyder 1997).

Recent literature has devoted increasing attention to the inter-community allocative performance of decentralised governance in a number of developing countries. Personal home bias was demonstrated in an incentive compatible choice experiment by Hoffmann et al. (2017) in the allocation of water infrastructure projects by elected county councillors in rural Kenya between different wards under their jurisdiction. Many other papers show evidence of partisan bias. Azulai (2017) used a triple difference specification to show that rotation of national ministers in Brazil between 2009 and 2016 was associated with corresponding fluctuations in the grants allocated to municipalities controlled by the same political party. Finan and Mazzocco (2021) used a structural approach to estimate a model of allocation of grants across regions within the Brazilian state of Roraima. They found that 25 per cent of these allocations were distorted by electoral incentives relative to social planner's optimum. In the Indian state of West Bengal, Dey and Sen (2016) showed that following floods in 2013 the dominant party in the state allocated employment programmes to favour those local areas where it won rather than lost by a narrow margin. Shenoy and Zimmerman (2020) used West Bengal data spanning 2011–16 to show that local residents and associated political brokers mobilising votes in the area were rewarded with increased employment benefits when the same party (narrowly) secured control of the local government council. Bardhan et al. (2020) used West Bengal data for an earlier period (2004–11) to show that local government areas redistricted into more competitive state legislature constituencies received larger (or smaller) private benefit programmes if they were controlled by the same (or rival) political party. Studying three South Indian states between 2008 and 2019, Tarquinio (2021) found that drought relief declarations made by state legislators discriminated across local areas based on the electoral competition motives of the party controlling the state legislature. This helped explain why one in three drought-affected areas did not receive any relief, while a third of the relief declarations went to areas without any drought.

3.3 Institutional reforms

The distortions described in previous sections raise some obvious questions about possible ways of reforming the institutions of decentralised governance. These include enhanced monitoring and oversight mechanisms, delegating authority to different sets of local agents, and recentralisation initiatives that limit the range of powers devolved to local governments.

Enhanced monitoring and verification via e-governance

Recent advances in information technology have augmented the capacity of state and central governments to monitor the behaviour of local government officials and control corruption. Large-scale e-governance field experiments were carried out in two different Indian states by research teams in collaboration with state government officials in an effort to reduce corruption in NREGA, a programme managed by local governments that employed village residents to build local infrastructure. In Andhra Pradesh, Muralidharan, Niehaus, and Sukhtankar (2016) showed that using biometric identification cards to verify employment beneficiaries nominated by local officials resulted in a 41 per cent reduction in programme leakages associated with 'ghost' beneficiaries. Beneficiaries were paid more quickly and reported earnings rose by 24 per cent, while programme costs did not change.

Similarly, Banerjee et al. (2019) studied an experiment in the state of Bihar where a manual system of requests for advances from local governments (submitted for verification by higher-tier officials) was replaced by a just-in-time system where payments were automatically triggered by entering the details of beneficiaries in a financial database. The initiative resulted in a reduction of ghost beneficiaries by 5 per cent and in wealth disclosed by upper-tier officials by 14 per cent. At the same time, programme expenditures declined by 24 per cent, while the employment benefits and number of beneficiaries were unaffected. However, after seven months the Bihar experiment was abruptly stopped, in the face of intense pressure from NREGA officials. None the less, the experiment formed the basis of a subsequent nationwide roll-out that realised similar reductions in programme expenditures. It is important to note that the scope of both e-government reforms was limited to reducing corruption (that is, cases where intermediate officials manage to divert benefits into their own private rents, rather than distributing them to local residents). They were not intended to reduce the severity of elite capture or political clientelism, or other forms of misallocation of benefits between local residents.

Delegating authority to others

One of the main virtues of decentralisation is that it can potentially harness specialised information about local needs and priorities that is possessed by community members or others in close proximity to beneficiaries. Hence an alternative to political decentralisation is to delegate the design and implementation of development projects instead to community leaders or groups. Such community-driven development programmes have been actively sponsored by the World Bank in nearly 90 low- and middle-income countries.[3] These were included in the review of Mansuri and Rao (2013), who noted that such programmes are also frequently subject to elite capture, because community elites can gain more direct control over such programmes.[4]

Alternative options include contracting with local members of the community who are hired as 'agents', with screening of eligible candidates and performance-based incentives. Examples include government health services contracted with local community agents in Zambia to deliver AIDS prevention services, where the effectiveness of the hired agents varied with their pro-social motivation and the nature of rewards offered (Ashraf, Bandiera, and Jack 2014). Maitra et al. (2022) conducted an experiment in West Bengal where the selection of beneficiaries from an agricultural micro-credit programme was delegated to local community members hired as commission agents (where commissions were linked to loan repayments): here agents were hired either from local trader-lenders or appointed by the local government.

While both treatments led to similarly high levels of take-up and loan repayment, only the treatment using trader-lender private sector agents resulted in significant increases in farm income for recipients. These results suggest the need for greater experimentation along these lines. A third option is to delegate implementation to independent non-government organisations (NGOs). While NGOs have played a large and growing role in the implementation of development programmes around the world, there are very few studies comparing their performance to programmes delegated to local governments.

A fourth option is for upper-level governments to contract directly with private sector providers, as in the case of grants offered to private schools in Pakistan that competed with traditional government schools (Andrabi et al. 2020). Services delivered by NGOs or private sector providers typically compete with those provided by local governments, resulting in complex interaction effects. They may enhance accountability pressures on government providers due to greater competition or they may result in shrinking government services in ways that end up adversely affecting those citizens who continue to rely on government providers. For instance, in Uganda, Deserranno, Nansambaz, and Qian (2021) found that the entry of NGO health clinics in areas with pre-existing government health workers induced government workers to move to the NGO clinics (which offered higher salaries), resulting in a worsening of infant mortality and overall health care. In areas without pre-existing government health workers, on the other hand, overall health care improved in the absence of any negative spillovers.

Limiting discretion over inter-community allocations: formula-based geographic targeting

Another type of reform works by restricting the scope for opportunistic manipulation of inter-community allocations by elected officials, and instead replacing them with formula-based allocations. Three of the papers described above studied inter-community misallocation also examined the likely consequences of this kind of reform. Recall the experimental study by Hoffmann et al. (2017) in which local councillors in Kenya exhibited bias in favour of their own ward in allocating water purification projects. When councillors' authority to select the inter-ward allocation was removed and replaced by an equal treatment mandate, this home bias was substantially reduced. However, the same intervention raised the councillors' demand for greater control over the management of the project within each ward, owing possibly to an increase in corruption incentives (that is, via collecting bribes from users within wards).

After finding geographic misallocation in funds allocated by Brazilian federal legislators across municipal governments in Roraima state, Finan and Mazzocco (2021) simulated the effect of two counterfactual political reforms intended to reduce partisan bias. They concluded that approval voting would have only small effects on reducing partisan bias. By contrast, introducing single-term limits for legislators was predicted to be more effective in reducing geographical misallocation. However, overall welfare was expected to fall owing to greater diversion of funds to personal interests by single-term incumbents – echoing a concern also raised by Hoffmann et al. (2017) in the Kenyan context.

In rural West Bengal, Mookherjee and Nath (2020) used proxy means tests based on household surveys to estimate what improvements in pro-poor targeting would result if grants to village-level governments were based on a formula recommended by the state finance commission rather than the discretion of upper-tier officials. The formula was based on measures of village need – incorporating population, remoteness, literacy, food insecurity, occupational structure, and the population share of scheduled castes and tribes. In the counterfactual policy, benefit allocations within each village would continue to be delegated to respective village governments. The authors found that formula-based grants would actually *lower* pro-poor targeting slightly. Moreover, altering weights assigned to different criteria used by the Finance Commission could improve pro-poor targeting, but only to a slight degree. This reflects partly the low information content of the criteria used by the Finance Commission to predict the regional distribution of poverty, and partly the political incentives of upper-tier officials to target poorer areas in a clientelistic setting. In addition, the reform would leave unchanged the targeting patterns within villages, where a proportion of benefits end up being allocated to households that are not poor.

Removing local discretion: formula-based transfer (private) benefits

A more drastic reform would eliminate any scope for local discretion in the allocation of 'private good' benefits to households (or individuals), in favour of a formula based on household- or individual-level measures of need, based on the demographic information (for example, gender, age, education, location, family size) available to the government. This would essentially replace existing welfare systems in developing countries with something similar to social security benefits in the US and European welfare states, or the conditional cash transfer programmes that originated in Mexico (Progresa) and Brazil (Bolsa Familia). The centralised system would both determine people's eligibility for benefits and set up a system to deliver the benefits directly to recipients. The system would not rely any longer on local government officials – their role would thereafter be restricted to providing and managing local public goods.

A priori, it is hard to predict what the outcome of such a reform may be. A formula-based programme might be less effective in targeting the poor if (i) local officials are better informed about the incidence of poverty across households and regions than could be captured by the criteria incorporated in the formula; and if (ii) these officials have the incentive to direct benefits to poorer households. But if local officials are either less well informed, or if they have a strategic incentive to target less-poor households (maybe because these are the kinds of households they personally favour, or that would be more responsive with their votes), the reform would improve pro-poor targeting.

Some developing countries in Asia have recently been experimenting with reforms of this kind. Haseeb and Vyborny (2021) evaluated a nationwide overhaul of the Benazir Income Support Program (BISP) in Pakistan. Prior to the reform, elected officials identified poor households that would receive the transfers. The reform followed creation of a new administrative database of households and assets with the assistance of the World Bank, which enabled the creation of 'proxy means tests' (PMTs) that were then used for targeting instead. The programme effects were identified by differences in the pre- and post-reform changes in the transfers received by households connected to (that is, belonging to the same village and clan as) officials that won elections, compared with other observationally similar households connected to political candidates that had lost elections. This study found that the reform reduced favouritism (that is, the role played by recipients' connections to elected officials) and improved pro-poor targeting. Moreover, it increased positive perceptions of social protection programmes, both in constituencies that had supported the government and in those that had supported the opposition, with a larger impact on the latter. The costs of implementing the reform, including collection of a nationwide household survey used to create an administrative database, amounted to less than 2 per cent of the total amount paid out in transfers in 2016.

A related experiment was carried out in Indonesia by Banerjee et al. (2021). They randomised the roll-out of a formula-based cash voucher scheme replacing an in-kind food assistance programme administered by local government officials. This combined two different dimensions of reform at the same time: cash versus in-kind transfers, and a centralised rather than a decentralised implementation. It is therefore difficult to separate the roles of these two dimensions. However, the combined change resulted in a significant improvement in pro-poor targeting, with a sharper concentration of benefits among poor households (that is, a reduction in errors from including the non-poor). There was a 45 per cent rise in benefits per capita among those who continued to receive benefits. The administrative costs amounted to 4 per cent of the benefits disbursed.

These last two experiences suggest that drastic reforms have the potential to improve pro-poor targeting quite significantly. They also indicate that the administrative costs and logistical challenge of implementing such a reform are not large enough to render them infeasible in low-income countries, owing to recent improvements in information technology.

3.4 Rules versus discretion: assessing pros and cons

The preceding results suggest the need to consider a rather drastic reform of decentralised governance, where delivery of private welfare benefits would no longer be delegated to elected local officials but instead would use a 'big data' approach to create a formula based on PMTs predicting the level of poverty of each household or individual in the country on the basis of administrative surveys. Eligibility for cash or in-kind transfers would be set by the formula, and the programme implemented using a nationwide household or individual-level ID system with biometric identification, combined with direct electronic transfers from central agencies to individuals' bank accounts or mobile phones. The studies cited point to the difficulties of partial reforms, such as formula-based geographic targeting where local officials continue to retain some discretion (over 'last-mile delivery'), while the extent of such discretion is curtailed. The benefits of such reforms are that they could enhance targeting to the truly needy, and lower waste and corruption. Additional benefits would include a reduction in the scope of elite capture and clientelism, which could reduce socio-economic inequality within communities, while enhancing political competition and accountability of local government officials. The main responsibility and focus of the latter would be on delivery of local public goods such as roads, irrigation, health, and education, which are likely to have a greater long-run development impact compared to short-term 'private good' benefits.

What are other potentially important implications of such drastic centralising reforms? The studies reviewed above examine the effect of reforms on targeting in favour of poor households, where poverty is estimated using proxy means tests relying on underlying household attributes in ways that predict consumption expenditures. Such measures can overlook relevant criteria (such as land quality) observed by members of the local community but not captured in household surveys. They also ignore temporary shocks experienced by households, such as illness or crop failure, which lower people's incomes but are difficult to verify and therefore hard to incorporate into administrative information about household need. Providing security against such shocks is an important objective of government income support programmes. Removing the scope for local discretion by transitioning completely to formula-bound income transfer programmes may then result in a loss of such insurance.

How important is this concern? The answer depends on whether decentralised welfare programmes actually do provide insurance against idiosyncratic shocks. The evidence on this issue varies across contexts. In a study of 300 households in central Java, Trachtman, Permana, and Sahadewo (2021) compared community-based assessments of individual households' needs with those assessed by the households themselves. They found a low correlation (0.16) between community and own-household assessments of weekly (per capita consumption) need, and a higher correlation (0.45) of assessments of asset value. This happens even among families that know each other (for example those who are in close physical and social proximity), suggesting that local communities do not seem to be well-informed about the main temporary shocks experienced by individual households. Community assessments therefore focus on long-term rather than short-term measures of poverty.

In Malawi, Basurto, Dupas, and Robinson (2019) evaluated targeting effectiveness (measured by weekly consumption expenditures) achieved in actual allocations of subsidised farm inputs and food aid by tribal chiefs against a counterfactual PMT-based formula. Both the chiefs and the formula failed to identify a substantial fraction of poor people, with chiefs making bigger errors on average. Moreover, chiefs were more likely to target food subsidies to their relatives. On the other hand, compared to the formula-based allocation, the chiefs did provide higher subsidies to people experiencing droughts, floods, cattle death, and crop disease. Hence this study finds evidence that the decentralised allocation provides more insurance than might be achieved by a PMT-based formula. At the same time, chiefs' allocations were associated with poorer targeting on average, implying that the degree of risk (or inequality) aversion would matter in determining the likely overall welfare impact of such a shift.

In similar vein, Dal Bó et al. (2020) found that intermediate supervisors of agricultural extension workers in Paraguay had valuable information about the relative value of distributing scarce cell phones to different extension workers within their jurisdiction, and favoured workers with higher marginal treatment effects when given this discretion in how to allocate them. A scheme that delegates the allocation to supervisors therefore achieves a higher average treatment effect overall, compared to a randomised allocation. However, a more sophisticated centralised allocation using a formula based on the observable characteristics of workers turned out to outperform the delegation mechanism.

Administrative challenges

While the experiences of Pakistan and Indonesia suggest that the administrative costs of transfer reforms are unlikely to be large, there may be a number of administrative challenges associated with implementation, particularly during the transition to a new system. Policymakers need to create a nationwide identification system; initiate surveys to generate the PMT formula; conduct censuses to collect the asset and demographic data to be used in applying the PMT formula to identify beneficiaries; find ways of integrating this data with the bank accounts or mobile phone accounts to be used for depositing cash transfers; and coordinate with public service institutions involved in delivering any in-kind transfers. In describing the roll-out of the biometric identification smartcards for verifying recipient identity in the Indian state of Andhra Pradesh, Muralidharan, Niehaus, and Sukhtankar (2016, p.2897) stated:

> After two years of program rollout, the share of Smartcard-enabled payments across both programs in treated subdistricts had reached around 50 percent. This conversion rate over two years compares

favourably to the pace of electronic benefit transfer rollout in other contexts. For example, the United States took over 15 years to convert all Social Security payments to electronic transfers, while the Philippines took 5 years to reach about 40 percent coverage in a cash transfer program. In AP [Andhra Pradesh], the inability to reach a 100 percent conversion rate (despite the stated goal of senior policymakers to do so) reflects the nontrivial logistical, administrative, and political challenges of rolling out a complex new payment system.

In India, there have been problems in integrating the nationwide identification system, Aadhar, with the public distribution system of food to the poor. The difficulties included denial of benefits to those who lacked the Aadhar ID cards and increased transport costs incurred by recipients, as widely reported in the Indian media and verified in a randomised control trial by Muralidharan, Niehaus, and Sukhtankar (2020). These problems were particularly pronounced for vulnerable groups such as manual workers, widows, and elderly people. The limited inclusion of these vulnerable groups within the financial system has further compounded the problem. Despite the Indian government's ambitious 'Jan Dhan' programme, promoting affordable bank accounts (which was launched in 2014), Pande et al. (2020) estimated that six years later half of all poor women still did not have a Jan Dhan account, and 23 per cent had no form of bank account.

A further challenge occurs where individuals' benefit eligibility is tied to a specific location. Here temporary migrants from rural to urban areas are ineligible for government benefits because their entitlement is tied to their area of origin. In turn, this set-up creates strong disincentives for migration, constraining a significant channel for poverty reduction and growth in developing countries. This problem was highlighted by the acute plight of large numbers of migrants that were trapped in urban areas of India without local support when the Covid-19 shock resulted in sudden loss of employment (Jesline et al. 2021). To create portable benefits that would address this problem, the transfers and social security system in a country would need to be centralised with nationwide identification and eligibility.

Broader implications for federalism and democracy

Changing to rule-based direct transfer systems would amount to a substantial recentralisation of the public expenditure system in developing countries, lowering the autonomy of state and regional governments in allocating aid. The balance of power between central and regional governments would alter, with possibly significant implications for federalism and democracy. A number of authors have highlighted strategic political economy considerations in decentralisation reforms. Cheema, Khwaja, and Qadir (2006) described how successive waves of decentralisation and recentralisation in Pakistan were related to the conflict between authoritarian rulers at the central level and populist democrats at the regional level. In particular, local governments were created by the former to create a central–local patronage structure that would enable them to bypass regional leaders. In India, since 2014 the BJP-controlled central government has sought to scale back funding for programmes (such as the national rural employment guarantee programme) administered by state and local governments, which appeared to increase the vote share of rival political parties that control state governments, and introduce a set of new welfare programmes more directly identified and controlled by the central government, which raised BJP vote share (Deshpande, Tillin, and Kailash 2019). Martinez-Bravo et al. (2022) provided evidence that in China during the 1980s and 1990s, locally elected village mayors were accompanied by an increase in locally popular policies. Some of these (such as weaker implementation of the one-child policy) were at odds with the goals of central policymakers. After 2000, enhancements of monitoring and bureaucratic capacity of the central government in Beijing enabled them to implement recentralisation reforms that reduced local leaders' autonomy. These experiences suggest that a transition to formula-based programmes will tend to lower the autonomy and political power of regional governments. If rival political parties control the central and regional governments, this will shift the balance of political power between these parties.

Conclusions

This chapter has reviewed recent literature pertaining to problems of corruption, elite capture, and political clientelism that limit the scope for decentralised governance to achieve the social welfare goals of cost-effectiveness and targeting the delivery of government benefits to deserving households. A range of reforms intended to curb these problems have varied in their method, scope, and effectiveness. The ones that seemed the most effective involved replacing discretionary authority of locally elected officials over the distribution of targeted transfers of individual/'private good' benefits with PMT-based, formula-based transfers. However, the key evidence so far has been limited to only two reform efforts carried out in Indonesia and Pakistan. Studies of these reforms also raised questions regarding the proxy means data that the formulae were based on, their administrative feasibility and some wider concerns for federalism and democracy. Clearly, much remains to be learnt from further experimentation with similar reforms in the future, combined with continued research and discussion about their outcomes.

Acknowledgements

This chapter is based on my presentation at the LSE Conference on Decentralized Governance, December 2021, and subsequently at various seminars, under a different title, 'Reassessing Decentralization'. I am grateful to participants at these venues, as well as Jean-Paul Faguet, Karthik Muralidharan, and Sarmistha Pal for their detailed comments.

Endnotes

[1] See Mookherjee 2015 for an elaboration of these respective literatures.

[2] The long-run welfare impacts of clientelism for partisan supporters may differ from short-run impacts if the systemic consequence of clientelism limits the accountability of incumbents by sheltering them from political competition. This is discussed further below.

[3] See https://www.worldbank.org/en/topic/communitydrivendevelopment.

[4] Again there are some exceptions to this. For instance, in field experiments in Indonesia, Alatas et al. (2012) found that safety net programme targeting achieved by community leaders and community-based groups were similar to those based on PMTs constructed from detailed household surveys of consumption and assets, while recording higher levels of community satisfaction; targeting patterns did not vary with local inequality, remoteness, or social connectedness.

References

Acemoglu, Daron; Reed, Tristan; and Robinson, James (2013) 'Chiefs: Economic Development and Elite Control of Civil Society in Sierra Leone', *Journal of Political Economy*, vol.122. https://doi.org/10.1086/674988

Alatas, Vivi; Banerjee, Abhijit; Hanna, Rema; Olken, Ben; and Tobias, Julia (2012) 'Targeting the Poor: Evidence from a Field Experiment in Indonesia', *American Economic Review*, vol.102, no.4, pp.1206–40. http://dx.doi.org/10.1257/aer.102.4.1206

Anderson, Siwan; Francois, Patrick; and Kotwal, Ashok (2015) 'Clientelism in Indian Villages', *American Economic Review*, vol.105, no.6, pp.1780–816. http://dx.doi.org/10.1257/aer.20130623

Andrabi, Tahir; Das, Jishnu; Khwaja, Asim; Ozyurt, Selcuk; and Singh, Niharika (2020) 'Upping the Ante: The Equilibrium Effects of Unconditional Grants to Private Schools', *American Economic Review*, vol.110, no.10, pp.3315–49. http://dx.doi.org/10.1257/aer.20180924

Ashraf, Nava; Bandiera, Oriana; and Jack, Kelsey (2014) 'No Margin, No Mission? A Field Experiment on Incentives for Public Service Delivery', *Journal of Public Economics*, vol.120, pp.1–17. https://doi.org/10.1016/j.j

Azulai, Michel (2017) 'Public Good Allocation and the Welfare Costs of Political Connections: Evidence from Brazilian Matching Grants', London School of Economics Working Paper. https://www.sv.uio.no/econ/english/research/news-and-events/events /guest-lectures-seminars/job-market/dokumenter/azulai-public-good -allocation-and-the-welfare-costs-of-political-connections.pdf

Bandiera, Oriana; Burgess, Robin; Deserranno, Erika; Morel, Ricardo; Rasul, Imran; and Sulaiman, Munshi (2020) 'Development Policy through the Lens of Social Structure', STICERD Working Paper, London School of Economics. https://sticerd.lse.ac.uk/dps/eopp/eopp69.pdf

Banerjee, Abhijit; Hanna, Rema; Olken, Ben; Satriawan, Elan; and Sumarto, Sudarno (2021) 'Food vs. Food Stamps: Evidence from an At-Scale Experiment in Indonesia', MIT Dept of Economics Working Paper. https://papers.ssrn.com/sol3/papers.cfm?abstract_id=3819544

Banerjee, Abhijit; Duflo, Esther; Imbert, Clement; Mathew, Santosh; and Pande, Rohini (2019) 'E-governance, Accountability, and Leakage in Public Programs: Experimental Evidence from a Financial Management Reform in India', *American Economic Journal: Applied*, vol.12, no.4, pp.39–72. http://dx.doi.org/10.1257/app.20180302

Bardhan, Pranab and Mookherjee, Dilip (2000) 'Capture and Governance at Local and National Levels', *American Economic Review*, vol.90, no.2 135–39. http://dx.doi.org/10.1257/aer.90.2.135

Bardhan, Pranab and Mookherjee, Dilip (2005) 'Decentralizing Anti-Poverty Program Delivery in Developing Countries', *Journal of Public Economics*, vol.89, pp.675–704. https://doi.org/10.1016/j.jpubeco.2003.01.001

Bardhan, Pranab and Mookherjee, Dilip (2006a) 'Decentralisation and Accountability in Infrastructure Delivery in Developing Countries', *Economic Journal*, vol.116, pp.107–33. https://doi.org/10.1111/j.1468-0297.2006.01049.x

Bardhan, Pranab and Mookherjee, Dilip (2006b) 'Pro-poor Targeting and Accountability of Local Governments in West Bengal', *Journal of Development Economics*, vol.79, pp.303–27. https://doi.org/10.1016/j.jdeveco.2006.01.004

Bardhan, Pranab; Mitra, Sandip; Mookherjee, Dilip; and Nath, Anusha (2020) 'How Do Voters Respond to Welfare vis-a-vis Public Good Programs? An Empirical Test of Political Clientelism', Department of Economics Working Paper, Boston University. https://people.bu.edu/dilipm/wkpap/WbclSep2021.pdf

Basurto, Maria; Dupas Pascaline; and Robinson, Jonathan (2019) 'Decen- tralization and Efficiency of Subsidy Targeting: Evidence from Chiefs in

Rural Malawi', *Journal of Public Economics*, vol.185.
https://doi.org/10.1016/j.jpubeco.2019.07.006

Burgess, Robin; Jedwab, Remi; Miguel, Edward; Morjaria, Ameet; and Padró
i Miquel, Gerard (2015) 'The Value of Democracy: Evidence from Road
Building in Kenya', *American Economic Review*, vol.105, no.6, pp.1817–51.
http://dx.doi.org/10.1257/aer.20131031

Cheema, Ali; Khwaja, Asim; and Qadir, Adnan (2006) 'Decentralization in
Pakistan: Context, Content and Causes', in Bardhan, Pranab and Mookherjee, Dilip (ed) *Decentralization and Local Governance in Developing
Countries: A Comparative Perspective*, Cambridge, MA: MIT Press.
http://dx.doi.org/10.2139/ssrn.739712

Dal Bó, Ernesto; Finan, Frederico; Li, Nicholas; and Schechter, Laura (2020)
'Information Technology and Government Decentralization: Experimen-
tal Evidence from Paraguay', University of California, Berkeley Working
Paper. https://doi.org/10.3982/ECTA17497

Deshpande, Rajeshwari; Tillin, Luise; and Kailash K.K. (2019) 'The BJP's
Welfare Schemes: Did They Make a Difference in the 2019 Elections?',
Studies in Indian Politics, vol.7, no.2, pp.219–33.
https://doi.org/10.1177/2321023019874911

Deserranno, Erika; Nansambaz, Aisha; and Qian, Nancy (2021) 'The
Unintended Consequences of NGO-Provided Aid on Government
Services in Uganda', NBER Working Paper 26928.
http://www.nber.org/pap

Dey, Shubhashis; and Sen, Kunal (2016) 'Is Partisan Alignment Electorally
Rewarding? Evidence from Village Council Elections in India', IZA
Working Paper No.9994. http://dx.doi.org/10.2139/ssrn.2835536

Dunning, Thad; Nazareno, Marcelo; Stokes, Susan; and Brusco, Valeria
(2013) *Brokers, Voters, and Clientelism: The Puzzle of Distributive Politics*,
New York, NY: Cambridge University Press.
https://doi.org/10.1017/CBO9781107324909

Finan, Fred; and Mazzocco, Mauricio (2021) 'Electoral Incentives and the
Allocation of Public Funds', *Journal of European Economic Association*,
vol.19, no.5, pp.2467–512. https://doi.org/10.1093/jeea/jvaa055

Frey, Anderson (2019) 'Cash Transfers, Clientelism and Political Enfranchisement: Evidence from Brazil', *Journal of Public Economics*, vol.176,
pp.1–17. https://doi.org/10.1016/j.jpubeco.2019.05.002

Hamilton, Alexander; Madison, James; and Jay, John (1937 [originally
published, 1787]) *The Federalist Papers*, New York: Tudor.

Haseeb, Mohammad and Vyborny, Kate (2021) 'Data, Discretion and Institutional Quality', *Journal of Public Economics*. https://doi.org/10.1016/j.jpubeco.2021.104535

Hicken, Allen (2011) 'Clientelism', *Annual Review of Political Science*, vol.14, pp.289–310. https://doi.org/10.1146/annurev.polisci.031908.220508

Hoffmann, Vivian; Jakiela, Pamela; Kremer, Michael; Sheelyy, Ryan; and Goodkin-Gold, Matthew (2017) 'There is No Place Like Home: Theory and Evidence on Decentralization and Politician Preferences', Department of Economics Working Paper, Harvard University. https://scholar.harvard.edu/files/kremer/files/there_is_no_place_like_home_17.11.09a_date_changed.pdf

Jesline, Joshy; Romate, John; Rajkumar, Eslavath; and George, Allen (2021) 'The Plight of Migrants during COVID-19 and the Impact of Circular Migration in India: A Systematic Review', *Humanities and Social Science Communication*, vol.8, p.231. https://doi.org/10.1057/s41599-021-00915-6

Khemani, Stuti (2015) 'Buying Votes versus Supplying Public Services', *Journal of Development Economics*, vol.117, pp.84–93. https://doi.org/10.1016/j.jdeveco.2015.07.002

Levitt, Steven and Snyder, James (1997) 'The Impact of Federal Spending on House Election Outcomes', *Journal of Political Economy*, vol.105, no.1, pp.30–53. https://doi.org/10.1086/262064

Maitra, Pushkar; Mitra, Sandip; Mookherjee, Dilip; and Visaria, Sujata (2022) 'Decentralized Targeting of Agricultural Credit Programs: Private versus Political Intermediaries', Boston University Working Paper. https://people.bu.edu/dilipm/wkpap/TRAIL_GRAILNov22.pdf

Malik, Adeel; Mirza, Rinchan; and Platteau Jean-Philippe (2021) 'Entrenched Political Dynasties and Development under Competitive Clientelism: Evidence from Pakistan', Economic Development and Institutions Network Working Paper. https://edi.opml.co.uk/wpcms/wp-content/uploads/2021/08/Entrenched-Political-Dynasties-and-Development-Under-Competitive-Clientelism-Evidence-from-Pakistan.pdf

Mansuri, Ghazala and Rao, Vijayendra (2013) *Localizing Development: Does Participation Work?* World Bank Policy Research Report, Washington, DC: World Bank. https://doi.org/10.1007/s00712-014-0394-4

Martinez-Bravo, Monica; Padro Miguel, Gerard; Qian, Nancy; and Yao, Yang (2022) 'The Rise and Fall of Local Elections in China' *American Economic Review*, vol 112, no.9. https://doi.org/10.1257/aer.20181249

Mehmood, Sultan and Seror, Avner (2021) 'Religion, Politics and Judicial Independence: Theory and Evidence', Economic Development and Institutions Network Working Paper. https://ideas.repec.org/p/hal/wpaper/halshs-02481060.html

Mookherjee, Dilip (2015) 'Political Decentralization', *Annual Review of Economics*, vol.7, pp.231–49. https://doi.org/10.1146/annurev-economics-080614-115527

Mookherjee, Dilip; and Nath, Anusha (2021) 'Clientelistic Politics and Pro-Poor Targeting: Rules versus Discretionary Budgets', Institute for Economic Development Working Paper, Boston University. https://doi.org/10.35188/UNU-WIDER/2021/065-8

Muralidharan, Karthik; Niehaus, Paul; and Sukhtankar, Sandeep (2016) 'Building State Capacity: Evidence from Biometric Smartcards in India', *American Economic Review*, November. https://doi.org/10.1257/aer.20141346

Muralidharan, Karthik; Niehaus, Paul; and Sukhtankar, Sandeep (2020) 'Identity Verification Standards in Welfare Programs: Experimental Evidence from India', NBER Working Paper 26744. https://doi.org/10.3386/w26744

Pal, Mahi (2019) 'Dr. B.R. Ambedkar, Dalits and Decentralized Rural Governance in India', *Mainstream*, vol.LVII, no.17, 13 April. https://www.mainstreamweekly.net/article8636.html

Pande, Rohini; Schaner, Simone; Moore, Charity; and Stacy, Elena (2020) 'A Majority of India's Poor Women May Miss COVID-19 PMJDY Cash Transfers', Center for Economic and Social Research, Yale University. https://egc.yale.edu/sites/default/files/COVID%20Brief.pdf

Shenoy, Ajay and Zimmerman, Laura (2020) 'The Workforce of Clientelism: The Case of Local Officials in the Party Machine', Department of Economics Working Paper, University of California, Santa Cruz. http://hdl.handle.net/10419/238109

Stokes, Susan (2005) 'Perverse Accountability: A Formal Model of Machine Politics with Evidence from Argentina', *American Political Science Review*, vol.99, no.3, pp.315–25. https://doi.org/10.1017/S0003055405051683

Tarquinio, Lisa (2021) 'The Politics of Drought Relief: Evidence from Southern India', Department of Economics Working Paper, University of Western Ontario. http://dx.doi.org/10.2139/ssrn.4163045

Trachtman, Carly; Permana, Yudistira; and Sahadewo, Gumilang (2022) 'How Much Do Our Neighbors Really Know? The Limits of Community-Based Targeting', University of California, Berkeley Working Paper.

Vera-Cossio, Diego (2022) 'Targeting Credit through Community Members', *Journal of the European Economic Association*, vol 20, no.2, pp.778–821, https://doi.org/10.1093/jeea/jvab036

Wade, R. (1997) 'How infrastructure agencies motivate staff: canal irrigation in India and the Republic of Korea', in Mody, Ashoka (ed.), *Infrastructure Strategies in East Asia*, Washington DC: World Bank.

World Bank (2004) 'World Development Report 2004 Making Services Work for Poor People', World Bank and Oxford University Press. https://doi.org/10.1596/0-8213-5468-X

PART 2
Politics

4. Realising the promise of partial decentralisation

Shantayanan Devarajan and Stuti Khemani

Summary

A well-established argument, pioneered by Musgrave (1959) and Oates (1972), states that devolving responsibility to subnational governments leads to better economic and governance outcomes. However, the empirical evidence on this has been mixed. In explaining these mixed outcomes, this chapter identifies two factors missing from this analysis on the impact of decentralisation, namely: that it depends upon prevailing political incentives that govern the behaviour of public sector bureaucrats and service providers, and that the design of decentralisation is inherently a political decision that may deviate from economically efficient solutions. Incorporating these factors, this chapter shows that most decentralisations are partial, specifically with regard to fiscal decentralisation, often with a mismatch between devolved responsibilities and accountability. It concludes that, nevertheless, increased contestation in local elections has the potential to lead to improved service delivery through increasing legitimacy of government and changing social norms.

It is easy to be pessimistic about decentralisation in developing countries today. Three decades of increasing responsibility of subnational governments has not improved service delivery outcomes. One reason is that the accountability of service providers is an important ingredient in service delivery (World Bank 2003), and it has not always been devolved. In Pakistan, while responsibility for education has been given to districts, teachers remain accountable to the central administration rather than to local-level politicians. Some countries are reversing course. Tanzania, for example, has recentralised revenue-raising

How to cite this book chapter:

Devarajan, Shantayanan and Khemani, Stuti (2023) 'Realising the promise of partial decentralisation', in: Faguet, Jean-Paul and Pal, Sarmistha (eds) *Decentralised Governance: Crafting Effective Democracies Around the World*, London: LSE Press, pp. 75–98. https://doi.org/10.31389/lsepress.dlg.d License: CC BY-3.0 IGO authority, making local governments even more dependent on fiscal transfers from the centre. In addition, the wave of authoritarianism that has swept the world in recent years (2014–22) has greatly reduced the policymaking and fiscal powers of local governments.

We strike a more optimistic note here for two, related reasons. First, improvements in service delivery come about not just from bureaucrats' being accountable to elected political leaders but also from changes in the professional norms governing behaviour in public service. Second, the past two decades have witnessed a rise in political contestation at the local level. And the characteristics of local political contestation – the quality of candidates running, reduced 'vote-buying', voters' knowledge of local corruption and other performance criteria – have been shown to improve policy outcomes. They do so by strengthening the legitimacy of government in general and by influencing the norms of local-level bureaucrats and service providers even if they are not accountable to local politicians. Taken together, these findings make a case for decentralisation as an inescapable part of the process of economic development.

The chapter has four parts. In Section 4.1, we review the original argument for decentralisation based on economic efficiency, following Musgrave (1959) and Oates (1972), and note its mixed results. In Section 4.2 we interpret the disappointing outcomes as stemming from two factors missing from the Musgrave–Oates principles. The impact of decentralisation depends upon prevailing political incentives that govern the behaviour of bureaucrats and service providers in the public sector. And the design of decentralisation is inherently a political decision that may deviate from the economically efficient solution. Incorporating these factors, we show that most decentralisations are partial, often with a mismatch between devolved responsibilities and accountability. Furthermore, this partial decentralisation is an equilibrium that balances competing political forces, making it difficult to improve development outcomes by tinkering with the allocation of functions. Nevertheless, in Section 4.3, we show how the increased contestation in local elections and the characteristics of these elections has the potential to lead to improved service delivery. The fourth section describes the key mechanism here, which is based on increasing legitimacy of government and changing social norms. The conclusions briefly assess the prospects for decentralisation's realising its original promise.

4.1 The promise and shortcomings of decentralisation

Why should devolving responsibility to subnational governments lead to better outcomes? The original arguments, pioneered by Musgrave (1959) and Oates (1972), rest on two, separate foundations. The first, often called the 'subsidiarity principle', stems from the allocative function of government in Musgrave's three functions of government (the other two being stabilisation and redistribution). When there is an externality or public good, government should intervene to allocate resources so that the externality is corrected or the public good provided. When this externality or public good has a spatial dimension, then the responsibility should be given to the smallest jurisdiction that encompasses that area. For example, sanitation services should be provided by the government of the local community that generates the solid waste.

The second foundation is based on the heterogeneity of preferences. Different communities will have different demands for publicly provided goods and services. For instance, communities with young families may have greater demand for public schools than those with older people. Subnational governments responding to local preferences would lead to a better distribution of public resources than a central government responding to average citizens' preferences.

Compelling as these arguments are, the experience with fiscal decentralisation in developing countries has been decidedly mixed. The delivery of basic services did not improve across the board. Previously under-represented groups, such as the poor and ethnic minorities, did not see their preferences systematically reflected in policy decisions at the subnational level (Mansuri and Rao 2012). Several countries including Brazil ran into macroeconomic difficulties as some large provinces over-borrowed, knowing they were 'too big to fail' (Rodden, Eskeland, and Litvack 2003).

The Musgrave–Oates arguments were founded on the assumption of a benevolent government, which was clearly violated in the real world. Even if it were appropriate (for spatial reasons) for a subnational government to be responsible for the public good, the incentives and capacity of the local administration to deliver were often severely limited. In Uganda, lower tiers of government lacked proper accounting practices that were a requirement for receiving funds. As a result, they received less money than before decentralisation and spending on primary health care fell (Akin, Hutchinson, and Strumpf 2001). In addition, many subnational entities suffered from elite capture, so that local preferences were not reflected in local service delivery. Indonesia introduced 'village governments' with locally chosen village heads accountable to village councils that would determine budget priorities. But, since the village heads chose the members of the council, accountability to the villagers was weak: only 3 per cent of the village proposals were included in the district budget (World Bank 2001). Decentralisation here simply multiplied the problems of patronage politics. Finally, Musgrave's subsidiarity principle applied only to the allocative function of government; decentralisation may have undermined the stabilisation function.

Different stakeholders responded to the shortcomings of decentralisation in different ways. International development partners, such as the World Bank and USAID, intensified what they were already doing, but at the subnational level. Noting that subnational administrations lacked capacity, the World Bank scaled up its capacity-building programmes to train local officials in public expenditure management. Observing the potential for elite capture at the local level, USAID accelerated its participatory programmes at both national and subnational levels. As we show below, these efforts were addressing the proximate, rather than the underlying, causes of the problem.

Where countries had embarked on major decentralisation efforts only to see development outcomes deteriorate, their governments often reacted by slowing down, stopping, or even reversing the decentralisation. In Pakistan, while political decentralisation to the third tier had been achieved, fiscal decentralisation started slowly and, when the results in terms of service delivery were not encouraging, slowed down even further – to the point where the fiscal system in the country is still described as 'centralised' (Tunio et al. 2020). A review of Tanzania's Local Government Reform Program suggests that, while the structures of decentralised governance were in place, the real power remained at the national level, partly due to lack of capacity at the local level to counteract that power. As a result, Ewald and Mhamba (2019) suggested that Tanzania's local government programme is entering a phase of 'recentralisation'.

These responses did not address the underlying problem, as our co-authors and we suggested (Ahmad et al. 2006). That problem is one of politics as the foundational driver of incentives and norms of behaviour in public sector organisations (Khemani 2019; Horn 1995; World Bank 2003; World Bank 2016). Although prolific work in political science has entered into the 'black-box' of government agencies for years, the focus has mostly been on the formal institutions of bureaucracy set up by elected legislators in developed countries like the United States, the United Kingdom, and New Zealand. (Horn (1995) is an early comprehensive account that remains relevant).

The World Bank's (2003) report 'Making Services Work for Poor People' brought an economic framework to the accountability problem of government and service delivery in developing countries. It suggested that the success of government intervention to correct market failures or achieve redistribution depended on two accountability relationships: (i) between policymakers and service providers; and (ii) between politicians and citizens. When one or both of these relationships is weak (for example, teachers are absent from school, social transfers are given to the non-poor, and so on), then service delivery outcomes are disappointing, at both national and subnational levels.

While decentralisation could in principle strengthen accountability – by enabling policymakers to monitor service providers more closely and citizens to vote local politicians into or out of office based on their performance – the way it was practised risked making existing problems worse. Politics in the developing world has suffered acutely from the maladies of patronage and vote-buying (World Bank 2016). Yet decentralisation reforms proceeded by ignoring politics and focused on capacity-building among local officials and fiscal transfers from central ministries. For instance, Callen et al. (2020; 2018) showed that political incentives in Pakistan drove how many doctors were provided to constituencies but not their performance in their jobs. Absenteeism among doctors was widespread, and particularly so among those doctors with political connections. District bureaucrats reported political interference when they attempted to discipline absent doctors. Politics is often geared towards providing patronage jobs in government, rather than holding workers accountable for service delivery. Decentralisation in Pakistan simply extended this form of patronage politics to local levels (Liaqat et al. 2019).

Although decentralisation meant that citizens could influence decisions about their district's budget allocations, if those local governments lacked their own tax base, they were dependent on the central government for revenues. Even when these revenues were determined by a formula governing intergovernmental transfers (as in India or South Africa), they were subject to political manipulation by central governments (Khemani 2007). Some local governments in Nigeria blamed their failure to deliver services on the capricious nature of transfers from central government (Khemani 2006; Rodden 2002).

The various responses by stakeholders to the mixed record of decentralisation sometimes exacerbated the problem. Strengthening capacity by training officials in accounting could not help if those officials were not held accountable for their actions. Moreover, the reason these officials were unable to manage budgets may be because they had not had the experience of managing budgets. If local officials gain some experience with managing budgets, they may over time improve outcomes. But, if at the first sight of poor performance the decision is made to recentralise, they may never gain that experience, so outcomes remain weak. Likewise, in the case of education in Pakistan, one way to address the problem of mismatched accountability of teachers and the education system may be to make the teachers employees of the district – that is, to further decentralise. Yet the reaction has been to slow down the decentralisation process.

These difficulties appear in sharp relief when we realise that all decentralisations are partial, in the sense that not all sectors or functions are devolved to subnational units (Devarajan, Khemani, and Shah 2009). For instance, in Pakistan responsibility for education was transferred to the districts but teachers remained employees of the provincial government. In South Africa, expenditure responsibility for health, education, and social security was devolved to provincial governments without the corresponding revenue responsibility (Ahmad et al. 2006). In Brazil, it was the reverse – revenue responsibility was devolved but without expenditure authority. In many countries, local governments have discretion over current expenditures but the central government prescribes or controls capital expenditures.

The implication of decentralisation being partial is that local governments cannot be held responsible by citizens for the allocation of the local budget, and hence for the outcomes of local public spending. Voters cannot make the local government accountable for performance. In fact, citizens are more likely to hold national government to account for performance – even on items that are the responsibility of the local government.[1] Knowing this, local politicians do not have an incentive to provide the best budgetary allocation to their citizens. They may instead choose to target resources to narrow interest groups who would vote for them. Indeed, disadvantaged groups may vote for people who are 'close' to them (that is, based on their identity) if the local government does not have enough discretion in protecting them from harassment and violence (Varshney 2005). This kind of identity-based voting further undermines political accountability and hence outcomes.

Meanwhile, the central government will be held accountable for public policy outcomes, and so it may use fiscal transfers as a way of ensuring its re-election, by targeting those local politicians who provide political benefits and returns while withholding funds from those who do not. The result is a low-level equilibrium where partial decentralisation has failed to strengthen (and may have weakened) the two accountability relationships for service delivery. Partial decentralisation also undermines the two foundational principles of Musgrave and Oates. Functions may not be devolved to the smallest jurisdiction that encompasses the externality if some of the functions are retained at a higher level. And lower-level governments may not be able to reflect local citizens' preferences if higher-level governments either provide some of these public goods, or lack the incentives to design decentralisation to reflect local preferences.

Even more troubling is that fact that the degree and nature of partial decentralisation are typically the result of multiple, opposing forces (Faguet and Shami 2021). Central-level bureaucrats resist decentralisation because it reduces the 'rents' they earn by controlling service providers. Conversely, these service providers may resist being accountable to local-level politicians who can observe their behaviour more closely. The outcome could be the complex decentralisation observed in Pakistan's education (with teachers being employees of the provincial government, but schools a district responsibility). This may also explain why, when the initial results of decentralisation are poor, there is often a groundswell of support from political and bureaucratic elites to slow down or reverse the decentralisation, rather than to further decentralise.

So politically driven partial decentralisation may lead to a governance trap, calling into question many conventional recommendations made to correct the shortcomings of decentralisation. For example, simply asking central governments to increase their allocation to local governments may not help if those local governments are not held accountable for allocating their budgets. Not devolving responsibility in essential functions (like health and education) because local governments 'lack capacity' is also unhelpful. Local-level governments cannot be held accountable by their citizens unless they have discretion over their budgets, and they may not be able to build capacity unless citizens can closely scrutinise public expenditure management.

Not only is the analysis and empirical evidence leading to discouraging prospects for decentralisation, but recent developments seem to reinforce the pessimism. The rise of political authoritarianism at the national level in the last five years (2017–22) seems to have created hurdles for fostering political representation at the local level. Yet, despite these underlying flaws and concerning developments in the real world, the prospects of decentralisation remain promising.

4.2 Political decentralisation has taken hold, even as fiscal decentralisation remains partial

Decentralisation in developing countries relies on instituting local elections to select local political leaders able to wield some power over local taxation, public spending, and implementation of national policies. While the degree of local fiscal and policy autonomy varies across countries and over time, a common feature of decentralisation is the establishment of political contestation for local government leadership positions.

In India, the immediate implication of the 1993 landmark decentralisation reform, the Panchayati Raj Act, was in local politics. Even as fiscal powers provided to local governments varied across state governments, the new constitutional amendment effectively mandated the holding of regular elections for the political leadership of local government bodies. Although panchayat institutions had existed historically, the decentralisation reform brought a sea change in how the leaders of those local governance institutions would be selected. After decades of no elections in villages and districts, post-1993 India has been holding local elections regularly.

In countries across Africa, decentralisation has primarily consisted of creating space for local political leaders to monitor the existing local administration, where bureaucrats are appointed to implement national policies (Habyarimana, Khemani, and Scot 2018). With political decentralisation, local administrative units (districts) have taken on a distinctive characteristic of local government: the sharing of powers and responsibilities between bureaucrats appointed by the national government and politicians elected by the people to the local council. With local governments dependent on the central government for fiscal revenues, the chief administrative officers appointed in districts are accountable to national ministries for the spending of transferred revenues. Local politicians have autonomy over spending any local revenues they collect through taxation or fees. But their revenue generation powers are both restricted by national governments and underutilised by local politicians. In Tanzania, when local politicians controlled local property taxes up to 2016, they had weak incentives to collect these taxes, because the incidence of property taxes would primarily fall on the local propertied class, who tended to be local politicians (Government of Tanzania, Prime Minister's Office for Regional and Local Government 2013). From 2016 property tax collection was recentralised.

In Brazil and Pakistan, political decentralisation was pursued by military dictators as a way to build their legitimacy (Faguet and Shami 2021; Ferraz,

Finan, and Martinez-Bravo 2020). In Indonesia, political decentralisation was part of the overall democratisation of the country following the downfall of the Suharto regime in 1998 (Hofman and Kaiser 2006; Martinez-Bravo 2014). Research on decentralisation in historically centralised countries has highlighted a shared explanation: the incentives of national leaders to pursue *political* decentralisation (Faguet and Shami (2021) and Khemani (2015) provide a review). The extent to which the newly created or invigorated local political jurisdictions would have powers over local public policy and service delivery, or receive revenue transfers to spend at their discretion, remained a decision of central governments, which controlled key revenue bases. While the fiscal, service delivery, and policymaking powers of local political leaders have waxed and waned, the enduring feature of decentralisation is local elections for leadership positions in local government.

Cross-country data on local elections began to be available in the early 2010s, starting with Wave 6 of the World Values Survey (WVS; Haerpfer et al. 2022). Waves 6 and 7 asked people whether they voted in local elections. Figure 4.1 plots the 32 countries covered by both waves according to the percentage of respondents who answered that they vote 'always' or 'usually' in local elections. In most countries, more than 70 per cent of respondents

Figure 4.1: Per cent of respondents who say they vote in local elections

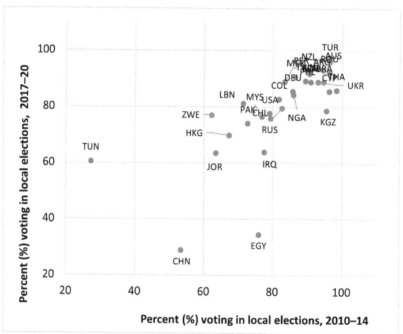

Source: World Values Survey waves: Wave 6, question V226, https://www.worldvaluessurvey.org/WVSDocumentationWV6.jsp; and Wave 7, question Q221, https://www.worldvaluessurvey.org/WVSDocumentationWV7.jsp

reported voting in local elections. China is an outlier (although still not zero, because of its village elections). Egypt stands out as having moved from 76 per cent voting in local elections in 2012 to only 34 per cent in 2018, while Tunisia moved in the opposite direction.

In addition to voting, citizens also participate as contenders for local leadership positions. While there is no similarly comparable cross-country data, micro-empirical research in countries as varied as Brazil, India, Indonesia, Pakistan, and Uganda shows significant political contestation in local government elections. In the Indian state of Bihar, an average of 10 people contest for the position of village *mukhiya*, or head of the village government (Khemani, Chaudhary, and Scot 2020). In Brazil, decentralisation helped dilute the influence of local economic elites, enabling new political contenders to emerge (Ferraz, Finan, and Martinez-Bravo 2020). In Yogyakarta, Indonesia, a detailed field study documented a dramatic change in village government leadership over the previous 10 years, away from the control of the traditional landed elite and towards leaders from more modest family backgrounds (Berenschot, Capri, and Dhian 2021). An experiment to encourage 'good' citizens to enter village politics in Pakistan had a large impact, suggesting that citizens were willing to become local political leaders to serve their communities (Gulzar and Khan 2021).

Figure 4.2: People think having *honest* elections is important, even in countries with low confidence in elections

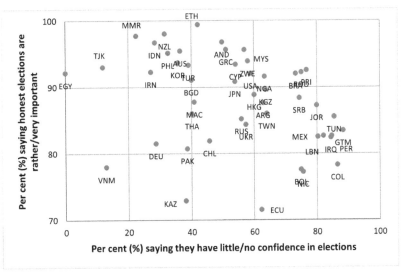

Source: World Values Survey, Wave 7 (2017–20), Q234,
https://www.worldvaluessurvey.org/WVSDocumentationWV7.jsp
Notes: The questions asked: 'How important is having honest elections?' and 'How much confidence do you have in elections?' The questions are about elections generally; the WVS does not distinguish between respondents' views of national vs. subnational elections.

Even where traditional leaders play a role in local governance (as in Africa), locally elected leaders are the agents tasked with managing public goods and services financed by the state (Baldwin and Raffler 2019). For example, in rural Zimbabwe, 79 per cent of respondents to Round 4 of the Afrobarometer survey cited traditional leaders as having some or a great deal of influence over local governance – but the areas of that influence were restricted to community matters such as dispute resolution. Responsibility for managing schools and clinics was assigned to local and central government.

The WVSs also explored people's aspirations for improving the quality of elections, even when they found low confidence in how elections were currently functioning. In Figure 4.2, the vast majority of respondents across countries thought that having 'honest' elections is very/rather important for their lives. Another module asks whether the respondent has 'confidence' in different institutions, including elections.[2] In the median country in the sample, 56 per cent of respondents say they have little or no confidence in elections. Among the countries with more than 80 per cent reporting little or no confidence in elections are Iraq, Lebanon, and Tunisia, countries with weaker institutions of democracy and growing political unrest in recent years. Yet, even in these countries, more than 80 per cent say that having 'honest' elections would be very/rather important.

4.3 The potential of political decentralisation

How can increased contestation in local elections lead to improved service delivery? At any level (national, regional or local) elections influence public policies and service delivery, and thence development outcomes, through three channels:

a. Incentives: local political leaders could take actions to further objectives of election/re-election into public office for the rents or benefits that office holding brings.
b. Intrinsic motivation: local elections could change the types of citizens who enter political contests and get selected as local leaders.
c. Norms and preferences: local elections could shape people's views and expectations about others' political behaviour (norms), and what to demand from public policy and political representatives (preferences).

The first two channels are well studied by economists,[3] while the third is an emerging area of such research in economics.[4] The impact of *local* elections through any of these channels depends upon what powers are decentralised and what actions locally elected leaders can take. In the context of partial decentralisation, when limited formal powers are assigned to locally elected leaders, informal channels of intrinsic motivation and norms may play a larger role. For example, in Uganda, locally elected leaders play informal roles of monitoring and supervision of frontline service providers, rather than wielding formal powers over the nature of contracts with these providers (Habyarimana, Khemani, and Scot 2018).

The impact of elections, whether national, regional, or local, also depends upon whether the electoral mechanism is indeed working fairly (opposition candidates are not prevented from running; votes are counted fairly, and so on). These issues cannot be taken for granted. For example, if votes can be purchased through cash or the promise of other targeted benefits in exchange for the vote, local elections are likely to yield different incentives and different types of contenders than if votes cannot be bought.[5] The WVS asked a series of questions about malpractices in elections – whether votes were counted fairly, opposition candidates were prevented from running, voters were bribed, violence was involved, or the media was captured. Bribing of voters was a robust correlate of low confidence in elections (Figure 4.3). The overall picture emerging from the WVSs was that voters were aware of electoral malpractice (and thus reported low confidence in elections) but nevertheless had hopes for honest elections.

Figure 4.3: Reports of vote-buying are correlated with low confidence in elections

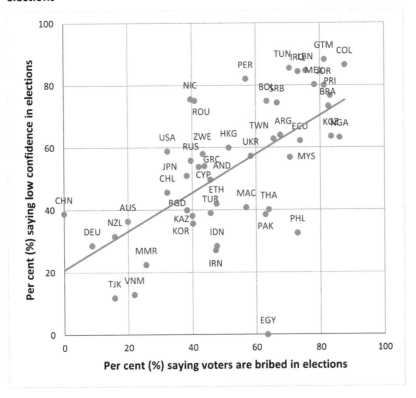

On average, electoral institutions tend to strengthen incentives of political leaders to perform better at both national and local levels (World Bank 2016). Yet there are clear examples where autocracies outperform democracies (Besley and Kudamatsu 2008; World Bank 2016). Research examining these differences suggests that the key question is whether leaders are selected and sanctioned based on performance in delivering public goods (Khemani 2019; World Bank 2016).

Why are some settings, within both autocracies and democracies, successful in selecting and sanctioning leaders based on performance in providing public goods, and others disastrous at it? The answer appears to be rooted in culture or norms. In the language of game theory, political institutions are games of multiple equilibria where shared expectations of how others are playing the game pin down an equilibrium (Bidner and Francois 2013; Myerson 2006; Schelling 1960). Initial sets of beliefs and expectations about how others are behaving shape an individual's behaviour, leading to an outcome of collective behaviour, whether one of high expectations and performance or one of low expectations and rampant corruption.

Viewing politics as a game with multiple equilibria (or collective outcomes, depending upon which initial beliefs are held by people), Myerson (2006) argues that decentralisation to a number of units of local government is more likely to yield successful outcomes than centralisation of power in one national government. The reason is that having several units, rather than one, makes it more likely for political leaders to emerge with a reputation for effective governance. The substantial variation within countries in governance outcomes at local levels supports this view. Evidence from studies on the persistent effect of institutions that have long since disappeared can be interpreted in terms of historical experience shaping beliefs and norms (World Bank 2016).[6] For example, Dell, Lane, and Querubin (2018) found that in present-day Vietnam norms of cooperation for local public goods are more likely to be found in places that were in the past governed by strong state institutions (Dai Viet) rather than weak states (the Khmer empire of Cambodia). This evidence can be interpreted as supporting Myerson's theoretical argument of reputation being built through the experience of good governance, changing beliefs, and allowing local governments and society and the economy at large to function better.

Public policy therefore could focus on the potential of decentralisation to help shift beliefs and norms and enable better quality leaders to emerge – that is, to facilitate the selection of better equilibria along the lines of Myerson's characterisation of political institutions as games of multiple equilibria. This means approaching the design of government agencies as a technical problem – asking which tasks of public policy and how much fiscal resources to assign to which type of agent, elected politician, or appointed bureaucrat. Political decentralisation – the existing jurisdictions where local political leaders are being selected – sets the context in which policymakers can design the most appropriate agency mechanisms through which to achieve government objectives.

For some emergent policy objectives (such as mitigating and adapting to climate change or managing an influx of refugees), government agencies find themselves needing to address problems of misinformation among citizens. For example, in advanced democracies, where electoral institutions are functioning well, the 'median' or 'pivotal' voter can vote against environmental regulations and taxes because they do not believe the science of climate change, and for right-wing parties that refuse refugees, because they are susceptible to misinformation about the impact of refugees.[7] In developing countries, raising revenues to finance public goods for economic development runs into tax avoidance by citizens.[8] Tariff policies to cover the costs of utilities that provide water and electricity are protested by citizens.[9] Restrictions on the quantity of water that can be abstracted are met with farmers' agitations and non-compliance.[10] These are examples of government addressing a public or social problem that individuals or markets cannot. The role of government is not only one of responding to citizens' demands and being held accountable for it but also of shaping those demands as problems of a 'public good' nature that become evident to technical agencies. To pursue these roles, government agencies would need to build legitimacy for taxation, price reforms (such as removal of energy subsidies), and environmental regulations (such as quantity restrictions on the use of scarce water resources).[11]

4.4 Building legitimacy and changing norms through decentralisation

Even after we take full account of the growth of concerns about local capacity and elite capture, as well as reluctance to give up powers and resources, we seek to show how decentralisation can nevertheless be designed to pursue objectives that are in the interests of national policymakers and the public. Local political contestation holds untapped potential to build legitimacy of government agencies. It can also strengthen professional norms in bureaucracies to improve service delivery. This potential lies in the selection of local leaders with intrinsic motivation to pursue the public good, and the role of local politics in shifting norms in public bureaucracies.

For example, Habyarimana, Khemani, and Scot (2018) found that district bureaucracies in Uganda perform better at delivering public health services in places where locally elected politicians have higher integrity, measured using survey modules developed by psychologists to assess moral disengagement. Case studies of Ugandan districts suggest that locally elected politicians can play both negative and positive roles in the delivery of services – interfering to obstruct versus monitoring to facilitate better services. The integrity of local politicians determines whether they obstruct or support technical officers in delivering services within the complex organisation of local government. Other studies in different contexts, such as Callen, Gulzar, and Rezaee (2020), referred to earlier, show how the integrity of local politicians can shape whether they collude with frontline service providers to extract rents or encourage them to perform.

Research on how local politics might shape norms of behaviour in bureaucracies and policy preferences among citizens is nascent. Nevertheless, available analysis of the persistent effects of historical institutions points to norms and preferences as important channels to investigate (as mentioned earlier, and argued in World Bank (2016) and studies like Dell, Lane, and Querubin (2018)). Another example is Pandey (2010), who provided evidence linking historical institutions to current political behaviour and the delivery of public services (or lack thereof). She took advantage of historical variation in the power given to landlords across districts in colonial India. Landlord districts that had more oppressive revenue systems gave greater power to elite landlords rather than to peasants. In districts with non-landlord control, village bodies that were more representative of peasants were responsible for collecting revenue. The results show that, in formerly landlord-controlled districts, village elections today are more likely to be won by leaders belonging to high-caste groups, who are the social elite. These high-caste groups are less likely to send their children to the public schools in the villages compared with low-caste groups. Teacher effort is significantly lower in villages in ex-landlord districts. When results are analysed by teacher caste, the difference in teacher effort between ex-landlord and ex-non-landlord districts is significant for high- and mid-caste teachers. For low-caste teachers, the difference in effort between ex-landlord and ex-non-landlord areas is not significant. Finally, student test scores and school infrastructure are significantly worse in villages belonging to ex-landlord districts.

The above example shows that behaviour varies a great deal across and within villages sharing the same formal political institutions of local democracy and economic conditions. The variation in behaviour can be traced to historical institutions of colonial revenue administration and even older institutions of caste networks, suggesting that these behaviours can be described as long-standing norms. The distinction between norms and incentives is important because long-standing norms among thousands of state personnel limit the ability of reform leaders to change incentives simply by changing the formal rules of the game. Banerjee, Duflo, and Glennerster (2008) and Dhaliwal and Hanna (2017) provided evidence from India that reformers who tried to use new technology to monitor frontline health workers and strengthen their incentives ultimately failed to implement or sustain these reforms.

Political norms of behaviour – what citizens demand from the state, and how they expect others to be acting in the public sector – can explain why even well-intentioned reformers in powerful political positions find it difficult to institute change. Consider the following example. Rational expectation among 'ordinary' (that is, non-office-bearing) citizens is that other citizens will vote for politicians who share their identity or ideology, and who provide targeted private benefits. This applies even though, in equilibrium, the consequences are harmful for everybody, since voting on the basis of identity and private benefits weakens political incentives to provide public goods. Among those who have leadership or entrepreneurial qualities and become contenders for political power, the rational expectation will be that other contenders are entering the fray to seek private rents from public resources. Among office-bearing citizens or state personnel, all the way from high-level bureaucrats to frontline providers, the rational expectation is that their peers do not care about doing their jobs well because there are few formal or informal (sanctions) rewards for (bad) good performance. The service delivery organisations of the state would thus lack both incentives and non-pecuniary sources of motivation (such as peer pressure and professional norms). When a reform leader tries to strengthen incentives in this low-performance setting, those reforms are often resisted and thwarted by well-organised interest groups, such as unions of teachers and doctors, or other politicians who seek rents from the status quo.

Theoretical analysis of how changes in norms come about points to a triggering role for political contestation and the leaders selected through it. Leaders can be 'prominent agents' who signal a shift in beliefs among society at large (Acemoglu and Jackson 2015). Growing experience with political engagement and the learning that comes from it, such as through frustration and indignation with bad outcomes, can create fertile conditions for change in political norms (Bidner and Francois 2013). Recent theoretical developments on the management of complex organisations, in both the private and public sectors, also point to the role of leaders in shaping organisational culture. For example, Akerlof (2015; 2017) defines the concept of 'legitimacy' of leaders as one of getting lower-level personnel to follow the organisation's objectives of their own accord, through peer-to-peer interaction, without incentive payments and monitoring from the top.

In each of these theories, changes in norms, information, and communication that shift expectations about how others are behaving are the necessary elements. Where norms support a less-than-desirable outcome, shifting to a new norm requires information sharing and communication among the actors to update their beliefs about how others are behaving. In some models, the information is communicated through the types of leaders who are selected (Acemoglu and Jackson 2015). In others, information is gathered and shared over time among citizens through the experience of political participation (Bidner and Francois 2013). The role of political leaders and processes of political participation as *the* channels for sharing information that shifts norms is reminiscent of Ostrom's (2000) classic work on norms for collective action.

The literature on the persistent effects of historical institutions, long after the formal institutions have disappeared and been replaced by others, is useful in supporting the argument that changing norms need not involve changing formal institutions. An example is the difference in economic performance across democracies and autocracies (Besley and Kudamatsu 2008; World Bank 2016). Shifting norms need not involve introducing elections into authoritarian regimes or, conversely, removing elections or changing electoral rules in democracies. The growing evidence of significant variation in economic outcomes within countries, across places sharing the same formal political institutions, shows how the *functioning* of political contestation is what matters. To illustrate what this means, it may be worth repeating an example cited earlier – in places where the currency of political contestation is, literally, to buy votes, municipal governments under-invest in public health services and a larger proportion of children are undernourished (Khemani 2015).

The easy part of politics is strengthening the incentives of political leaders to defeat opponents and remain in office. The difficult part is to change the political norms of thousands of ordinary citizens, not to mention mid-level bureaucrats and frontline providers, so that winning strategies move away from things like vote-buying and exploiting ideological divisions among voters towards pursuing broader public goods. Prevalent political norms explain why, despite intense electoral competition and powerful leaders who emerge speaking the language of reforms, it is hard to get frontline service providers, such as teachers and community health workers, to deliver (Callen, Gulzar, and Rezaee 2020; Callen et al. 2016). Even though they wield formal power over the frontline workers of the state, reform leaders can be thwarted in their attempts to exact accountability from them (Banerjee, Duflo, and Glennerster 2008; Dhaliwal and Hanna 2017). Effective reform in this context is not the passage of a new law or act. The reform that matters is in the minds of the thousands of human beings who run state bureaucracies and implement public policies.

At the same time, the evidence of persistent effects of history and path dependency raises the question of historical determinism. Are countries doomed to run the long course of history and evolve norms over time? Can policy actors do anything in the short run to change norms? Political decentralisation offers opportunities for reform leaders to change political norms in the short run by raising three questions: (i) what is the goal the state hopes to achieve? (ii) Who are the agents whose actions will collectively shape that outcome? (iii) What resources and incentives do each of those agents have?

The policy experience of the Brazilian state of Ceará illustrates how a mechanism design approach can work for reform leaders to bring about dramatic change in the short run (Khemani 2019; Tendler and Freedheim 1996). The goal of a series of reformist governors of Ceará was to effectively deliver public health services, such as vaccination. The agents whose actions would collectively shape whether vaccinations are effectively delivered were the frontline health workers, as well as the locally elected mayors and the nurses these mayors hired, who had supervisory powers over frontline workers. Apart from the physical resources (such as vaccines, cold chain, and other equipment) needed to accomplish the goal, the governors confronted the lack of incentives and professional norms among nurses and health workers because of local patronage politics. A new cadre of health workers was meritocratically recruited by the governor's office, trained, and given credible signals that their career trajectory would depend upon their performance. Credibility came from broadcasting information about the hiring of these workers, the goals they were expected to pursue, the welfare gains that would come from achieving them, and what people could do if they did not see these workers performing. Those candidates who did not get the job effectively became monitors of those who did. Radio broadcasts about the new cadre of workers made public health services politically salient, changing the incentives of mayors. Mayors began to compete on facilitating health workers to deliver rather than distributing government jobs as patronage.

To be sure, the kind of initiative undertaken by the governors of Ceará is far from guaranteed to work in other places. Incumbent political parties in other places may not have the credibility to be effective with media broadcasts, or they may not enjoy the fiscal and political space for meritocratic recruitment of a new cadre of workers. Mayoral politics at the local level in other places may be more clientelistic and resistant to change, even after a media blitz. However, approaching the problem of state capacity as a problem of incentives and norms that is rooted in local politics (the Ceará strategy) is instructive. And it can be adapted to the unique contexts of different countries. The starting point would be to identify the existing local-level jurisdictions where political contestation is happening and examine how this local-level politics shapes incentives and norms across different types of state agencies.

Conclusions

The mixed results of fiscal decentralisation in developing countries called into question the original Musgrave–Oates foundations of subsidiarity and matching local policies to local preferences. Research on government policymaking and service delivery as a series of accountability relationships, and the fundamental role of politics in shaping those relationships, reinforces this questioning of traditional public finance conclusions based on assumptions of benevolent government. It also suggests that all decentralisations will remain partial, in a low-level equilibrium. The tendency towards greater autocracy around the world could lead to greater pessimism about decentralisation in the future.

In this chapter, we have tried to strike an optimistic note by exploring the potential of political contestation at local government levels. Political decentralisation has taken hold in the developing world and is likely to remain an important feature of the landscape. It offers opportunities to improve service delivery outcomes even if fiscal decentralisation is only partial. Political decentralisation has led to more and better-motivated people seeking public office in local elections. In turn, this phenomenon has the potential to strengthen the legitimacy of government as a whole and shift social norms so that bureaucracies perform better. Neither of these changes is guaranteed. However, approaching fiscal decentralisation as a mechanism design problem geared towards strengthening state legitimacy and shifting norms can harness the potential of decentralisation to deliver on its original promise of better outcomes and higher welfare.

Acknowledgements

Disclaimer: The arguments in this chapter are entirely those of the authors. They draw on work for the World Bank but they do not necessarily represent the views of the International Bank for Reconstruction and Development/ World Bank and its affiliated organisations, or those of the executive directors of the World Bank or the governments they represent.

Endnotes

[1] Chhibber, Shastri, and Sisson (2004) asked voters in India which tier of government they held responsible for the public goods they cared most about: medical facilities, drinking water, roads, education. The majority indicated it was the state government.

[2] Elections generally; the WVS does not distinguish between respondents' views of national vs. subnational elections.

[3] Some pioneering contributions are: Tirole (1994); Dewatripont et al. (1999); Francois (2000); Dixit (2002); Besley and Ghatak (2005); Besley (2006); Acemoglu et al. (2008); Alesina and Tabellini (2007; 2008). Dal Bo and Finan (2018) reviewed the recent accumulation of evidence on political selection.

[4] Bidner and Francois (2013) provided a model where people learn about how others are behaving in deciding whether to punish corrupt politicians. Acemoglu and Jackson (2015) provided a model where 'prominent agents' signal a shift in norms in society.

[5] Khemani (2015) found variation across local governments in the Philippines in the extent to which voters are bribed, and this variation is correlated with the performance of local governments in delivering public health services. Fujiwara (2015) found complementary evidence that more effective enfranchisement (in Brazil) leads to better public health services.

[6] Reviewed in Nunn (2009).

[7] Blanchard and Tirole (2020) described the protest movement in France being triggered by a 'green' tax on gasoline. Alesina and Stantcheva (2020) described how misinformation about immigration that is prevalent among European voters shapes their preferences for public policies.

[8] For example, Besley (2020) provided a view of the problem of non-compliance with taxation in developing countries.

[9] Ianchovichina, Burger, and Witte (2020)

[10] Al-Alaween et al. (2016)

[11] Khemani (2020) discussed the issue of legitimacy of government agencies to pursue policies in the public interest.

References

Acemoglu, Daron and Jackson, Matthew O. (2015) 'History, Expectations, and Leadership in the Evolution of Social Norms', *The Review of Economic Studies*, vol.82, no.2, pp.423–56. https://doi.org/10.1093/restud/rdu039

Acemoglu, Daron; Kremer, Michael; and Mian, Atif (2008) 'Incentives in Markets, Firms, and Governments', *The Journal of Law, Economics, and Organization*, vol.24, no.2, pp.273–306. https://doi.org/10.1093/jleo/ewm055

Ahmad, Junaid; Devarajan, Shantayanan; Khemani, Stuti; and Shah, Shekhar (2006) 'Decentralization and Service Delivery', in Ahmad, Ehtisham and Brosio, Giorgio (eds) *Handbook of Fiscal Federalism*, Cheltenham: Edward Elgar Publishing.

Akerlof, Robert (2015) 'A Theory of Authority', University of Warwick Working Paper. https://www.worldbank.org/content/dam/Worldbank/Event/DEC /ABCDE/ABCDE-2015/99.%20Robert%20Akerlof.pdf

Akerlof, Robert (2017). 'The Importance of Legitimacy', *The World Bank Economic Review*, vol.30, Supplement 1, pp.S157–65. https://doi.org/10.1093/wber/lhw009

Akin, John; Hutchinson Paul; and Strumpf, Koleman Samuel (2001) 'Decentralization and Government Provision of Public Goods: The Public Health Sector in Uganda', Abt Associates: MEASURE Evaluation Project Working Paper No.01-35, Bethesda, MD. https://doi.org/10.1080/00220380500187075

Al-Alaween, Mufleh; Jacobson, Maria; Jaraiseh, Alice; and Weinberg, Josh (eds) (2016) 'Water Integrity in the Middle East and North Africa Region: Synthesis Report of Water Integrity Risks Assessments in Jordan, Lebanon, Morocco, Palestine and Tunisia', UNDP Water Governance Facility at SIWI, Stockholm. https://siwi.org/wp-content/uploads/2016/11/synthesis-report-water -integrity-in-the-mena-region-web.pdf

Alesina, Alberto and Stantcheva, Stefanie (2020) 'Diversity, Immigration, and Redistribution', *AEA Papers and Proceedings*, vol.110, pp.329–34. https://doi.org/10.1257/pandp.20201088

Alesina, Alberto and Tabellini, Guido (2007) 'Bureaucrats or politicians? Part I: a single policy task', *American Economic Review*, vol.97, no.1, pp.169–79. https://doi.org/10.1257/aer.97.1.169

Alesina, Alberto and Tabellini, Guido (2008) 'Bureaucrats or politicians? Part II: Multiple policy tasks', *Journal of Public Economics*, vol. 92, no.3–4, pp.426–47. https://doi.org/10.1016/j.jpubeco.2007.06.004

Baldwin, Kate and Raffler, Pia (2019) 'Traditional Leaders, Service Delivery, and Electoral Accountability', in Rodden, Jonathan and Wibbels, Erik (eds) *Decentralized Governance and Accountability*, Cambridge: Cambridge University Press, pp.61–90. http://piaraffler.com/wp-content/uploads/2018/12/Baldwin_Raffler_TraditionalandElectedLeaders.pdf

Banerjee, Abhijit; Duflo, Esther; and Glennerster, Rachel (2008) 'Putting a Band-Aid on a Corpse: Incentives for Nurses in the Indian Public Health Care System', *Journal of the European Economic Association*, vol.6, no.2–3, pp.487–500. https://doi.org/10.1162/JEEA.2008.6.2-3.487

Berenschot, Ward; Capri, Wigke; and Dhian, Devy (2021) 'A Quiet Revolution? Village Head Elections and the Democratization of Rural Indonesia', *Critical Asian Studies*, vol.53, no.1, pp.126–46. https://doi.org/10.1080/14672715.2021.1871852

Besley, Timothy (2006) *Principled Agents? The Political Economy of Good Government*, Oxford University Press. https://epge.fgv.br/we/Graduacao/EconomiaPolitica/2007?action=AttachFile&do=get&target=Besley+completebook.pdf

Besley, Timothy (2020) 'State Capacity, Reciprocity, and the Social Contract', *Econometrica*, vol.88, no.4, pp.1307–35. https://doi.org/10.3982/ECTA16863

Besley, Timothy and Ghatak, Maitreesh (2005) 'Competition and Incentives with Motivated Agents', *American Economic Review*, vol.95,no.3, pp.616–36. https://doi.org/10.1257/0002828054201413

Besley, Timothy and Kudamatsu, Masayuki (2008) 'Making Autocracy Work', in E. Helpman (ed.) *Institutions and Economic Performance*, Cambridge, MA: Harvard University Press.

Bidner, Chris and Francois, Patrick (2013) 'The Emergence of Political Accountability', *The Quarterly Journal of Economics*, vol.128, no.3, pp.1397–448. https://doi.org/10.1093/qje/qjt014

Blanchard, Olivier and Tirole, Jean (2020) 'The major future economic challenges', France Strategie commission. https://www.strategie.gouv.fr/english-articles/major-future-economic-challenges-olivier-blanchard-and-jean-tirole

Callen, Michael; Gulzar, Saad; and Rezaee, Arman (2020) 'Can Political Alignment Be Costly?' *Journal of Politics*, vol.82, no.2, pp.612–26. https://doi.org/10.1086/706890

Callen, Michael; Gulzar, Saad; Syed, Hasanain, Ali; and Khan, Yasir (2018) 'The Political Economy of Public Sector Absence: Experimental Evidence from Pakistan', No. w22340. National Bureau of Economic Research. https://doi.org/10.3386/w22340

Chhibber, Pradeep; Shastri, Sandeep; and Sisson, Richard (2004) 'Federal arrangements and the provision of public goods in India', *Asian Survey*, vol.44, no.3, pp.339–52. https://doi.org/10.1525/as.2004.44.3.339

Dal Bó, Ernesto and Finan, Frederico (2018) 'Progress and Perspectives in the Study of Political Selection', *Annual Review of Economics*, vol.10, pp.541–75. https://doi.org/10.1146/annurev-economics-080217-053221

Dell, Melissa; Lane, Nathan; and Querubin, Pablo (2018) 'The Historical State, Local Collective Action, and Economic Development in Vietnam', *Econometrica*, vol.86, no.6, pp.2083–121. https://doi.org/10.3982/ECTA15122

Devarajan, Shantayanan; Khemani, Stuti; and Shah, Shekhar (2009) 'The Politics of Partial Decentralization', in Ahmad, E. and Brosio, G. (eds) *Does Decentralization Enhance Service Delivery and Poverty Reduction?* Edward Elgar Publishing. https://ideas.repec.org/b/elg/eebook/13565.html

Dewatripont, Mathias; Jewitt, Ian; and Tirole, Jean (1999) 'The Economics of Career Concerns, Part II: Application to Missions and Accountability of Government Agencies', *The Review of Economic Studies*, vol.66 no.1, pp.199–217. https://doi.org/10.1111/1467-937X.00085

Dhaliwal, Iqbal and Hanna, Rema (2017) 'The Devil Is in the Details: The Successes and Limitations of Bureaucratic Reform in India', *Journal of Development Economics*, vol.124, pp.1–21. https://doi.org/10.1016/j.jdeveco.2016.08.008

Dixit, Avinash (2002) 'Incentives and organizations in the public sector: An interpretative review', *Journal of Human Resources*', pp.696–727. https://doi.org/10.2307/3069614

Ewald, Jonas and Mhamba, Robert (2019) 'Recentralisation? Interrogating the State of Local Democracy, Good Governance and Development in Tanzania', Research Report No.13., Swedish International Center for Local Democracy. https://icld.se/wp-content/uploads/files/forskningspublikationer/icld -researchreport-13-2019-web.pdf

Faguet, Jean-Paul and Shami, Mahvish (2021) 'The Incoherence of Institutional Reform: Decentralization as a Structural Solution to Immediate Political Needs', *Studies in Comparative International Development*, vol.57, pp.82–109. https://doi.org/10.1007/s12116-021-09347-4

Ferraz, Claudio; Finan, Frederico; and Martinez-Bravo, Monica (2020) 'Political Power, Elite Control, and Long-Run Development: Evidence from Brazil', National Bureau of Economic Research Working Paper No.27456. https://doi.org/10.3386/w27456

Francois, Patrick (2000) '"Public Service Motivation" as an Argument for Government Provision', *Journal of Public Economics*, vol.78, no.3, p.275–99. https://doi.org/10.1016/S0047-2727(00)00075-X

Fujiwara, Thomas (2015) 'Voting Technology, Political Responsiveness, and Infant Health: Evidence from Brazil', *Econometrica*, vol.83, no.2, pp. 423–64. https://doi.org/10.3982/ECTA11520

Government of Tanzania, Prime Minister's Office of Regional and Local Government (2013) 'A Study on Local Government Authorities' Own Source Revenue Collection'.

Gulzar, Saad and Khan, Muhammad (2021) '"Good Politicians": Experimental Evidence on Motivations for Political Candidacy and Government Performance'. http://dx.doi.org/10.2139/ssrn.3826067

Haerpfer, C.; Inglehart, R.; Moreno, A.; Welzel, C.; Kizilova, K.; Diez-Medrano J.; Lagos, M.; Norris, P.; Ponarin, E.; and Puranen, B. (eds) (2022) World Values Survey: Round Seven – Country-Pooled Datafile Version 3.0'. Madrid and Vienna: JD Systems Institute & WVSA Secretariat. https://doi.org/10.14281/18241.20

Hofman, Bert and Kaiser, Kai (2006) 'Decentralization, Democratic Transition, and Local Governance in Indonesia', in Pranab Bardhan and Dilip Mookherjee (eds) *Decentralization and Local Governance in Developing Countries: A Comparative Perspective*, MIT Press, pp.81–124. https://doi.org/10.7551/mitpress/2297.003.0004

Horn, Murray (1995) *The Political Economy of Public Administration: Institutional Choice in the Public Sector*. Cambridge University Press.

Ianchovichina, Elene; Burger, Martijn; and Witte, Caroline (2020) 'Why Are People Protesting', Brookings. https://www.brookings.edu/blog/future-development/2020/01/29/why-are-people-protesting

Khemani, Stuti (2019) 'What Is State Capacity?' World Bank Policy Research Working Paper No.8734, Washington DC. https://ssrn.com/abstract=3335607

Khemani, Stuti (2015) 'Political Capture of Decentralization: Vote Buying through Grants to Local Jurisdictions', in Faguet, Jean-Paul and Pöschl,

Caroline (eds) *Is Decentralization Good for Development? Perspectives from Academics and Policy Makers*, Oxford University Press, USA. https://doi.org/10.1093/acprof:oso/9780198737506.003.0009

Khemani, Stuti (2007) 'Does Delegation of Fiscal Policy to an Independent Agency Make a Difference? Evidence from Intergovernmental Transfers in India', *Journal of Development Economics*, vol.82, no.2, pp.464–84. https://doi.org/10.1016/j.jdeveco.2006.04.001

Khemani, Stuti (2006) 'Local Government Accountability for Health Service Delivery in Nigeria', *Journal of African Economies*, vol.15, no.2, pp.285–312. https://doi.org/10.1093/jae/eji029

Khemani, Stuti; Chaudhary, Sarang; Scot, Thiago (2020) 'Strengthening Public Health Systems: Policy Ideas from a Governance Perspective', Policy Research Working Paper, No. 9220, Washington, DC: World Bank,. http://hdl.handle.net/10986/33663

Liaqat, Asad; Callen, Michael; Cheema, Ali; Khan, Adnan; Naseer, Farooq; and Shapiro, Jacob N. (2019) 'Political Connections and Vote Choice: Evidence from Pakistan', Harvard University Working Paper. https://www.povertyactionlab.org/sites/default/files/research-paper /Political_connections_vote_choice_Liaqat_et_al._September2019.pdf

Mansuri, Ghazala and Rao, Vijayendra (2012) 'Localizing Development: Does Participation Work?' World Bank Policy Research Report. http://hdl.handle.net/10986/11859

Martinez-Bravo, Monica (2014) 'The Role of Local Officials in New Democ-racies: Evidence from Indonesia', *American Economic Review*, vol.104, no.4, pp.1244–87. https://doi.org/10.1257/aer.104.4.1244

Myerson, Roger (2006) 'Federalism and Incentives for Success of Democracy', *Quarterly Journal of Political Science*, vol.1, no.1, pp.3–23. https://escholarship.org/uc/item/9940s9bv

Musgrave, Richard A. (1959) *The Theory of Public Finance*, New York: McGraw Hill. http://digilib.fisipol.ugm.ac.id/handle/15717717/11954

Nunn, Nathan (2009) 'The Importance of History for Economic Develop-ment', *Annual Review of Economics*, vol.1, no.1, pp.65–92. https://doi.org/10.1146/annurev.economics.050708.143336

Oates, Wallace E. (1972) *Fiscal Federalism*, New York: Harcourt Brace Jova-novich. https://ideas.repec.org/b/elg/eebook/14708.html

Ostrom, Elinor (2000) 'Collective Action and the Evolution of Social Norms', *Journal of Economic Perspectives*, vol.14, no.3, pp.137–58. https://doi.org/10.1257/jep.14.3.137

Pandey, Priyanka (2010) 'Service Delivery and Corruption in Public Services: How Does History Matter?' *American Economic Journal: Applied Economics*, vol.2, no.3, pp.190–204. https://doi.org/10.1257/app.2.3.190

Rodden, Jonathan (2002) 'The Dilemma of Fiscal Federalism: Intergovernmental Grants and Fiscal Performance around the World', *American Journal of Political Science*, vol.46, no.3, pp.670–87. https://doi.org/10.2307/3088407

Rodden, Jonathan; Eskeland, Gunnar; and Litvack, Jennie Ilene (eds) (2003) *Fiscal Decentralization and the Challenge of Hard Budget Constraints*, MIT Press.

Schelling, Thomas C (1960) *The Strategy of Conflict*, Cambridge, MA: Harvard University Press.

Tendler, Judith and Freedheim, Sara (1994) 'Trust in a Rent-Seeking World: Health and Government Transformed in Northeast Brazil', *World Development*, vol.22, no.12, pp.1771–91. https://doi.org/10.1016/0305-750X(94)90173-2

Tirole, Jean (1994) 'The Internal Organization of Government', *Oxford Economic Papers*, vol.46, no.1, pp.1–29. https://www.jstor.org/stable/2663521

Varshney, Ashutosh (2005) 'An Electoral Theory of Communal Violence?' *Economic and Political Weekly*, 24 September, pp.4219–24. https://www.jstor.org/stable/4417194

World Bank (2001) 'Indonesia Poverty Report', Washington, DC: World Bank.

World Bank (2003) 'World Development Report 2004: Making Services Work for Poor People', Washington, DC: World Bank. [by Ahmad, Junaid Kamal; Commins, Stephen; Devarajan, Shantayanan; Filmer, Deon P.; Hammer, Jeffrey; Pritchett, Lant Hayward; Reinikka, Ritva S.; Shah, Shekhar; Soucat, Agnès.] http://documents.worldbank.org/curated/en/832891468338681960 /World-Development-Report-2004-making-services-work-for-poor-people

World Bank (2016) 'Making Politics Work for Development', World Bank Policy Research Report, Washington, DC. [by Khemani, Stuti; Dal Bó, Ernesto; Ferraz, Claudio; Finan, Frederico Shimizu; Stephenson Johnson, Corinne Louise; Odugbemi, Adesinaola Michael; Thapa, Dikshya; Abrahams, Scott David] http://documents.worldbank.org/curated/en/268021467831470443 /Making-politics-work-for-development-harnessing-transparency-and -citizen-engagement

5. Devolution under autocracy: evidence from Pakistan

Adeel Malik, Rinchan Mirza,
and Jean-Philippe Platteau

Summary

Authoritarian regimes often direct the course of electoral politics in ways that allow them to concentrate and consolidate power. This observation applies well to Pakistan and its three autocratic regimes under military rulers General Ayub Khan (1958–69), Zia-ul-Haq (1977–88), and General Parvez Musharraf (1999–2008). The political reforms enacted by Zia-ul-Haq, his devolution programme, and his mode of channelling development funds via elected politicians exerted an enduring impact on the country's political system. Specifically, we argue that institutional changes under Zia's regime have stimulated the rise of family politics in replacement of party politics, resulting in the formation and consolidation of political dynasties. They have also contributed to the capture of local bureaucracy by elected politicians thereby entrenching clientelism.

Authoritarian regimes often direct the course of electoral politics in ways that allow them to concentrate and consolidate power (Gandhi and Przeworski 2007; Gandhi 2015; Svolik 2012). While a growing body of literature has devoted attention to studying politics under authoritarian rule, devolution under dictatorship remains a relatively understudied aspect. Why do autocrats devolve power to the local level and what are the long-run impacts of such devolution on political outcomes? In this chapter, we study the impact of local government reforms carried out by Pakistan's military regime under General

---

How to cite this book chapter:

Malik, Adeel; Mirza, Rinchan and Platteau, Jean-Philippe (2023) 'Devolution under autocracy: evidence from Pakistan', in: Faguet, Jean-Paul and Pal, Sarmistha (eds) *Decentralised Governance: Crafting Effective Democracies Around the World,* London: LSE Press, pp. 99–134. https://doi.org/10.31389/lsepress.dlg.e
License: CC BY 4.0

Zia-ul-Haq on the subsequent trajectory of electoral politics. Drawing on a rich data set on genealogies of political families in Pakistani Punjab, we show how Zia's devolution provided the staging ground for the entry of new family-backed elites into electoral politics, and how these political elites persisted long after his departure in 1988. The process was facilitated by the changes that he brought to the modus operandi of electoral politics and to the way of channelling funds earmarked for the provision of local public goods.

Our focus on Pakistan is derived from its relevance for studying devolution under dictatorship. All three major devolution attempts were carried out by the country's military dictators, Generals Ayub, Zia, and Musharraf. Rather paradoxically, these reforms were guided by a desire to centralise political power in the hands of a non-representative government and to bypass party politics (Cheema, Khwaja, and Khan 2005). Relatedly, facing a legitimacy deficit in a formally democratic set-up, the three military autocrats tried to fill this deficit by cultivating alliances with local elites and powerbrokers. More precisely, devolution and the associated channelling of financial resources to local elites allowed military rulers to develop and maintain, outside the realm of mainstream political parties, a network of political patrons that were dependent on them for access to state patronage and political survival. Studying the Pakistani experience can therefore provide important insights for the understanding of authoritarianism in the context of electoral politics. Situating our analysis in the emerging literature on politics under authoritarianism, we argue that local government elections held by Pakistan's respective military regimes provided important instances of authoritarian power-sharing through which military rulers co-opted elites by distributing the benefits of 'joint rule' (Svolik 2012; Auriol et al. 2023). More precisely, we adduce quantitative evidence to the effect that the rise of General Zia to supreme power was associated with a clear strengthening of political dynasties, and we highlight the mechanism that plausibly lies behind this relationship.

Our central argument is that the local government reforms introduced by General Zia-ul-Haq and the associated institutional interventions were a critical juncture in Pakistan's electoral history in the sense that, after the interlude of Zulfikar Ali Bhutto's regime, they not only marked a return to the old mode of politics dominated by influential political clans and families but also changed the political landscape in a deeper and more durable manner carrying profound implications for dynastic politics. In effect, the Zia-era changes brought back, with a reinforced vigour and longevity, a dynastic trend whose traces could already be found in the Ayub period. This prior is based on at least four factors that distinguish the Zia era from Pakistan's other military regimes. First, Zia took drastic measures to kill mass politics in the form of a populist party that operated outside the military's control. Second, while the devolution under General Ayub Khan (Pakistan's first military dictator) maintained a bureaucratic representation in local bodies, Zia completely dispensed with this practice so that local bodies were now under the total control of elected representatives. Third, a more elaborate system of dispensing state patronage through special development funds was devised that solidified the electoral hold of local elites and ushered in a new period of electoral clientelism. This resulted in the political capture of state resources earmarked for development. It has also led to a greater 'localization and personalization of politics' (Wilder 1999). Finally, owing to his ideological leaning and, even more importantly, owing to his political opportunism and pragmatism, Zia wooed religious elites into the electoral fold. This was especially evident in the case of shrine-based religious families who have solidified their position in electoral politics since the 1980s. For all these reasons, the Zia period is especially relevant and significant for studying the long-run impact of authoritarian devolution on political outcomes.

Our analysis contributes to several related strands of literature. To begin with, we complement prior works on the political economy of devolution, in India (Bardhan and Mookherjee 2006), and Pakistan in particular (Cheema, Khan, and Myerson 2010; Cheema, Khwaja, and Khan 2005; Khan, Khan, and Akhtar 2007). In this respect, we contribute by highlighting the role of local government elections in authoritarian regimes and probing their impact on dynastic politics. Our analysis holds relevance for the emerging literatures on authoritarian politics (Boix and Svolik 2013; Gandhi and Lust-Okar 2009; Gehlbach, Konstantin, and Svolik 2016) and democratic transitions (Geddes 1999; Murtin and Wacziarg 2014). While the two literatures have sometimes developed in isolation, we show how political institutions under autocratic rule can shape electoral politics after autocracy has given way to democracy. Finally, our work makes a distinct contribution to the niche literature on dynastic politics (Besley and Reynal-Querol 2017; Dal Bó, Dal Bó, and Snyder 2009; Querubin 2016). While prior work has established the persistence of dynasties and explored their impact on economic development, we shed light on the institutional processes that trigger dynastic formation. Specifically, we show how institutional interventions under a military regime led to the formation of new political dynasties and consolidated the power of pre-existing families.

Before proceeding further, two clarifications are in order. The first point relates to the frequent reference to the term 'devolution' in this chapter. We recognise that devolution is typically a political decision that is, at least in part, guided by pressures from below and is a result of 'political negotiations around the division of powers among levels of government' (Bresser-Pereira 2004, p.3). On the other hand, 'decentralisation' is a top-down decision that is usually part of a strategy for public management. Both processes involve devolution of power to subnational levels of government and can possibly involve delegation of fiscal authority. While recognising these distinctions, our core argument is essentially around local government reforms and the associated elections for local bodies. Owing to lack of data, we are not able to go below the provincial level to measure election outcomes. This should not seriously affect our results, however, since politicians sitting in provincial assemblies have typically graduated from preceding wins in local body elections. In addition, it is at the provincial and national levels that we expect to see the most important changes, since the system of special development funds initiated by Zia was implemented in favour of elected members of provincial assemblies. Our second clarification concerns our methodology used in the empirical analysis. The evidence presented there is largely descriptive in nature and establishes robust empirical patterns. But at this stage we do not claim to have established any causal relationship.

The chapter is organised as follows. In Section 5.1, we provide a background to the devolution reforms enacted by the military rulers of Pakistan, Ayub, Zia, and Musharraf. Next (Section 5.2), we briefly review the political science literature dealing with the role of elections in autocracies. In Section 5.3 we propose a plausible mechanism linking the military regime of Zia to the rise of political families and dynastic politics in Pakistan. Insights are also provided about the post-Zia persistence of this phenomenon. The fourth section then offers descriptive statistical evidence consistent with the suggestion that the Zia's regime represented a discontinuity in the incidence of dynastic politics and the extent of electoral competition. Our conclusions summarise the argument.

5.1 Devolution under Pakistan's authoritarian regimes

Pakistan is a federal state with seven administrative units, including four different provinces (Punjab, Sindh, Balochistan, and the Khyber Pakhtunkhwa), one federal territory (Islamabad Capital Territory), and two parts of territories disputed with India. Within all of Pakistan's provinces and territories the next tier down consists of divisions, which are further subdivided into districts, and then tehsils, which are in turn partitioned into union councils. By far the most important province is Punjab, which is the area that we are concerned with in this chapter. In terms of political constituencies, the highest level is the National Assembly (NA) where groups of elected representatives from the four provinces sit together. Below the NA, we find provincial assemblies (PAs), one for each province. Members of PAs come from political constituencies that correspond either to a district (when the district has a small size) or a subdistrict (when the district is heavily populated and subdivided into several subunits). Finally, the lowest tier of the political structure is made up of local bodies, which represent several villages and/or towns grouped for the purpose of local elections.

Unfortunately, because we do not have the data pertaining to the latter, lowest tier of elections, our empirical analysis in later parts of the chapter rests on data from NA and PA elections. What needs to be stressed, however, is that the politicians who emerged as PA and NA members in the first post-Zia election in 1985 overwhelmingly came from the local elections that were held in the preceding period from 1979 to 1983. And this strong relationship between the 'national/provincial' and 'local' tiers of the electoral system has been maintained afterwards.

Turning to the devolution efforts of Pakistan's three military rulers, major attempts at decentralisation were carried out by Ayub Khan in the 1960s, Zia-ul-Haq in the 1980s, and Parvez Musharraf in the 2000s, which have been well covered in the seminal contributions by Cheema, Khwaja, and Khan (2005), Khan, Khan, and Akhtar (2007), and Cheema, Khan, and Myerson (2010). (Pakistan's civilian regimes have occasionally tried to devolve power to the local level, but these attempts were mostly half-hearted and remain peripheral to our analysis.[1]) Additional analyses on devolution reforms include special reports by the International Crisis Group and the US Institute of Peace, which mainly focus on the post-Musharraf reforms (Ali 2018; ICG 2004). Rather than reinventing the wheel, we synthesise prior work and highlight both similarities and differences across the three military rulers' main devolution attempts, setting the stage for the conceptual and empirical discussion in Sections 5.3 and 5.4.

Military rulers typically began their political life by dissolving national and provincial assemblies and imposing some form of presidential rule. Soon after assuming power, they initiated serious attempts at decentralisation of political power in favour of local tiers of government. The decision to hold local elections was motivated by the need to fill a critical legitimacy gap and co-opt local political elites in the service of authoritarian rule. It bears emphasis that decentralisation entailed only constrained forms of representation, so that political power remained essentially centralised in the hands of the military. It is thus not coincidental that devolution was partial and incomplete, involving only limited administrative and financial autonomy. Because state resources were distributed to allied local politicians who could then direct a portion of them to their clientele, military regimes tried to build a stable political constituency. Furthermore, elections for local bodies were organised on a non-party basis, thereby allowing military rulers not only to weaken the influence of grassroots participation via political parties, but also to strengthen the role of local brokers who were able to leverage their de facto power to garner public support. To achieve this, military regimes did not hesitate from disqualifying political opponents.

General Ayub Khan (1958–69)

There are some important historical continuities in the manner in which 'non-representative regimes such as the British during the pre-independence period and the military during the post-independence period' have favoured local elected governments in a bid to centralise power (Cheema, Khwaja, and Khan 2005). Local governance under British rule was limited in scope and explicitly driven by the need to support central imperial administration. Local panchayats in that period were more representative of a village's social and economic structure and subordinated to central bureaucratic authority. Pakistan's successive military regimes patronised the same system of indirect rule through local elites.

In particular, the first military ruler of independent Pakistan, Ayub Khan, adopted a local government system that closely followed the colonial template: like the latter, it offered limited representation to local politicians while retaining significant bureaucratic oversight. Akin to the British, Ayub's local governance arrangements had a distinct rural bias in terms of distribution of resources, an expected consequence of the fact that local governments were dominated by rural elites who provided the basic support for his regime. During the 1950s, significant budgetary shares had been allocated to urban areas, partly a response to the influx of Muslim refugees from India who settled in large numbers in urban centres. This budgetary trend was reversed by Ayub, who restored the British policy of favouring rural areas in development expenditures (Cheema and Mohmand 2003).

The Basic Democracies Ordinance (1959), introduced by Ayub soon after he seized power (in 1958), provided for a multi-tiered system with villages (rural) and town committees (urban) at the lowest tier. The local government system consisted of both elected and unelected members who were both ultimately subordinated to bureaucratic authority. While the lowest tier consisted of members directly elected through adult franchise, the upper tiers included both members who were indirectly elected and members nominated by government officials. Limited political representation was thus combined with bureaucratic control, the ultimate objective being to consolidate political power. This was first done by using the 80,000 so-called Basic Democrats in local bodies as the electoral college for the election of the president. Local governments were therefore used as a limited representative tool to 'legitimise' presidential elections under the 1962 constitution. A second instrument for consolidation of political power in the hands of the dictator was achieved through explicit bureaucratic control vested in the offices of commissioners and deputy commissioners. As Cheema, Khwaja, and Khan (2005, p.6) noted, bureaucratic authority could be used to 'quash the proceedings; suspend resolutions passed or orders made by any local body' and to prohibit actions undertaken by local bodies. Moreover, even if local bodies enjoyed some 'regulatory and development functions', these were effectively circumscribed by limited fiscal capacity (Cheema, Khwaja, and Khan 2005; Siddiqui 1992).

Zia-ul-Haq (1977–88)

The second major attempt at reviving local governments happened during a six-year period, 1979–85. Soon after staging a military coup, Zia-ul-Haq issued special decrees and ordinances for local governments. Elections for local bodies were held in 1979–80 and, subsequently, in 1983. Like Ayub's experiment with Basic Democracies, Zia's local bodies elections were an attempt to centralise political power and co-opt local politicians. The need for centralised political control in the hands of the military was felt even more acutely as a populist political party, the Pakistan People's Party (PPP), led by Pakistan's first democratically elected leader, Zulfikar Ali Bhutto, had gained ascendancy during the years that preceded the coup. During this run-up, a broad anti-Bhutto mobilisation of petty traders, religious parties, and the urban middle classes brought people to the streets to express their discontent against some policies favoured by Bhutto. Through clever political engineering, Zia disallowed PPP stalwarts from participating in elections. Using the Martial Law Order No 65 and through a series of amendments in the Political Parties Act of 1962, Zia thus disqualified a large number of PPP-linked candidates. Many of Bhutto's diehard supporters were thrown into jail or driven to exile. Zia's extensive disqualifications radically altered the course of electoral politics and the Peoples Party's decision to boycott elections created a political void that was either filled by new political actors or led to the entrenchment of powerful local intermediaries who participated in elections according to the new rules of the game. The elections were held on a non-party basis in the sense that candidates could not reveal their party affiliations. This implied that party-based competition was replaced by a contest between personalities who were leaders of so-called 'voting banks'. In this context, candidates relied on alternative structures of political mobilisation linked to society's natural formations, such as clans, kinship groups, religious status, and wealth.

In contrast to the programmatic politics of Zulfikar Ali Bhutto, Zia put in place a powerful system of clientelistic politics based on the co-option of local elites enticed by egregious advantages and privileges. It is not only the case that, as Mohmand (2019, p.75) argues, 'district councils were given considerable power to raise and spend money, turning them quickly into an alternative source of patronage' but also, and more ominously, members elected for the national and provincial assemblies in 1985 were given direct access to development funding in their constituencies. Such access to special development funds granted elected politicians direct and unaudited control over the provision of local public goods. They could therefore identify which development schemes are approved for their regions – and where and how they are implemented. While, previously, central planners and the bureaucracy had a greater say over public goods provision, Zia's government entrusted elected politicians with the task of devising and controlling development schemes. In this way, local politicians could avail themselves of plentiful opportunities of lucrative contracts to offer to allied contractors and of juicy commissions that they could themselves earn in the process. Even worse, they were allowed to influence transfers and postings of local bureaucrats responsible for service delivery in health, education, and irrigation departments.

It bears emphasis that the system of special development funds and the allocation of party tickets and ministries as a result of individual bargaining between powerful local brokers and party leaders has continued unabated under all civilian governments after Zia and it continues to grease the wheels of patronage politics until today. In this way, moved by his ambition to suppress popular parties, Zia laid the groundwork for an enduring change in the way electoral politics functions in Pakistan (Hasnain 2008, p.145; Martin 2016, p.74; Ziring 1988, p.804).

It is evident that the rising influence of local politicians and the growing nexus between them and officials would not have been possible if the autonomy of the bureaucracy had not been seriously impaired. Pakistan's inherited colonial legacy of a strong bureaucratic state and weak representative institutions meant that elected politicians only had an 'advisory role' and were effectively subordinated to an executive rule where the military and the civilian bureaucrats called the shots. In the words of Wilder (2010, p.3), '[f]rom 1947 to 1971 the civilian bureaucracy played the dominant role in Pakistan's policymaking and, as such, was insufficiently controlled or influenced by elected politicians. During this period, there was limited scope for interference from politicians on the bureaucracy.'

Zulfiqar Ali Bhutto, Pakistan's first popularly elected leader (in office 1971–77), was effectively the first ruler to have attempted to reverse the legacy of 'executive rule' and to redress the 'imbalance between elected and unelected institutions'. Toward this purpose, he brought significant changes to the civil service, which ended up swinging the pendulum to the other extreme by politicising the civil service (Wilder 2010, p.4). These changes included the removal of the constitutional protection available to civil servants and the possibility of lateral entry into the civil service ranks. The effect was to undermine the professional independence of civil servants and to make their postings, transfers, and promotions subject to political interference (Mufti 2020).

Initiated under Bhutto, the politicisation of civil service was significantly accelerated during the Zia era. Overruling the recommendations of the Civil Services Reform Commission, which was set up by his own regime, Zia not only retained the measures taken by Bhutto but further reinforced the subordination of bureaucracy to elected politicians (World Bank 1998).[2] In parallel, Zia opted for devolution reforms requiring that all members of local bodies be elected, dispensing with the past practice of combining elected with unelected officials. Direct bureaucratic representation in local governments was thus throttled in order to create greater autonomy for the elected tier at the local level, which obtained total control over local bodies (Cheema, Khwaja, and Khan 2005, p.28). At the same time, however, the power of local representative institutions was circumscribed by limited financial and administrative autonomy. They were also subordinated to provincial governments, which could summarily dismiss them or undo the actions of local governments.

In sum, central power was considerably reinforced under Zia's regime and the way this was done proved to be highly detrimental to the political fabric of the country. Unlike what was observed in South Korea and Taiwan, for example, it entailed the erosion of the bureaucracy's independence and the proliferation of a system of clientelistic politics in which the lust for power and its advantages replaced commitment to ideas and programmes of economic and social change. More power was devolved to locally elected politicians who showed loyalty to the regime, but at the same time they were dependent on funds and other privileges dispensed by the highest level of the political machine, the presidency.[3] Together with the absence of party-based political competition and control over development funds that the Zia regime gave to members of parliament, the subordination of bureaucracy to local politicians carried profound repercussions. It turned them into gatekeepers of the state who mediated voters' access to essential services provided by government institutions (Cheema, Naqvi, and Siddiqi 2007), as vividly illustrated by a growing body of fieldwork-based research.

One such study, devoted to Sargodha district by Nicolas Martin (2016), thus highlights that 'most voters participate not because of socio-economic dependence but because they need access to a distant and unresponsive state that the leader is able, or at least promises, to provide' (p.214). The Zia period ushered a noticeable shift in the structural sources of elite dominance: rather than being directly derived from their ownership of land and the employment they can thereby provide to local people, the staying power of traditional landed elites increasingly stemmed from their control over the state apparatus. Prior to Zia, these traditional elites were mobilising a hierarchical social structure that they dominated to their electoral advantage. In the post-Zia period, by contrast, many landlords lost their absolute dominance and land ownership became a less important determinant of electoral success. Instead, 'control over the state apparatus' became more 'central to landlords' strategies of accumulation and dominance' (p.4). In urban areas, the political space vacated by mass disqualifications of PPP loyalists was taken up by new political actors, often traders and businessmen, who became more adept at playing by the new rules of the game. Their success was measured by entrenchment of their political position over time.

General Parvez Musharraf (1999–2008)

In a familiar pattern, Parvez Musharraf's dictatorial rule also started with a promise to devolve power. One year after imposing a military coup, Musharraf introduced a plan in the year 2000 to hold local body elections under a new framework for devolution that differed in some respects from previous experiments. Firstly, Musharraf's devolution programme substantially altered the structure of local governments and made the local bureaucratic administration (for example, deputy commissioners) responsible to elected heads of district councils. Second, Musharraf's devolution reforms expanded the scope of local governments in the sense of a greater decentralisation of public service delivery to local tiers of government. Third, the reforms did away with the rural–urban divide in the administrative and financial operations of local governments.

Despite the expanded scope of reforms, Musharraf's devolution was limited by several factors. Local governments lacked the capacity to generate revenues and continued to be constrained by the absence of financial decentralisation. While the devolution plan of 2000 did succeed in transferring some powers from provincial to local level, the transfer of power from federal to provincial governments was limited. As a result, the system retained significant centralisation at the federal level. There was also variation in the extent of devolution between departments. Thus, key departments, such as police and irrigation, remained controlled at the provincial level. Even for departments witnessing a devolution of power, certain functions and services were exempt. Clearly, the devolution reforms of 2000 gave more executive authority to mayors (*nazims*), who were only indirectly elected and had a more elevated status than the union councillors representing the lowest tier of government. The indirect elections of mayors encouraged vote-buying and corrupt practices (Cheema, Khan, and Myerson 2010). Furthermore, the local union councils were elected through a multi-seat proportional representational system outside party lists. Commonly known as single non-transferable voting (SNTV), this electoral arrangement is widely recognised as favouring local brokers, including moneyed elites and tribal leaders 'who exercise authority in patron-client relationships' (Cheema, Khan, and Myerson 2010).

Looking across all three military regimes, a final observation applies: they not only imposed a system of electoral contests run through local bodies that they could control; they also engaged in political engineering aimed at manipulating the election process. Each of the devolution attempts was thus preceded by a wave of political disqualifications that selectively targeted political opponents. For example, after usurping power, Ayub Khan promulgated the Public Offices Disqualification Order (PODO) in 1959, and later the Elective Bodies Disqualification Order (EBDO), which resulted in the disqualification of about 6,000 politicians and officials (Noman 1988). Similarly, Zia-ul-Haq disqualified an entire generation of political actors affiliated with the PPP, whose leader, Zulfiqar Ali Bhutto, was deposed by Zia. A similar template was rolled out by Musharraf when he used the process of selective accountability to disqualify non-compliant politicians. He also set out a minimum educational criterion for public office holders, effectively excluding several leading political faces from the electoral race. In addition, by holding elections for local bodies on a non-party basis, military regimes not only weakened the influence of grassroot participation through the channel of political parties but also strengthened the role of local brokers, who were able to leverage their de facto power to garner public support.

5.2 Electoral politics in autocracies

How should we understand the underlying logic of the reforms undertaken by the military rulers of Pakistan? The wider political science literature offers some key pointers. Autocratic states often hold local and national-level elections, whether they are single-party communist states, military dictatorships, or monarchic regimes. In fact, a large proportion can be characterised as 'electoral' autocracies where some formal institutions of politics exist alongside autocratic rule (Luhrmann, Tannenberg, and Lindberg 2018). Even if such avenues for political representation are limited or subject to manipulation, the question remains: why do autocratic regimes permit electoral politics? Why do citizens and candidates, including those hailing from opposition, participate in these contests?

Dominant analyses of authoritarian politics show that, like any ruler, a dictator essentially cares about their regime's survival. For autocrats this is predicated on the challenge of authoritarian control and power-sharing (de Mesquita et al. 2003; Gehlbach, Konstantin, and Svolik 2016; Svolik 2012). The basic idea is that repression is never sufficient to guarantee the sustainability of dictatorial rule, nor the regime's ability to counter the threats not only of a popular uprising from the majority excluded from power, but also of an internal rebellion fomented by members of the ruling coalition or rivals within the autocrat's clique.[4] The second threat is especially important in the light of available evidence suggesting that two-thirds of rulers have been removed by insiders. The use of repression must therefore be combined with other tactics, foremost among which are legitimacy-building and elite co-option (Gerschewski 2013). The three tactics may be seen as complementary or as imperfect substitutes. Thus, strong legitimacy dispenses the ruler with resorting to some repression, and it may also reduce the need to have recourse to elite co-option.

To obtain legitimacy, authoritarian rulers need to build 'active consent' and structures of voluntary obedience. In many Muslim societies, autocrats have leaned on Islam and religious classes to legitimate their rule. For example, the Islamization of the economy and the polity, and the ensuing patronage for religious clerics, can be viewed as an effort to legitimate military rule. The regimes of Zia-ul-Haq in Pakistan and of Nimeiry and al-Bashir in Sudan are appropriate illustrations of this possibility. In other regimes, appeals to a nationalist and pan-Arab ideology have served the same purpose, as epitomised by the Ba'athist regimes of Saddam Hussein in Iraq and theal-Assad (father and son) in Syria. In Latin America, on the other hand, military rulers in the 1960s and 1970s often mobilised support by using anti-communism to justify their seizure of power. In a medium- or long-term perspective, perhaps the best way of building legitimacy is by implementing effective development policies that have the effect of significantly improving the levels of living of a great number of people. Examples that come to mind here are South Korea under Park and Taiwan under Chiang Kai-shek (see Bourguignon and Platteau, 2023, Ch. 8).

Another way of building legitimacy, achievable in a shorter time span, is by organising local elections in such a way as to allow the emergence of supporting elites. In return for the 'spoils' of office, these elites can form the basis of a class of 'collaborative politicians' who act as a conduit between local-level constituencies and the non-representative centre' (Boix and Svolik 2013, p.24). When state patronage is effectively tied to electoral participation and success, elite defection is kept under control and political opponents have to think twice about the costs of non-participation (remember the boy-cott of the first post-Zia election by the PPP in Pakistan) or of denouncing the ruling regime. Moreover, autocrats can skilfully use elections to divide the opposition. This is especially evident when military-supervised elections are based on competitive clientelism. In a wide-ranging review of elections under authoritarianism, Gandhi and Lust-Okar (2009) argue that elections are a preferred means of distributing resources to citizens and elites in many regimes, where both candidates and voters participate in the electoral process to access state resources. As in democratic contexts, authoritarian regimes create electoral business cycles where contests for access to state resources intensify during the election period (Blaydes 2006).

Finally, according to Geddes (1999), autocracies that hold elections are more stable than those that do not. Gerschewski (2013) refines this proposition by adding that electoral autocracies resting on formal avenues for co-option seem to provide a surer way toward regime durability than those in which informal means of co-option (such as cronyism) are predominant. Formal mechanisms can rely on a stable configuration defined by a diffused pattern of support for the ruler, lower levels of repression, and extensive co-option through local governments and legislatures. Several important works emphasise that, in an environment dominated by commitment and moral hazard problems, both the autocrat and the ruling coalition can benefit from formal political insti-tutions, such as parties and legislatures (Blaydes 2006; Boix and Svolik 2013).

Perhaps the most important problem plaguing the interactions between the ruler and societal and elite actors is the autocrat's inability to make cred-ible commitments (Acemoglu and Robinson 2006). Their promises carry little weight because institutions under authoritarian rule lack commitment power (the autocrat can change his or her mind) and have limited ability to resolve conflicts. Another problem stems from the fact that the interactions between the ruler and the dominant coalition are permeated by imperfect and asymmetric information (Gehlbach, Konstantin, and Svolik 2016). Because they suppress all opposition, autocrats have poor information about the true extent of support they command from the elites and the masses. Further-more, authoritarian rule is defined by secrecy and opacity, which allow the ruler to exploit his privileged access to information. At the same time, how-ever, secrecy runs against the interests of the autocrat's allies, limiting their ability to monitor the ruler's compliance to the promises they have made. In addition, the ruling coalition also has imperfect information about the ruler's actions, which makes it difficult to organise a rebellion.

The central dilemma in dictatorships is therefore to establish mecha-nisms that commit a dictator and their allies to 'joint rule' (Boix and Svolik 2013; Svolik 2012). Institutionalised interactions between the autocrat and the ruling coalition precisely contribute to the stability of authoritarian rule based on power-sharing. In particular, formal institutions, such as local governments, facilitate regular contacts between the autocrat and his allies, conferring a consultation and decision-making role on the latter. Moreover, rules defining the procedures, membership and jurisdiction of formal insti-tutions 'embody the power sharing compromise between the dictator and his allies' (Boix and Svolik 2013). Indeed, compliance with rules and procedures constitutes a 'publicly observable signal' of the autocrat's commitment to share power. Moreover, elections under autocratic rule serve a critical infor-mational role: local bodies elections help rulers to determine who among their potential political agents and allies command greater popular support (Gandhi and Lust-Okar 2009). Likewise, local electoral contests reveal which geographic areas are important opposition strongholds. As Blaydes (2006) has shown in the context of Egypt, regions dominated by legislators of the Muslim brotherhood were systematically disadvantaged by the regime in terms of access to development funding.

In this vein, we can understand the local government reforms designed and implemented by Pakistan's military regimes as allowing them to: (i) foreclose political mobilisation around party platforms; (ii) create non-party represent-ative structures dependent on the autocrat's administrative machinery for the exercise of authority; and (iii) institutionalise the ruling coalition through formal rules and establish tiers of patronage aimed at awarding payoffs to the regime's allies. The major turning point corresponded to Zia's regime. It insti-tuted special development funds as a key patronage instrument in the hands of the central state, and it encouraged the politicisation of the administration, which thereby suffered a major blow in the form of a dramatic loss of inde-pendence and ability to direct development.

5.3 Dynastic politics in Pakistan: revival and persistence

A crucial additional feature of the Zia regime was the acceleration of dynastic politics. To facilitate the entry into politics of new actors and their local kin-ship networks, financial resources, and brokerage capacity, Zia used local bro-kers with a foothold in local politics. These political families were catapulted into provincial and national politics during and after Zia's rule. Although more an outcome than a purposeful policy effort itself, the revival of dynastic politics proved to be remarkably resilient even after Zia's demise.

Why did dynastic politics first increase under Zia?

What were the precise mechanisms behind the resurgence of dynastic poli-tics, and how was this new political landscape causally linked to Zia's devo-lution reforms? A plausible answer is that the main purpose of Zia's changes or 'reforms' was to annihilate political parties, understood as mass-based machines driven by programmatic agendas and coalesced around a reformist ideology. This definition applied very well to the populist party, the Pakistan People's Party (PPP), constructed by Zulfikar Ali Bhutto, which Zia saw as a direct threat to order and the integrity of the Pakistani nation.

The extensive political purge of PPP-linked politicians created a new electoral space that was filled by new political actors in urban areas. Many of them first honed their electoral skills in local body elections and subsequently moved up the political ladder to become provincial- and national-level legislators. These families were more likely to form new urban political dynasties in the post-Zia period. During Bhutto's rule, candidates for elections were fielded by political parties, and money played a less important role in electoral politics. By closing the political space to well-organised parties and allowing candidates to enter the political stage on their individual account in a party-less contest, Zia created a new problem, namely how campaigning expenses and other political mobilisation resources would be financed in the absence of a supporting party machine. Powerful families and their personalised networks now effectively offered a substitute for party-based mobilisation because they were well-established and well-to-do; indeed, they could provide the financial and manpower resources required to run an effective campaign and maintain a political clientele. In the absence of party machines and distinct ideological platforms, money thus came to acquire a more salient role in electoral competition, and patronage resources became an essential means of creating and maintaining a political following.

Yet the capacity to supply political resources is to no avail if it is not accompanied by the potential participants' willingness to engage in the new political game. For two main reasons, notable or big families were primed to respond more positively to this emerging opportunity. First, they were not interested in ideology or broad policy programmes but in power and in the preservation of their own status and privileges. Therefore, the new political set-up in which seats could be contested on the basis of identity suited them well. A second appealing feature of the new politics was the clientelistic logic inherent in the way that special development funds earmarked for the provision of local public goods were disbursed by the central state. Coupled with the predominance of elected politicians over bureaucrats in all sorts of strategic matters, these funds came to constitute an additional source of patronage to which big families were quite sensitive. Not only could the families thus expect to recover their campaigning expenditures but also, and most importantly, they were given a golden opportunity to enlarge the set of their own followers and to increase their influence.

For these same two reasons, Zia and his military successors were also interested in motivating the big families to enter the political field afresh or to strengthen their existing presence. First, Zia wanted to anchor his regime in the actions of non-ideological agents, people who were least likely to think of changing the social and political order and who did not want to call into question the manner in which central politics was run. Second, big families are considered privileged sources of political support because in their constituencies they wield great social prestige and influence, allowing them to control large networks of dependent followers and allies, and to form strong and stable voting blocs. So, co-opting and reinforcing the means of patronage available to these families makes perfect sense for military rulers who (by definition) lack legitimacy.

As an important illustration of this, consider those families that have acquired a high traditional status thanks to their occupation of a pre-eminent position within Sufi orders, the dominant religious organisation in the Pakistani countryside. For a long time, the Syed and Qureshi families have enjoyed a sacred status derived from their lineage associated with a holy Muslim saint. Members of these families are commonly respected under the honorific title of Makhdoom, and in many cases they fulfil the function of caretakers of a shrine. Across Pakistan shrines have been built to venerate saints credited with the merit of originally bringing local tribes into the fold of Islam. The religious authority associated with these shrines is conferred on the family rather than an individual, and it is transmitted from one next generation to the next, thereby ensuring intra-family continuity of the function and status. The political capital attached to guardianship of a shrine is maintained and accumulated within the family that originally built it and is usually able to claim blood ties with the saint. Shrine families are typically rich not only because they own large landholdings but also because they collect regular donations from the faithful.

The same families have historically acted as natural contenders for political power and have participated in elections held under both colonial rule and Ayub's era (Ewing 1983; Gilmartin 1988). However, the Zia era marked a decisive shift in their politicisation and propelled a significantly larger number of shrine families into electoral politics, as illustrated in the next section (Malik and Malik 2017; Malik and Mirza 2022). One might think that Zia, himself a devout Muslim, gave prime importance to enlisting the support of shrine families. Yet the reality was different. For such a cunning and opportunistic politician as Zia, the interest they represented was a more mundane matter: they were influential and potentially command large vote banks.

A plausible consequence of the replacement of party-affiliated by individual candidates is an increase in political competition as measured, in particular, by the average number of candidates per seat in election contests. This will happen automatically if the number of families entering the political stage is larger than the number of parties which were present before the change of electoral system. In the context of Punjab, such an outcome is the more likely as participating families do not correspond to whole extended clans but to family factions or subclans and allies. A given *biraderi* (kinship groups or 'brotherhoods') may actually be divided into different factions (*dharras*) because of personality rivalries or the perceived need to diversify risks. In the former instance, factions can ally themselves with outsiders against their own clan members and even their close kin (owing to competition over land or over local dominance), sometimes leading to violent and enduring feuds. Bitter fights involve religious as well as secular elites. In the latter instance, the *biraderi*'s potential voting influence is put into several baskets (vote blocs) so as to avoid being stuck with a losing candidate.[5] Factions are then the outcome of a coordinated decision. Their insurance function is especially important in contexts where, eager to retain its erstwhile power and prerogatives, the landed elite compete vigorously for vote bloc members (Lyon 2019, p.109; Mohmand 2019, p.250; Yadav 2020, p.1053). In many cases, the core of a faction seems to be based on cooperation between male siblings and preferential cousin marriages, as it yields prestige to keep daughters within the *biraderi* (Martin 2016, pp.96, 117).

In short, not only did rural politics become more 'parochial and kinship-based' under military rule but immediate siblings (rather than extended *biraderis*) also tended to command people's political loyalties. As personalised ties became more central than programmatic agendas in determining the political allegiances of both politicians and their followers, private feuds and tensions often intensified inside big families (Martin 2016, pp.94, 118–19). By implication, candidates were not necessarily the heads of lineages or large clans. They could (and can) be local brokers mediating between voters and big political families, or middle-level landlords or lesser figures in these families that stand on their own. In his in-depth study of Sargodha district, Martin (2016) explained the useful role of brokers thus:

> When villagers needed to resolve a dispute or required patronage with a government institution, these [middle-level] Gondals (notables) were more readily accessible than were the members of the leading families ... during elections they played an important role as brokers between the powerful Gondals [from leading families] and poorer villagers. (pp.41–42)

Another indicator of enhanced pressures exerted by political competition following Zia's devolution reforms has been the rising cost of elections for candidates (Wilder 1999). Combined with evidence about the higher average number of candidates per seat (see the next section), the increased cost of electoral participation seems to confirm that the shift from party-based to family-based politics has, indeed, given rise to growing political competition.

More specifically, we can ask why the rise of family-based politics in the wake of Zia's devolution reforms took the form of *dynastic* politics. What needs to be borne in mind here is that the patronage provided by politicians is not confined to public goods financed by the state development funds that accrue to them if elected. It also includes key services valued by voters, such as protection against the police; legal defence in local courts; the obtaining of jobs, licences, contracts, and identity cards (which condition access to subsidised subsistence goods); and even providing fake high-school matriculation certificates. For this reason, the de facto power of politicians hinges on their connections to persons who matter inside strategic departments and offices of the administration, and on their capacity to activate them when their intervention is required. This networking and mobilising capacity can be considered important components of a candidate's political capital, and building them up obviously involves big sunk costs. In this respect, the families that managed to jump aboard the running train of Zia's politics and establish the right kind of contacts with the government machine gained a significant edge over other political competitors. This leverage quickly translated into an incumbency advantage.

To be successful in the long term, a political family therefore needs to possess two abilities: the ability to harness resources, finance and manpower, for campaigning and patronage purposes, and the ability to accumulate and maintain the precious political capital that leads to patronage power (for related arguments, see Fiva and Smith 2018; Gandhi and Lust-Okar 2009). In the same line, it is interesting to observe that many candidates and families graduated from holding offices in local government councils to winning provincial- and national-level elections in 1985. In fact, close to 50 per cent of the elected members of the Punjab Assembly had previously been local counsellors (Niazi 1994).

Why did dynastic politics persist after Zia?

By 1988, when Pakistan's political parties returned after Zia's departure, they had been extensively transformed from machines articulated around a programmatic and ideological platform to machines instrumental for realising the ambitions of powerful families and their close allies. The institutional ecosystem for electoral politics that took root during Zia's rule persisted over time and continues to cast a long shadow at the time of writing. Zia's non-party elections 'decisively shifted the political initiative towards electoral candidates', and this aspect continued to define the political landscape (Waseem 1994, p.15; Wilder 1999). Even when they returned, the political parties remained weakly institutionalised, and there was no return of programmatic and ideological politics. Instead, political parties continued to serve as machines that served as instruments for ambitious powerful families and their close allies. As Cheema, Khwaja, and Khan (2005) note,

> [s]ince the current members of the provincial and national assemblies are, in a very large number of cases, a product of the 1979 non-party local elections they are more interested in organizing local-level payoffs than pursuing legislative questions. (p.27)

Factionalism, extended lineages, clan networks, religious status, and wealth all continued to yield important electoral advantages. Political brokerage rather than legislative action became the main purpose of electoral politics. Mainstream political parties also avoided holding within-party elections. Such is the salience of 'electable' families that Waseem (2021) noted that '[t]he first rule of thumb is: no electables, no party as an election entity' (p.193).

In the absence of political parties centred on a distinct programmatic platform or an ideology representing specific redistributive preferences, it has been easy for political opportunists to jump from one political party to another. Frequent shifts of party allegiances before elections have now become a pervasive feature of Pakistan's electoral politics, especially among leading political families. This feature is entirely consistent with the fact, common to all political parties, that members of provincial and national assemblies emerged as gatekeepers to state benefits in the post-Zia period. Their political survival thus came to depend on continued access to the state administration, and these personalised links achieved more importance than loyalty to any party platform or discipline. Focusing on the case of the Muslim League, a mainstream political party that has perfected the art of survival, Waseem (2021) emphasises the crucial role of such party switches:

> The Muslim League [PML]'s electables and legislators trafficked between the civilian-led and military led factions with great ease. Therefore, we can argue that this party is the symbol of the status quo in terms of representing the dynastic families from the districts ... The PML's organizational fluidity kept the boundaries of the party porous, which kept it as a fallback option for all kinds of political careerists. The party has typically shunned ideology. As a club of locally respectable and electable persons, the party's real concern is to acquire potential access to the state's administrative resources for [the] articulation of the interests of their own members and their cohorts and constituents. (p.192)

Another institution inherited from the Zia era has proven remarkably resilient, namely the distribution of development funds through elected members of parliament. Despite the succession of many political governments and regular elections, the involvement of members of provincial and national assemblies in the provision of local public goods has remained intact. Curiously, in his speeches Imran Khan has been the only mainstream political leader to have challenged the Zia-era policy of involving MPs in the distribution of development funds. His party's 2018 election manifesto emphasised the need to terminate the role of elected politicians in providing public goods and to carry out wide-ranging reforms. However, after subsequently coming to power, he failed to implement these reforms owing to stiff resistance from within his own party's ranks.

The post-Zia period has also been characterised by a lack of enthusiasm among elected civilian governments for holding local government elections.[6] One reason is that political parties have viewed local governments as a 'competing tier of patronage' to themselves (Cheema, Khwaja, and Khan 2005; Wilder 1999). Another reason is that the parties are dominated by established political families and local brokers, who fear the prospect of facing competition from potential new entrants emerging from local elections. This is a classic illustration of what Acemoglu and Robinson (2006) have termed the 'political replacement effect', the idea that incumbent political elites tend to oppose reforms that can potentially threaten their future political power.

When political parties went back in action, the higher degree of political competition compared to pre-Zia times is yet another feature that persisted. The factional logic of family politics penetrated into the fabric of the parties, thus causing them to reflect the vested interests of the dominant member family. As pointed out by Waseem (2021):

> Divisions and sub-divisions in the political community are reflected through the personal cliques and factions that contribute to the increasing number of parties as players on the political stage. Conversely, parties formed new coalitions based on a shared interest to have access to state patronage, irrespective of divergent ideological or policy orientations. (p.195)

Because there has been fierce competition for tickets inside the mainstream political parties, many prominent candidates who did not receive a party endorsement ended up forming their own party or running in the election as 'independents'.

Political competition and the Zia era

Which new patterns of political competition came about around Zia's military coup? To address this issue, we created a comprehensive data set of constituency elections held on five occasions from 1951 to 1977 (the pre-Zia period) and eight elections held between 1985 and 2013 (the post-Zia period). We used five different measures of political competitiveness. The first is the *number of candidates per seat*. Figure 5.1 shows that in post-Zia elections there were much higher numbers of candidatures per seat for both the national and provincial assemblies in Punjab province than had been the case for pre-Zia elections, virtually twice as many in both cases.

This measure reflects the overall pool of candidates who contested the election for a given parliamentary seat and indicates the extent of the choice available to voters. However, what matters for competition is not just how many candidates there are (since many minor candidacies may not be electorally significant) but how competitively votes are divided between them. A well-accepted key measure of political competition is the Herfindhal–Hirschman index of political competition, which in political applications and across political science is universally used in the form 1/HH, a measure known as *the effective number of parties (or candidates) in terms of votes*

Figure 5.1: The average number of candidates per seat competing in Punjab elections in the pre-Zia period (1951–77) and the post-Zia period (1985–2013)

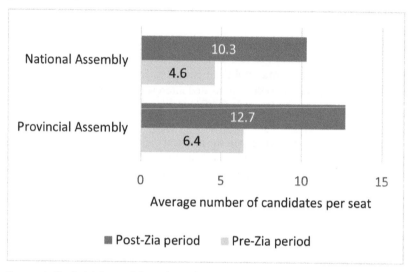

Average number of candidates per seat

■ Post-Zia period   ■ Pre-Zia period

Source: Author's database of dynastic candidates in constituency contests in Punjab province at all elections.

(ENPv). This equals 1 divided by the sum of squares of the decimal vote shares of each candidate running for election in a constituency (that is, $1/\Sigma VS_i$, where VS_i is the vote share of candidate i). Essentially, ENPv measure reweighs parties by the size of their vote shares, with larger parties counting most and the smallest parties least. Like any index, ENPv has some limitations (Dunleavy and Boucek 2003) but it also has some value in being intuitively interpretable. The lowest possible number for ENP*votes* is not 0 but 1, when the top party wins all the votes. In liberal democracies, ENPv is normally at least 2 (often denoting significant competition among two close top rivals), and in PR systems it may rise above 4 or 5 if party fragmentation increases. In the Punjab, Table 5.1(a) shows that the number of parties for NA elections stood at just over 2.4 before the Zia period, and changed only a bit (to just over 2.5) after it. In provincial elections there was more pronounced change, from just over 1.7 before (denoting top party/candidate dominance) to nearly 2.9 after the Zia regime (showing a clear increase in competitive elections).

The table also shows three other measures useful for gauging competition. Table 5.1(b) gives *the share of votes not included in the top candidate's winning margin.* Higher values on this measure reflect a lower victory margin of the winning candidate and, therefore, stronger political competition. There was a clear increase in provincial assembly elections, but only a modest rise at national level. Next, Table 5.1(c) shows *the combined percentage vote share of all the non-winning candidates.* From the pre- to post-Zia periods this

Table 5.1: Changes in indices of political competition between the pre-Zia elections (1970–77) and the post-Zia elections (1985–2013) for the national and provincial assemblies in Punjab province

	Pre-Zia period	Post-Zia period	Comment
(a) Average effective number of parties (ENP votes)			
National Assembly	2.42	2.53	Not much change
Provincial Assembly	1.72	2.86	Clear increase
(b) Average 100% minus winner's margin of victory (%)			
National Assembly	74.4	83.7	Some increase
Provincial Assembly	48.6	84.3	Clear increase
(c) Average 100% minus top party's vote share (%)			
National Assembly	45.1	50.4	Some increase
Provincial Assembly	31.4	54.3	Clear increase
(d) Average vote share of all third and lower placed candidates (%)			
National Assembly	15.8	17.1	Not much change
Provincial Assembly	14.3	24.3	Some increase

Source: Author's database of constituency contests in Punjab province at all elections.
Notes: Data in Table 5.1 shows averages (mean values) in the Punjab as a whole for the two pre-Zia elections and eight post-Zia elections, at National and Provincial Assembly elections.

measure rose noticeably for NA elections, but far more sharply in provincial elections. Finally, we looked at the *vote shares going outside the combined vote shares of the top two candidates* (that is, to third, fourth or subsequent parties) in Table 5.1(d). This metric was stable at national level but grew somewhat at provincial level. Looking across Table 5.1, the reasons for different patterns of change at the NA and provincial assembly levels are not immediately clear and would therefore warrant further investigation.

Overall, the profound institutional shifts under Zia corresponded to an important historical inflection point, or critical juncture, since the impact of the decisions and choices then made by the military regime continue to reverberate till today. Electoral politics continues to be shaped by the same rules of the game and the wheels of electoral politics continue to be greased by clientelism, the salient role of money and family status, and the ability of candidates to mediate the voters' access to the state. The establishment of dynastic political families and their interest in controlling special development funds channelled through politicians, an institution that persists to this date, ensures that the system endures and the bureaucracy remains essentially captured by political actors. Thus, the initial advantages conferred on specific groups in society have been significantly reinforced over time, and beneficiaries of these policies have become important gatekeepers of the existing institutional set-up. These important shifts have also occurred against a background of sharply increasing political competition in provincial elections, and somewhat increased contestation in national elections. Here is a vivid illustration of institutional persistence in the sense that, once profound institutional shifts are set in motion, individual political actors are pushed onto a path that is hard to reverse, thereby creating a powerful 'lock-in' effect (Pierson 2000).

5.4 Analysing post-dynastic politics and competition in detail

We examine here in more detail how the Zia-era reforms led to a step change in the rate at which members of dynastic families both 'contested' and 'won' elections, and a clear emergence of new political dynasties after Zia seized power. After having analysed how various measures of political competition increased as the power of dynasties persisted when the Zia regime ended, we present evidence on political dynasties, which is descriptive in nature. It should therefore be considered as being 'strongly suggestive', as opposed to 'causal' interpretation, for which we would need an empirical strategy that 'identifies' the impact of Zia-era reforms on the formation and consolidation of political dynasties. We lack such a strategy, but nevertheless believe that the patterns traced here provide an important step to an empirically more comprehensive study of the Zia era's impacts.

Description of the data

We compiled an extensive database on political genealogies in Punjab province that dates back around a century and covers the period 1921–2013. To our knowledge, this is the most comprehensive data collection effort on political families carried out for Punjab to this date. We have been able to map dynasties that range from having just one relative who contested in an election to having dozens of relatives participating in different election rounds. Most importantly for our purposes, we have been able to precisely identify the date of entry into electoral politics of each dynastic family in our data set, defined as the date at which the founder of the dynasty formally entered an electoral cycle for the first time. Our data allows us to chart much of the evolution of dynasties over time, which is crucial to determining whether dynasticism increases around the time of Zia's military coup.

In addition to political genealogies, we also collected detailed data on all 10 elections held in the Punjab from 1970 to 2013. For each we were able to compile constituency-level information on candidate names, candidate party affiliation, candidate votes, total votes polled, and the total number of registered voters. Such level of detail allows us to construct a range of time-varying measures of political competitiveness which we then use to look at patterns of political competition before and after the Zia coup. Ideally, we would have liked to extend our electoral results data set right back to first elections held in the Punjab in 1921. However, detailed data on elections prior to 1970 was hard to find despite our efforts at scouring through many different sources.

The impact of the Zia regime on the dynastic hold over parliaments

Figure 5.2 shows the number of dynastic candidates running in each election that took place in post-independence Pakistani Punjab. What emerges is an almost doubling in the number of dynastic candidates running for both the national and provincial assemblies in 1985, the first elections held under the Zia regime. And in both assemblies the increase in the dynastic pool of candidates under Zia was sustained and even increased over time during the post-Zia period.

One concern is the possibility that the upward trend in the pool of dynastic candidates could be affected by the mechanical effects of an increase in the sizes (that is, number of seats) of both assemblies over time. However, Annex Figure 5A (in the data annex at the end of this chapter) normalises the number of dynastic candidates running in each election by the number of seats contested, and so separates out the mechanical effect of an increase in the number of seats from the overall increase in the number of dynastic candidates that run for elections. The Zia-era effect appears to be actually reinforced. The number of dynastic candidates per seat for the NA increased from 0.75 to 1.4 in 1985 and the ratio for the provincial assemblies from 0.51 to 0.91, with both increases also persisting throughout the post-Zia period. Annex Figure 5B also shows that some of the same trends in the evolution of candidacies are visible when attention is limited to the religious, shrine-guardian families in the period since 1970, albeit with some more stability and less consistent growth in the post-Zia period.

Did the Zia regime also influence the political dynasties' success rates in winning seats and thus their overall hold over parliaments? The two parts of Figure 5.3 show the proportion (%) of dynastic members holding seats in the Punjab for all post-independence national and provincial assemblies. The number of dynastic members per seat did not increase uniformly during the pre-Zia period: while it went up markedly between 1951 and 1962–65, it fell during the period 1970–77. In 1985, under Zia, it surged to levels surpassing the previous maximum at the NA level and stayed there afterwards. At the Punjab provincial level, the number of dynastic members increased sharply in 1985 and has stayed at levels above or at the previous maximum in 1965. At both levels the Zia-era reforms permanently boosted and clearly consolidated the overall hold of dynasts over the national and provincial parliaments. Rather than being a structural shift from party- to family-based politics, the Zia regime revived and reinvigorated a prior characteristic of Pakistan's

Figure 5.2: The number of dynastic candidates in Punjab at Pakistani elections, 1951–2013, at national and provincial levels

a. National elections

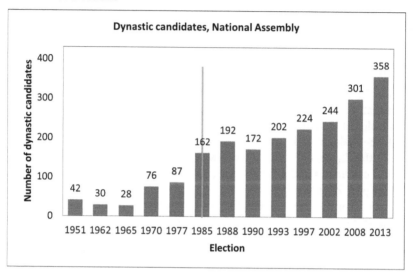

b. Provincial elections

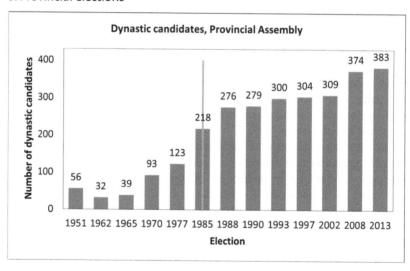

political system as well as putting it on a more stable footing, after the sharp dips in the 1970s under Zulfikar Ali Bhutto.

Before Bhutto, the opening of the political space to parties (conceived as platform-based organisations) was restricted and the bureaucracy was largely independent. Under Bhutto, the political landscape was inverted, as the political space became more open, and the autonomy of the state bureaucracy

Figure 5.3: Dynastic members as a percentage of seat-holders in the Punjab at national and provincial elections, 1951–2013

a. National assembly

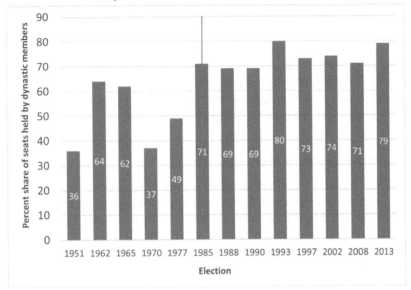

b. Provincial assembly

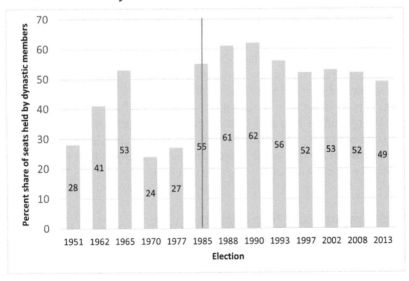

was seriously encroached upon. Bhutto was himself the scion of a big land-lord family, but his brand of politics can be characterised as populist. His approach was designed to break the hold of rural notables who had been courted in turn by the British colonisers, the Muslim League (at the time the new nation was formed), and General Ayub Khan. By taking politics to the grassroots and mobilising them around a common ideological platform, Bhutto brought a radical change into Pakistan's rules of political game. However, Zia did not only signal a return to the old political practices but he also modified the political landscape in a deeper and more durable manner. He considerably reinforced the subordination of the bureaucracy to politicians initiated under Bhutto, but in a different direction; he also expanded politicians' scope for political clientelism via control of development funds, as well as by disqualifying and repressing a wide range of political actors. The result was the opening, or the reopening, of a larger space for political families willing to play by the new rules of the political game.

Zia and the emergence of new dynasties

Did the Zia regime simply encourage *more* dynastic candidates to run for elections and increase their probability of success conditional upon running? Or did it also encourage *new* dynasties to be formed from scratch? In Figure 5.4 we examine the change in the number of founders of dynasties from Punjab who entered the national and provincial assemblies (that is, gained a seat) for the first time before, during, and after Zia. In both cases, it is obvious that a clear majority of founders of dynasties entered parliament for the first time in the two elections that were held under or immediately after the Zia regime – 1985 and 1988. For the NA, Figure 5.4a shows that 124 individuals founded political dynasties between 1977 and 2013, of whom 58 (or 47 per cent) entered parliament for the first time in either 1985 or 1988. Similarly, for the provincial assemblies, Figure 5.4b shows that of the 189 individuals who founded political dynasties between 1977 and 2013, 96 (or 51 per cent) entered parliament for the first time during the Zia era. Again, we normalised the numbers shown in Figures 5.4 by the number of assembly seats in each election year, without any major effects on the results. The ratio between the number of founder members who entered parliament for the first time and the number of seats was unusually high for the 1985 election nationally and provincially. In the case of the Punjab Provincial Assembly, it was more than double the ratio for any of the other election years.

Political persistence of Zia-era dynasties

To what extent did the new entrant families under Zia continue to contest and win elections in once autocratic rule was removed, that is, from 1990 to 2013? The proportion of dynastic families in the Punjab contesting elections fell very gradually over this period and averaged around a quarter of all families at most elections.

Did the families' fortunes decline once autocracy ended? We looked at what proportion of families won seats from 1990 to 2013. In the NA elections this

Figure 5.4: The number of founder members who first entered the legislature in Punjab, 1970–2013

a. National assembly

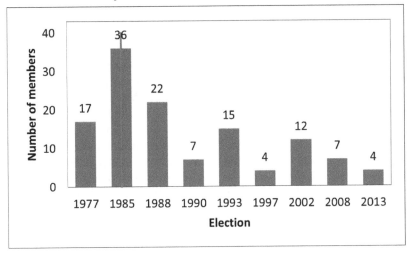

b. Provincial assembly

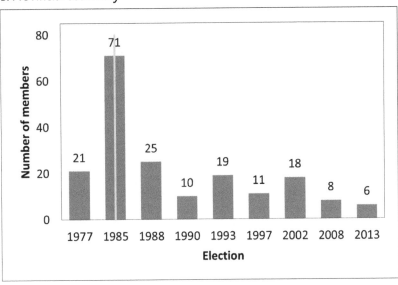

averaged around a quarter of families, but this share fell slightly to a fifth for the 2008 and 2013 elections. In provincial elections, 39 per cent of families won a seat in 1990, but thereafter it levelled off to around a quarter of families. Clearly, the families persistently stayed in electoral politics and enjoyed quite high rates of 'electoral success', suggesting that the Zia-era changes produced durable political dynasties. (For more detailed charts that support the interpretation of this section, see Figures S1 to S6 of this chapter's Supplementary Materials.[7])

Next, we examined how the Zia changes played out spatially. Urban areas witnessed significant political mobilisation during the Bhutto period (1970–77) and saw many new professional actors arriving on the political stage, including lawyers, doctors, and trade union activists. The anti-Bhutto movement was led by a right-wing political alliance of nine political parties and paved the way to Zia's military coup, and it too was also primarily centred in urban regions. After the coup, Zia purged the urban political landscape of Bhutto loyalists, encouraged the entry of new urban actors into electoral politics, and gave them access to state patronage. We should therefore expect a strong urban dimension to dynasticism in the post-Zia period.

To shed light on this, we looked at Punjab constituencies for the national and provincial assemblies in three more recent elections (2002, 2008, and 2013) that can be easily classified as urban – using a broad definition, a medium definition and a narrow definition of 'urban' seats.[8] The broad definition included predominantly urban areas, majority urban areas, and semi-urban areas. We calculated the proportion of elected dynasties that were either formed during the Zia period or after. In NA elections this index rose from 26 per cent in 2002 to 38 per cent in 2008 and 2013, and in provincial elections it rose from 20 per cent to 29 per cent. This ratio of urban dynasties first entering electoral politics during the Zia period increased slightly if we used a more restrictive definition of what constitutes an urban constituency, that is, if we exclude semi-urban areas, and it rose again if we focused only on predominantly urban constituencies. By 2013 on this most restrictive definition, 47 per cent of the total urban elected dynasties in the NA were formed during the Zia period, and 44 per cent in the provincial assemblies. (For more detailed charts supporting this analysis, please see Figures S7 to S12 of this chapter's Supplementary Materials.[9])

Finally, it may appear paradoxical that political competition actually increased in the wake of Zia's reforms, as we showed in Section 5.3, alongside the growing political importance of dynastic families. The puzzle can be resolved if we bear in mind that enhanced competition between individual candidates at the constituency level can co-exist with consolidation of dynastic power. As a matter of fact, a dynastic political family may have several members contesting elections in multiple constituencies and, while one member may fail to win the seat in one constituency, another may be more successful in another constituency.

Conclusions

A key challenge confronting all autocratic regimes is how to build legitimacy and commit the ruler and his allies to 'joint rule'. Electoral politics offers one such mechanism to stabilise autocratic rule. This logic applies well to Pakistan, where the country's three long-serving military rulers, Generals Ayub, Zia, and Musharraf each began their tenure by holding local government elections. As prior research has shown, devolution experiments can be effectively used to undercut party-based politics and concentrate power in the hands of autocrats. In this chapter, we adduced evidence that the local government elections held by Pakistan's respective military regimes were important instances of elite co-option and authoritarian power-sharing.

Zia-ul-Haq's political and administrative interventions left the most profound and enduring legacy for electoral politics. Apart from the brief 1970s interlude of Zulfiqar Ali Bhutto's popularly elected government, political families have played a more important role than party-based politics. The Zia period restored the pre-Bhutto political equilibrium but in ways that not only further reinforced the pre-Bhutto order but also tilted the political landscape decisively. Zia was able to do so through a more intensive political purge, more political subordination of the bureaucracy, and greater political instrumentalisation of development spending. The resulting institutional ecosystem significantly expanded the scope for the emergence and consolidation of political dynasties and they clearly took advantage of these new opportunities.

As the literature on historical institutionalism has argued, critical junctures are shaped by 'antecedents': what happened before shapes the available policy choices. Zia brought into play a combination of the worst aspects of the two preceding regimes by suppressing party-based politics, and dramatically increasing politicisation of the bureaucracy. That political legacy continues to shape modern electoral politics in Pakistan. When political parties, at least the most important among them, were allowed to contest elections again, they had now become machines largely controlled by dominant families, who tried to consolidate their power through political clientelism.

Beyond Pakistan, our analysis has important implications for the role of elections in other authoritarian contexts in the Muslim world, such as Egypt and Jordan, where ideology-based affiliations have been rendered insignificant relative to ties based on family, clan, tribe, or religion. The findings in this chapter also cast a grim light on equating elections with democratisation. As the recent political experiences of Iraq, Afghanistan, and Libya indicate, competitive elections without multiple institutions backing 'clean' politics are often reduced to a contest between different factions over control of state resources. Finally, our analysis has clear implications for donor agencies that support political and administrative devolution in developing countries by extending technical and financial assistance. When such support is given to autocratic regimes, foreign donors may effectively reinforce or help stabilise a system of authoritarian power-sharing.

While our evidence here is innovative and strongly suggestive of the soundness of our interpretations, it should be treated with a degree of caution. Without rigorous statistical analysis it is not possible to attribute a causal interpretation to the empirical patterns charted here. We nevertheless contend that the patterns we have documented shed an important and original light on the relation between political strategies of authoritarian regimes and the dual processes of dynastic 'formation' and 'consolidation'.

Annex: Detailed statistics on competition and dynastic families' involvement at national and provincial elections in the Punjab

Figure 5A: The number of dynastic candidates per seat at Punjab elections, 1951–2013

a. National level

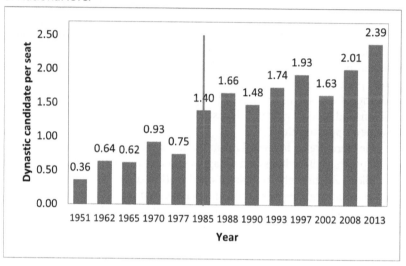

b. Provincial level

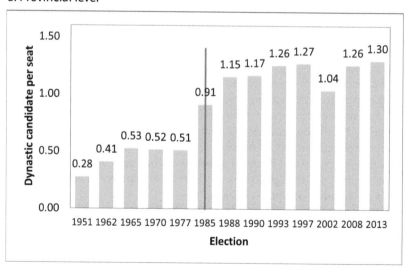

Figure 5B: The number of shrine dynastic candidates per seat at Punjab elections, 1970–2013

a. National level

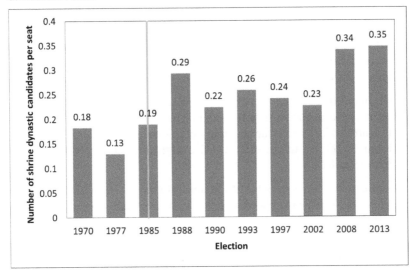

b. Provincial level

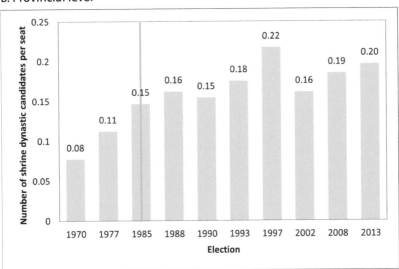

Endnotes

Supplementary material for this chapter is available on LSE Press's Zenodo site (https://zenodo.org/communities/decentralised_governance/). See: *Supplementary material for*: Adeel Malik, Rinchan Mirza, and Jean-Philippe Platteau (2023) 'Devolution under autocracy: Evidence from Pakistan', in Jean-Paul Faguet and Sarmistha Pal (eds) *Decentralised Governance: Crafting Effective Democracies Around the World*, London: LSE Press. https://doi.org/10.5281 /zenodo.7920785

[1] Given our focus on devolution under military regimes, the recently instituted local government reforms in Khyber-Pakhtunkhwa (KP) and Punjab also lie beyond the core remit of this chapter (see Gulzar and Khan (2021) for experimental evidence on the impact of devolution reforms in KP).

[2] Rather than inducting political appointees in the civil service through lateral entry, Zia encouraged his fellow military staff to enter the civil service.

[3] Dependence from central political authority was especially strong in rural constituencies. Indeed, Zia maintained separate jurisdictions for rural and urban regions (introduced under Ayub), the former being defined as district councils and the latter as town committees and municipal corporations. The rural–urban divide was important in terms of income and revenue generation. At a time when rapid urbanization was resulting in growing revenues for town and municipal committees, these resources could thus not be shared with rural areas, which remained relatively resource-starved and strongly dependent on provincial governments (Cheema, Naqvi, and Siddiqi 2005, pp.10–12).

[4] According to the selectorate theory of de Mesquita et al. (2003), any political system, including autocracies, can be characterized as consisting of the following groups: the population, a subset of the population called a 'selectorate', in which groups select their own leader, and the winning coalition. The latter, in turn, forms a subset of the selectorate whose support is crucial for the ruler's survival.

[5] Internal fights are illustrated by the old confrontation between the Gilani and Quraishi pîr families in Multan district.

[6] It is only recently that the elected government of Imran Khan has held local body elections in one province after the Supreme Court intervened on the matter.

[7] Supplementary material for: Adeel Malik, Rinchan Mirza, and Jean-Philippe Platteau (2023) 'Devolution under autocracy: Evidence from Pakistan', in Jean-Paul Faguet and Sarmistha Pal (eds) *Decentralised Governance: Crafting Effective Democracies Around the World*, London: LSE Press. https://doi.org/10.5281/zenodo.7920785

[8] The definition is based on the classification of FAFEN (Free and Fair Election Network).

[9] Supplementary material, https://doi.org/10.5281/zenodo.7920785

References

Acemoglu, Daron; and Robinson, James (2006) 'Economic Backwardness in Political Perspective', *American Political Science Review*, vol.100, no.1, pp.115–31. https://doi.org/10.1017/S0003055406062046

Ali, Syed Mohammad (2018) 'Devolution of Power in Pakistan', Washington, DC: United States Institute of Peace. https://www.jstor.org/stable/resrep17667

Auriol, Emmanuelle; Platteau, Jean-Philippe; and Verdier, Thierry (2023) 'The Quran and the Sword', *Journal of European Economic Association*, forthcoming.

Bardhan, Pranab and Mookherjee, Dilip (eds) (2006) *Decentralization and Local Governance in Developing Countries: A Comparative Perspective*, Cambridge: MIT Press.

Besley, Timothy and Reynal-Querol, Marta (2017) 'The Logic of Hereditary Rule: Theory and Evidence', *Journal of Economic Growth*, vol.22, no.2, pp.123–44. https://doi.org/10.1007/s10887-017-9140-4

Blaydes, Lisa (2006) 'Who Votes in Authoritarian Elections and Why? Determinants of Voter Turnout in Contemporary Egypt', Annual Meeting of the American Political Science Association, Philadelphia, PA, August.

Bourguignon, François and Platteau, Jean-Philippe (2023) *Institutional Challenges at the Early Stages of Development: Lessons from a Multi-Country Study*, Cambridge University Press: Cambridge.

Bresser-Pereira, Luiz Carlos (2004) *Democracy and Public Management Reform: Building the Republican State*, New York: Oxford University Press. https://doi.org/10.1093/0199261180.003.0017

Boix, Carle and Svolik, Milan W. (2013) 'The Foundations of Limited Authoritarian Government: Institutions, Commitment, and Power-Sharing in Dictatorships', *The Journal of Politics*, vol.75, no.2, pp.300–316. https://doi.org/10.1017/S0022381613000029

Cheema, Ali; Khwaja, Asim Ijaz; and Khan, Adnan Qadir (2005) 'Decentralization in Pakistan: Context, Content, and Causes', Faculty Research Working Papers Series RWP05-034, Kennedy School of Government, Harvard University. https://dx.doi.org/10.2139/ssrn.739712

Cheema, Ali; Khan, Adnan Q.; and Myerson, Roger B (2010) 'Breaking the Counter-Cyclical Pattern of Democracy in Pakistan', International Growth Centre Working Paper. Lahore.

https://www.theigc.org/sites/default/files/2014/11/Cheema-Et-Al-2010
-Working-Paper.pdf

Cheema, Ali and Mohmand, Shandana Khan (2003) *Local Government Reforms in Pakistan: Legitimizing Centralization or a Driver for Pro-poor Change?* Karachi: Collective for Social Science Research.

Cheema, Ali; Naqvi, Asjad; and Siddiqi, Bilal (2007) 'The Long-Run Impacts of Colonial Village Institutions on Development: Evidence from Pakistan'. Lahore University of Management Sciences (LUMS).

Dal Bó, Ernesto; Dal Bó, Pedro; and Snyder, Jason (2009) 'Political Dynasties', *The Review of Economic Studies*, vol.76, no.1, pp.115–42. https://doi.org/10.1111/j.1467-937X.2008.00519.x

De Mesquita, Bruce Bueno; Smith, Alastair; Siverson, Randolph M; and Morrow, James D. (2003) *The Logic of Political Survival*, Cambridge, MA: MIT Press.

Dunleavy, Patrick and Boucek, Françoise (2003) 'Constructing the Number of Parties', *Party Politics*, vol.9, no.3. https://doi.org/10.1177/1354068803009003002

Ewing, Katherine (1983) 'The Politics of Sufism: Redefining the Saints of Pakistan', *The Journal of Asian Studies*, vol.42, no.2, pp.251–68. https://doi.org/10.2307/2055113

Fiva, Jon H. and Smith, Daniel M. (2018) 'Political Dynasties and the Incumbency Advantage in Party-Centered Environments', *American Political Science Review*, vol.112, no.3, pp.706–12. https://doi.org/10.1017/S0003055418000047

Gandhi, Jennifer (2015) 'Elections and Political Regimes'. *Government and Opposition*, vol.50, no.3, pp.446–68. https://doi.org/10.1017/gov.2015.11

Gandhi, Jennifer and Przeworski, Adam (2007) 'Authoritarian Institutions and the Survival of Autocrats', *Comparative Political Studies*, vol.40, no.11, pp.1279–301. https://doi.org/10.1177/0010414007305817

Gandhi, Jennifer and Lust-Okar, Ellen (2009) 'Elections under Authoritarianism', *Annual Review of Political Science*, vol.12, pp.403–22. https://doi.org/10.1146/annurev.polisci.11.060106.095434

Geddes, Barbara (1999) 'What Do We Know about Democratization after Twenty Years?' *Annual Review of Political Science*, vol.2, no.1, pp.115–44. https://doi.org/10.1146/annurev.polisci.2.1.115

Gehlbach, Scott; Konstantin, Sonin; and Svolik, Milan W. (2016) 'Formal Models of Nondemocratic Politics', *Annual Review of Political Science*, vol.19, pp.565–84. https://doi.org/10.1146/annurev-polisci-042114-014927

Gerschewski, Johannes (2013) 'The Three Pillars of Stability: Legitimation, Repression, and Co-optation in Autocratic Regimes', *Democratization*, vol.20, no.1, pp.13–38. https://doi.org/10.1080/13510347.2013.738860

Gilmartin, David (1988) *Empire and Islam: Punjab and the Making of Pakistan*, Berkeley: University of California Press.

Gulzar, Saad and Khan, Muhammad (2021) '"Good Politicians": Experimental Evidence on Motivations for Political Candidacy and Government Performance'. http://dx.doi.org/10.2139/ssrn.3826067

Hasnain, Zahid (2008) 'The Politics of Service Delivery in Pakistan: Political Parties and the Incentive for Patronage, 1988-1999', *The Pakistan Development Review*, vol.47, no.2, pp.129–51.

International Crisis Group (ICG) (2004) 'Devolution in Pakistan: Reform or Regression', ICG Asia Report Number 77, Islamabad/Brussels: International Crisis Group. https://gsdrc.org/document-library/devolution-in-pakistan-reform-or-regression

Khan, Shahrukh Rafi; Khan, Foqia Sadiq; and Akhtar, Aasim Sajjad (2007) *Initiating Devolution for Service Delivery in Pakistan: Ignoring the Power Structure*, Karachi: Oxford University Press. https://ideas.repec.org/b/oxp/obooks/9780195472219.html

Lührmann, Anna; Tannenberg, Marcus; and Lindberg, Staffan I. (2018) 'Regimes of the World (RoW): Opening New Avenues for the Comparative Study of Political Regimes', *Politics and Governance*, vol.6, no.1, pp.60–77. https://doi.org/10.17645/pag.v6i1.1214

Lyon, Stephen M. (2019) *Political Kinship in Pakistan: Descent, Marriage, and Government Stability*, Lexington Books.

Malik, Adeel and Malik, Tahir (2017) 'Pīrs and politics in Punjab, 1937–2013', *Modern Asian Studies*, vol.51, no.6, pp.1818–61. https://doi.org/10.1017/S0026749X16000949

Malik, Adeel and Mirza, Rinchan Ali (2022) 'Pre-colonial Religious Institutions and Development: Evidence through a Military Coup', *Journal of the European Economic Association*, forthcoming. https://doi.org/10.1093/jeea/jvab050

Martin, Nicolas (2016) *Politics, Landlords and Islam in Pakistan*, London: Routledge.

Mohmand, Shandana Khan (2019) *Crafty Oligarchs, Savvy Voters: Democracy under Inequality in Rural Pakistan*, Cambridge: Cambridge University Press. https://doi.org/10.1017/9781108694247

Mufti Masood (2020) *Do-Minar: A Reportoire*, Karachi: Oxford University Press.

Murtin, Fabrice and Wacziarg, Romain (2014) 'The Democratic Transition', *Journal of Economic Growth*, vol.19, no.2, pp.141–81. https://doi.org/10.1007/s10887-013-9100-6

Niazi, M.A. (1994) 'Local Bodies: The History', *The News International*, 30 September.

Pierson, Paul (2000) 'Increasing Returns, Path Dependence, and the Study of Politics', *American Political Science Review*, vol.94, no.2, pp.251–67. https://doi.org/10.2307/2586011

Querubin, Pablo (2016) 'Family and Politics: Dynastic Persistence in the Philippines', *Quarterly Journal of Political Science*, vol.11, no.2, pp.151–81. http://dx.doi.org/10.1561/100.00014182

Siddiqui, Kamal (ed.) (1992) *Local Government in South Asia*, Dhaka: University Press.

Svolik, Milan W. (2012) *The Politics of Authoritarian Rule*, Cambridge: Cambridge University Press. https://doi.org/10.1017/CBO9781139176040

Waseem, Mohammed (1994) *Politics and the State in Pakistan*, Islamabad: National Institute of Historical and Cultural Research.

Waseem, Mohammad (2021) *Political Conflict in Pakistan*, London: Hurst.

Wilder, Andrew (1999) *The Pakistani Voter: Electoral Politics and Voting Behaviour in the Punjab*, Karachi: Oxford University Press.

Wilder, Andrew (2010) 'The Politics of Civil Service Reform in Pakistan', *Journal of International Affairs*, 1 May. https://www.jstor.org/stable/24384170

World Bank (1998) 'A Framework for Civil Service Reform in Pakistan', Washington, DC. https://documents1.worldbank.org/curated/en/307081468774919191/pdf/multi-page.pdf

Yadav, Vineeta (2020) 'Political Families and Support for Democracy in Pakistan', *Asian Survey*, vol.60, no.6, pp.1044–71. https://doi.org/10.1525/as.2020.60.6.1044

Ziring, Lawrence (1988) 'Public Policy Dilemmas and Pakistan's Nationality Problem: The Legacy of Zia ul-Haq', *Asian Survey*, vol.28, no.8, pp.795–812. https://www.jstor.org/stable/2644587

6. Social fragmentation, public goods, and local elections: evidence from China

Monica Martinez-Bravo, Gerard Padró i Miquel, Nancy Qian, and Yang Yao

Summary

This study examines how the economic effects of local elections in rural China depend on voter heterogeneity, as captured by religious fractionalisation. We first document religious composition and the introduction of village-level elections for a nearly nationally representative sample of over 200 villages. Then, we examine the interaction effect of heterogeneity and the introduction of elections on village government provision of public goods. The interaction effect is robustly negative. We interpret this as evidence that voter heterogeneity constrains the potential benefits of local elections for public goods provision.

The introduction of municipal elections is often a component of governance reforms towards decentralisation. However, the national-level experience suggests that the introduction of democracy in developing countries during the 20th century has often failed to produce the public policy changes that Western European countries historically experienced when they democratised (for example, Acemoglu and Robinson 2000; Lizzeri and Persico 2004). One potential answer, as argued by the *modernisation* (Lipset 1959) and the *critical junctures* hypotheses (Acemoglu et al. 2008), is that democracy can only survive and succeed in contexts where certain historical preconditions exist. However, existing studies provide little concrete evidence on what the

---

How to cite this book chapter:

Martinez-Bravo, Monica; Padró i Miquel, Gerard; Qian, Nancy and Yao, Yang (2023)
'Social fragmentation, public goods, and local elections: evidence from China',
in: Faguet, Jean-Paul and Pal, Sarmistha (eds) *Decentralised Governance: Crafting Effective Democracies Around the World*, London: LSE Press, pp. 135–179.
https://doi.org/10.31389/lsepress.dlg.f License: CC BY 4.0

exact preconditions are and which economic outcomes are sensitive to these conditions. This chapter addresses this gap in the literature by examining how the introduction of village elections interacts with *voter fragmentation*, defined as the clustering of citizens in different groups with potentially distinct identities, in determining the allocation of government-provided public goods in rural China.

Our analysis here has four main sections, plus an online annex. We begin by giving a look ahead to the core approaches used and some of the most salient findings. Section 6.2 discusses the conceptual framework and the empirical strategy we used. We next describe the data in Section 6.3, and the results achieved in Section 6.4. The final main section (6.5) considers the robustness of our results. In addition, extensive background information is available in the chapter's Supplementary Materials, which cover more descriptive material on the overall role of village elections in China, the importance and measurement of religion across the country, and other issues relevant to understanding our approach and findings.[1]

6.1 The core approach and findings of our study

Village elections were introduced during the 1980s and 1990s to address challenges in local governance that had led to severe under-provision of public goods in rural China, among other problems. These elections partially replaced the Communist Party appointment system that had previously determined village leadership and represent a marginal shift towards democracy in village government (on which more below). Consistent with the belief that electoral accountability incentivises village leaders to improve public goods provision, several studies have found that the introduction of elections increases average local public goods provision (for example, Luo et al. 2010; Mu and Zhang 2011; Zhang et al. 2004; Martinez-Bravo et al. 2022). These results on the average effect of elections, together with the size and diversity of China's socio-geographic landscape, make China a natural context for studying the relationship between the underlying heterogeneity in villages and the effectiveness of elections in determining public goods.

A priori, the sign of the interaction between heterogeneity and elections on government-provided public goods is ambiguous. Following the seminal work of Alesina, Baqir, and Easterly (1999), an extensive literature suggests that a number of factors (lack of trust, lower altruism across groups, preference divergence) can cause social fragmentation to reduce the government's ability and willingness to raise revenues to provide public goods.[2] However, the literature has not addressed whether the advantages of introducing elections should be larger or smaller in more fragmented polities. The reason is that the mechanisms emphasised in the literature should, in principle, hold for both appointed and elected governments. However, the sign of the interaction depends on whether this relationship is *stronger* under an elected government or under an appointed one. For instance, if fragmentation limits the benefits of elections because it weakens electoral accountability, the interaction would be negative. In contrast, if heterogeneous villages have more to gain from the introduction of elections, because elections better aggregate conflicting preferences, the interaction would be positive. Therefore, whether the benefits of introducing elections are larger or smaller in heterogeneous polities is ultimately an empirical question.

There are two main challenges in studying the interaction effect of democratisation and voter heterogeneity on public goods provision: identification and data. The main concern for identification is that voter heterogeneity is typically correlated with other factors (such as a history of conflict or weak administrative capacity) that could influence the quality of institutions. Similarly, voter heterogeneity could be an outcome of democratisation. For example, across countries, if democracies are more tolerant of diversity and are better able to provide public goods for reasons unrelated to diversity, the sign of the interaction effect would not necessarily reflect whether heterogeneity is an important precondition for a working democracy.

The second difficulty is finding high-quality data from the appropriate context. A study on the interaction effects of voter heterogeneity and the introduction of elections, or any democratisation reforms, requires a context that fulfils the following criteria:

(i) the units of observation must be responsible for determining and financing public goods;
(ii) these units must undergo a similar and well-defined shift towards democracy;
(iii) there must be variation in voter heterogeneity across the populations in these units;
(iv) the introduction of democracy should be exogenous to heterogeneity; and
(v) these units should be otherwise similar so that they are comparable for statistical analysis.

While cross-national analyses struggle with (ii), (iv) and (v), within-country comparisons tend not to satisfy (i) and (ii). The introduction of village-level elections in China and the natural variation in local population mixes across this large country provide a context in which these difficulties can be successfully addressed.

Our study proceeds in two steps. First, we document the introduction of elections, public goods expenditures and provision, and social composition of villagers in each village for a nearly nationally representative sample of over 200 villages and 20 years. The Village Democracy Survey (VDS), the main source of the data, is a unique survey conducted by the authors that digitised data from village records. This data set is supplemented with demographic variables from the National Fixed Point Survey (NFS), which is collected by the Ministry of Agriculture each year in the same villages as the VDS.

For practical reasons, we focus on religious fragmentation as a proxy for voter heterogeneity. Of the three dimensions of ethnic, religious, and linguistic fragmentation that dominate the literature on diversity, religion is the only one that varies substantially across the villages in our sample. Religious heterogeneity is interesting in its own right owing to the re-emergence of religion in China after years of state repression, its importance for economic performance, its salience for political attitudes around the world (for example, Alesina et al. 2003; Montalvo and Reynal-Querol 2005; Guiso, Sapienza, and Zingales 2003), and its place in the historical Chinese context (for example, Weber 1968).[3] Religious conflict is practically non-existent in our context. Therefore, we interpret religious fragmentation broadly as a proxy for social fragmentation. In practice, our study also reveals the importance of religion as a dimension for social clustering in post-Mao rural China.

The second step is to use the data to examine the interaction effect of the introduction of elections (which varied in time across villages) and a time-invariant measure of the level of average religious fragmentation that differs across villages.[4] Because data for religious population shares is not available every year, we use the *average* of religious fragmentation over time to maximise our sample size. The baseline specification controls for

- village fixed effects, which absorb all time-invariant differences across villages;
- year fixed effects, which control for all changes over time that affect all villages similarly, such as macroeconomic changes taking place in China during this period; and
- province–time trends, which control for the growing economic divergence across regions during the reform era.

Our strategy is similar to a triple differences estimate that compares public goods in villages before and after the introduction of elections, between villages that have already introduced elections to those that have not, and between fragmented and less fragmented villages.

Religious fragmentation is a non-random variable that is correlated with other factors that can influence elections and public goods. To address this problem our baseline equation controls for the *interaction* of year fixed effects with a large number of potential correlates of fragmentation: village size, the average share of religious population in the village, and, most importantly, religious fragmentation itself. The latter set of controls is extremely conservative because it controls for *all* time-varying omitted variables that correlate with fragmentation, allowing villages with different levels of fragmentations to evolve across different paths over time in a fully flexible manner. It forces our estimates to be identified only from a systematic change in the difference in public goods between fractionalised and less fractionalised villages from the year that elections are implemented.

Our interpretation of the interaction effect relies on two assumptions. First, our measure of religious fragmentation must not be an outcome of elections. We support this by showing that elections have no effect on the time-varying measure of religious fragmentation, and that average religious fragmentation is uncorrelated with the timing of the introduction of elections. Second, we assume that, conditional on our baseline controls, the interaction of the introduction of elections and religious fragmentation is not jointly determined with public goods. In other words, we assume that fragmentation is not correlated with other factors (beyond the baseline controls) that can influence the effect of elections on public goods. This is highly likely because of the baseline controls for the interaction of fragmentation and year fixed effects. Nevertheless, we provide a large body of evidence against alternative explanations in the section on robustness (Section 6.5). Note that the interpretation of the interaction effect as causal does not require that the timing in the introduction of elections was random.

The main results show that, prior to the introduction of elections, village government expenditure on public goods was very similar across villages with different degrees of fragmentation; elections increase public goods expenditure, and the magnitude of the effect *declines* with fragmentation. We find similar results when examining proxies for public goods provision as the dependent variable, which supports our interpretation of expenditure as reflecting provision. Taken literally, the estimates imply that approximately 92 per cent of the villages in rural China were homogenous enough to experience some increase in public goods expenditures after the introduction of elections, while 8 per cent of villages were so heterogeneous that elections reduced village public goods expenditure. The high share of villages that experienced some increase from elections is not surprising given the homogeneity of most Chinese villages.

In addition, we show that the changes in public goods expenditure occurred exclusively for village-raised funds (that is, funds collected from village households). In contrast, we found no effect of elections or the interaction for public goods funded by transfers from upper levels of government. Together with the large number of robustness checks we conduct, these results show that mechanisms local to the village were causing heterogeneous villages to experience lower gains from elections. In particular, there were two possible and non-mutually-exclusive mechanisms, both related to the fact that elections increase accountability: (i) heterogeneous villages have a lower preference for public goods, and elected village leaders better reflect this underlying preference; and (ii) homogeneous villages are better able to hold their elected leaders accountable.[5] Importantly, we were able to rule out the alternative explanation that our results are driven by poor implementation of the electoral reforms in fragmented villages by showing that there is no relationship between heterogeneity and the quality of election implementation.

In terms of its links to earlier work, this study complements a large empirical literature studying the relationship between heterogeneity and public goods provision (for example, Alesina, Baqir, and Easterly 1999; Alesina and La Ferrara 2000; Alesina and La Ferrara 2002; Alesina and La Ferrara 2005).[6] Our analysis differs in that we investigate how heterogeneity modulates the effects of institutional change on public goods instead of the cross-sectional effect of heterogeneity on public goods. In focusing on heterogeneity, local governance and public goods in a developing country, we are approaching it in a similar way to studies such as Bardhan and Mookherjee (2006) and Bandiera and Levy (2010), which analysed the effect of heterogeneity on local governance in India and Indonesia; Khwaja (2009), Okten and Osili (2004), and Miguel and Gugerty (2005), who found that social fragmentation reduces collective action towards public goods in Pakistan, Indonesia, and Kenya; Chattopadhyay and Duflo (2004), Ferraz and Finan (2008), Olken (2010), and Besley, Pande, and Rao (2012), who examined local democratic governance in India, Brazil, and Indonesia; and Banerjee, Iyer, and Somanathan (2005), Banerjee and Somanathan (2007), and Munshi and Rosenzweig (2008), who examined how groups mobilise through the political system to obtain public goods in India.[7] In focusing on religious fragmentation as our measure of heterogeneity, we contribute to the macro-empirical literature on the effect of religious fragmentation on growth (for example, Alesina et al. 2003; Montalvo and Reynal-Querol 2005).

We also add to the studies discussed earlier on Chinese elections by taking a first step towards understanding the preconditions under which elections work. In our companion paper (Martinez-Bravo et al. 2022), we show that local elections pose a trade-off from the autocrat's point of view, which allows us to characterise the conditions under which they are introduced. In Martinez-Bravo et al. (2015), we explored the interaction of elections with social capital. Since the average effect reflects the conditions of a very specific context, an analysis of the preconditions is crucial towards obtaining generalisable lessons for policymakers. In addition, in the discussion of China's transition, religion has recently become an object of academic interest and systematic data collection.[8]

Our study is the first to provide direct and rigorous empirical evidence on the interaction of formal institutional reform and pre-existing conditions. For China, the results show that the presence of distinct groups in society can severely limit the effects of a democratic transition for public goods provision. To the best of our knowledge, we produce the first village-level data set that documents regional religious composition during the modern era, which, together with the other data we have collected, makes a general contribution by facilitating future research on the relationship between informal and formal institutions and economic outcomes in China.

6.2 Conceptual framework

This section surveys the theoretical mechanisms that link public goods provision, social heterogeneity, and democratic choice and accountability.

Throughout the discussion we refer to contextual factors in rural China to assess plausibility. For a deeper description of the background of this study, please refer to the chapter's Supplementary Materials.[9]

Social heterogeneity and public goods

The first step towards conceptualising the relationship between religious diversity, government-provided public goods, and elections is to focus on the different mechanisms that link social heterogeneity and public goods, regardless of institutions. Existing research has proposed several channels to explain the often-observed negative cross-sectional correlation between fragmentation and public goods provision. This literature, reviewed in Alesina and Ferrara (2005), often considers a public goods game in which citizens willingly contribute to the public good. In the case of rural China, the village government needs to collect contributions from villagers to provide goods, but has limited enforcement power. Hence, the insights of this literature are applicable to this context: by refusing to cooperate, villagers have the ability to significantly increase the cost of collecting contributions for the village government. These increased costs will decrease the provision of public goods through a mechanism similar to the voluntary contribution public goods game.

Among the proposed mechanisms, the most plausible in the context of rural China is that religious activity induces altruism, trust, and willingness to join efforts with other members of the religious group (Alesina and Ferrara 2000; Guiso, Sapienza, and Zingales 2003; Vigdor 2004). Rituals, practices, and festivals throughout the year induce repeated and intense interactions among those who share the same faith, facilitating communication, trust and empathy. As in many other contexts, each religious group builds a strong social identity that helps accumulate these different dimensions of within-group social capital. Theoretically, in the extreme case in which religious participants fully internalise the preferences of the other followers of their faith, a religiously homogeneous village would enjoy optimal voluntary contributions to the public good. By the same logic, to the extent that altruism and trust are limited to the religious group, the more fragmented the village, the lower the willingness to contribute to public goods.[10] Similarly, social sanctions might be weaker for members of other religious groups, which results in less social leverage for enforcing contributions in fragmented villages (Miguel and Gugerty 2005). Note that this mechanism would be active even if there were consensus on which public good to provide and what the ideal level of expenditure would be.

A different mechanism posits that preferences differ across groups. In particular, groups might prefer different varieties of public goods, and technological constraints may be such that only one variety can be provided (Alesina, Baqir, and Easterly 1999). In a fragmented village, villagers might refrain from contributing since they suspect they will not get their preferred variety. In the context of rural China, this mechanism would be most directly relevant when the public good under consideration is schooling, since different religions might have diverging preferences over the religious orientation of education. However, note that, even if all citizens prefer the same public good, such as better irrigation, groups can still differ on their preferences over the location of the public amenity, since individuals of similar religions often cluster into neighbourhoods within villages (see Cohen 1992). Hence religious diversity may also result in preference divergence for public goods due to the geographic differences across groups.[11]

Finally, Tsai (2007) provided evidence suggesting that village officials who are embedded in encompassing social groups have an easier time discharging their duties. In fragmented villages, social groups will not generally encompass the entire village and officials cannot belong to all of them. To the extent that this mechanism applies, the effective cost of providing public goods in fragmented villages should be higher, likely resulting in lower expenditure. In the extreme case, divergent preferences can generate wasteful conflict between groups (Esteban and Ray 1999; Montalvo and Reynal-Querol 2005). Such conflict could also result in lower public good provision. However, given the scant anecdotal evidence of conflict across religious affiliations in China today, this does not appear to be a first-order mechanism for our context.

The interaction of social heterogeneity and elections in determining public goods

The mechanisms discussed so far predict a negative cross-sectional relationship between fragmentation and public goods provision given a fixed institutional environment. Hence, we would expect the level of public goods to be higher in homogeneous villages under *both* appointed leaders (for example, our baseline before the electoral reforms) and under elections (for example, after the electoral reforms). However, there are two main differences between the two institutional situations: elections increase the accountability of village government to villagers; and elections provide a mechanism for preference aggregation. As we now discuss, these two functions of elections have opposite predictions on the sign of the interaction effect of fragmentation and the introduction of elections.

If elected leaders are more directly accountable than appointed leaders to citizens, we can posit two reinforcing effects. First, accountable governments should better reflect the preferences of the population. If fragmented villages have a lower preference for public goods, the relationship between heterogeneity and public goods provision should be stronger (more negative) under elected leaders than under appointed leaders, since the former are more responsive to the underlying preferences of the village than the latter. Second, all else being equal, rational citizens are more willing to contribute to the village government for public goods when they feel that they can hold the government accountable. A necessary condition for effective government accountability under elections is that some citizens need to gather and distribute information on government performance. Since these monitoring activities are public goods in themselves, and public goods are better provided in homogeneous villages for the reasons stated earlier, elected officials are more accountable in homogeneous villages.[12] This effect causes villagers to be more willing to contribute to the government for public goods when the government is elected rather than appointed, and more so in homogeneous villages. These two mechanisms predict that the interaction effect of elections and heterogeneity is *negative*.

On the other hand, elections also serve as a mechanism for aggregating voter preferences. In fragmented villages, with low communication and contentious relationships between groups, it is likely to be more difficult for appointed village leaders to determine the most preferred public goods by the majority of villagers. Their inability to propose the majority-preferred public good will cause villagers to resist contributing to the public goods that the leader chooses. Hence, in terms of preference aggregation, heterogeneous villages will have more to gain from the introduction of elections. This mechanism predicts that the interaction effect of elections and heterogeneity is *positive*. This mechanism is likely to be stronger if the pre-election correlation between heterogeneity and public goods is highly negative, since it is predicated on heterogeneous villages catching up to homogeneous villages.

As we show below (with context given in the chapter's Supplementary Materials), in rural China public goods provision was extremely low and not correlated with fragmentation prior to the implementation of elections. This was most probably a result of lack of accountability: since the village leaders were appointed by upper levels of government, they could both safely ignore the preferences of the villagers and shirk the work necessary to accomplish public goods provision, with two main consequences.

First, since the relationship between heterogeneity and public goods is non-existent before elections, and the theoretical discussion suggests that the interaction between elections and heterogeneity will be negative, there is very little catching up that heterogeneous villages can do. As a consequence, the accountability mechanisms described above should dominate. Hence, we will interpret a negative interaction between religious fragmentation and the introduction of elections as reflecting the mechanism that the accountability introduced by elections works better in homogeneous villages. This effect should be reinforced when in heterogeneous villages preferences are such that public goods games result in lower provision, and the newly introduced accountability induces the elected government to closely reflect this.

Second, because there is no relationship between heterogeneity and public goods under the appointment regime, our empirical analysis is silent regarding the different mechanisms that the existing literature proposes for the cross-sectional relationship between heterogeneity and public goods. For this reason, we focus on the well-identified change caused by the introduction of elections.

Case studies

In order to understand the likely mechanisms behind the patterns in the data, we spent significant time observing village meetings, interviewing villagers, reading local newspapers, and interviewing scholars of modern religion in China and religious activist groups to find detailed case studies to provide concrete examples of how fractionalisation matters for public goods provision. We summarise the insights here.

Consider fractionalised village A, where Muslims wished to provide religious education to their children outside of school and were legally prohibited from teaching religion in school or having private schools in China. They did not wish public funds to be spent in the village school. By contrast, the Buddhists, Daoists, and Animists/Atheists (that is, almost everyone else) wished to improve the village school, because their need for spiritual education was satisfied by the existing non-Judeo-Christian infrastructure (for example, village temple, ancestral temples, and so on).

In village B, all groups wished to improve irrigation, for example by drilling tube wells to increase agricultural profits. However, the availability of water for all farmers over time depended on correct usage (not over-pumping). Individuals belonging to the same religion interacted frequently with each other, and thus found it easier to monitor each other's water usage and also to punish bad behaviour with social sanctions. However, individuals could not easily monitor or punish those from different groups. In this context, increased fractionalisation would reduce investment in irrigation. It is interesting to note that in this village it was clear that increased interaction within a religion could crowd out interaction with others.

In village C, villagers disagreed about which roads to pave, and the village could only pave a few roads at a time. The Buddhists, Daoists, and Animists worshipped in different locations (there were no Christians or Muslims in this village). Each argued that the roads near their temple should be paved first, not trusting that more money could be raised in the future to pave other roads.

In village D, non-Christians and Christians were in verbal conflict. In village meetings, Christians accused others of being backwards and argued that the village needed to invest in modern infrastructure (for example, a computer for the village school). The others accused the Christians of acting superior and not really looking out for the interest of all villagers, and simply refused to contribute anything.

Note that these anecdotal accounts suggest the mechanisms discussed above can all be active in different villages, since they are not mutually exclusive. We also found that, in most villages, leaders had little incentives to raise funds and provide public goods prior to the introduction of elections. The introduction of elections forced leaders to address the pent-up demand for public goods. However, as leaders tried to do so, the issues generated by social fragmentation became a problem.

Religious fractionalisation

We measure religious fragmentation with an index of fractionalisation, which proxies for the lack of trust and altruism and the difference in preferences regarding the type of public goods across religious groups (for example, Alesina et al. 2003). This can be written as:

$$F_i = 1 - \sum_{j=1}^{N} s_{ij}^2 \tag{1}$$

The fractionalisation index for village i is equal to one minus the sum of the squares of s_{ij}, the population share of religion j in village i, where N is the total number of religions. This index captures the probability that two randomly drawn villagers belong to different groups.

An alternative index used to measure heterogeneity is the polarisation index (for example, see Esteban and Ray 1994; Montalvo and Reynal-Querol 2005). In principle, this index captures the conflict potential of a given group composition. However, in our context, there is little known conflict across religious groups. In addition the correlation with the fractionalisation score is 0.98 across villages and statistically significant at the 1 per cent level, as Figure 6.1 shows. So, we focus on the fractionalisation index for brevity. Nonetheless, when we present the baseline estimates, we will show that our results hold when we use the polarisation index. The polarisation index is:

$$P_i = 1 - \sum_{j=1}^{N} \left(\frac{0.5 - s_{ij}}{0.5} \right)^2 s_{ij} \tag{2}$$

The main outcome we examine is village government expenditure on public goods. To estimate the impact of voter heterogeneity on expenditures induced by the introduction of elections, we estimate the following equation:

$$\begin{aligned} Y_{ijt} &= \alpha_1 E_{ijt} + \alpha_2 (E_{ijt} \times H_{ij}) + \beta_1 O_{ijt} + \beta_2 (O_{ijt} \times H_{ij}) \\ &+ \mu_t H_{ij} + \gamma X_{ijt} + t\theta_j + \delta_i + \rho_t + \epsilon_{ijt} \end{aligned} \tag{3}$$

where the outcome of interest for village i in province j during year t is a function of: the interaction effect of fragmentation, H_{ij}, and the introduction of elections, E_{ijt}; the interaction term of fragmentation and the introduction of open nominations in each village, O_{ijt}; the main effects of the introduction of elections and open nominations; the interaction of fragmentation with year fixed effects, μ_t; a vector of village–year specific controls, X_{ijt}; province–year trends, $t\theta_j$; village fixed effects, δ_i; and year fixed effects, ρ_t.

Our main estimates cluster the standard errors at the village level to correct for serially correlated shocks within each village. Given the top-down nature of the reform, one may also be concerned about correlated shocks within

Figure 6.1: Fractionalisation versus polarisation scores in our full sample

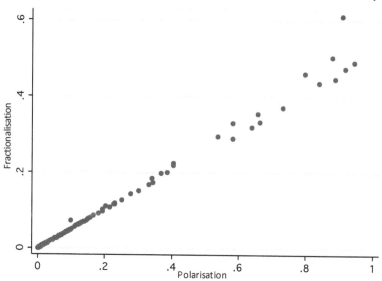

provinces. To address this, we will also present the standard errors clustered at the province level and show that they are very similar.

In this equation, the village fixed effects control for all differences across villages that are time-invariant (for example, geography, the main effect of fragmentation), and the year fixed effects control for all changes over time that affect villages similarly (for example, macroeconomic growth, economic liberalisation). Province–time trends control for the regional economic and cultural divergence across China during our period of study (for example, the coastal regions experienced more rapid economic growth and were more exposed to outside cultural influences).[13] Because elections were introduced rapidly across villages within provinces, we do not have enough variation in the data to control for province–year fixed effects. However, after we present the main results, we will show that our estimates are robust to controlling for province–time trends with other functional forms.

To address possible concerns about omitted variables, the vector of controls, X_{ijt}, includes several variables. First, we control for village population, which addresses the fact that there may be economies of scale in public goods provision or that it may be more difficult to coordinate larger populations. Second, we control for the share of village population that is religious, which is highly correlated with religious heterogeneity and could affect the provision public goods. Since we use it as a time-invariant measure, we control for its interaction with the full set of year dummy variables to allow its influence to vary flexibly over time.

Finally, and most importantly, we control for the interaction of religious heterogeneity and year fixed effects, $\mu_t H_{ij}$. Since our heterogeneity measure is time-invariant at the village level, we interact it with the full set of year fixed effects to allow villages to differ according to the level of fragmentation in a way that is fully flexible over time. Hence, our estimate of the interaction of heterogeneity and the introduction of elections is very conservative in that any underlying reason why villages with different levels of fragmentation evolve along different paths is absorbed by this exacting set of controls. The estimate is determined only by the systematic change in public goods after the introduction of elections in villages with higher versus lower levels of heterogeneity, net of any other time divergence across these villages.

To interpret the estimates, consider the case of religious fragmentation. For villages with no fragmentation, $H_i = 0$ and so α_1 is the total effect of the introduction of elections. For villages where there is a high ('infinite') degree of fragmentation, $H_i = 1$ and $\alpha_1 + \alpha_2$ is the total effect of the introduction of elections. So α_2 is the differential effect of the introduction of elections between these two types of village. The hypothesis that religious fragmentation limits the benefits of the introduction of elections predicts that $\hat{\alpha}_2 < 0$. In contrast, if fragmentation has no influence, then $\hat{\alpha}_2 \approx 0$.

Conceptually, our empirical strategy is similar to a triple differences estimate (DDD). We compare public goods investment: in villages before and after the introduction of elections (first difference); between villages that have already introduced elections to those that have not (second difference); and between villages that have high heterogeneity to villages with low heterogeneity (third difference). Our identification strategy makes two assumptions. One is that we assume our measure of religious fragmentation is not affected by the introduction of elections. We will demonstrate that this is true with the data before we present the main results. A second assumption is that, conditional on the baseline controls, our measure of heterogeneity is not correlated with other factors that influence the effects of elections on public goods expenditures. We do not take this as given and provide a large body of evidence to address this concern after our main results. It is important to note that our differences strategy does not rely on the timing of the introduction of elections being random.

6.3 Data

Our data forms the most comprehensive data on village-level reforms and village-level outcomes ever constructed, as well as the first data to document religious composition of rural villages in post-Mao China. It covers a larger and more nationally representative sample, and spans a longer time horizon than any other existing data of rural China that are available to researchers. It mainly uses village- and year-level data from a panel of 217 villages for the years 1986–2005 from the Village Democracy Survey (VDS), a unique retrospective survey conducted by the authors of this chapter. In 2006, our survey recorded the history of electoral reforms and public goods expenditures. In

2011, we returned to the same villages to collect data on the presence of voluntary social organisations and on the number of households per surname for the four most prevalent surnames in the village roster (in 2011), which we will use in the robustness exercises.[14] Our main variables are obtained from village records, and therefore are not subject to reporting or recall biases.

We supplement the VDS with annual data collected each year since 1986 by the Ministry of Agriculture in the National Fixed Point Survey (NFS), which surveys the same villages as the VDS. These surveys are nationally representative and the villages are updated over time. The two surveys are merged at the village and year level to form the sample that we use for estimating the main results. It comprises a balanced panel of 217 villages for the years 1986–2005.

In addition, the NFS surveys a random sample of approximately 100 households per village each year (out of approximately 420 households per village on average) with detailed questions regarding household expenditures. We were able to obtain this additional household data for approximately a third of the villages in the total sample. The panel aspect of our data means that we can control for village fixed effects and year fixed effects. Since we have many villages from each province, we can also control for province–year trends, which are important for addressing the growing economic divergence across regions in China. An additional advantage of the data is the accuracy and uniformity of the historical public expenditures data, which come from administrative records overseen by the Ministry of Agriculture.

In the supplementary material to this chapter, Section B provides a detailed account of how religion was measured in the NFS survey and how the religious fractionalisation index was calculated.[15] We also include full details of the descriptive statistics for our villages and of the correlates with religious fragmentation. It is important to note here that the average village has 420 households. By the end of our sample, all villages had introduced elections, but only half of them had introduced open nominations. Indeed, 50 per cent of villages introduced elections between 1984 and 1993. Looking at whether there were more candidates than positions, we find that 1,002 out of 1,071 elections we observed had more candidates than positions. Thus, around 94 per cent of elections were competitive.

Finally on data, it is important to note two pieces of information relating to our approach. First, religious fractionalisation is uncorrelated with the average pre-election level of government spending on public goods, and the fraction that is financed by villagers. This is consistent with the belief that there was little difference in government public goods provision across villages prior to elections because provision was universally low and that any existing differences were unrelated to social heterogeneity. Second, fractionalisation is uncorrelated with the timing in the introduction of elections (or open nominations), which supports the notion that fractionalisation did not affect the way elections were rolled out.

It is important to emphasise that the correlation between average fractionalisation and other variables does not confound our baseline estimates per se because the baseline controls of the interaction of average fractionalisation and year fixed effects control for *all* differences between fragmented and less fragmented villages in a way that is fully flexible over time. In Section 6.5 we demonstrate the robustness of our baseline estimates by controlling for the interaction of these correlates (and other variables) with the introduction of elections.

6.4 Results

To allay concerns that our measure of average fractionalisation is endogenous, we first establish that the introduction of elections has no effect on a time-varying measure of religious fractionalisation. To support this claim, we regress the time-varying measure of fractionalisation on the introduction of elections.[16] The sample for this regression is smaller than the full sample because it is restricted to villages that held their first election after 1993, when the NFS began to collect religious population data. The post-election dummy in Table 6.1 column 1 shows that there is no effect: the coefficient is small in magnitude and statistically insignificant. Together with the descriptive statistics, which show that average fractionalisation and election timing are uncorrelated, we conclude that there is no direct relationship between religious fractionalisation and elections.[17] Henceforth, we only consider the time-invariant measure of average religious fractionalisation since this allows us to extend the empirical analysis to the mid-1980s.

For the rest of Table 6.1, the dependent variable is government public goods expenditure, measured in RMB 10,000s. In column 2 we estimate a similar equation to Equation [3], except that we replace the village fixed effects with the religious fractionalisation main effect to examine the pre-election difference in public goods expenditure across villages of different levels of fractionalisation. The estimate of the uninteracted fractionalisation effect, which reflects the effect of fractionalisation prior to the introduction of elections, is small in magnitude and statistically insignificant. This is consistent with the qualitative and correlational evidence shown earlier that fragmented and homogeneous villages had very similar public goods expenditures prior to the first election.

Column 3 presents our baseline estimate. The main effect of elections is positive and the interaction effect with religious fractionalisation is negative. Both are statistically significant at the 1 per cent level. To assess the magnitude of the coefficients, note that the estimates for the main effect of post-election in column 3 show that the introduction of elections increased government public goods expenditure by RMB 207,300 (Constant 2000 US$ 37,914) for villages with zero fractionalisation. For villages with the mean level of fractionalisation of 0.053, elections increased government public goods expenditure by 150,590 RMB (21,194 Constant 2000 USD, $(-107 \times 0.053 + 20.73) \times 10,000 = 150,590$). This is shown at the bottom of the table in column 3.

Table 6.1: The effect of religious fragmentation × the introduction of elections

| | Dependent variables | | | | |
| | Government public goods expenditure | | | | |
	(1) Time-varying measure of religious fractionalisation	(2)	(3) Baseline	(4)	(5)
Post 1st Election × Religious Fractionalisation		−4.645 (34.81)	−107.4** (46.84)	−142.1** (55.88)	
Post 1st Election × Religious Polarisation					−53.79** (23.42)
Religious Fractionalisation (Average)		−7.02 (35.94)			
Post 1st Election	0.00638 (0.007999)	10.65 (8.397)	20.73** (9.351)	21.35** (9.507)	20.61** (9.301)
Post-Open Nominations	−0.00116 (0.00557)		6.168 (10.20)	5.245 (9.963)	6.483 (10.25)
Post-Open Nominations × Religious Fractionalisation			−3.443 (49.68)	10.07 (71.15)	
Controls Village FE	Y	N	Y	Y	Y
Year FE	Y	Y	Y	Y	Y
Village Population	Y	Y	Y	Y	Y
Population Share of All Religions × Year FE	N	Y	Y	Y	Y
Religious Fractionalisation × Year FE	N	N	Y	Y	Y
Province–Year Trends	Y	Y	Y	Y	Y
Pop Share of Each Religion × Year FE	N	N	N	Y	N
Post-Open Nominations × Religious Polarisation	N	N	N	N	Y
Level of Clustering	Village	Village	Village	Village	Village
Observations	1773	4,340	4340	4,340	4340
R-squared	0.911	0.034	0.117	0.119	0.117
Avg Effect: Post 1st Election + Post 1st Election × Rel Frac × 0.053 (0.202 for Imputed Rel Frac)			15.04	13.82	

(Continued)

Table 6.1: Continued

	Dependent variables Government public goods expenditure		
	(6) Cluster SE at the province level	(7) Cluster SE at the province level, wild bootstrap	(8) Imputed measure of fractionalisation
Post 1st Election × Religious Fractionalisation	−107.4** (42.76)	−107.4** (47.29)	−200.5** (85.02)
Post 1st Election × Religious Polarisation			
Religious Fractionalisation (Average)			
Post 1st Election	20.73** (9.058)	20.73** (10.00)	55.50** (23.24)
Post-Open Nominations	6.168 (9.466)	6.168 (9.90)	12.32 (19.85)
Post-Open Nominations × Religious Fractionalisation	−3.443 (44.26)	−3.443 (40.63)	−32.17 (82.09)
Controls Village FE	Y	Y	Y
Year FE	Y	Y	Y
Village Population	Y	Y	Y
Population Share of All Religions × Year FE	Y	Y	Y
Religious Fractionalisation × Year FE	Y	Y	Y
Province–Year Trends	Y	Y	Y
Pop Share of Each Religion × Year FE	N	N	N
Post-Open Nominations × Religious Polarisation	N	N	N
Level of Clustering	Province	Province	Village
Observations	4340	4340	4340
R-squared	0.117	0.117	0.118
Avg Effect: Post 1st Election + Post 1st Election × Rel Frac × 0.053 (0.202 for Imputed Rel Frac)	*15.04*	*15.04*	*15.00*

Notes: The variable Religious Fractionalisation (Average) was not used in Models 5 to 8.

Another way to assess the magnitude is to ask how many villages experienced increases in public goods due to the introduction of elections given their levels of religious fractionalisation. Dividing the absolute values of the main effect by the interaction effect (20.73 / 107), we find that a village with a fractionalisation index below 0.193 will experience some increase in public goods from the introduction of elections. This includes approximately 92 per cent of the villages in our sample. Therefore most villages were homogenous enough to experience some increase in public goods following the introduction of elections.

In terms of standard deviations, we find that a one standard deviation increase in fractionalisation (0.105) causes the increase in public goods expenditure due to elections to decline by RMB 112,350 ($0.105 \times -107 = 11.235$), which is 0.08 standard deviations of average public goods expenditure ($11.235 / 135.466 = 0.083$). Thus, our estimates imply a strong, yet plausibly sized effect of heterogeneity.

In column 4, we additionally control for the average population share of each religion, each interacted with year fixed effects. This addresses the concern that the presence of a particular religion may both be correlated with fractionalisation and affect public goods expenditure after the introduction of elections. Our main interaction estimate does not change.

In column 5 we examine the interaction of religious polarisation and the introduction of elections while controlling for all of the baseline controls. The estimated interaction effect is negative and statistically significant at the 1 per cent level, and the magnitude is about half of that of fractionalisation in column 1. Since the standard deviation of polarisation doubles that of fractionalisation, the implied effects for heterogeneity are essentially the same, which is not surprising since these two variables are highly correlated in the data.[18]

In column 6, we address the concern that the top-down nature of electoral reforms means that correlated shocks within provinces may cause our main estimates to under-reject hypotheses. Therefore, we alternatively estimate the baseline equation by clustering the standard errors at the province level. The standard errors are very similar to those clustered at the village level. However, one may be concerned that having 29 provinces can induce small-sample bias when we cluster at the province level. In column 7, we address this by correcting for potential biases with wild-bootstrapped standard errors as recommended by Cameron, Gelbach, and Miller (2008). The standard errors, presented in columns 6 and 7 are almost identical. Since the different levels of clustering make little difference to our estimates, we will continue to present standard errors clustered at the village level. Finally, we note that the estimated effect of the introduction of open nominations and religious fractionalisation is always small in magnitude and statistically insignificant, as is the main effect of open nominations. For this reason we will not report these coefficients in the rest of the regressions.[19] We return to discuss the estimate in column 7 later in the chapter.

These results, combined with the lack of correlation between fractionalisation and public goods expenditure before the introduction of elections, are consistent with our interpretation: prior to the elections, the village government was not incentivised to raise money and invest in public goods. Therefore, fractionalisation was not binding. With the introduction of elections, accountability increased and village leaders had to respond to the existing demand in public goods. Hence, it is only after elections are introduced that fractionalisation became binding in constraining the government's ability to raise money and invest for reasons discussed in Section 6.2. In other words, before elections, the village leaders did nothing, so disagreement among villagers was immaterial to public goods. After elections, village leaders tried to raise money to invest in public goods. This was harder to do in fractionalised villages, resulting in relatively lower provision in such villages, post-elections.

Timing of the effects

In order to ensure that the estimated effects are a consequence of the introduction of elections and not of spurious changes that may have occurred in the pre- or post-election periods, it is important to examine the timing of our estimated effects. We estimate the following equation:

$$y_{ijt} = \sum_{\tau=-3}^{4} \alpha_\tau e_{it\tau} + \sum_{\tau=-3}^{4} \beta_\tau (e_{it\tau} \times H_i) + \sum_{\tau=-3}^{4} \theta_\tau O_{it\tau} + \sum_{\tau=-3}^{4} \lambda_\tau (o_{it\tau} \times H_i)$$
$$+ \mu_t H_{ij} + \gamma X_{ijt} + t\theta_j + \delta_i + \rho_t + \epsilon_{it}$$

where $e_{it\tau} = 1$ if village i experienced the introduction of elections τ years ago in year t, and $o_{it\tau} = 1$ if village i experienced the introduction of open nominations τ years ago in year t. The other variables have the same notation as in the baseline equation.[20] α_τ is a vector of coefficients that capture the effect of the number of years since the first election for villages with zero fractionalisation ($H_i = 0$), and β_τ is a vector of coefficients that reflects the differential effect of elections between hypothesised villages with fractionalisation equal to 1 and villages with zero fractionalisation, for each year since the election. θ_τ and λ_τ are the analogous estimates for the introduction of open nominations.

For our identification strategy, we would like to establish that there are no pre-trends in public goods expenditure in the years leading up to the first election ($\hat{\beta}_\tau \approx 0$ when $\tau < 0$); that, for villages with no fractionalisation, the positive effect on public goods expenditure occurs with the introduction of elections ($\hat{\alpha}_\tau > 0$ when $\tau \geq 0$); and that public goods expenditure between homogenous and heterogeneous villages diverge when elections are introduced ($\hat{\beta}_\tau < 0$ when $\tau \geq 0$).

The coefficients of the dummy variables for the years since the first election and the coefficients of their interaction with religious fractionalisation are

Figure 6.2: The estimated effects on government public goods expenditure for each year since the first election

a. The coefficients for villages where fractionalisation = 0 and the differential effects between villages where fractionalisation = 0 and fractionalisation = 1

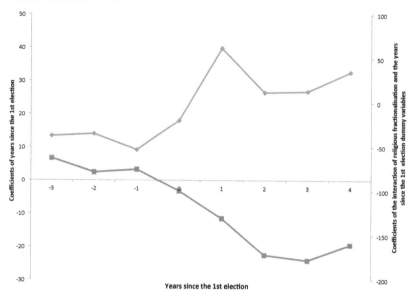

b. The effect for the average village with fractionalisation = 0.053

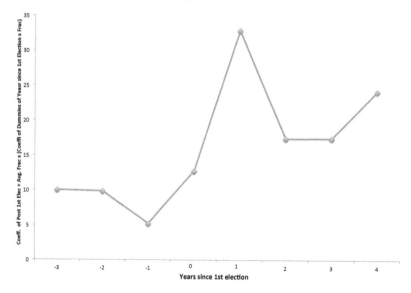

plotted in Figure 6.2a (on two different vertical axes for presentational purposes).[21] It shows that there is no pre-trend in government spending on public goods in the years leading up to the first election for either homogenous or heterogeneous villages. Consistent with the 'parallel trends' assumption, the pre-election coefficients move in parallel between the two types of villages. The spending in the two types of villages diverge exactly when elections were introduced – they increased for very homogenous villages and decreased for very heterogenous villages. These estimates provide strong support for our identification strategy and interpretation.

In Figure 6.2b, we plot the effect of elections on public goods provision over time for the village with the average level of fractionalisation ($\hat{\alpha}_\tau + 0.053\hat{\beta}_\tau$). This number shows that the average village experienced no change in public goods expenditure over time prior to the introduction of elections, but then experienced an increase when elections were introduced. The large increase in the first year after elections are introduced may reflect the newly elected government's response to latent demand for public goods. However, the important fact to note is that, although spending is somewhat lower in the second and third years after the first election, all post-election spending is nevertheless positive and much higher than pre-election years.[22]

Public goods provision and private expenditure

Our main results focus on public goods expenditure mainly because the data quality for this measure is better than for the data on public good provision. However, we are able to proxy for the provision of two public goods that together approximately constitute a quarter of total public goods expenditure by the village government; we proxy for irrigation with the amount of arable land in a village, and for schooling with primary school enrolment rates. This is based on the logic that increases in spending on irrigation should increase the amount of arable land and increases in spending in schooling should increase enrolment rates. In our sample, 83 per cent of the villages have a school and 94 per cent of these are primary schools (the others are middle schools). These data are not available for all years, which reduces the precision of our estimates. Table 6.2 columns 2 and 3 show that the estimated interaction effect of religious fractionalisation and the introduction of elections on these proxies for provision are negative and the main effects of the introduction of religion are positive, as in the baseline equation, restated in column 1. The interaction effects are statistically significant at the 15 per cent and 10 per cent levels. These results suggest that actual public good provision followed the same pattern as recorded expenditure and support our interpretation of changes public goods expenditure as reflecting changes in public goods provision.

Note that an interesting implication of the changes in provision is that the increase in public expenditure is unlikely to have completely crowded-out private expenditure on public goods. If there is complete crowd-out, we

Table 6.2: The effect of religious fragmentation × the introduction of elections on public goods provision and private expenditure

	(1) Total government public expenditure	(2) Ln arable land	(3) Primary school enrolment rate	Dependent variables (4) Household expenditure on agricultural products	(5) Ln arable land	(6) Household expenditure on schooling	(7) Primary school enrolment rate
Dependent variable mean	14.28	7.35	96.42	8.81	7.95	5.19	96.8
Post 1st election × Religious fractionalisation	−107.4** (46.84)	−4.204 (2.864)	−30.02* (17.06)	−95.93** (36.68)	−8.511*** (2.847)	11.98** (4.827)	−6.422 (10.35)
Post 1st election	20.73** (9.351)	0.145* (0.0809)	1.752* (1.056)	10.73 (9.491)	0.391 (0.239)	−2.186 (1.415)	0.589 (1.25)
Observations	4340	3291	2682	873	769	873	841
R-squared	0.117	0.873	0.311	0.551	0.914	0.835	0.303

Notes: All regressions control for post-open nomination and its interaction with religious fractionalisation and the full set of baseline controls: religious fractionalisation*year FE, the share of religious population FE, village population, province–year trends, and village and year FE. The standard errors are clustered at the village level. Columns 1–3 use data from all village. Columns 4–7 use data from villages for which we have household-level data. The number of observations vary across columns 1–3 and across columns 4–7 because data on arable land and school enrolment is not available for every year.

should observe no change in provision.[23] For a third of the sample, we can investigate this more directly by examining private expenditures on irrigation and schooling as outcomes in columns 4 and 6 (columns 5 and 7 repeat the estimates for public goods provision on a similarly restricted sample of villages for comparison purposes). Column 4 shows that household expenditures parallel public expenditure for irrigation, but, interestingly, this is not the case for expenditure in schooling, in column 6. For the latter, it seems that there is some substitution of public and private expenditure.

Interpreting the results – local funds for public goods

The main results show that elections increased public goods expenditure, but that this increase was smaller in fragmented villages. Following the discussion in Section 6.2, we interpret our results as evidence that voter heterogeneity causes elected governments to be unwilling or unable to finance public goods. In Table 6.3, we examine alternative explanations that might threaten this interpretation.

First, we examine government expenditure on public goods separately according to the source of the funds. A comparison of columns 1 and 2 shows that the main results on total public goods is entirely driven by financing from villagers. In contrast, column 3 shows that there is no effect on funds from the upper government. Consistent with our interpretation, this provides strong evidence that the effect of heterogeneity is local to the village and that elections were not confounded with other reform at higher levels of government.

Column 4 examines tax payments made by households to local governments. Unfortunately, this measure includes payments to the county and township as well as to the village governments and is only available for a third of the villages in our sample. Nevertheless, it is interesting to note that the signs of the main effect and interaction effect are consistent with those in columns 1–3. This estimate is insignificant but it also points in the direction of our interpretation.

We interpret religious fragmentation as a proxy for reduced cross-group social capital caused by social clustering along religious lines. While we cannot test for this directly, we can investigate whether there is a difference in terms of the presence of social organisations between homogeneous and heterogeneous villages. The VDS survey measures the presence of organisations that are voluntary, do not exclude any villager, and are partly or wholly funded and organised by villagers. Approximately 14 per cent of our village–year observations have at least one such organisation. Column 5 shows that the interaction effect on voluntary village-wide social organisations is large in magnitude and negative in sign. However, it is not statistically significant. Thus, we interpret this as weak suggestive evidence consistent with heterogeneous villages having reduced village-wide social capital also after the introduction of elections.

Table 6.3: The effect of religious fragmentation × the introduction of elections on public goods expenditure from villagers and election quality

	Dependent variables				
	(1) All	(2) Villagers	(3) Non-villagers	(4) Township and county governments	(5) Voluntary social organisation dummy
Dependent variable mean	14.279	9.769	4.422	176.19	0.143
Post 1st Election × Religious Fractionalisation	−107.4**	−97.20**	−11.53	−54.99	−0.777
	(46.84)	(48.55)	(11.68)	(193.9)	(0.566)
Post 1st Election	20.73**	21.09**	−0.159	32.71	0.0157
	(9.351)	(9.586)	(2.074)	(24.69)	(0.0279)
Observations	4340	4340	4340	1300	3900
R-squared	0.117	0.107	0.076	0.573	0.805
SUR: p-value			0.047		

Alternative mechanisms

An obvious alternative to our preferred interpretation is that the central government changed public goods targeting when elections were introduced such that it favoured homogenous villages. However, our finding that the interaction effect of the introduction of elections and fractionalisation on public goods expenditures financed with funds from the upper government is 0 makes this alternative highly unlikely.

Another potential threat for our interpretation is that our main results may be driven by poor implementation of the electoral reforms in fragmented villages. For instance, this would be the case if the limited interaction across religions makes it more difficult to inform villagers of proper electoral procedures, and therefore allows more corrupt elections. If this were true, then the correct interpretation of our main results would be that heterogeneous communities underwent less formal institutional change. To investigate this hypothesis, we collected data on the occurrence of the most common aberrations in elections from village records. These include the presence of roving ballot boxes, not having anonymous ballots, and allowing voting by proxy without a signed permission form by the individual who is away. We create a dummy variable that equals 1 if any of these aberrations occurred. In our sample, 85 per cent of the observations have poor-quality elections. We examine this variable as the dependent variable in our main estimating equation. Table 6.4 column 1 shows that the coefficient of the interaction term between fractionalisation and post-first election is very small in magnitude and statistically insignificant. Thus, we conclude that our estimates are not driven by differences in electoral quality between heterogeneous and homogenous villages.

Similarly, we can examine other political outcomes that may reflect the quality of elections such as voter participation or the probability that the newly elected VC was persecuted during the Cultural Revolution, was from a family that was officially classified as a rich farmer or landlord in the initial communist land reforms during the early 1950s, or was a party member before entering office. As a placebo, we can also examine the characteristics of the party secretaries (PSs), who were not directly affected by elections. These data are recorded by the VDS and vary slightly in the number of observations because records were not always available. The estimates in columns 2–8 are all statistically zero. There is no evidence that elections were implemented or interpreted differently across villages of different levels of heterogeneity. Consistent with the anecdotal evidence, there is no effect on the PSs.

Finally, note that mean reversion is extremely unlikely to have caused our results, since we find that there is little difference in pre-election public goods expenditure between homogeneous and heterogeneous villages (Table 6.4 column 2).

Table 6.4: The effect of religious fragmentation × the introduction of elections on electoral quality and village leader characteristics

	(1) Electoral procedure error dummy	(2) Voter participation (%)	(3) VC was persecuted during Cultural Revolution	(4) PS was persecuted during Cultural Revolution	(5) VC family was rich farmer or landlord in 1949	(6) PS family was rich farmer or landlord in 1949	(7) VC was party member before entering office	(8) PS was party member before entering office
Dependent variable mean	0.85	74.11	0.05	0.05	0.21	0.17	0.72	0.94
Post 1st Election × Religious Fractionalisation	0.214 (0.291)	−7.253 (8.455)	0.022 (0.557)	−0.0108 (0.183)	0.594 (0.624)	0.368 (0.355)	−0.428 (1.271)	0.115 (0.155)
Post 1st Election	−0.213*** (0.0561)	87.59*** (1.854)	0.0614 (0.053)	0.0197 (0.025)	0.113* (0.0659)	0.0114 (0.0465)	0.0358 (0.169)	−0.00702 (0.0226)
Observations	4196	4112	3658	3984	3677	4004	3641	4024
R-squared	0.628	0.961	0.625	0.657	0.607	0.687	0.538	0.774

Notes: All regressions control for post-open nomination and its interaction with religious fractionalisation and the full set of baseline controls: religious fractionalisation*year FE, the share of religious population, village population, province–year trends, village FE and year FE. The standard errors are clustered at the village level.

6.5 Robustness

We examine five possible issues for the robustness of our analysis – mismeasurement of religious composition; breaking down fractionalisation; correlates of religious fractionalisation; additional controls; and sample selection.

Mismeasurement of religious composition

The NFS data on religious composition do not distinguish between Catholics and Protestants and only report officially sanctioned religions, which will cause individuals who follow folk religion to be miscategorised as non-religious. These errors in measurement will likely cause our data to understate fragmentation.

To address this, we construct an alternative measure of fractionalisation using the most reliable data available on actual religious populations in China. These data are collected by anthropologists, ethnographers, and sociologists and are only available at the national level. Lai (2003) summarises these estimates, which we report in Table A1 of this chapter's Supplementary Materials.[24] Column 6 shows that, according to these estimates, our data may underreport Buddhism (Mahayana) by 46.6 per cent and Christianity by 66.7 per cent (where Protestants are underreported by 67 per cent and Catholics are underreported by 100 per cent). They also show that approximately 28.5 per cent of Christians are Catholics.

To impute the true religious population, we first divide Christians in each village into two categories – Protestants and Catholics, where we assume that 28.5 per cent of the Christian population is Catholic. Then, we adjust the number of religious individuals for each group by the estimated difference shown in column 6. Then we add the category of folk religion by assuming that 20 per cent of the total village population follow folk religious practices. The descriptive statistics for the imputed measures are shown in the Supplementary Materials Table A1 columns 7–9. A comparison with the measures constructed from the raw NFS data shows that the share of all religious population increases from approximately 5 per cent to 26 per cent. Average fractionalisation increases from approximately 0.053 to 0.2. Note that the cross-sectional correlation between the imputed measure of religious fractionalisation and the reported measure is 0.71 and is statistically significant at the 1 per cent level.

We re-estimate the baseline equation using the imputed measure of religious fractionalisation. Table 6.1 column 7 shows that the estimated interaction effect of fractionalisation and the introduction of elections is very similar to the baseline estimate, which we restate in column 1. It is also statistically significant at the 5 per cent level.

A shortcoming of our imputation exercise is that it attributes mismeasurement equally across all villages. To be cautious, we have conducted several alternative imputations where we assigned higher mismeasurement to villages that gained more from elections. For example, we can divide the villages into two groups according to whether they are in the top half or bottom half in terms of the gains in public goods from elections. We can then assume that religious composition is correctly reported by the NFS for the bottom half, but use the imputed measures for the top half, and re-estimate the baseline equation. This exercise yields very similar results as the ones presented.[25] We conclude that it is highly unlikely that our main results are driven mismeasurement of the religious population.

Breaking down fractionalisation

The fractionalisation index (or any measure of fragmentation) is a function of the number of groups and the distribution of the population shares across groups. In Table 6.5, we attempt to 'decompose' the fractionalisation index to examine whether our main results are driven by the number of groups, the distribution of groups sizes, or the combination of the two. We use several alternative ways to measure the number and sizes of the groups.[26] The results in columns 2–3 show that the number of groups does not interact with the introduction of elections. In columns 4–6, the interaction effects of elections with the standard deviation of groups sizes and the size of the largest group and have large but statistically insignificant coefficients. Together with the fact that our main interaction effect is always negative and similarly large in magnitude as the baseline in column 1, these results show that the fractionalisation index captures the combined effects of the number of groups and the distribution of group sizes, and is not driven by one component.

To check the sensitivity of the fractionalisation index to any particular religion, we can alternatively omit each religion and recalculate the fractionalisation index. Note that this does not require omitting observations. We simply group the given religion with non-religious individuals. In results available from the authors, we find that our estimates are similar in sign and statistically similar in magnitude to the baseline regardless of which religion we ignore.

Correlates of religious fractionalisation

The baseline controls of the interaction of average fractionalisation and year fixed effects control for *all* differences between fragmented and less fragmented villages in a way that is fully flexible over time. However, to fully eliminate concerns of omitted variable bias, it is important to show that our main effect is robust to allowing these correlates to have a differential effect when elections are implemented.

The correlates, shown in Table A2 of this chapter's Supplementary Materials,[27] are: the average share of villagers that belong to any religion, the presence of a village temple, the number of temples historically in the same county, dummy variables for whether the village is in a hilly or mountainous area, and average pre-election household income for the 10th-, 50th-, and 90th-percentile households.[28]

Table 6.5: The effect of religious fragmentation × the introduction of elections, the number of religious groups × the introduction of elections, and the distribution of religious group sizes × the introduction of elections

	(1)	(2)	(3)	(4)	(5)	(6)	(7)
	Government public goods expenditure						
Post 1st Election × Religious Fractionalisation	-138.7 (61.41)	-191.7 (195.1)	-192.3 (264.5)	-172.6 (75.86)	-302.6 (179.5)	-168.3 (74.22)	-470.7 (242.4)
Post 1st Election × number of Religious Groups	8.934 (6.225)						10.19 (6.553)
Post 1st Election × number of Religious Groups (excl Non-Religious)		29.11 (33.15)					
Post 1st Election × Std. Dev. of Group Size			-239.5 (716.9)				-407.7 (241.3)
Post 1st Election × Std. Dev. of Group Size (excl Non-Religious)				144.8 (95.14)			
Post 1st Election × Pop Share of Largest Group					-241 (183.4)		
Post 1st Election × Pop Share of Largest Group (excl Non-Religious)						66.93 (44.83)	
Post 1st Election	10.03 (7.134)	-21.5 (36.14)	128.1 (320.3)	21.35 (9.475)	263.1 (188.5)	21.29 (9.452)	418.4 (242.3)
Observations	4340	1880	4340		4340		
R-squared	0.119	0.141	0.117	0.117	0.117	0.117	0.12

Notes: All regressions control for post-open nomination and its interaction with religious fractionalisation and the full set of baseline controls: religious fractionalisation*year FE, the share of religious population, province–year trends, village FE, and year FE. In addition, all regressions control for the interaction of post-open nominations and the relevant explanatory variable. The standard errors are clustered at the village level. The explanatory variables are the following. In column 1, we measure the number of religious groups as reported by the NFS data. In column 2, we measure the number of groups according to our imputed measures. In column 3, we calculate the standard deviation of groups sizes using the NFS data. In column 4, we calculate the standard deviation of groups for the religious population (non-religious individuals do not enter into this measure). In column 5, we calculate the population share of the largest group. In column 6, we calculate the population share of the largest group that is not the non-religious group.

Table 6.6: The effect of religious fragmentation × the introduction of elections – robustness to controlling for the correlates of religious fragmentation

Dependent variable: total government public goods expenditure

	(1)	(2)	(3)	(4)	(5)	(6)	(7)	(8)	(9)	(10)	(11)	(12)	(13)	(14)
Post 1st Election × Religious Fractionalisation	-107.4 (46.84)	-126.7 (61.15)	-162.9 (68.46)	-117.7 (51.16)	-89.63 (41.30)	-110.1 (48.19)	-106.2 (47.12)	-105.3 (46.97)	-100.7 (42.60)	-99.17 (43.20)	-109 (49.85)	-108.2 (47.76)	-132 (59.02)	-158 (69.14)
× Share of All Religious Population		24.87 (27.76)												
× Temple			49.85 (23.09)											42.25 (20.43)
× Temple in 1820				17.29 (13.92)										-12.91 (13.65)
× Hilly					-12.68 (17.30)									-9.815 (17.52)
× Mountainous					-18.82 (18.15)									8.864 (12.81)
× Surname Fractionalisation						41.62 (33.76)								5.54 (46.81)
× Surname Polarisation							-15.73 (56.82)							
× Pop Share of Top 2 Surnames								-17.81 (32.77)						-23.51 (55.61)

(Continued)

Table 6.6: Continued

	(1)	(2)	(3)	(4)	(5)	(6)	(7)	(8)	(9)	(10)	(11)	(12)	(13)	(14)
	Dependent variable: total government public goods expenditure													
× Lineage Group									39.94 (16.96)					23.23 (15.07)
× Avg Pre-Election Tot Gov Pub Goods Exp										2.292 (1.198)				−1.37 (1.257)
× Average Pre-Election HH Income (10th Percentile)											0.0147 (0.0263)			0.0227 (0.0244)
× Average Pre-Election HH Income (50th Percentile)											−0.0208 (0.0219)			−0.0162 (0.0172)
× Average Pre-Election HH Income (90th Percentile)											0.00516 (0.00384)			0.00179 (0.00207)
× Average Pre-Election Gini												42.16 (98.56)		24.6 (149.7)
× Village Population													0.151 (0.0484)	0.109 (0.0403)
Post 1st Election	20.73 (9.351)	20.75 (9.400)	7.797 (4.681)	11.95 (6.827)	27.54 (16.26)	−6.754 (20.03)	30.83 (34.52)	29.88 (21.97)	0.733 (5.060)	12.2 (7.139)	30.12 (14.76)	9.004 (25.45)	−41.3 (16.00)	−30.83 (68.71)
Observations	4340	4340	4340	4340	4340	3880	3880	4340	4340	4340	4340	4340	4,340	3,880
R-squared	0.117	0.117	0.124	0.119	0.119	0.119	0.119	0.117	0.123	0.121	0.124	0.118	0.131	0.142

In addition, we also control for other potentially important factors: surname fragmentation, the presence of a lineage group (for example, the presence of a family that has an ancestral hall or family tree), the population share of the two most popular surnames, the pre-election average public goods expenditure, the pre-election average Gini coefficient, and village population each interacted with the introduction of elections and open nominations.[29]

The estimates for these tests are shown in Table 6.6. In column 2 we omit our usual baseline controls of the interaction of the average share of villagers that belong to any religion and year fixed effects when we control for the interaction of post-election and the average share of villagers that belong to any religion due to collinearity. In column 14, we control for all of these interactions in one equation (except the interaction of surname polarisation because it is highly correlated with surname fractionalisation, and the interaction of the average share of villagers that belong to any religion because it is highly correlated to our baseline controls that interact the same variable with all year fixed effects). Our main result is very robust and similar to the baseline, which we restate in column 1. This provides strong evidence that our main results are not driven by spurious correlations.

There are several interesting results to note in addition to the robustness of our main results. First, the interaction of surname fragmentation and the introduction of elections is small in magnitude and statistically insignificant. This suggests that religion is more important as a factor of social clustering in rural China than extended kinship networks in the context of the effectiveness of elections for increasing public goods.[30]

Additional controls

In Table 6.7 columns 2–4, we control for additional factors that could potentially influence the effect of elections on public goods: the interaction of a dummy variable indicating that a village is a suburb of an urban area and year fixed effects; a dummy variable indicating that the Tax and Fee Reform has been introduced; and a dummy variable for whether a village ever experienced an administrative merger interacted with year fixed effects. In columns 5 and 6, we alternately control for quadratic and cubic province–time trends.

In column 7, we control for all of the additional variables in columns 2–4 simultaneously. The estimates show that our main result is robust to controlling for any or all of these additional controls. In column 8, we omit the control for the introduction of open nominations. The results are nearly identical to the baseline. Finally, in column 9, we check whether the main results are driven by electoral accountability. We omit all years following an uncompetitive election (that is, where the number of candidates did not exceed the number of positions). The effects are, if anything, more pronounced than the full sample baseline estimate, which is consistent with the importance of electoral accountability.

Table 6.7: The effect of religious fragmentation × the introduction of elections – robustness to additional controls

	(1)	(2)	(3)	(4)	(5)	(6)	(7)	(8)	(9) ~
	Dependent variable: total government public goods expenditure								
Post 1st election × Religious fragmentation	-107.4**	-97.64**	-104.6**	-105.0**	-107.4**	-107.4**	-92.67	-106.3**	-127.5**
	(46.84)	(45.64)	(46.54)	(47.05)	(46.85)	(46.86)	(45.43)	(46.24)	(55.21)
Post 1st Election	20.73**	20.41**	20.46**	20.09**	20.72**	20.71**	19.62**	21.13**	25.65**
	(9.531)	(9.390)	(9.207)	(9.705)	(9.348)	(9.345)	(9.621)	(9.858)	(11.16)
Controls	N	Y	N	N	N	N	Y	N	N
Near City*Year FE	N	N	Y	N	N	N	Y	N	N
Post Tax and Fee Reform	N	N	N	Y	N	N	Y	N	N
Ever Merged*Year FE	N	N	N	N	Y	N	N	N	N
Province–Year Squared	N	N	N	N	N	Y	N	N	N
Province–Year Cubic	N	N	N	N	N	N	N	N	Y
Open Nominations × Religious Fractionalisation	Y	Y	Y	Y	Y	Y	Y	N	Y
Observations			4340				4340		3,586
R-squared	0.117	0.123	0.118	0.122	0.117	0.117	0.129	0.117	0.149

Notes: All regressions control for the full set of baseline controls: religious fractionalisation*year FE, village population, province–year trends, village FE and year FE. Regressions in columns 1 to 7, and 9 also control for post-open nomination and its interaction with religious fractionalisation. 'Y' and 'N' indicate the inclusion or exclusion of controls. The standard errors are clustered at the village level. Additional sample restrictions are stated in the column headings.
~ In Model 9 the years after uncompetitive elections are omitted.

Table 6.8: The effect of religious fragmentation × the introduction of elections – robustness to sample selection

	Dependent variable: total government public goods expenditure				
	(1) Full sample, baseline	(2) Omit if Religious Share = 0	(3) Omit if Religious Fractionalisation = 0	(4) Dep variable is a dummy for Gov Pub Exp > 0	(5) Omit if Pub Goods Exp = 0
Post 1st Election × Religious Fractionalisation	−107.4 (46.84)	−174.9 (88.57)	−174.9 (88.49)	−0.272 (0.161)	−135.2 (226.5)
Post 1st Election	20.73 (9.351)	33.64 (17.5)	33.66 (17.48)	0.0708 (0.0278)	51.59 (33.52)
Observations	4340	3280	3300	4340	954
R-squared	0.117	0.111	0.111	0.194	0.346

Notes: All regressions control for post-open nomination and its interaction with religious fractionalisation and the full set of baseline controls: religious fractionalisation*year FE, the share of religious population*year FE, village population, province–year trends, village FE and year FE. The standard errors are clustered at the village level.

Sample selection

In our context, the majority of the population is not religious, so one might be concerned that our results are mainly given by the comparison between fully atheist villages and the rest. Table 6.8 columns 2–3 show that our estimates are robust to the exclusion of villages with no religious population or zero fractionalisation. Similarly, public goods expenditures are not made every year, but the estimates in column 5 show that our results are robust to the exclusion of village–year observations that make no public goods expenditure. Alternatively, column 4 examines a dummy variable for whether any public expenditure is made. The estimated coefficients have the same sign as the main results in column 1. Thus, our main results on expenditures recorded reflect the frequency of expenditures as well as the total amount of expenditures. In summary, the results in this section show that the main results are extremely robust to a large set of additional controls and sensitivity checks.

Conclusions

Between 1970 and 2003, the average Polity Index for the world increased from approximately −2 to +3, meaning that the world as a whole experienced a dramatic increase in institutional openness. It is also true that this rise in democratisation was mainly driven by poor countries. Therefore, understanding the preconditions for successful democratisation and the underlying mechanisms must rank among the most important questions for researchers and policy-makers in development economics and political economy.

The study takes a first step in providing rigorous empirical evidence on the necessary preconditions for successful democratisation in the context of grassroots elections in rural China and local public goods provision. The centrally determined electoral reforms in China provide a stark example of how an identical reform can have very different effects depending on the pre-existing level of voter heterogeneity. Specifically, we find that voter heterogeneity – that is, religious fragmentation – significantly reduces the gains from introducing elections.

The findings suggest that the dominant force behind the differential effects of elections in heterogeneous versus homogeneous villages was that elections increased the accountability of local governments towards villagers; this increase was larger in homogeneous villages owing to their capacity to better monitor the leader. In addition, the elected village leader was induced to implement policies that reflected the underlying preferences of villagers for public goods. It is particularly noteworthy that our main result on total government public goods expenditure is entirely driven by differences in expenditure financed by villagers. Neither the introduction of elections nor its interaction with religious fragmentation has any effect on expenditure financed by other revenue sources.

A general lesson from our results is that preconditions are very important for determining the impact of institutional reforms. Since the influence of religion in China has been significantly weakened by the historical presence of a strong secular state, our estimates provide a striking illustration of a high lower bound on the influence of social fragmentation on elections and public goods.

Generalisations aside, we believe that understanding the determinants of the impact of electoral reforms in China is inherently important, since they are among the largest democratisation reforms in history and have changed the lives of almost one billion individuals. For those interested in the social organisation of rural China, our findings identify religion as an important dimension for group clustering during the post-Mao era. Indeed, we find that religion has overtaken other important traditional differences such as those across kinship groups.

There are two important caveats to keep in mind for interpreting our results. First, when attempting to extrapolate our results to other contexts, it is important to realise that the estimated sign and magnitude of the interaction effect are specific to our context. For example, we interpret the increase in public goods expenditure as beneficial because of the severe under-provision of public goods prior to the introduction of elections. Had public goods expenditure been excessive relative to demand from villagers prior to the electoral reforms (for example, high taxation and elite rent-seeking), the increased accountability caused by elections would reduce public goods expenditure on average, and would cause the interaction with heterogeneity to be positive. Second, although the severe under-provision of public goods prior to the electoral reforms is consistent with elections improving efficiency and heterogeneity reducing it, the inability to measure demand or total public goods provision means that welfare assessments are beyond the scope of this chapter. This is an important topic for future research.

Acknowledgements

We thank Abhijit Banerjee, Esther Duflo, Luigi Guiso, and Chris Udry for their insights; the participants at the Paris School of Economics/Sciences Po Political Economy Seminar, 'The Conference on Governance in China' at Stanford University, BREAD, and the EIEF Macro Lunch Workshop for useful comments; the discussant and participants at the NBER Political Economy Workshop; and Carl Brinton, Louis Gilbert, Yunnan Guo, Yiqing Xu, and Jaya Wen for excellent research assistance. We acknowledge financial support from the National Science Foundation Grant 0922087, the European Union's Seventh Framework Programme (FP/2007–2013)/ERC Starting Grant Agreement no.283837, the Ramón y Cajal Grant (RYC–2013–14307) and the Whitney and Betty MacMillan Center for International and Area Studies.

Endnotes

Supplementary material for this chapter is available on LSE Press's Zenodo site (https://zenodo.org/communities/decentralised_governance/). See: *Supplementary materials for:* Monica Martinez-Bravo, Gerard Padró i Miquel, Nancy Qian, and Yang Yao (2023) 'Social fragmentation, public goods and local elections: evidence from China', in Jean-Paul Faguet and Sarmistha Pal (eds) *Decentralised Governance: Crafting Effective Democracies Around the World*, London: LSE Press. https://doi.org/10.5281/zenodo.7920700

[1] See *Supplementary materials for:* Monica Martinez-Bravo, Gerard Padró i Miquel, Nancy Qian, and Yang Yao (2023) 'Social fragmentation, public goods and local elections: Evidence from China', Chapter 6 in Jean-Paul Faguet and Sarmistha Pal (eds) *Decentralised Governance: Crafting Effective Democracies Around the World*, London: LSE Press. https://doi .org/10.5281/zenodo.7920700

[2] There is a large body of literature that finds a negative relationship between social heterogeneity and public goods in different contexts. Please see the discussions towards the end of the introduction and in Section 6.2.

[3] We discuss the re-emergence of religion in rural China in the chapter's Supplementary Materials. We do not have reliable data for other dimensions of heterogeneity such as the education composition of villagers, and income is not a stable dimension of social clustering since elections may have caused income redistribution. Another potentially relevant dimension of heterogeneity in this context is kinship networks. However, several studies by sociologists find that extended kinship networks have become less important in China over time owing to factors such as the collectivization of agriculture during the Maoist era and the rapid economic growth and social modernization that followed (for example, Cohen 1992; Jiang 1995). For completeness, we will examine the influences of fragmentation along kinship lines and other sources of heterogeneity such as pre-election income after we present the main results on religious fragmentation.

[4] In most of the chapter, we measure fragmentation by constructing an index of fractionalization. This particular choice of measurement is not important for our results, which are robust to using an alternative polarization index. This is shown and discussed in more detail later in the chapter. See Alesina et al. (2003), Duclos, Esteban, and Ray (2004), Esteban and Ray (2007), and Montalvo and Reynal-Querol (2005) for discussions of the different measures of fragmentation.

[5] Please see the discussion in Section 6.2.

[6] The seminal paper in the cross-sectional literature is Alesina, Baqir, and Easterly (1999), which generated a literature that is surveyed in Alesina and Ferrara (2005). Luttmer (2001) and Alesina and La Ferrara (2002) found that fragmentation affects preferences towards neighbors. See also Munshi, Rosenzweig and Wilson (2010) for an analysis of the origin and transmission of fragmentation in the United States.

[7] See also Glennerster, Miguel, and Rothenberg (2010) and Dayton-Johnson (2000) for analyses of this relationship in Sierra Leone and Mexico, and Habyarimana et al. (2007) for an experimental study in Uganda. Our study is loosely related to cross-country studies of the relationship between ethnic/linguistic/religious fragmentation and macroeconomic performance that was pioneered by Easterly and Levine (1997). See also Desmet, Ortuno-Ortin, and Wacziarg (2009) and Alesina et al. (2003).

[8] See for instance the recent release of the first Spatial Explorer of Religion (accessible at http://chinadataonline.org/religionexplorer), a joint initiative of Purdue University and University of Michigan.

[9] See *Supplementary materials*, https://doi.org/10.5281/zenodo.7920700

[10] For example, Guiso, Sapienza, and Zingales (2003) found that religious people are more intolerant of diversity than non-religious ones regardless of the type of religion, although some religions are worse than others.

[11] This has been documented historically in mainland China (for example, Yang 1961, pp.98, 158) and in a modern context in Taiwan (for example, Deglopper 1975, p.65). Unfortunately, our data does not allow us to identify the geographic location of households within villages.

[12] For a review of reasons why democracy works better in high social capital environments, see Boix and Posner (1998). See also Banerjee and Pande (2007), Bandiera and Levy (2010), and Padró i Miquel (2007) for other reasons strongly fragmented polities find it difficult to keep elected leaders accountable.

[13] We can alternatively control for distance to the coast interacted with year fixed effects, province GDP, province GDP growth, or other province-level time-varying controls. The estimates are very similar and we do not present these alternative results for brevity. They are available upon request.

[14] For administrative reasons, the 2011 wave includes only 195 of the original villages.

[15] See *Supplementary materials*, https://doi.org/10.5281/zenodo.7920700

[16] Workers in China often migrate temporarily for work. However, the household registration system (known as *hukou* or *huji*) that ties access to public goods and government benefits makes permanent migration costly. Also, rural residents are also disincentivized to migrate permanently away because that results in the loss of the right to farmland.

[17] Please see Table A.2 in the Supplementary Materials. One may also be concerned that religious fragmentation is affected by the implementation or the competitiveness of elections. In results available from the authors we show that there is no correlation between fragmentation and procedural aberrations or the competitiveness of elections.

18 We do not control for fractionalisation and polarisation simultaneously owing to their high correlation. Hence, our results cannot distinguish the role of cross-group conflict from the other mechanisms discussed in Section 6.2. However, the lack of documented open conflict between religious groups in the provinces of our study suggests that the most plausible mechanism behind the deleterious effect of heterogeneity on elections is given by the interaction of the lack of trust, empathy and divergent preferences with the increase in accountability brought about by the reform.

19 The results are also similar if we exclude the open nominations controls. They are available upon request.

20 Note that, although we examine a similar window of time before and after each reform for consistency, we do not exclude any observation. Instead, we follow convention to maximize the information in our estimation and group all of the observations that are four or more years prior to the first reform together, and they constitute the reference group; and, similarly, we group all of the observations that are four or more years after the reform together.

21 Results in the form of regression tables are available upon request.

22 Our main pre–post estimates are very similar when we exclude the first year after the first election. For brevity, these estimates are not presented.

23 See Hungerman (2007) and the studies referenced within for empirical evidence on private-expenditure crowd-out in other contexts. See our Online Annex for details on private provision of public goods.

24 See *Supplementary materials*, https://doi.org/10.5281/zenodo.7920700

25 We tried several alternative ways of assigning mismeasurement differentially across villages. For example, we can only adjust the number of Catholics upwards in the provinces known to have more Catholics (Hebei, Shaanxi, Guangxi, Gansu, and Xinjiang (Lai 2003)). Regardless of how we adjust the data, the results are always very similar. For brevity, they are not reported but are available upon request.

26 In column 1, we measure the number of religious groups as reported by the NFS data. In column 2, we measure the number of groups according to our imputed measures. In column 3, we calculate the standard deviation of groups sizes using the NFS data. In column 4, we calculate the standard deviation of groups for the religious population (non-religious individuals do not enter into this measure). In column 5, we calculate the population share of the largest group. In column 6, we calculate the population share of the largest group that is not the non-religious group.

27 See *Supplementary materials*, https://doi.org/10.5281/zenodo.7920700

[28] Controlling for the presence of temples is motivated by the concern that our main results may be confounded by the potential influence of other dimensions of social capital. Studies in political science such as Tsai (2007) interpret village temples as plausible proxies for social capital because they are not specific to any one religion and are used to worship a range of local deities by all villagers, are funded and maintained by voluntary villagers, and are an important venue for village events such as fairs, festivals, and public discussions. In short, functioning temples are civic organizations that could be behind the differential effect of elections.

[29] We use surname fragmentation and the presence of lineage groups to proxy for the presence of kinship networks, which are a historically important feature of rural life and could be another dimension of social clustering.

[30] Several scholars have observed that kinship networks have declined in importance relative to other dimensions of social clustering as China modernises (for example, Cohen 1992; Jiang 1995). The decline of the importance of kinship networks has also been observed for societies that are culturally Chinese outside the People's Republic of China. For example, in a description of villages in Taiwan during the 1970s, Deglopper (1975, p.65) states that '[n]eighborhoods ... are composed of diverse populations who bear different surnames, who earn a living in different ways, and whose income ranges from high to very low. They have nothing in common except residence in an arbitrarily and rather vaguely defined area, and they do nothing in common except worship. This is because the other traditional social divisions – guilds and surnames – no longer matter today.'

References

Acemoglu, Daron and Robinson, James A. (2000) 'Why Did the West Extend the Franchise? Democracy, Inequality and Growth in Historical Perspective', *The Quarterly Journal of Economics*, vol.115, pp.1167–99. https://doi.org/10.1162/003355300555042

Acemoglu, Daron; Johnson, Simon; Robinson, James A.; and Yared, Pierre (2008) 'Income and Democracy', *American Economic Review*, vol.98, no.3, pp.808–42. https://doi.org/10.1257/aer.98.3.808

Alesina, Alberto; Baqir, Reza; and Easterly, William (1999) 'Public Goods and Ethnic Divisions', *The Quarterly Journal of Economics*, vol.114, no.4, pp.1243–84. https://doi.org/10.1162/003355399556269

Alesina, Alberto; Devleeschauwer, Arnaud; Easterly, William; Kurlat, Sergio; and Wacziarg, Romain (2003) 'Fractionalization', *Journal of Economic Growth*, vol.8, no.2, pp.155–94. https://doi.org/10.1023/A:1024471506938

Alesina, Alberto and La Ferrara, Eliana (2000) 'Participation in Heterogeneous Communities', *The Quarterly Journal of Economics*, vol.115, no.3, pp.847–904. https://doi.org/10.1162/003355300554935

Alesina, Alberto and La Ferrara, Eliana (2002) 'Who Trusts Others?' *Journal of Public Economics*, vol.85, no.2, pp.207–34. https://doi.org/10.1016/S0047-2727(01)00084-6

Alesina, Alberto and La Ferrara, Eliana (2005) 'Ethnic Diversity and Economic Performance', *Journal of Economic Literature*, vol.43, no.3, pp.762–800. https://doi.org/10.1257/002205105774431243

Bandiera, Oriana and Levy, Gilat (2010) 'Diversity and the Power of the Elites in Democratic Societies: A Model and a Test', STICERD Economic Organisation and Public Policy Discussion Papers Series 018, Suntory and Toyota International Centres for Economics and Related Disciplines, LSE. https://papers.ssrn.com/sol3/papers.cfm?abstract_id=1707855

Banerjee, Abhijit; Iyer, Lakshmi; and Somanathan, Rohini (2005) 'History, Social Divisions, and Public Goods in Rural India', *Journal of the European Economic Association*, vol.3, no.2–3, pp.639–47. https://doi.org/10.1162/jeea.2005.3.2-3.639

Banerjee, Abhijit and Pande, Rohini (2007) 'Parochial Politics: Ethnic Preferences and Politician Corruption', Discussion Papers 6381, C.E.P.R. https://papers.ssrn.com/sol3/papers.cfm?abstract_id=1136706

Banerjee, Abhijit and Somanathan, Rohini (2007) 'The Political Economy of Public Goods: Some Evidence from India', *Journal of Development Economics*, vol.82, no.2, pp.287–314. https://doi.org/10.1016/j.jdeveco.2006.04.005

Bardhan, Pranab and Mookherjee, Dilip (2006) 'Pro-poor Targeting and Accountability of Local Governments in West Bengal', *Journal of Development Economics*, vol.79, no.2, pp.303–27. https://doi.org/10.1016/j.jdeveco.2006.01.004

Besley, Timothy; Pande, Rohini; and Rao, Vijayendra (2012) 'Just Rewards? Local Politics and Public Resource Allocation in South India', *World Bank Economic Review*, vol.26, no.2, pp.191–216. https://doi.org/10.1093/wber/lhr039

Boix, Carles and Posner, Daniel N. (1998) 'Social Capital: Explaining Its Origins and Effects on Government Performance', *British Journal of Political Science*, vol.28, no.4, pp.686–93. https://doi.org/10.1017/S0007123498000313

Cameron, A. Colin; Gelbach, Jonah B.; and Miller, Douglas L. (2008) 'Bootstrap-Based Improvements for Inference with Clustered Errors', *The Review of Economics and Statistics*, vol.90, no.3, pp.414–27. https://doi.org/10.1162/rest.90.3.414

Chattopadhyay, Raghabendra and Duflo, Esther (2004) 'Women as Policy Makers: Evidence from a Randomized Policy Experiment in India', *Econometrica*, vol.72, no.5, pp.1409–43. https://doi.org/10.1111/j.1468-0262.2004.00539.x

Cohen, Myron L. (1992) 'Religion in a State Society: China', in *Asia Case Studies in the Social Sciences*, Armonk, NY: ME Sharpe, pp.17–31. https://doi.org/10.4324/9781315288178

Dayton-Johnson, Jeff (2000) 'Determinants of Collective Action on the Local Commons: A Model with Evidence from Mexico', *Journal of Development Economics*, vol.62, no.1, pp.181–208. https://doi.org/10.1016/S0304-3878(00)00080-8

Deglopper, Donald R. (1975) 'Religion and Ritual in Lukang', in Wolf, Arthur (ed.) *Religion and Ritual in Chinese Society*, Stanford, CA, and London: Stanford University Press.

Desmet, Klaus; Ortuno-Ortin, Ignacio; and Wacziarg, Romain (2009) 'The Political Economy of Ethnolinguistic Cleavages', NBER Working Papers 15360, National Bureau of Economic Research. https://www.nber.org/system/files/working_papers/w15360/w15360.pdf

Duclos, Jean-Yves; Esteban, John; and Ray, Debraj (2004) 'Polarization: Concepts, Measurement, Estimation', *Econometrica*, vol.72, no.6, pp.1737–72. https://doi.org/10.1111/j.1468-0262.2004.00552.x

Easterly, William and Levine, Ross (1997) 'Africa's Growth Tragedy: Policies and Ethnic Divisions', *The Quarterly Journal of Economics*, vol.112, no.4, pp.1203–50. http://www.jstor.org/stable/2951270

Esteban, Joan and Ray, Debraj (1994) 'On the Measurement of Polarization', *Econometrica*, vol.62, no.4, pp.819–51. https://doi.org/10.2307/2951734

Esteban, Joan and Ray, Debraj (1999) 'Collective Action and the Group Size Paradox', IEE Working Papers 23, El Instituto de Estudios Economicos de Galicia Pedro Barrie de la Maza 1999.

Esteban, Joan and Ray, Debraj (2007) 'A Comparison of Polarization Measures', UFAE and IAE Working Papers 700.07, Unitat de Fonaments de l'Analisi Economica (UAB) and Institut d'Analisi Economica (CSIC) https://ddd.uab.cat/record/45293

Ferraz, Claudio and Finan, Frederico (2008) 'Exposing Corrupt Politicians: The Effects of Brazil's Publicly Released Audits on Electoral Outcomes', *Quarterly Journal of Economics*, vol.123, no.2, pp.703–45. https://doi.org/10.1162/qjec.2008.123.2.703

Glennerster, Rachel; Miguel, Edward; and Rothenberg, Alexander (2010) 'Collective Action in Diverse Sierra Leone Communities', NBER Working Papers 16196, National Bureau of Economic Research. https://doi.org/10.3386/w16196

Guiso, Luigi; Sapienza, Paola; and Zingales, Luigi (2003) 'People's Opium? Religion and Economic Attitudes', *Journal of Monetary Economics*, vol.50, no.1, pp.225–82. https://doi.org/10.1016/S0304-3932(02)00202-7

Habyarimana, James; Humphreys, Macartan; Posner, Daniel N.; and Weinstein, Jeremy M. (2007) 'Why Does Ethnic Diversity Undermine Public Goods Provision?' *The American Political Science Review*, vol.101, no.4, pp.709–25. https://doi.org/10.1017/S0003055407070499

Hungerman, Daniel M. (2007) 'Diversity and Crowd-Out: A Theory of Cold-Glow Giving', NBER Working Papers 13348, National Bureau of Economic Research. https://doi.org/10.3386/w13348

Jiang, Lin (1995) 'Changing Kinship Structure and Its Implications for Old-Age Support in Urban and Rural China', *Population Studies*, vol.49, no.1, pp.127–45. https://doi.org/10.1080/0032472031000148286

Khwaja, Asim Ijaz (2009) 'Can Good Projects Succeed in Bad Communities?' *Journal of Public Economics*, vol.93, no.7–8, pp.899–916. https://doi.org/10.1016/j.jpubeco.2009.02.010

Lai, Hongyi Harry (2003) 'The Religious Revival in China', *Copenhagen Journal of Asian Studies*, vol.18, pp.40–64. https://doi.org/10.22439/cjas.v18i0.19

Lipset, Seymour Martin (1959) 'Some Social Requisites of Democracy: Economic Development and Political Legitimacy', *The American Political Science Review*, vol.53, no.1, pp.69–105. https://doi.org/10.2307/1951731

Lizzeri, Alessandro and Persico, Nicola (2004) 'Why Did the Elites Extend the Suffrage? Democracy and the Scope of Government with an Application to Britain's "Age of Reform"', *The Quarterly Journal of Economics*, vol.119, pp.707–65. https://doi.org/10.1162/0033553041382175

Luo, Renfu; Zhang, Linxiu; Huang, Jikun; and Rozelle, Scott (2010) 'Village Elections, Public Goods Investments and Pork Barrel Politics, Chinese-style', *Journal of Development Studies*, vol.46, no.4, pp.662–84. https://doi.org/10.1080/00220380903318061

Luttmer, Erzo F.P. (2001) 'Group Loyalty and the Taste for Redistribution', *Journal of Political Economy*, vol.109, no.3, pp.500–28. https://doi.org/10.1086/321019

Martinez-Bravo, Monica; Padró i Miquel, Gerard; Qian, Nancy; and Yao, Yang (2022) 'The Rise and Fall of Local Elections in China', *American Economic Review*, vol.112, pp.2921–58. https://doi.org/10.1257/aer.20181249

Martinez-Bravo, Monica; Padró i Miquel, Gerard; Qian, Nancy; Xu, Yiqing; and Yao, Yang (2015) 'Making Democracy Work: Formal Institutions and Culture in Rural China', Technical Report 21058, NBER Working Paper. https://gerardpadro.com/working-papers/scap_20170606.pdf

Miguel, Edward and Gugerty, Mary Kay (2005) 'Ethnic Diversity, Social Sanctions, and Public Goods in Kenya', *Journal of Public Economics*, vol.89, no.11–12, 2325–68. https://doi.org/10.1016/j.jpubeco.2004.09.004

Montalvo, Jose and Reynal-Querol, Marta (2005) 'Ethnic Diversity and Economic Development', *Journal of Development Economics*, vol.76, no.293–323. https://doi.org/10.1016/j.jdeveco.2004.01.002

Mu, Ren and Zhang, Xiaobo (2011) 'The Role of Elected and Appointed Village Leaders in the Allocation of Public Resources: Evidence from a Low-Income Region in China', IF-PRI Working Paper International Food and Policy Research Institute. http://www.ifpri.org/sites/default/files/publications/ifpridp01061.pdf

Munshi, Kaivan; and Rosenzweig, Mark (2008) 'The Efficacy of Parochial Politics: Caste, Commitment, and Competence in Indian Local Governments', NBER Working Papers 14335, National Bureau of Economic Research. https://doi.org/10.3386/w14335

Munshi, Kaivan; Rosenzweig, Mark; and Wilson, Nicholas (2010) 'Identity and Mobility: Historical Fractionalization, Parochial Institutions, and Occupational Choice in the American Midwest', Department of Economics Working Papers 2010–22, Williams College. https://core.ac.uk/download/pdf/6223838.pdf

Okten, Cagla and Osili, Una Okonkwo (2004) 'Contributions in Heterogeneous Communities: Evidence from Indonesia', *Journal of Population Economics*, vol.17, no.4, pp.603–26. https://doi.org/10.1007/s00148-004-0189-y

Olken, Benjamin A. (2010) 'Direct Democracy and Local Public Goods: Evidence from a Field Experiment in Indonesia', *American Political Science Review*, vol.2, pp.243–67. https://doi.org/10.1017/S0003055410000079

Padró i Miquel, Gerard (2007) 'The Control of Politicians in Divided Societies: The Politics of Fear', *The Review of Economic Studies*, vol.74, pp.1259–74. https://doi.org/10.1111/j.1467-937X.2007.00455.x

Tsai, Lily Lee (2007) *Accountability without Democracy: Solidary Groups and Public Goods Provision in Rural China*, New York: Cambridge University Press. https://doi.org/10.1017/CBO9780511800115

Vigdor, Jacob L. (2004) 'Community Composition and Collective Action: Analyzing Initial Mail Response to the 2000 Census', *Review of Economics and Statistics*, vol.86, no.1, pp.303–12. https://doi.org/10.1162/003465304323023822

Weber, M. (1968) *The Religion of China: Confucianism and Taoism*, New York: Free Press.

Yang, Ching Kun (1961) *Religion in Chinese Society: A Study of Contemporary Social Functions of Religion and Some of Their Historical Factors*, Los Angeles, CA: University of California Press.

Zhang, Xiaobo; Fan, Shenggen; Zhang, Linxiu; and Huang, Jikun (2004) 'Local Governance and Public Goods Provision in Rural China', *Journal of Public Economics*, vol.88, pp.2857–71. https://doi.org/10.1016/j.jpubeco.2003.07.004

7. How does fiscal decentralisation affect local polities? Evidence from local communities in Indonesia

Anirban Mitra and Sarmistha Pal

Summary

How fiscal decentralisation (FD) affects the selection of local leaders remains largely unexplored. We utilise Indonesia's important fiscal decentralisation to local communities in 2001 to study such issues. Using the 1997 and 2007 Indonesian Family Life Survey (IFLS) data, we observed communities practising majority voting (electoral democracy), consensus-building (participatory democracy) and also oligarchy (leaders selected by the local elite). The incidence of democracy (voting and consensus-building taken together) did not increase significantly after FD. Leader selection by consensus-building declined while that by voting increased. We show that community homogeneity has been an important driver of leader selection by consensus-building. However, after decentralisation, ethnically diverse communities increasingly opted for choosing leaders by voting. Furthermore, voting (relative to consensus-building) communities registered higher income and development spending after FD, suggesting the salience of local political entrepreneurship. In a fiscally decentralised environment, enterprising local political leaders can facilitate the aligning of economic interests in ethnically diverse communities, especially if ambient economic inequality is low.

How to cite this book chapter:

Mitra, Anirban and Pal, Sarmistha (2023) 'How does fiscal decentralisation affect local polities? Evidence from communities in Indonesia', in: Faguet, Jean-Paul and Pal, Sarmistha (eds) *Decentralised Governance: Crafting Effective Democracies Around the World*, London: LSE Press, pp. 181–208. https://doi.org/10.31389/lsepress.dlg.g License: CC BY 4.0

Fiscal decentralisation involves the devolution of power to local authorities in terms of either or both of the following: (i) raising local revenue (through local taxes and so on) and (ii) making decisions regarding the spending of revenue at the local levels. In principle, this process can be quite distinct from political decentralisation, which involves the transfer of political power to local levels of government, sometimes resulting in the creation of local tiers of government. On its own, fiscal decentralisation (hereafter FD) leaves local governance unchanged – specifically, the rules regarding the election or selection of local leaders are not directly affected by the FD process. So, while it is quite natural to expect a different pattern of budgetary allocations and spending at the local level following FD, any potential changes in the *dynamics* of local polities are less obvious. However, this does not preclude the possibility that FD has an indirect effect on the dynamics of local governance structures. In fact, Bardhan and Mookherjee (2006) argued that these two processes are usually enmeshed:

> Many developing countries have thus begun to experiment with initiatives to increase accountability of service providers by providing greater control rights to citizen groups. These include decentralisation of service delivery to local governments, community participation, direct transfers to households and contracting out delivery to private providers and NGOs. The programmes include a wide range of infrastructure services (water, sanitation, electricity, telecommunications, roads) and social services (education, health and welfare programmes).

We explore the broad issue of the link between FD and the dynamics of local polities with a view to identifying their key drivers. We highlight the potential implications of fiscal devolution on the change in local leadership regimes and suggest how specific socio-economic factors may be relevant to explaining the flux in local leadership selection following expenditure shifts. To the best of our knowledge, this is a vastly under-researched area. While there is a rich literature on FD, there has been little or no work on examining its ramifications for the organisation of local governance.

Our empirical investigation is motivated by the experience of Indonesia, a large emerging economy. The country undertook a comprehensive programme of FD at the turn of the millennium, which roughly coincided with the end of President Suharto's rule. Indonesia is also diverse along many socio-economic markers and forms of local governance, thus making it a very apt candidate for the issues we seek to explore. The remainder of this chapter is organised as follows. We begin by describing how FD was implemented within Indonesia, and how this change combined with the different ways in which communities selected their local leaders. Section 7.2 gives a brief critical review of related literature and sets out our hypotheses. The third section covers our data and empirical analysis approaches, and Section 7.4 presents our empirical findings.

7.1 Fiscal decentralisation in Indonesia

FD in post-Suharto Indonesia has its roots in Law 22/99 and Law 25/99, enacted in January 2001. The change involved was largely an exogenous event for the communities under consideration. It gave local communities more autonomy in raising local revenues, while enforcing strict budgetary cuts on the central government leadership to supply development grants to these communities. It also granted administrative authority to local governments to hire staff and conduct local government affairs with minimum intervention from the central government. Local community governments were made responsible to the district (instead of the central) government, and the district provided the bulk of their funds after FD.

It is fair to claim that the centre of power moved from the central government in Jakarta to the 357 districts (*kabupaten*s), located in the district headquarters after FD. This institutional set-up allows us to study the impact of exogenously given FD on transition of local polities within districts. Using the Indonesian Family Life Survey (IFLS) data, we consider these 312 local communities drawn from 13 provinces (representing 83 per cent of Indonesian population) in 1997 and 2007, two years separated by the introduction of Law 22/99 and Law 25/99 in 2001, which were largely exogenous for the communities under consideration. The communities represent the lowest level of administrative structure in Indonesia within a district that still have an independent political identity. They can be rural villages (*desa*s) or urban townships (*kelurahan*s). The IFLS data allow us to categorise local polities as 'democratic' if the community leader is elected by voting or consensus-building among all citizens, and 'non-democratic' (or oligarchic) if the leader is 'chosen' by a few citizens including the local elite, local institutions, and/or outside influence.

Our method of characterising local political transition focuses on changes to the method of leader selection in a given community (within a district that governed them) after FD. In particular, our analysis lets us distinguish between electoral (majority voting) and participatory (*Musyawarah-Mufakat*) democracies prevalent in Indonesia. The latter is a form of Indonesian customary decision-making based on deliberation and consensus-building, which has regularly been recognised in village gatherings. The term *Musyawarah-Mufakat* (together with the terms *koperasi* and *gotong royong*) has to do with the obligations of the individual toward the community, the compatibility of power, and the relation of state authority to traditional social and political systems.

The method of leader selection is important in terms of policy implementation at the local level and the provision of local public goods, especially in a fiscally decentralised setting. Whether the leader of a community reflects the preferences of the entire populace or is only sensitive to the needs of a select few ('the local elite') is likely to determine the pattern of local public spending and thereby social welfare in the community. In fact, the greater the control over the local 'purse strings' (courtesy of FD), the more crucial the role of the local leadership's preferences become, underlying the need for a fuller understanding of how community leaders are selected. With the introduction of the '1979 village law', village affairs were brought under the supervision and close control of higher authorities. Since 1979, the heads of villages classified as '*desa*' have been elected in village-level elections held every eight years, while the heads of '*kelurahan*' villages (urban/city) were appointed by upper levels of administration. Hence, Indonesia has been a culturally and politically decentralised nation even though local leader selections may have been controlled by the central regime under Suharto. While one may debate the de facto politically decentralised status under Suharto's regime, the nation was unambiguously within the tight grips of central fiscal control until 2001.

The FD changes led to a dramatic shift in the sources of revenues for village governments, also shown in Table 7.1. Data from the village governance module in the IFLS shows a substantial increase in the share of revenues that came from the district-level government and a corresponding decline in the share of revenues from the central government, between 1997 and 2007. In 1997, on average, nearly a third of the revenue came from direct grants made by the central government in Jakarta. By 2007, the central government's average contribution in village budgets had drastically fallen to under 7 per cent. By contrast, the average contribution from the district-level government to communities had risen from just 9 to 41 per cent between 1997 and 2007. The share of total revenues generated *within* the village itself remained roughly unchanged between 1997 and 2007.

Electoral versus participatory democracies in Indonesia

Consensus-building or participatory democracy has its root in *Musyawarah-Mufakat*, which is a form of Indonesian native culture of consensus-building. It has been adopted as one of the foundational philosophical theories of the Indonesian state (*Pancasila*) and become a method of decision-making in the wider Indonesian government. *Musyawarah-Mufakat* is borrowed from Islamic learning, which prioritises a peaceful approach (*Sulh*) in settling a conflict. During Sukarno's time of 'guided democracy', the 1945 Constitution included approval of *Mufakat* (unanimous consent) as the basis for decision-making for the legislature. This was promoted for upholding the Indonesian identity and as a rejection of the Western majority voting rule, which was seen as driving the parties to battle for their own narrow interests at the cost of the national interests. The establishment of *Musyawarah* is an implementation of the *gotong royong* (that is, mutual cooperation or assistance) philosophy prevalent in most Indonesian village communities.

Table 7.1: Fiscal decentralisation and changes in community revenues and spending

Variables	1997 Mean	(StdDev)	2007 Mean	(StdDev)
Total spending (’000 Rp) [3] on				
social infrastructure	164	(318)	1,057.2	(2633)
physical infrastructure	75.1	(135)	1,540	(2659)
Share of spending (%) on				
social infrastructure	10.8	(11.5)	12.8	(19.6)
physical infrastructure	6.58	(8.4)	49.9	(36.9)
Total revenue (’000 Rp) [3] from				
central government	67.3	(164)	146.6	(528)
provincial government	135.2	(376)	673.8	(2086)
district government	2,214	(63.4)	523.3	(898.4)
local income	235.5	(726)	2,393.7	(10,0961)
Share of revenues (%) coming from				
central government	32.9	(31.2)	6.6	(17.5)
provincial government	14.4	(29.2)	13.5	(26.8)
district government	9.1	(18.8)	40.7	(34.8)
local income	37.9	(37.8)	39.3	(32.6)

Source: Authors' calculation using the IFLS data sample.
Note: The table summarises the average revenue and spending details (both total and as shares of the total) of the sample communities before (1997) and after (2007) FD. All nominal variables are measured at 2010 price level. Std Dev = standard deviation. *Total community spending* includes spending on new investment (social and physical infrastructure), maintenance of existing infrastructure and also that on paying staff salaries and transfers.
Total community revenue is generated from grants from central, provincial and district governments and also funds raised from local communities. The remaining balance is accounted for by various governmental transfers under different development programmes.

Under the Suharto government, although village heads were elected by villagers, they were generally perceived to be part of the government's state apparatus, and, because they controlled the entire village government, that was in turn perceived to be part of the central state apparatus (Hidayat and Antlov 2004). As such, the role of *Musyawarah-Mufakat* might have been limited. The fall of the Suharto government in 1998 marked the introduction of the Reformation Era as democratisation and decentralisation laws were launched. This period bore witness to (i) the provincial and district governments using their new authority to adopt local laws on a range of ethical and spiritual issues, and (ii) a reawakening of customary law, based on the implementation of *Musyawarah-Mufakat*.

The 1997 and 2007 rounds of the IFLS survey asked community leaders about how a leader was selected in their area, which we use to classify these communities. Answers to this question were coded as: A voting, B all residents, C local elites, D local institutions, and E others. Because it is not clear how the 'others' (code E) selected their local leaders, we excluded these communities from our analysis. We classified the remaining local polities as follows: 'democratic' if a leader is selected by free and fair elections, with voters being all community members (codes A and B), and 'oligarchic' if a leader is selected by community elites (codes C and D), who then remain uncontested. Further, we subdivide democratic communities into two categories: 'electoral' when the leader is elected by majority voting (code A) and 'participatory' when the leader is selected by consensus-building (code B).

Table 7.2 shows that, in 1997, 36 per cent of sample communities practised majority voting and 29 per cent consensus-building; the remaining 35 per cent of communities were oligarchic. In 2007, the share of communities adhering to democracy (voting plus consensus-building taken together) changed only very slightly, from 65 to nearly 68 per cent, which in turn means that the incidence of oligarchy stayed at a third of the sample communities. However, the percentage of communities opting for voting went up to 57 per cent, and those choosing consensus-building fell below 11 per cent. In general, a higher proportion of rural communities adhered to democracy while a higher proportion of urban communities adhered to oligarchy in both years.

Table 7.2: The proportion (%) of communities using different methods to select community leaders

Method of selection	1997			2007		
	Rural	**Urban**	**Total**	**Rural**	**Urban**	**Total**
Voting	53.3	26.0	36.5	83.3	40.6	57.1
Consensus	31.7	27.6	29.2	12.5	9.4	10.6
Oligarchy	15.0	46.4	34.3	4.2	50.0	32.4
Total	**100%**	**100%**	**100%**	**100%**	**100%**	**100.1%**
N of cases	120	192	312	120	192	312

Source: Authors' calculation using the IFLS data sample.
Notes: The original sample of communities totalled 317, but five cases where the mode of leadership selection could not be determined in both 1997 and 2007 were left out of the sample, leaving N = 312.
The table summarises the methods of selection of community leaders in rural and urban communities in 1997 and 2007 in our sample. We classify communities into three types: 'consensus-building' among community members, 'voting' and 'oligarchies' where the leader is elected by the local elite (religious or legal leaders) or government officials. 'Consensus' = 1 if the community leader is selected by consensus-building through meetings; 'Voting' = 1 if the community leader is elected by voting; 'Oligarchy' = 1 if the community leader is selected by few elites. Each cell represents the percentage (%) of communities as a share of the column total.

In part, this was the result of Village Law 1979, which retained the power of the government to select leaders for urban communities. Incidence of oligarchy was more prevalent in urban communities, which further increased after FD. About 71 per cent of sample communities tend to be politically stable. Only 91 of 312 total sample communities (that is, about 29 per cent of the total) saw a change in the local polity.

Nearly two-thirds of the communities did *not* change local polity after FD and were 'stable' voting (30 per cent), or 'stable' consensus-building (14 per cent) or 'stable' oligarchies (19 per cent). Moreover, there were 107 communities in 1997 that were oligarchic and the number only slightly dipped to 102 in 2007 – so there was no drastic trend towards democratisation on the heels of FD. Table 7.2 shows that about 16 per cent of participatory democracies (that is, consensus-building) and 12 per cent of oligarchies had opted for majority voting after FD. There were also some instances of new oligarchies being created: somewhat under one in 20 voting communities and one in 11 consensus-building communities turned oligarchic in 2007.

The IFLS data also provided information on the process of decision-making used within the sample communities. As with leader selection, this could be classified into voting decisions, consensus-building, and oligarchies (determined by local elites and local institutions) in both 1997 and 2007. Overall, two-thirds of the communities practised consensus-building for decision-making in 1997 and 2007. The elites dominated the decision-making process in about 29 per cent of communities. So, the use of voting remained negligible for decision-making in both years. The picture does not change much even when we consider the communities where the leader was elected through voting. In other words, any change in outcomes at the community-level would essentially arise from the change in the process of leader selection rather than that of decision-making per se. Whether the leader of a community reflects the preferences of the entire populace or is sensitive only to the needs of a select few would determine the pattern of local public spending/development and thereby shape social welfare in the community.

Democratic processes and ethnic diversity

Electoral democracies rely on obtaining majoritarian support and thus minorities tend to get overlooked. Given this issue with electoral democracy, some scholars (for example, Mansuri and Rao 2013; Sanyal and Rao 2018) have advocated direct and participatory democracy to enable the forming of a consensus. However, the success of such schemes relies (too) heavily on the presence of community homogeneity. This is because discourse tends to be similar among communities characterised by similarities in language, culture, and institutions. If this is indeed the case, good governance via participatory democracy would tend to be elusive in ethnically diverse societies.

And, to look ahead a little to our analysis results (Section 7.4), we do indeed find a robust and consistent association between the extent of ethnic diversity at the community level and the changes to the method of leader selection in the wake of fiscal decentralisation. Ethnically diverse (homogeneous) communities were more likely to choose electoral (participatory) democracy after FD. Moreover, the emergence of new electoral democracies is significantly higher in the ethnically diverse rural (relative to urban) communities. In sum, ethnically diverse communities tend to opt for 'voting' rather than 'consensus-building' as the method for leader selection, and this phenomenon is accentuated in rural areas. Our finding here suggests that ethnically diverse communities recognise the futility of consensus-building (given the inherent differences) and opt for the ballot.

To explore this matter in more depth, Indonesia offers an ideal 'laboratory'. It is one of the most ethnically diverse countries in the world and consists of 1,300 ethnic groups, with at least 95 per cent native to the archipelago. The six largest ethnic groups make up more than two-thirds of the country's total population: they are the Javanese, Sundanese (western Java), Batak (north Sumatra), Sulawesi, Madurese (predominantly Muslims), and Betawi (native Jakartan). Minority groups who were originally migrants (such as the Chinese, Arab, and Indian populations) make up the remaining 5 per cent. Additionally, our analysis shows that, after FD, communities, especially more ethnically diverse ones that chose electoral democracies, had greater ability to raise local incomes (both from self-reliant efforts and total income) and development spending (both total and as share of total community spending).

So, what may be the possible channels through which FD influences the observed dynamics in local polity? The core idea is the following: FD offers greater local autonomy and thus increases the perceived 'rents' (psychological, pecuniary, and so on) from holding office at local levels of government. Hence, the identity of the local leader assumes extra importance. In ethnically homogeneous communities, consensus-building continues to hold sway. In ethnically diverse communities, however, the increase in 'rents' received post-decentralisation exacerbates the existing differences among the various groups. Thus, consensus-building becomes untenable and there is a movement towards electoral democracy. Moreover, the high stakes (post-FD) environment leads to the emergence of entrepreneurial local leaders in these communities. The ones who are able to align the economic interests of the ethnically diverse groups tend to succeed and also help raise local incomes and generate more development. This is understandably easier where economic inequality is lower.[1] We document some evidence in support of this mechanism in terms of greater leader turnover too.

In sum, it appears that FD in Indonesia provided an additional impetus to ethnically diverse communities to lead to a reorganisation of their local polities. Our analysis highlights how entrepreneurial local leaders in an electoral democracy may successfully align economic interests of ethnically diverse citizens after FD. These results may have wider implications for other ethnically diverse emerging economies beyond the Indonesian border.

7.2 Literature and hypotheses

There is a burgeoning literature on decentralisation, particularly, FD. Several of these studies analyse the effects of some aggregate measure of decentralisation on public policy and development in cross-country set-up (for example, Enikolopov and Zhuravskaya 2007). Relatedly, the substantial literature on capture by interest groups via vote-buying, co-optation, and patronage networks at a more local level is closer to our study.[2] Our finding that the dynamics in local polities relied on local politicians who can generate local income/spending decisions finds support in Besley, Pande, and Rao (2005), who also focused on how the identity of the local politicians affects the quality of decentralised governance.

There has been a general consensus in development economics that ethnic diversity is detrimental to development.[3] This view is being challenged by more recent findings. For instance, Ashraf and Galor (2013) pointed out that diversity could have both positive and negative impacts on economic outcomes. The findings of Gomes (2020) in the context of health outcomes have a similar flavour. We shall see below that our analysis also supports the argument that ethnically diverse electoral democracies may promote income and development more when inequality is not too high.

The literature on political entrepreneurship is also relatively sparse. William Riker (1986) showed how a political entrepreneur can advantageously transform existing political coalitions, especially by adding a new dimension to political debates. In this perspective political entrepreneurs are people who change the course of a policy (Schneider and Teske 1992). We add to this literature by exploring how local entrepreneurship can help overcome collective action problems in ethnically diverse societies, thus promoting income and development in electoral democracies.

Our focus on local leadership resonates with several studies that document how the leader's identity (ethnic or gender) can matter for various policy outcomes. Earmarking political office for members from various marginalised ethnic groups has sometimes been found to be effective – in the sense of fostering their interests. For instance, Pande (2003) and Chin and Prakash (2011) provided supportive evidence in the case of India, where reservation has been in place for decades in favour of historically disadvantaged groups called the scheduled castes (SCs) and the scheduled tribes (STs). Other studies suggest that the effects may be heterogeneous within the minorities (Mitra 2018) or may not be persistent (Bhavnani 2017; Jensenius 2015). In the context of Kenya during the 1963–2011 period, Burgess et al. (2015) found strong evidence of ethnic favouritism in road-building during periods of autocracy.

Our work adds to the literature on local governmental policy in emerging economies. In ethnically diverse societies, Bandiera and Levy (2011) argued that the elite are able to distort policy in their favour, owing to the difference in ethnicity-based preferences among the non-elites. Their empirical analysis using the 1997 Indonesian Family Life Survey data showed that democratic policy outcomes were closer to the elite preferences in ethnically diverse decentralised communities. Padró i Miquel, Qian, and Yao (2014 and Chapter 6 in this volume) examined the case of rural China to demonstrate that one of the preconditions for exogenously introduced grassroots democracy to be effective is the degree of community homogeneity in some vertical attribute (religion in their case) that allows better provision of public goods. Within decentralised communities in Indonesia, Mitra and Pal (2021) documented that the adverse effects of ethnic diversity could be counteracted by social norms that promote cooperative behaviour. Mansuri and Rao (2013) assessed the impact of large-scale, policy-driven efforts to induce participation in decentralised communities. They found that the participants tended to be wealthier and more politically connected, indicating a high cost of participation for the poor. Relatedly, Martinez-Bravo, Mukherjee, and Stegmann (2017) showed that allowing agents of the old-regime to remain in office during democratic transitions was a key determinant of the extent of subsequent elite capture.[4]

We add to the above literature here by highlighting an important difference between ethnically homogeneous and ethnically diverse communities following FD – namely, their different proclivities towards participatory and electoral democracies. Our findings also highlight that local political entrepreneurship may help align the economic interests of citizens in ethnically diverse electoral democracies, thus aiding efforts to overcome the collective action problems in ethnically diverse societies, especially if inequality is relatively low.

Hypotheses

The existing literature shows specific advantages of voting (electoral democracy) over consensus-building (participatory democracy).[5] Mansuri and Rao (2013) posited that the poor are often excluded from the process of consensus-building, raising concerns about genuine representation of all interests in this set-up. We draw upon this literature to build our key hypotheses for explaining a community's choice between electoral and participatory democracy.

Ethnic homogeneity and leader selection after FD. FD increases the importance of the local leader. Hence, all constituent ethnic groups take greater interest in the selection of the leader. If a community is largely ethnically homogeneous, the selection can take place by consensus-building; after all, the associated costs of discussion and deliberation are low owing to the uniformity in culture and thereby preferences over public goods, and so on. Such costs, however, are substantially higher for ethnically diverse communities which might derail consensus-building. Therefore, these communities tend toward electoral democracy for selecting leaders post-FD. This generates our first hypothesis, which is recorded below.

Hypothesis 1: Ethnically homogeneous (heterogeneous) communities are more likely to choose participatory (electoral) democracy to select leaders.

Local polity and local entrepreneurship after decentralisation. Following FD, the ethnically diverse communities that choose electoral democracy 'open up' the political space for competition. Given the possibility of higher 'rents' from holding (local) office in the post-FD scenario, this spurs the more entrepreneurial potential leaders into action. As a result, these communities tend to have higher local incomes and more development. Moreover, this effect is accentuated in communities where the ambient economic inequality is low – it is easier for the leader to implement better policies when the economic interests are more closely aligned. This leads us to the following hypothesis.

Hypothesis 2: Ethnically diverse communities choosing electoral democracies after FD generate higher local incomes and more development, especially when the ambient economic inequality is low.

7.3 Empirical analysis

Our analysis is based on the community-level data obtained from 1997 and 2007 rounds of Indonesian Family Life Survey (IFLS) from a sample of 312 rural and urban communities, drawn from 13 provinces including Jakarta, Bali, Java (central, east and south), Sumatra (north, west and south), Lampung, West Nusa Tenggara, and South Kalimantan, representing 83 per cent of Indonesian population.[6] This is a particularly rich data set that provides community-level information on a whole range of demographic characteristics, local governance and its public finances, and citizens' participation in planning and implementation of local development projects, as well as a range of public utilities, infrastructure and transport, health, and education facilities. (See Frankenberg and Thomas (2000) and Strauss et al. (2009) for the study design and overview of the data set.)

The IFLS data available for the adjacent years 1998 and 2000 reveal that there were no local elections in the sample communities during those two years. This is not unexpected as the country faced widespread economic and political turmoil during 1997–99. The first elected president (Wahhid) took office in October 1999. Things started to get back to normal from the turn of the century, paving the way for Law 22/99 and Law 25/99 to be introduced officially in January 2001. Community-level elections in the post-FD period did not all take place at the same time. About 80 per cent of post-FD local elections had been completed by 2003 since they involved a fair amount of administrative change as part of the new decentralisation rules (Rodriguez and Meirelles 2010). Although we cannot observe the precise timing of the local elections for the sample communities, we observe the tenure of the community leaders in 1997 and 2007. Given that the term of office of a community leader since 2001 has been five years, it is most likely that those community leaders in power in 2007 were ones selected or elected from 2002 onwards.

Following FD, the central government provided grants to district authorities using a 'fiscal needs' formula based on various district-level characteristics (Pal and Wahhaj 2017). These factors are invariant across communities *within* the same district. By employing *district fixed effects*, our estimation strategy compares various aspects of local polities before and after FD within a district.

The effect of community homogeneity on choice of local polity

First, we explore Hypothesis 1, about the effect of community homogeneity on local polity (voting, consensus-building, or democratisation) following FD. We take community homogeneity to be exogenous, because the population composition has remained largely invariant over the decade between 1997 and 2007 in the sample communities. The dependent variable Y accordingly takes the form of the following three variables in alternative specifications:

a. democratisation (status_v): takes the value 1 if a community leader is selected by voting (code A) or consensus-building (code B) and 0 otherwise (denoting oligarchy);
b. consensus-building (consensus): takes the value 1 if a community leader is selected by consensus-building (code B) and 0 otherwise; and
c. voting (voting): takes the value 1 if a community leader is selected by voting (code A) and 0 otherwise.

This motivates the following empirical specification in community i in district j in year t:

$$\begin{aligned} Y_{ijt} = {} & \beta_0 + \beta_1 FD_t + \beta_2 Homog_{ijt} + \beta_3 (FD_t x \beta_2 Homog_{ijt}) \\ & + \beta_4 X_{ijt} + \beta_5 (FD_t x X_{ijt}) + D_j + \upsilon_{ijt}, \end{aligned} \quad [1]$$

Equation [1] thus allows us to identify the determinants of the likelihood of a local polity choosing a leader by voting, consensus-building or more generally democratisation, thus giving rise to Model 1, Model 2, and Model 3, respectively:

$$\begin{aligned} \text{Model 1:} \quad Consensus_{ijt} = {} & \beta_0 + \beta_1 FD_t + \beta_2 Homog_{ijt} + \beta_3 (FD_t x \beta_2 Homog_{ijt}) \\ & + \beta_4 X_{ijt} + \beta_5 (FD_t x X_{ijt}) + D_j + \upsilon_{ijt}, \end{aligned}$$

$$\begin{aligned} \text{Model 2:} \quad Voting_{ijt} = {} & \beta_0 + \beta_1 FD_t + \beta_2 Homog_{ijt} + \beta_3 (FD_t x \beta_2 Homog_{ijt}) \\ & + \beta_4 X_{ijt} + \beta_5 (FD_t x X_{ijt}) + D_j + \upsilon_{ijt}, \end{aligned}$$

Model 3:

$$Democratisation_{ijt} = \beta_0 + \beta_1 FD_t + \beta_2 Homog_{ijt} + \beta_3 (FD_t \times \beta_2 Homog_{ijt})$$
$$+ \beta_4 X_{ijt} + \beta_5 (FD_t \times X_{ijt}) + D_j + \upsilon_{ijt},$$

The explanatory variables included in all three models are the same as listed below:

Measure of fiscal decentralisation: we proxy fiscal decentralisation by the binary variable *FD* that takes a value 1 for the year 2007 and 0 for 1997.

Measure of community homogeneity: our key explanatory variable is ethnic homogeneity (*Homog*) of the community. In this respect, we consider two measures of homogeneity. We observe the size of the top three population groups, 1, 2, 3, in the sample communities in 1997 and 2007, which together exhaust the total community population. The median value of the largest population group across our sample communities is 91 per cent. Our first measure of ethnic homogeneity is: *Pop1_91*, which equals 1 if the population of the largest group in the community is greater than or equal to the median value; it is 0 otherwise. Our second index is *Pop1_100*, which equals 1 if the population of the largest group in the community is 100 per cent and is 0 otherwise.[7]

X contains other community characteristics that may also influence the outcome variables to mitigate omitted variables bias. These include the community's population, its geographic size (in hectares), whether it is rural or urban, and whether Islam is the main religion. We also include interactions of all these community characteristics with the fiscal decentralisation dummy *FD* as included in $FD_t \times X_{ijt}$ to account for the differential effects of FD by community characteristics.

Finally, we include a set of district dummy variables *Dj* for the *j*th district in our sample. Inclusion of these district-level dummies accounts for time-invariant unobserved factors at district level that may also influence the outcomes of interest.

FD accounts for the common shock to all districts after fiscal decentralisation. The coefficient of interest is β_3, which is the coefficient of the interaction term with community homogeneity ($FD_t \times Homog_{ijt}$). This captures the differential effect of local homogeneity on various measures of local polities after FD, after controlling for all other factors.

Local polity and local political entrepreneurship

Next, we examine Hypothesis 2, which concerns the link between local polity and local political entrepreneurship. We measure the local entrepreneurship of the community leader by the size of local income and local development spending in the community. We proxy local income by local revenue generated from various sources. Local development is measured by spending on new social and physical infrastructure plus the maintenance of existing social infrastructure (such as schools and health facilities) and physical infrastructure (such as roads and transport connections) at the local community level.

Given that some concerns may arise about biased estimation, owing to the simultaneity between local polities and local revenue/development spending in sample communities, we use propensity score matching (PSM) methods to compute the average treatment effects on the treated (ATT). In particular, we consider voting and consensus-building for selection of community leaders as the two possible treatments in alternative specifications; the rest are considered as a control. A successful implementation of PSM methods requires that the treatment and control groups are comparable in terms of all observable covariates. We use the same set of covariates X as in Equation [1] to determine the likelihood of relevant local polities, that is, *voting* and *consensus*. The propensity score is the probability of receiving a treatment T, conditional on the observable covariates X. The idea is to compare communities that have a very similar probability of receiving the treatment (similar propensity score) based on some observables X, but where some localities received the treatment while others did not. Thus, for a given propensity score, the exposure to treatment is random and therefore the treated and control units should be observationally identical.

Next, we classify our sample communities into blocks of observations with similar propensity scores for both treatment (T) and control (C) groups. Within each block of communities, the means of the outcomes (O) of interest are the natural logarithm of total local income and total local development spending. We test whether they are equal in the treatment and control groups. Thus, we derive the average treatment effect on the treated ATT for each outcome variable as follows:

$$ATT = (O_T - O_C)_{2007} - (O_T - O_C)_{1997} \qquad [2]$$

We use Equation [2] to determine the ATT for local income and local development spending for the chosen treatments (*voting* and *consensus*) relative to the control in 2007 (relative to 1997).

7.4 Results

We start with the effects of community homogeneity, as in Equation [1], on measures of local polity including consensus-building, voting, and any form of democratisation that includes both consensus-building and voting together. Next, we present the effects of the local polity on local income and development in our sample, as in Equation [2]. Finally, we explore some possible mechanisms that may lie behind our results.

The effects of community homogeneity on the local polity

We begin here with Table 7.3, which summarises the ordinary least squares (OLS) estimates in our full sample following Equation [1]. Columns 1–3 show

Table 7.3: Effects of community homogeneity on local polities

a. Homogeneity measured by the top ethnic group having above median population (pop1_91)

Explanatory variables	Dependent variable showing effects *(standard errors)*					
	Model 1: Consensus		**Model 2: Voting**		**Model 3: Democratisation**	
FD (shock)	−0.454	*(0.460)*	1.001*	*(0.523)*	−0.1633	*(0.198)*
pop1_91	−0.107	*(0.072)*	0.185***	*(0.054)*	0.0273	*(0.040)*
pop1_91×FD	0.178**	*(0.068)*	−0.093*	*(0.055)*	0.097*	*(0.052)*
Constant	0.567	*(0.352)*	−0.256	*(0.269)*	1.1941***	*(0.289)*
Other controls	Yes		Yes		Yes	
District dummies	Yes		Yes		Yes	
Observations	616		616		616	
R-squared	0.158		0.351		0.500	

b. Homogeneity measured by the top ethnic group having 100% or not (pop1_100)

Explanatory variables	Dependent variable showing effects *(standard errors)*					
	Model 4: Consensus		**Model 5: Voting**		**Model 6: Democratisation**	
FD (shock)	−0.522	*(0.369)*	1.021**	*(0.500)*	−0.036	*(0.158)*
pop1_100	−0.107	*(0.073)*	0.145**	*(0.069)*	0.112	*(0.069)*
pop1_100×FD	0.219***	*(0.071)*	−0.137	*(0.088)*	0.010	*(0.037)*
Constant	0.5482	*(0.328)*	−0.1481	*(0.255)*	1.1797***	*(0.290)*
Other controls	Yes		Yes		Yes	
District dummies	Yes		Yes		Yes	
Observations	616		616		616	
R-squared	0.160		0.341		0.502	

Source: As for Table 7.2.
Note: All estimates are clustered by districts; cluster-robust standard errors are shown in parentheses and italics. Significance levels: ***$p < 0.01$, **$p < 0.05$, *$p < 0.1$. We pool data for 1997 and 2007 together to run the regressions. The total number of regression observations is less than the 624 (312 + 312) cases shown in Table 7.2 because of some missing observations for some variables.

the estimates of Models 1–3 of three measures of local polities, namely consensus-building, voting, and any democratisation (status_v) using pop1_91 as the relevant measure of community homogeneity. Columns 4–6 do the same using pop1_100 instead as the measure of community homogeneity. We focus on the estimated coefficients on pop1_91×FD in columns 1–3 and that on pop1_100×FD in columns 4–6. These coefficients account for the differential effects of community homogeneity on measures of local polity after FD. Notice, the estimated coefficient on pop1_91×FD is positive for consensus-building (see column 1) and negative for voting (see column 2) and both coefficients are statistically significant. This means that homogeneous communities are more likely to choose participatory (rather than electoral) democracies. Similar results are obtained in columns 4 and 5 using the alternative homogeneity measure.

The table presents the estimates of local polities using alternative community homogeneity indices, pop1_91 and pop1_100, among others. Part (a) shows the estimates using the variable pop1_91, which takes a value 1 if the population share of the largest population group is greater than the median value and is 0 otherwise. Part (b) shows the corresponding estimates using the perfect homogeneity measure pop1_100 that takes a value 1 if the community has 100% population of one group only. We present estimates of three types of local polities here, namely consensus (column 1 in both parts), voting (column 2) and any democratisation proxied by the status_v variable (column 3). Consensus is a binary variable taking a value 1 if a leader is selected by consensus-building. Voting is a second binary variable taking a value 1 when a leader is selected by voting; otherwise, these two binary variables are 0. Status_v = 1 if a leader is selected either by voting or by consensus. Other controls used include community population, geographic size, whether it is rural, if Islam is the main religion, and also their interactions with FD. All regressions include district dummies too.

Next, consider the effects of community homogeneity on the likelihood of *any* democratisation status_v. Recall, this variable takes a value 1 for electoral or participatory democracy and 0 for oligarchy. Observe that the estimated coefficients on the interaction term pop1 91×FD (column 3) or pop1_100×FD (column 6) are both positive, though the effect is only statistically significant when using pop1_91 (column 3). This suggests that greater (or lesser) community homogeneity significantly boosts (lowers) the probability of any democratisation (relative to oligarchy).

We also test the robustness of our findings by employing a fractionalisation measure popular in the extant literature. Using $p1$, $p2$ and $p3$ to respectively represent the shares of the three constituent population groups in a community, we generate an ethnic fractionalisation index *Ethfrac* as 1 minus the sum of the squared decimal population shares of the top three ethnic groups. So:

$$Ethfrac = 1 - (p_1^2 + p_2^2 + p_3^2) \qquad [3]$$

These estimates are collected in Table 7.4. Since ethnic fractionalisation is inversely related to ethnic homogeneity, we expect a reversal in terms of the signs of the estimated coefficients. This is indeed what is observed in the table.

Table 7.4: Effects of ethnic fractionalisation on local polities

	Dependent variable showing effects *(standard errors)*					
Explanatory variables	**Model 4: Consensus**		**Model 5: Voting**		**Model 6: Democratisation**	
FD	−0.333	*(0.416)*	0.904*	*(0.514)*	−0.113	*(0.155)*
Ethnic frac	0.308**	*(0.139)*	−0.592***	*(0.139)*	−0.215**	*(0.104)*
Ethnic frac×FD	−0.444***	*(0.149)*	0.344**	*(0.162)*	−0.116	*(0.111)*
Constant	0.5065	*(0.331)*	−0.0433	*(0.265)*	1.2590***	*(0.267)*
Other controls	Yes		Yes		Yes	
District dummies	Yes		Yes		Yes	
Observations	605		605		605	
R-squared	0.160		0.358		0.502	

Notes: All estimates are clustered by districts; cluster-robust standard errors are shown in parentheses and italics. Significance levels: ***$p < 0.01$, **$p < 0.05$, *$p < 0.1$. The table presents the estimates of local polity using the ethnic fractionalisation index (ethfrac), which is given by: $1 - (p_1^2 + p_2^2 + p_3^2)$ where pi is the population share of the ith group. i = 1, 2, 3. See also the notes to Table 7.3.

Rural–urban heterogeneity

Next, we explore any potential rural–urban heterogeneity in our sample in terms of Hypothesis 1. Differential effects in rural and urban regions could arise from the fact that prior to FD, leaders in urban communities were nominated by the centre; this was not the case in rural areas.

The top halves of Tables 7.5a and 7.5b show the estimates for rural communities and the lower halves show those for urban communities. The layout of the regressions in each panel mirrors that in the baseline table (Table 7.3). Comparing the estimates in the (a) and (b) panels for the impacts of greater community homogeneity on the local polity after the FD shock shows that the (full sample) results observed in Table 7.3 were primarily driven by effects in the rural communities.

Effect of the local polity on local entrepreneurship

We now move on to test Hypothesis 2. Table 7.6 presents comparisons of the means of different components of local income and local development spending between voting and other communities. The top panel shows the full sample comparisons, while the bottom panel refers to just the 2007 (post-FD) comparisons.

We use the natural logarithm of income from self-reliant community sources as well as total local income from various local sources. We also

Table 7.5: Separate rural/urban estimates of homogeneity effects on the local polity of fiscal decentralisation

a. Homogeneity measured by a community falling above or below the mean homogeneity score (pop1_91)

Explanatory variables	Dependent variable showing effects *(standard errors)*					
	Model 1: Consensus		Model 2: Voting		Model 3: Democratisation	
RURAL communities						
FD	−1.247*	*(0.692)*	2.085***	*(0.746)*	0.046	*(0.151)*
pop1_91	−0.228**	*(0.104)*	0.269***	*(0.090)*	−0.050	*(0.039)*
pop1_91×FD	0.368***	*(0.107)*	−0.467***	*(0.092)*	0.009	*(0.053)*
Constant	0.7684	*(0.544)*	−0.6516	*(0.433)*	1.1371***	*(0.169)*
Other controls	Yes		Yes		Yes	
District FE	Yes		Yes		Yes	
Observations	255		255		255	
R-squared	0.224		0.323		0.466	
URBAN communities						
FD	0.279	*(0.486)*	0.308	*(0.458)*	−0.064	*(0.411)*
pop1_91	−0.089	*(0.103)*	0.143	*(0.089)*	0.082	*(0.063)*
pop1_91×FD	0.085	*(0.107)*	0.105	*(0.131)*	0.093	*(0.082)*
Constant	0.090	*(0.394)*	0.027	*(0.301)*	0.974**	*(0.401)*
Other controls	Yes		Yes		Yes	
District FE	Yes		Yes		Yes	
Constant	0.090	*(0.394)*	0.027	*(0.301)*	0.974**	*(0.401)*
Observations	361		361		361	

(Continued)

employ the natural logarithm of total development spending and the share of total development spending in total community spending. It is clear that voting communities were significantly more successful in generating greater local income as well as local development spending than were comparable consensus-building communities. This pattern holds for both self-reliant efforts and total local income, and for both total local development spending and its share in the full sample as well as in 2007 (post-FD) only.

Figure 7.1 captures the variation in local income and local development spending by local polity when plotted against the percentage share of largest population group. Note, the greater the share of largest population group, the higher (lower) is the ethnic homogeneity (diversity) of the community. This is done separately for the pre-FD round (1997) and the post-FD round (2007). The patterns are distinctly different across the two periods, with much of the

Table 7.5: Continued

b. Homogeneity measured by the top ethnic group having 100% or not (pop1_100)

Explanatory variables	Dependent variable showing effects (standard errors)					
	Model 1: Consensus		Model 2: Voting		Model 3: Democratisation	
RURAL communities						
FD	−1.069	(0.635)	1.851***	(0.673)	0.033	(0.149)
pop1_100	−0.112	0.2077**	0.148	(0.088)	−0.001	(0.028)
pop1_100×FD	0.208**	(0.085)	−0.290**	(0.110)	−0.021	(0.021)
Constant	0.684	(0.484)	−0.550	(0.355)	1.128***	(0.176)
Other controls	Yes		Yes		Yes	
District FE	Yes		Yes		Yes	
Observations	255		255		255	
R-squared	0.202		0.299		0.459	
URBAN communities						
FD	0.205	(0.453)	0.594	(0.474)	0.111	(0.320)
pop1_100	−0.206	(0.150)	0.173	(0.137)	0.414***	(0.124)
pop1_100×FD	0.330**	(0.123)	−0.032	(0.094)	−0.185*	(0.099)
Constant	0.0470	(0.388)	0.0260	(0.315)	0.9088**	(0.379)
Other controls	Yes		Yes		Yes	
District FE	Yes		Yes		Yes	
Observations	361		361		361	
R-squared	0.252		0.303		0.424	

Notes: All estimates are clustered by districts; cluster-robust standard errors are shown in parentheses and italics. Significance levels: ***$p < 0.01$, **$p < 0.05$, *$p < 0.1$. The table presents the estimates of local polity using the ethnic fractionalisation index (ethfrac), which is given by: $1 − (p_1^2 + p_2^2 + p_3^2)$, where pi is the population share of the ith group. $i = 1, 2, 3$. See also the notes to Table 7.3.

variation seen in the high ethnic diversity (relatively smaller size of the largest population group) zone. This is particularly evident for the 2007 round and holds for both local income and local development spending, supporting the validity of Hypothesis 2 graphically; it also justifies our use of the PSM method, which is well adapted to analysing such patterns. Accordingly, we compare income and development spending in voting and consensus-building communities relative to other comparable (in terms of observed characteristics including ethnic homogeneity/diversity) communities after 2007 (relative to 1997) using average treatment effects on the treated (ATT) as per Equation [2].

Table 7.6: Comparisons of mean local incomes and development expenditure in communities using voting and other communities

Indices	Voting communities	Other communities	T-stat
1997 and 2007			
Log (ln) of local income	14.73	7.53	11.020***
Log (ln) of self-reliant income)	9.72	4.52	8.136***
Log (ln) development expenditure	16.73	13.49	5.812***
% share of development expenditure in total expenditure	0.68	0.51	6.434***
2007			
Log (ln) of local income	16.26	12.35	4.659***
Log (ln) of self-reliant income)	10.38	6.92	3.527***
Log (ln) development expenditure	18.11	16.29	3.153***
% share of development expenditure in total expenditure	72	51	6.028***

Source: Authors' calculation using the IFLS data sample 1997–2007.
Notes: Significance levels: ***$p < 0.01$, **$p < 0.05$, *$p < 0.1$. The table summarises the mean comparisons of local income and local development spending using t-tests between voting and other communities in our sample. The top panel shows the full sample comparisons including both 1997 and 2007, while the bottom panel refers to the 2007 comparisons only.

Table 7.7 contains the ATT estimates as per Equation [2] above. We define *voting* and *consensus* as two possible treatments of interest (with all remaining polities as the control) and compare the outcomes, namely indices of income and development spending as defined above. For improved identification, we ensure that both the propensity scores and covariates are balanced between the treatment and the control groups for each outcome.

The table shows the average treatment effects on the treated (ATT) of local income and local development spending (both levels and shares) by local polities derived by using the propensity score matching (PSM) method. The first-stage estimates generating the propensity score estimates are shown in Table 7.3. The reference group for each polity is the comparable control group belonging to all other polities – comparable by observed percentage share of the largest population group, village size, village population, rural/urban location, FD dummy, and district dummies. ATT is the average treatment effect on the treated $= (O^T - O^C)_{2007} - (O^T - O^C)_{1997}$; T: treatment and C: control. The corresponding t-statistics are also shown.

In the case of *voting*, the top panel of Table 7.7 shows that the ATT estimate is positive and statistically significant for both income from self-reliant efforts and also total local income. This means that the extra income (total or self-reliant) in *voting communities* relative to non-voting communities in

Figure 7.1: Variation in local income and local development spending by local polity with the percentage share of largest population ethnic group

a. 1997 local income

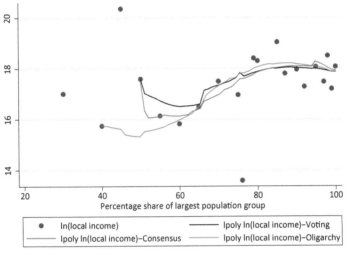

1997 local income

b. 2007 local income

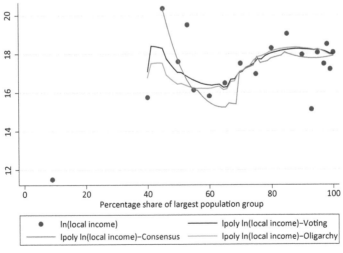

2007 local income

(Continued)

Figure 7.1: Continued

c. 1997 local development spending

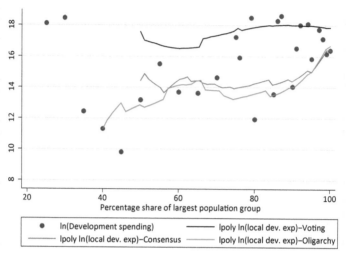

1997 local development spending

d. 2007 local development spending

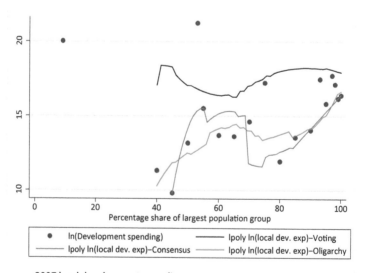

2007 local development spending

Sources: As per Table 7.2.
Notes: The figure shows the smooth local polynomial (Epanechnikov) of local income and local development spending against the percentage share of the largest population ethnic group for each type of local polity in 1997 and 2007.

Table 7.7: Treatment effects of local polity on local income in 2007

Treatment (type of local polity)	Ln (income from self-reliant efforts)		Ln (local income)	
	ATT estimates	T-stat	ATT estimates	T-stat
Consensus	−3.183***	−2.960	−4.421***	−7.356
Voting	2.463***	4.329	2.570 **	2.139
	% Share of development spending		Ln (local development spending)	
Consensus	−0.105	−1.634	−2.388**	−2.404
Voting	0.115***	5.474	1.332***	3.934

Note: Significance levels: ***p < 0.01, **p < 0.05, *p < 0.1.

2007 (relative to that in 1997) is positive and statistically significant at the 1 per cent level. The corresponding ATTs for natural log of local development spending and the percentage share of development spending are shown in the lower panel of Table 7.7: both the ATT estimates here are positive and statistically significant for voting communities. In contrast, the ATT estimates of income and development for consensus-building communities are always negative across the table and are statistically significant for the most part. Taken together, these ATT estimates suggest that the communities that elect their local leaders by allowing everybody to vote are also the ones to have significantly higher income (both measures) and development spending (both measures) when contrasted with those communities, which employ the process of 'consensus-building' or 'oligarchy'.

These results raise an obvious question: why may electoral democracies be more entrepreneurial? We explore a few possibilities here using the data at our disposal. First, the likelihood of leader turnover is significantly higher in voting relative to consensus-building communities in our sample. The likelihood of leader turnover from 1997 to 2007 is 0.60 in voting communities as opposed to only 0.38 in consensus-building ones and the mean difference is statistically significant (t-stat = 5.00). A greater chance of leader turnover could be an obvious mechanism to discipline leaders, and this likelihood is significantly higher in voting rather than consensus-building communities, thus inducing or encouraging a leader to be more entrepreneurial.

Second, we examine the extent of economic inequality in voting and non-voting communities. A more unequal society with ethnic diversity may dampen a democratically elected leader's accountability, since they cannot cater to everyone. The core logic in Bandiera and Levy (2011) can be easily adapted to establish that unequal communities with ethnic diversity are more prone to elite capture. An analysis of monthly per capita household expenditure data suggests that voting communities in our sample tend to be less unequal. In particular, the total income share of households in the top quartiles is significantly less in voting as opposed to consensus-building communities: the sample average is 19 per cent for voting communities as opposed to 27 per cent for consensus communities.[8] Similar patterns emerge when using the Gini coefficient and the coefficient of variation as alternative indices of inequality. These observations, taken together, suggest that leaders in voting communities are more likely to be entrepreneurial because they need to cater to all households in the community, which is also easier to do in less unequal communities.

Conclusions

We have examined the implications of a major nationwide programme of fiscal decentralisation in Indonesia for the structure and organisation of local political processes, an issue not hitherto explored in much detail. We offer a first glimpse into these complex inter-linkages using detailed community-level data from Indonesia, using data from 312 rural and urban communities, drawn from 13 provinces, before and after the introduction of FD in 2001.

We focused on two particular issues. First, we sought to highlight the factors that drove communities' choices between voting and consensus-building, exploring whether community homogeneity (dominance by a single ethnic group) had been a precondition for the initiation of participatory democracy (proxied by consensus-building) as opposed to electoral democracy (proxied by majority voting). Second, we studied the role of local polities in local income generation and development, exploring how the political entrepreneurship of local leaders may succeed in overcoming the collective action problems in ethnically diverse communities, especially after FD.

We observed that, after the decentralisation changes, local leader selection by consensus-building declined and that by voting increased significantly. Our analysis identifies community homogeneity as an important factor in boosting the likelihood of communities choosing to do leader selection by consensus-building. More ethnically diverse communities increasingly opted for voting as their means of selection after FD. Local political entrepreneurship played an important role in this political transition after FD. Our PSM analysis shows that voting communities were consistently more successful in raising local income and local development relative to comparable consensus-building communities. This highlights the significance of local political entrepreneurship in aligning the economic interests of ethnically diverse communities after FD in Indonesia. We argue that this can be attributed to the greater local accountability of leaders in electoral democracies, who must seek to cater to the everyone (including poorer households), especially when economic inequality is moderate. In a way, our findings conjoin the literature on ethnic diversity (Alesina and La Ferrara 2000; Ashraf and Galor 2013; Gomes 2020) with that on participatory developmental efforts (Mansuri and Rao 2013; Olken 2010). While we do not claim that these empirical associations are strictly causal, the consistency of their magnitude and significance means that we cannot dismiss them as a mere statistical oddity. In fact, we choose to interpret these results as a springboard for further careful exploration of the features of local entrepreneurship, which we believe lies at the heart of such transitions following FD.

Acknowledgements

We acknowledge the support of University of Kent and University of Surrey, where much of this research was based. We are grateful to Patrick Dunleavy, Jean-Paul Faguet, and Stuti Kehmani, as well as the participants in the online workshop on 'Decentralized Governance: Crafting Effective Democracies Around the World', for many constructive comments on an earlier draft. The usual disclaimer applies.

Endnotes

[1] It is easier for leaders to unite supporters when economic differences are lesser.

[2] For instance, see Bardhan (2002), Bardhan and Mookherjee (2006), Stokes (2005), and Larreguy, Montiel Olea, and Querubin (2017).

[3] See Easterly and Levine (1997), Alesina, Baqir, and Easterly (1999), Banerjee and Somanathan (2007), and Collier (2008), among others.

[4] See Martinez-Bravo (2014) for evidence on electoral fraud post-FD in Indonesia.

[5] See for example, Lind and Tyler (1988), Matsusaka (2004), and Olken (2010).

[6] Although IFLS data are available for the years 1993, 1998, and 2000 as well, information on local politics could be found only in the 1997 and 2007 surveys.

[7] About 51% of sample communities had a group 1 (that is, the largest ethnic group) comprising at least 91% of the community's population. Around 27% of sample communities were perfectly homogeneous ethnically.

[8] The mean difference in the share is significant too (t-stat = 2.12).

References

Alesina, Alberto; Baqir, Reza; and Easterly, William (1999) 'Public Goods and Ethnic Divisions', Quarterly Journal of Economics, vol.114, no.4, pp.1243–84. https://doi.org/10.1162/003355399556269

Alesina, Alberto and La Ferrara, Eliana (2000) 'Participation in Heterogenous Communities', *Quarterly Journal of Economics*, vol.115, no.3, pp.847–904. https://doi.org/10.1162/003355300554935

Ashraf, Quamrul and Galor, Oded (2013) 'The "Out of Africa" Hypothesis, Human Genetic Diversity, and Comparative Economic Development', *American Economic Review*, vol.103, no.1, pp.1–46. https://doi.org/10.1257/aer.103.1.1

Bandiera, Oriana and Levy, Gilat (2011) 'Diversity and the Power of the Elites in Democratic Societies: Evidence from Indonesia', *Journal of Public Economics*, vol.95, pp.1322–30. https://doi.org/10.1016/j.jpubeco.2011.04.002

Banerjee, Abhijit and Somanathan, Rohini (2007) 'The Political Economy of Public Goods: Some Evidence from India', *Journal of Development Economics*, vol.82, no.2, pp.287–314. https://doi.org/10.1016/j.jdeveco.2006.04.005

Bardhan, Pranab (2002) 'Decentralization of Governance and Development', *Journal of Economic Perspectives*, vol.16, no.4, pp.185–205. https://doi.org/10.1257/089533002320951037

Bardhan, Pranab and Mookherjee, Dilip (2000) 'Capture and Governance at Local and National Levels', *American Economic Review*, vol.90, pp.135–139. https://doi.org/10.1257/aer.90.2.135

Bardhan, Pranab and Mookherjee, Dilip (2006) 'Decentralization, Corruption and Government Accountability', in Rose-Ackerman, Susan (ed.) *International Handbook on the Economics of Corruption*, Edward Elgar. https://doi.org/10.4337/9781847203106

Besley, Timothy; Pande, Rohini; Rao, Vijayendra (2005) 'Participatory Democracy in Action: Survey Evidence from South India', *Journal of European Economic Association*, vol.3, no.2–3, pp.648–57. https://onlinelibrary.wiley.com/doi/abs/10.1162/jeea.2005.3.2-3.648

Bhavnani, Rikhil R. (2017) 'Do the Effects of Temporary Ethnic Group Quotas Persist? Evidence from India', *American Economic Journal: Applied Economics*, vol.9, no.3, pp.105–23. https://doi.org/10.1257/app.20160030

Burgess, Robin; Jedwab, Remi; Miguel, Edward; and Morjaria, Ameet; and Padró I Miquel, Gerrard (2015) 'The Value of Democracy: Evidence from Road Building in Kenya', *The American Economic Review*, vol.105, no.6, pp.1817–51. https://doi.org/10.1257/aer.20131031

Chin, Aimee and Prakash, Nishith (2011) 'The Redistributive Effects of Political Reservation for Minorities: Evidence from India', *Journal of Development Economics*, vol.96, no.2, pp.265–77. https://doi.org/10.1016/j.jdeveco.2010.10.004

Collier, Paul (2008) 'Growth Strategies for Africa', Commission on Growth and Development Working Paper; No.9. World Bank, Washington, DC. http://hdl.handle.net/10986/28011

Easterly, William and Levine, Ross (1997) 'Africa's Growth Tragedy: Policies and Ethnic Divisions', *The Quarterly Journal of Economics*, vol.112, no.4, pp.1203–50. https://www.jstor.org/stable/2951270

Enikopolov, Ruben and Zhuravskaya, Ekaterina (2007) 'Decentralization and Political Institutions', *Journal of Public Economics*, vol.91, pp.2261–90. https://doi.org/10.1016/j.jpubeco.2007.02.006

Frankenberg, Elizabeth and Thomas, Duncan (2000) 'The Indonesia Family Life Survey (IFLS): Study Design and Results from Waves 1 and 2', DRU-2238/1-NIA/NICHD. http://www.vanneman.umd.edu/socy699j/ifls2design.pdf

Gomes, Joseph Flavian (2020) 'The Health Costs of Ethnic Distance: Evidence from Sub-Saharan Africa', *Journal of Economic Growth*, vol.25, pp.195–226. https://doi.org/10.1007/s10887-020-09177-4

Hidayat, Syarif and Antlov, Hans (2004) 'Decentralization by Default in Indonesia', in Oxhorn, Philip; Tulchin Joseph S.; and Selee, Andrew (eds) *Decentralization, Civil Society, and Democratic Governance: Comparative Perspectives from Latin America, Africa, and Asia*, Washington, DC: Woodrow Wilson Center.

Jensenius, Francesca Refsum (2015) 'Development from Representation? A Study of Quotas for the Scheduled Castes in India', *American Economic Journal: Applied Economics*, vol.7, no.3, pp.196–220. https://doi.org/10.1257/app.20140201

Larreguy, Horacio; Montiel Olea, Cesar E.; and Querubin, Pablo (2017) 'Political Brokers: Partisans or Agents? Evidence from the Mexican Teachers' Union', *American Journal of Political Science*, vol.61, no.4, pp.877–91. https://doi.org/10.1111/ajps.12322

Lind, E. Allan and Tyler, Tom R. (1988) *The Social Psychology of Procedural Justice*, New York: Plenum Press.

Mansuri, Ghazala and Rao, Vijayendra (2013) 'Localizing Development: Does Participation Work?' World Bank Policy Research Report, Washington, DC. https://openknowledge.worldbank.org/handle/10986/11859

Martinez-Bravo, Monica (2014) 'The Role of Local Officials in New Democracies: Evidence from Indonesia', *American Economic Review*, vol.104, no.4, pp.1–45. https://doi.org/10.1257/aer.104.4.1244

Martinez-Bravo, Monica; Mukherjee, Priya; and Stegmann, Andreas (2017) 'The Non-Democratic Roots of Elite Capture: Evidence from Soeharto Mayors in Indonesia', *Econometrica*, vol.85, no.6, pp.1991–2010. https://doi.org/10.3982/ECTA14125

Matsusaka, John G. (2004) *For the Many or the Few: The Initiative, Public Policy, and American Democracy*, Chicago, IL: University of Chicago Press.

Mitra, Anirban (2018) 'Mandated Political Representation and Redistribution', *Economica*, vol.85, no.338, pp.266–80. https://doi.org/10.1111/ecca.12249

Mitra, Anirban and Pal, Sarmistha (2021) 'Ethnic Diversity, Social Norms and Elite Capture: Theory and Evidence from Indonesia', *Economica*, vol.89, no.356, pp.947–96. https://doi.org/10.1111/ecca.12423

Olken, Benjamin (2010) 'Direct Democracy and Local Public Goods: Evidence from a Field Experiment in Indonesia', *American Political Science Review*, vol.104, no.2. https://doi.org/10.1017/S0003055410000079

Padró-i-Miguel, Gerard; Qian, Nancy; and Yao, Yang (2014) 'Social Fragmentation, Public Goods and Elections: Evidence from China', CEPR Discussion Paper No. DP8975. https://www.nber.org/system/files/working_papers/w18633/w18633.pdf

Pal, Sarmistha and Wahhaj, Zaki (2017) 'Fiscal Decentralisation, Local Institutions and Public Good Provision: Evidence from Indonesia', *Journal of Comparative Economics*, vol.45, no.2, pp.383–409. https://doi.org/10.1016/j.jce.2016.07.004

Pande, Rohini (2003) 'Can Mandated Political Representation Increase Policy Influence for Disadvantaged Minorities? Theory and Evidence from India', *American Economic Review*, vol.93, no.4, pp.1132–1151. https://doi.org/10.1257/000282803769206232

Riker, William (1986). *The Art of Political Manipulation*. New Haven, CT: Yale University Press.

Rodriguez, Catherine and Meirelles Patricia (2010) 'Devolution and Accountability Effects in the Public Provision of Water Services in Indonesia', Documento CEDE No. 2010-39, Universidad de Los Andes, Colombia. https://papers.ssrn.com/sol3/papers.cfm?abstract_id=1755050

Sanyal, Paromita and Rao, Vijayendra (2018) *Oral Democracy: Deliberation in Indian Village Assemblies*, UK: Cambridge University Press. https://doi.org/10.1017/9781139095716.006

Schneider, Mark and Teske, Paul (1992) 'Toward a Theory of the Political Entrepreneur: Evidence from Local Government', *The American Political Science Review*, vol.86, no.3, pp.737–47. https://doi.org/10.2307/1964135

Stokes, Susan (2005) 'Perverse Accountability: A Formal Model of Machine Politics with Evidence from Argentina', *American Political Science Review*, vol.99, no.3, pp.315–25. https://doi.org/10.1017/S0003055405051683

Strauss, John; Witoelar, Firman; Sikoki, Bondan; and Wattie, Anna Marie (2009) 'The Fourth Wave of the Indonesian Family Life Survey (IFLS4): Overview and Field Report', WR-675/1-NIA/NICHD. https://microdata.worldbank.org/index.php/catalog/1044/download/20909

8. Can parliamentary sanctions strengthen local political accountability? Evidence from Kenya

Michael Mbate

Summary

This chapter uses administrative data from Kenya that directly matches parliamentary sanctions with incidences of corruption at the subnational level to demonstrate how party politics can impede the legislative oversight of local politicians. The results show that co-partisanship between parliamentarians serving in oversight committees and local politicians in Kenya tended to weaken oversight because of collusive behaviour and the need to preserve party credibility. However, this effect seems to decline substantially when committee members face an electoral threat and are motivated by career concerns. These findings suggest that the structure and composition of national legislative committees and the nature of political incentives faced by the legislature can influence local accountability outcomes.

Parliamentary oversight of all levels of government is crucial for enhancing the transparency and accountability of public resources (Gaines et al. 2019; Shaw 1998; Strøm 1998). In its absence, politicians are likely to misappropriate public resources for private gain, compromising the delivery of quality public services, decreasing political responsiveness to the needs of the electorate, reducing state legitimacy, and increasing poverty and inequality (Keneck-Massil, Nomo-Beyala, and Owoundi 2021). Resource misappropriation can also undermine public expenditure efficiency and the targeting, quantity,

---

How to cite this book chapter:

Mbate, Michael (2023) 'Can parliamentary sanctions strengthen local political accountability? Evidence from Kenya', in: Faguet, Jean-Paul and Pal, Sarmistha (eds) *Decentralised Governance: Crafting Effective Democracies Around the World*, London: LSE Press, pp. 209–231. https://doi.org/10.31389/lsepress.dlg.h License: CC BY 4.0

quality and outcomes of social spending (De Mendonça and Baca 2018; Transparency International 2014). Parliamentary audit institutions have the potential to enhance political and bureaucratic accountability in three main ways:

- Because of the constitutional powers bestowed upon the legislature, their recommendations can be legally enforceable, potentially changing the behaviour and incentives of those managing public finances.
- Audits quantify the incidence of resource misappropriation and so enable parliamentary institutions to make objective recommendations based on verifiable and credible sources.
- Parliaments often possess powers to summon politicians and bureaucrats, including the executive, to explain audit findings and respond to queries.

However, in most developing countries, the legislative accountability of government agencies mainly remains ineffective. According to the 2020 Global Report on Public Financial Management, 'legislative scrutiny is relatively weak on average', with 'legislatures performing better on scrutiny of budgets than on scrutiny of audits' (PEFA 2020, p.107). In most African countries, survey data have shown significant variation in the performance of parliamentary institutions and their capacity to hold the executive accountable (Opalo 2019). Poor coordination between the parliament and other government institutions is a critical factor contributing to the weak oversight. For instance, parliamentary committees often blame supreme audit institutions (SAIs) for providing highly technical audits, some of which are poorly conducted, politically motivated, or submitted late. Parliamentary committees also blame the National Assembly for a lack of effort and political will to adopt or enforce their recommendations.

In developing countries, the judiciary and anti-corruption agencies often point to low-quality audits and investigations as the basis for non-prosecutions. On the other hand, audit institutions point out the inability of parliamentary committees to either summon corrupt politicians and bureaucrats to account or deliver timely and appropriate sanctions. Both these explanations provide few insights into how to address the factors constraining the legislature in enhancing political accountability. Consequently, it has become something of an academic and policy priority to understand the root causes of institutional ineffectiveness and to identify potential policy remedies (Fashagba 2009; Opalo 2021).

This chapter examines the factors that influence the effectiveness of parliaments in promoting accountability at lower levels of government. The next section gives an advance look ahead explaining the study's rationale and value. Section 8.2 summarises the theoretical literature, while Section 8.3 presents the Kenyan institutional setting. Section 8.4 presents the research design, and Section 8.5 discusses the results.

8.1 The value of this study

Using a unique data set on legally binding disciplinary sanctions imposed by the legislature on local politicians and bureaucrats in Kenya, I examine how the variation in co-partisanship between the parliamentary accounts committee and local politicians affects the likelihood of decision makers getting sanctioned for misappropriating public funds. In addition, employing different metrics that capture the political incentives of committee members, I assess whether electoral competition alters the behaviour of committee members in exercising their oversight over local politicians.

Several factors make Kenya an appropriate setting to examine these questions. Local politicians (including the governors of the 47 counties) have substantial powers over spending decisions and often misappropriate public funds (D'Arcy and Cornell 2016). Given the sizeable resources controlled locally, parliamentary scrutiny can have important implications for both spending decisions and public service delivery. The country's institutional framework mandates the national Office of the Auditor-General (OAG) to carry out annual audits of the country's public finances and submit them to the parliament. Consequently, the efficiency of spending and service delivery outcomes at the subnational level is likely to be either determined or strongly influenced by the legislature (PEFA 2020). Taken together, these aspects permit an analysis of the role of vertical accountability systems in promoting local accountability.

The analysis generates two key findings. First, the organisation of legislative institutions and the nature of political incentives that their members face both influence legislators to hold local governments accountable for misappropriating public funds. Partisanship between parliamentarians and local politicians seems to generate unintended incentives to circumvent disciplinary sanctions, as the legislature promotes party interests. Second, electoral incentives tend to provide a mechanism through which committee members can align their oversight responsibilities with the public interest, suggesting a potential avenue for enhancing their oversight effectiveness.

The chapter contributes to a small but growing body of literature on legislative accountability in Africa (Opalo 2019; Osei 2020; Pelizzo and Kinyondo 2014; Pelizzo and Stapenhurst 2008). Unlike most studies assessing how local factors (such as elections and grassroots organisations) can improve accountability outcomes, the argument here focuses on the *interaction* between the central government (parliaments) and subnational governments. Doing so provides new insights on the importance of accountability institutions at the central government for local accountability outcomes.

The chapter also contributes to the growing body of empirical studies attempting to quantify parliamentary oversight's effectiveness (Foster 2015; Opalo 2021; Wehner 2006). The detailed nature of the parliamentary reports used in the analysis allows me to construct direct measures of sanctions, and match them with the different types of audit allegations. These measures improve on the conventional approach of measuring parliamentary oversight using proxies (such as visibility in media outlets or the number of parliamentary hearings) that are potentially biased or require subjective classification. In addition, by adopting a within-country analysis, these estimation techniques help control for the differences in institutional settings and political institutions that normally plague cross-country analysis (Mickler 2017).

Lastly, the chapter contributes to the literature on the institutionalisation of politics in Africa, which to date has only considered determinants of parliamentary responsiveness such as term limits, parliamentary proceedings, and the availability of adequate skills and resources (Stapenhurst, Jacobs, and Olaore 2016; Wehner 2006). By focusing on the deliberations of an influential legislative committee in Kenya, the results demonstrate that formal institutional rules related to the selection of committee members matter for local accountability outcomes. This finding adds to a literature documenting how the lack of separation of powers within the political sphere hinders good governance (Golooba-Mutebi 2016; Pelizzo and Kinyondo 2014).

Evidence that the legislature matters for political outcomes has been documented in different countries, irrespective of the degree of political interference (Hansen 2019; Holzhacker 2005; Keyes 2021). Yet, in fiscal decentralisation, where bottom-up accountability might be weak, the legislature may be well placed to act as an alternative source of political accountability. The current literature often examines legislative issues and subnational accountability in isolation. This chapter addresses this gap by systematically focusing on the interaction between the two in a specific case analysis of the Kenyan legislature, yet with findings relevant for a broader set of countries or contexts. It shows that the legislature can have some degree of efficacy even in a political system usually associated with significant local corruption.

8.2 The literature on legislative oversight and partisanship

Parliamentary committees have long been argued to be 'among the most important features of legislative organisations in contemporary democracies' (Strøm 1998 p.21). Although they vary in size, scope, and responsibilities, committees were often established by parliaments so as to provide oversight, help with legislation (law-making), strengthen policy formulation and consensus-building, and undertake fact-finding and deliberating around executive appointments (Gaines et al. 2019). Their effectiveness has generally been analysed using the principal–agent theory, where committees (acting as principals) develop oversight tools to hold the executive and other government institutions (their agents) accountable for their actions. Committees thus enable politicians to develop specialised knowledge, identify issues suitable for legislative review, and recommend appropriate courses of action to the national assembly, parliament, or congress.

Existing studies point to the academic and policy debate on the ideal organisational structure of institutions of accountability in the central government, especially parliamentary committees (Pelizzo and Kinyondo 2014). The motivation behind the *selection and composition* of committee members is considered a critical element that can determine how parliaments can effectively achieve meaningful checks and balances between different levels of government. Because committees comprise a subset of politicians, doubts may arise about whether they can effectively monitor and sanction each other. One way that politics affects legislative processes and outcomes is via parliamentary committees made up of politicians who are sometimes motivated by political interests. In Sweden, for instance, it has been observed that:

> Members of the Constitution Committee were placed in an impossible dual role. On the one hand, they were responsible for a statesman-like inspection of constitutional democracy. On the other, they were party politicians driven by a legitimate desire to maximize their votes in the coming election. (Norton 2020, p.221)

Several theories provide insights into how partisanship influences political accountability through legislative oversight (Longley and Davidson 1998; Pelizzo and Stapenhurst 2014). Those that focus on partisanship suggest a direct link between political parties and committee members, with party loyalties influencing or even organising the behaviour of individual legislators within committees (Mathews and Flinders 2015). Committee placements and sessions are here considered to be primarily instruments that serve to attain partisan goals (Shaw 1998). Just as legislative parties are formed to solve whole-chamber collection action problems faced by subsets of politicians, so do party members in parliamentary committees (Strøm 1998). Committees can thus undermine the legitimate purpose of the legislature by promoting party interests and disproportionately making policy decisions along partisan lines to maintain party credibility (Norton 2019; Zubek 2008). For instance, Stapenhurst, Jacobs, and Olaore (2016) found that the Public Accounts Committee (PAC) in Nigeria advanced political goals by constantly harassing the executive. In South Africa, de Vos (2013) found that the dominance of the ANC Party in parliament limited the scope for effective parliamentary oversight. Evidence from the US Congress suggests that partisan divisions negatively reduce the inclination of committees to perform their responsibilities (Hughes and Carlson 2015).

An alternative approach focuses on the individual incentives of politicians. The distributive theory views politicians as self-interested and inclined to maximise their political standing. The structure and composition of committees are highly political and configured to help achieve electoral gains or redistribute political benefits to a subset of politicians or legislators (Keyes

2021; Mickler 2017). Consequently, individual legislators favour partisan interests over the public interest since they benefit from the collective reputation of their parties on the ballot (Jensen, Kuenzi, and Lee 2020; Strøm 1998). They can also improve their career prospects by aligning their oversight responsibilities with their parties in exchange for access to state resources, allowing them to gain or retain positions of power or raise their political profiles (Mathews and Flinders 2015; Meriläinen and Tukiainen 2018). For instance, Dauda, Suhuyini, and Antwi-Boasiako (2020) found that Ghana's influential legislative committee members protect co-partisans. So, legislators serve in committees for politically strategic reasons, and political considerations dominate legislative matters.

An important implication of both approaches is that where members of the oversight committee belong to the same party as the politicians they supervise (either at the central and local levels) this co-partisanship is likely to reduce the effectiveness of legislative oversight. A key mechanism that could reinforce this link is potential collusive behaviour (Laffont and Tirole 1991). On the one hand, politicians under scrutiny can influence committee members through bribes, monetary contributions to political campaigns, or lobbying for them locally (Mwangi 2008). On the other hand, legislators who receive such benefits can commit to helping supervised politicians circumvent sanctions through political favouritism, resulting in a mutually beneficial outcome. Typically, for such collusion to occur, it must be enforceable, and, given its informal nature, partisanship offers a platform for cooperation and mutual interactions that can sustain such behaviour (Tirole 1986).

Finally, an extended form of the distributive theory posits that electoral incentives can constrain political behaviour (Besley and Case 1995; Finan and Mazzocco 2020). When political careers are decided at the ballot, those serving in parliamentary committees have strong incentives to protect their individual reputations by ensuring that committee deliberations and outcomes are aligned with the public interest. For instance, Pelizzo and Stapenhurst (2014, p.259) note that 'if there is an electoral reward for [politicians] who perform oversight, then it is in the self-interest of [politicians] to perform it adequately'. A key implication is that the structure of incentives faced by committee members can determine the quality of legislative oversight. Thus, committee members facing higher electoral incentives should be more likely to perform their oversight responsibilities in line with the public interest.

8.3 Kenya's institutional setting for audit

Consistent with theories of retrospective voting, Kenyan voters have increasingly punished politicians for poor performance, with political turnover increasing per electoral cycle. Several high-ranking politicians, especially those implicated in misappropriating public funds, have been fired following audit deliberations from auditors and commissions of inquiry (Bachelard

2010). Audits seem to play an essential role in affecting politicians' career concerns, through either the ballot or judicial processes (Supreme Auditor 2015).

Members of the national legislature tend to favour their co-partisans for at least two reasons. First, party politics in Kenya matter for electoral outcomes. Most legislators care about the reputation of their parties, because voters often have preferences for party labels rather than for individual politicians. Survey data shows that in the mid-2010s at least 70 per cent of Kenyan voters identified with a particular political party (Afrobarometer 2015). Parties have often been blamed when their politicians performed unsatisfactorily or when they mismanaged public resources. Maintaining party credibility is thus an essential component of political survival. In addition, voters sometimes engage in block voting, selecting all of the same party's candidates across different electoral positions based on their loyalty (Mboya 2020). Thus, politicians have relied on party identification for re-election, creating incentives for them to protect their party's reputation and, therefore, disproportionately impose fewer legislative sanctions on corrupt or ineffective officials from their party.

Second, political favouritism also occurs because of collusive behaviour in corruption scandals (Laffont and Tirole 1991). Misappropriation of public funds, especially in procurement, often involves strategic collaboration between government entities and bureaucrats (Coviello and Gagliarducci 2010). The proceedings of such illegal activities would then be shared with legislators, who, in return, must ensure that critical allegations are dismissed during parliamentary sessions. Evidence shows that parliamentarians in Kenya, including those in oversight committees, have been constantly implicated in corruption scandals and bribe-taking to resolve audit queries (Rugene 2009).

Past research on the Kenyan legislature provides further insights into the mechanisms of political favouritism (Burgess et al. 2015; Harris and Posner 2019; Jablonski 2014; Mai 2020) and how intra- and inter-party politics influences legislative decisions and policy outcomes (Akech 2011; Nyamori and Nyamori 2015), and the impacts on party polarisation in Kenya. Yet there is still limited knowledge about how the legislature interacts with subnational governments in its oversight responsibilities. For instance, Opalo (2021) argues that parliamentary committees in Kenya fail to uphold the public interest and instead manage intra-elite distributive policies, reflecting the broader political environment of patronage and clientelism. Survey data also shows that 84 per cent of Kenyans thought that at least some, if not most, of the MPs were corrupt (Afrobarometer 2015). This finding is consistent with Rugene (2009), who argues that corruption is rampant in the Kenyan parliament.

The Public Accounts Committee (PAC)

The PAC is one of the most influential parliamentary committees. It is established by law and derives its mandate from various issues of the government's standing orders and the Public Finance Management Act. The committee is responsible for ensuring the accountability of public finances by examining whether appropriated funds by entities (such as ministries, state departments, local counties, commissions, and independent offices) have been disbursed consistent with the government's financial regulations and procedures. Working with Kenya's independent supreme audit institution, the OAG, and other entities, the PAC holds government officials accountable for the efficiency and effectiveness of public spending.

The chairperson of the PAC is a crucial element in shaping the committee's effectiveness, given their powers to convene sessions, summon public officials, or control the agenda of the committee (McGee 2002; Stapenhurst, Jacobs, and Olaore 2016). The chairperson is often appointed from the main opposition party so as to enhance some separation of powers between the PAC and other government institutions (Pelizzo and Stapenhurst 2014). This practice enhances the committee's legitimacy by promoting more of a balance of power between the government and the opposition. In addition, it signals the willingness of the majority party and minority parties to work together in a bipartisan manner (Pelizzo and Stapenhurst 2008). Nonetheless, the selection process for the chair's position is highly politicised, given his or her ability to significantly influence the committee's procedures and outcomes (Nyamori and Nyamori 2015).

In addition to its chairperson, the PAC has no more than 16 other members. It is constituted immediately after each general election, and its members serve for an initial period of three calendar years. After this period, the committee is reconstituted to fill the remainder of the parliamentary term, which may extend another two years. During 2015–18, the committee members were drawn from seven different political parties, although the two main parties (the Orange Democratic Party and the Jubilee Party) constituted almost 75 per cent of all members (Figure 8.1). Five other parties were represented with a single committee member in the 2015–18 period, although the Wiper Democratic Movement gained two seats in 2018.

The PAC's deliberations regularly involve summoning accounting officers or county governors to respond to audit queries in sessions that have often been open to the public. (Accounting officers are those top public officials mandated to monitor, evaluate, and oversee the management of public finances in their respective government entities.) This summoning power makes the PAC very influential in the Kenyan parliament – it is one of the few institutions with legal authority to call upon senior government officials and bureaucrats. Nevertheless, the PAC's influence over oversight matters is restricted to offering recommendations and actions that are tabled and discussed with the National Assembly or the OAG. The PAC itself lacks prosecutorial powers. The OAG is responsible for making any follow-up actions and ensuring that accounting officers or their respective entities implement the PAC's recommendations.

Figure 8.1: The political parties of the Public Accounts Committee members in 2018 and 2017

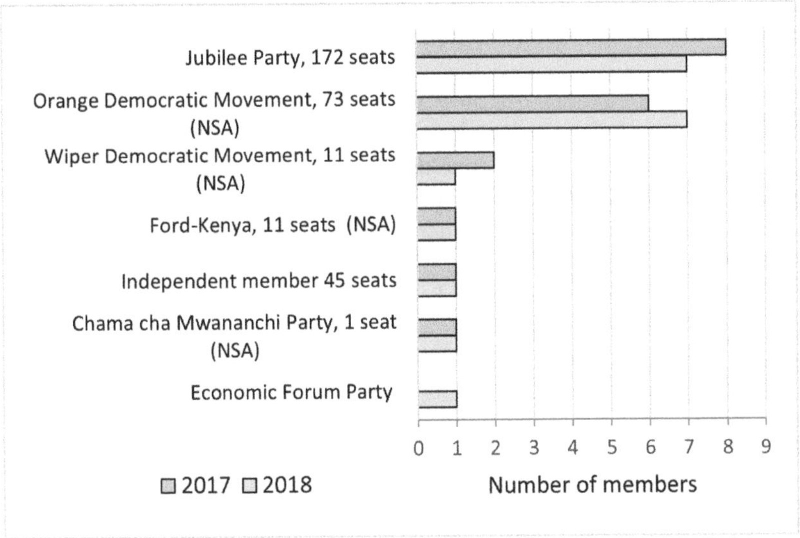

Source: Public Accounts Committee Reports (various issues).
Notes: The distribution of PAC members in 2016 and 2015 was the same as in 2017. The near-majority party in the 2017–22 legislature was the Jubilee Party, holding 172 (49 per cent) of the 350 members, with one of its members as speaker. The parties labelled (NSA) formed a 'National Super Alliance'.

8.4 Research design: data, measurement, and estimation strategy

The data deployed here comes from a variety of official government sources. First, data on legislative sanctions imposed on county officials was hand-coded from annual reports produced by the PAC that specify the type of allegation uncovered in the audits, the committee's observation and findings, and the recommendations made to the National Assembly and the Senate. In all, 156 sanctions were imposed between 2015 and 2018, a period selected because of data availability. Second, data was collected from the Independent Electoral and Boundary Commission on indicators such as the party affiliation of PAC members, the number of votes received by each committee member in their previous election as MP, and the number of their political opponents. Finally, data on the amounts of misappropriated funds was obtained from audit reports conducted by the OAG. Most audit queries relate to misappropriations such as irregular and unsupported payments, irregular procurements and tenders, unsupported balances, outstanding debts, and pending bills.

Turning to measurement, three different coding approaches were adopted to measure the intensity of sanctions – that is, how severe their implications were for county officials. The first classifies sanctions into two non-overlapping categories: severe and modest. Severe sanctions include those where the PAC recommended either that (i) the national government, through the cabinet secretary or National Treasury, recover the money owed by the county governments, or (ii) the director of criminal investigation and the Ethics and Anti-Corruption Commission investigate the county governments, or (iii) the judiciary reprimand the accounting officers. Modest sanctions refer to those where the PAC provided a cautionary warning or advised counties to institute corrective measures to comply with the PFM Act. (See this chapter's Supplementary Materials, Table 8.A for some examples.[1]) Figure 8.2 presents a descriptive analysis of sanctions' distribution by severity. Excluding 2017, modest recommendations appear to be the most predominant outcome of the PAC's deliberations, casting doubt on whether the PAC can impose stronger oversight over local politicians.

Figure 8.2: Severe and modest PAC sanctions, 2015–18

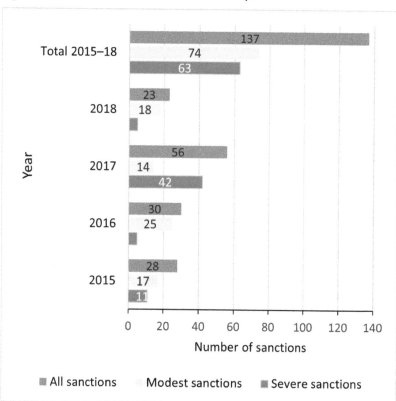

Source: Public Accounts Committee Reports (various issues).

Table 8.1: Resolved and unresolved PAC cases, 2015–18

Year	Resolved	Unresolved	Not clear	Total
2015	6	17	5	28
2016	9	11	16	36
2017	14	45	1	60
2018	17	14	1	32
Total	46	87	23	156
% of total	*29.5*	*55.8*	*14.7*	*100.0*

Source: PAC reports.

A second code distinguishes between resolved and unresolved allegations. Resolved cases are defined as those closed by the PAC, where no further action is required by the committee or county officials. Unresolved cases remain pending and need to be followed up by either the committee, county officials, or the OAG. This distinction is vital as some cases classified as having modest sanctions remain unresolved and were deferred for later periods. More than half of the audit allegations were unresolved (Table 8.1). Half of these cases occurred in 2017. Less than a third of cases were resolved, while there was no clear information for the remaining cases.

I also examined the relationship between the partisanship of the PAC chair and local politicians – co-partisanship between the two is associated with a low share of severe sanctions (less than 30 per cent across the period 2015–18) and also of modest sanctions (less than 21 per cent). Co-partisans were also more likely to have their allegations resolved without any sanctions. A significant share of sanctions was on local politicians who were not affiliated with the chairperson of the PAC. Overall, these patterns suggest a role for political favouritism. Also coded was the number of recommendations or sanctions imposed by the PAC on each allegation. For each audit allegation, the PAC can recommend several courses of action to counties, often varying from 1 to 3.

Co-partisanship between the PAC and counties was measured using four proxies. The first is a binary variable (chairperson-governor) that takes the value 1 if the chairperson of the PAC and the governor are co-partisans. The second proxy is a binary indicator (chairperson-senator) equal to 1 if the chairperson is a co-partisan with the senator. A third measure takes a value 1 if the majority of the committee members are co-partisans with the governor. The final measure takes a value 1 if the majority of the committee members and the senator are co-partisans.

Finally, to measure electoral incentives, the analysis takes advantage of the fact that the committee members are also parliamentarians and subject to re-election after each five-year term. Electoral competition is proxied by the margin of an MP's victory over the runner-up MP in the previous election. I assume that those with smaller margins face the highest electoral threat.

Estimation strategy

The baseline specification adopted to estimate how co-partisanship between the oversight committee and local politicians affects disciplinary sanctions takes the form:

$$y_{it} = \beta_0 + \beta_1 Alignment + \beta_2\, Controls + C_i + \varepsilon_{it} \qquad [1]$$

where y_{it} is the outcome variable of interest (proxied using the three indicators of number of sanctions imposed, a binary variable for case resolved or not, and whether sanctions were severe or modest). The subscript i indexes each audit allegation, and t denotes the year the sanction was imposed. Alignment is measured using the four different proxies (co-partisanship between the chair of the PAC and governor/senator or between the majority of the committee members and the governor/senator). The coefficient of interest is denoted by β_1 and measures the association between co-partisanship and oversights.

The control variables included in the regression are the location/character of the county (rural or urban) as a proxy of the visibility of a particular county at the national level; the size of the budget (to capture the overall resource avail-ability, because counties with higher budgets might have more incentives to misappropriate funds); a binary variable indicating whether a governor or sen-ator was a politician before 2013 (to capture any existing political relationships that could facilitate corrupt networks); and a variable indicating the number of years to the subsequent elections (to capture the timing of elections, which could provide incentives to engage in resource misappropriation). County fixed effects (C_i) are included to control for time-invariant county-level fac-tors that might affect the imposition of sanctions. This helps to minimise endogeneity concerns arising from omitted variables and minimises potential simultaneity between co-partisanship and the imposition of sanctions.

8.5 Results

Does co-partisanship undermine legislative oversight? Table 8.2 presents results from estimating Equation [1] using a linear probability model. Across the different specifications, the alignment coefficient has the anticipated sign and provides significant evidence in favour of the alignment hypothesis. Co-partisanship with the chairperson of the PAC reduces the likelihood of facing severe sanctions by 11 per cent (Panel A, column 1). Co-partisanship also reduces the proportion of recommendations by 27 per cent (Panel C, column 1). At the same time, it increases the possibility of having the audit resolved by 8 per cent (Panel B, column 1, a positive association since resolu-tion is better here).

Co-partisanship between the chairperson and the county senator is asso-ciated with a 12 per cent reduction in the likelihood of receiving severe sanctions (Panel A, column 2), 11 per cent lower likelihood of having cases resolved (Panel B, column 2), and 30 per cent lower likelihood of receiving

Table 8.2: Testing the co-partisanship alignment hypothesis

	Type of co-partisanship			
	1: Chair-governor	2: Chair-senator	3: Majority-governor	4: Majority-senator
Panel A: Outcome variable: severe or modest sanctions				
Alignment	−0.110*** (0.034)	−0.116** (0.06)	−0.05* (0.03)	−0.03*** (0.01)
Panel B: Outcome variable: resolved or unresolved				
Alignment	0.081** (0.04)	0.111** (0.04)	0.08* (0.06)	0.10** (0.04)
Panel C: Outcome variable: number of recommendations				
Alignment	−0.27** (0.14)	−0.30* (0.17)	−0.110** (0.04)	−0.08*** (0.04)
Controls	Yes	Yes	Yes	Yes
County fixed effects	Yes	Yes	Yes	Yes
Observations	133	133	133	133
R-squared	0.62	0.69	0.56	0.71

Notes: Robust standard errors in italics and parentheses. ***$p < 0.01$, **$p < 0.05$, *$p < 0.1$.

a higher number of recommendations (Panel C, column 2). These results reflect the nature of personalised politics between politicians at different levels of the government. This may help explain why survey evidence shows that only 20 per cent of Kenyans think that the parliament should scrutinise county officials (Afrobarometer 2015). These findings were also present with the alternative alignment measures shown in columns 3 and 4 of Table 8.2, which suggest that alignment increases the likelihood of having audit queries resolved and receiving fewer recommendations by around 10 per cent, statistically significant at the 5 per cent level.

Are these findings robust to alternative explanations? First, it might be plausible that the PAC considers the amount of misappropriated funds in its deliberations. If this were the case, the type and severity of sanctions would drive the results because low amounts of misappropriated funds would receive fewer sanctions. To address this concern, Equation [1] above was re-estimated but controls for the amounts of misappropriated funds associated with each audit allegation. Table 8.3 presents the results. Across the different specifications, the alignment coefficient is similar in sign and magnitude to Table 8.2. These results show that corruption does not confound the results but also strengthens the finding that co-partisanship was significantly associated with lower disciplinary sanctions and more resolution of audits.

A second concern relates to changes in the broader political climate that might influence the committee's deliberation. For instance, if the PAC were more lenient or strict in holding politicians accountable in specific years, this would affect the baseline estimates. To address this, Table 8.4 reports estimates obtained from re-estimating Equation [1], but separately for each

Table 8.3: Testing for the effect of the amount of misappropriated funds

| | Type of co-partisanship | | | |
	1: Chair-governor	2: Chair-senator	3: Majority-governor	4: Majority-senator
Panel A: Outcome variable: severe or modest sanctions				
Alignment	−0.111** (0.04)	−0.115** (0.05)	−0.08** (0.04)	−0.06* (0.05)
Panel B: Outcome variable: resolved or unresolved				
Alignment	0.087** (0.03)	0.116** (0.04)	0.10* (0.06)	0.15** (0.05)
Panel C: Outcome variable: number of recommendations				
Alignment	−0.25* (0.05)	−0.28* (0.05)	−0.13*** (0.05)	−0.09** (0.05)
Controls	Yes	Yes	Yes	Yes
County fixed effects	Yes	Yes	Yes	Yes
Observations	133	133	133	133
R-squared	0.22	0.43	0.42	0.47

Notes: Robust standard errors in italics and parentheses. ***$p < 0.01$, **$p < 0.05$, *$p < 0.1$.

Table 8.4: Testing for the effect of broader political events

| | Party of PAC chairperson and county governors aligned | | | |
	2015	2016	2017	2018
Panel A: Outcome variable: severe or modest sanctions				
Alignment	−0.05** (0.02)	−0.04** (0.02)	−0.01** (0.05)	−0.04* (0.02)
Panel B: Outcome variable: resolved or unresolved				
Alignment	0.01** (0.004)	0.001** (0.0004)	0.20* (0.11)	0.05 (0.05)
Panel C: Outcome variable: number of recommendations				
Alignment	−0.11** (0.04)	−0.06*** (0.02)	−0.18** (0.08)	−0.00 (0.02)
Controls	Yes	Yes	Yes	Yes
County fixed effects	Yes	Yes	Yes	Yes
Observations	23	20	59	31
R-squared	0.08	0.06	0.15	0.41

Notes: Robust standard errors in italics and parentheses. ***$p < 0.01$, **$p < 0.05$, *$p < 0.1$.

of the years under analysis. The analysis is restricted to alignment between the chairperson of the PAC and county governors, although the results were robust to the other measures of alignment. Across all the columns, the coefficient of the alignment variable has the expected sign and is statistically significant for most of the years. This result suggests that differences in annual political events, such as the setting of the committee's agenda, the allocation of resources from the central to the local governments, and the parliamentary schedule, were not confounding the main results.

Testing for collusive behaviour

Does co-partisanship undermine political accountability because of collusive behaviour? Empirically, testing for this mechanism is complicated because collusive behaviour is not directly observed. So, the analysis examines whether there were differentials in sanctions conditional on the type of audit allegation. This is consistent with the idea that certain kinds of corruption, especially those that require coordination between different politicians, generate resources that politicians could use to advance their careers.

To investigate this possibility, Table 8.5 presents the results obtained from re-estimating Equation [1] separately for each type of audit allegation. The results show significant variation in imposing disciplinary sanctions according to the kind of misappropriation. Across the columns, alignment varies in size, magnitude, and significance. The coefficients in columns 1 and 2 are statistically insignificant, suggesting that sanctions were not lower for pending bills or outstanding debts. These were typically audit allegations that can be traced back to either bureaucrats or debt interest payments. Pending bills consist of any amount related to goods and services received. Still, a commitment was

Table 8.5: Differences across types of cases

	Types of cases			
	1: Pending bills	2: Outstanding debts	3: Unsupported balance	4: Irregular procurement
Panel A: Outcome variable: severe or modest sanctions				
Alignment	0.05 (0.05)	0.101 (0.11)	−0.09*** (0.03)	−0.12** (0.06)
Panel B: Outcome variable: resolved or unresolved				
Alignment	0.005 (0.005)	0.000 (0.00)	0.32** (0.15)	0.11* (0.06)
Panel C: Outcome variable: number of recommendations				
Alignment	0.001 (0.001)	0.04 (0.05)	−0.14*** (0.05)	−0.09*** (0.03)
Controls	Yes	Yes	Yes	Yes
County fixed effects	Yes	Yes	Yes	Yes
Observations	40	45	33	38
R-squared	0.18	0.20	0.14	0.41

Notes: Robust standard errors in italics and parentheses. ***$p < 0.01$, **$p < 0.05$, *$p < 0.1$.

made to carry the bills over to the next financial year, thus drawing unnecessary interest charges.

However, the results in columns 3 and 4 are positive and significant at the 5 per cent level, suggesting that counties receive significantly fewer sanctions if audits revealed unsupported balances or irregular procurements. Unsupported balances are those transactions that take place during the financial year, but sufficient documents were not provided to show that the expenditure was authorised or that the counties made the payment and yet did not receive the goods and services. Irregularities in procurement refer the overpricing of contracts and tenders relative to the stipulated market price. Misappropriations are significantly associated with collusion as they entail coordination from different government entities.

This finding is consistent with the evidence of collusive behaviour within legislative committees in Kenya. For instance, Ayaga (2015) detailed how members of the PAC accused each other of bribe-taking to avoid scrutinising allegations of resource misappropriation. Akech (2011, p.372) noted that legislators can serve on committees,

> even though their membership would entail a conflict of interest—either because they face allegations of corruption, are allegedly allied to corruption cartels, or have commercial interests that these committees oversee.

Finally, Hope (2014) argued that bribes are paid to Kenya's MPs from internal sources such as their counterpart legislators, or external sources such as businesspersons to lobby legislators, to either debate or vote in ways favouring their interests.

Do electoral incentives influence legislative oversight?

According to several studies, career concerns predict the behaviour of political agents and can predict the effectiveness of the legislature in executing its mandate. Politicians, especially those serving in the committees, have incentives to signal their competence in performing their oversight responsibilities, either as a means of getting promoted to more influential positions in the government or to signal greater competence to voters, or to receive significant media attention. So those facing higher electoral threats are more likely to execute their oversight responsibilities more effectively than their counterparts, leading to more severe oversight outcomes.

To test this hypothesis, I examined how the structure of political incentives within parliamentary committees influenced the scrutiny of subnational governments. Equation [2] below introduces an interaction term between the alignment variable and political competition. Each MP's 2013 constituency margin of victory over the second runner-up was used as a proxy for the

Table 8.6: Do MPs' electoral incentives impact on the co-alignment effect?

Explanatory variables	Dependent variable		
	1: Intensity of sanctions	2: Resolved vs unresolved	3: No of recommendations
Alignment × Competition	0.16** (0.07)	−0.32*** (0.12)	0.23*** (0.07)
County fixed effects	Yes	Yes	Yes
Observations	80	87	90
R-squared	0.61	0.72	0.53

Notes: Robust standard errors in italics and parentheses. ***$p < 0.01$, **$p < 0.05$, *$p < 0.1$.

closeness of political competition, with slimmer margins assumed to improve legislative performance among committee members.

$$y_{it} = \beta_0 + \beta_1 Alignment + \beta_2\ Competition + \beta_3\ Alignment * Competition$$
$$+ \beta_4 Controls + C_i + \varepsilon_{it} \qquad [2]$$

By taking derivatives, the effect of political competition on legislative sanctions is given by $\beta_2 + \beta_3$ (competition), which is conditional on the strength of the electoral incentives of the committee members. The estimated coefficient of β_3, therefore, accounts for the differential effect of political competition for aligned (relative to non-aligned) committee members, which is reported in Table 8.6. The results suggest that aligned legislators with a smaller margin of victory in the previous elections were more likely to impose higher sanctions than those that did not. The point estimate of the interaction term in column 1 is statistically significant at the 5 per cent level, implying that electoral incentives increase the probability of having an audit allegation unresolved by 16 per cent. The point estimate in column 3 reveals that political competition increases the probability of receiving a higher number of recommendations by 23 per cent by an aligned committee member. The results in column 2 show that these incentives also lower the likelihood of having an audit allegation resolved by 32 per cent by an aligned committee member. These findings reflect a pattern where aligned committee members who serve in competitive constituencies portray stronger incentives to oversee county governments by imposing stricter sanctions for misappropriating public resources.

Conclusions

Using a unique data set that matches parliamentary sanctions with the political alignment of local and central government officials, this analysis shows that co-partisanship between legislative committee members and local politicians can undermine political accountability. Kenyan politicians affiliated with the chairperson of the PAC or the majority of committee members tended to receive lower sanctions than the unaffiliated ones. Additional analysis that merges electoral data with parliamentary sanctions shows that, when legislators faced a credible electoral threat, they tended to exercise their oversight responsibilities more in line with democratic principles.

Taken together, these findings point to some broad policy implications. First, concerted efforts should be made to ensure that the structure and composition of legislative committees are set up in ways that create political incentives to enhance their capacity to fulfil their oversight mandate. While party politics is a crucial feature of most parliamentary systems, increasing the institutional distance between the oversight committees and the politicians under scrutiny for misappropriating public funds can reduce the risk of political favouritism and enhance accountability outcomes. Useful measures here could include a more proactive role of different institutions (such as parliamentary budget offices and parliamentary subcommittees) to provide more bureaucratic and technical inputs into the oversight process. The literature has also advocated the establishment of several initiatives (such as open forums where top politicians are summoned to respond to parliamentary questions and independent bodies that examine the deliberations of oversight committees) to review or probe any inconsistencies in sanctioning (Pukelis 2016; Strøm, Müller, and Smith 2010). Efforts should be made to increase the transparency of oversight committees. In addition, redistributing some of the powers of the chairperson to other committee members could reduce the political salience of that position, and place the decision-making process with a larger set of members whose interests might differ from the chair.

A more robust civil society or media surveillance that ensures committee members carry out their mandates in line with the public interest could also play an important role. Mostly, there is limited public information on their work that can provide insights into their effectiveness and capacity to influence public policy. Providing such information is integral to assessing their effectiveness and could also provide voters with critical information to hold politicians accountable. At the minimum, African parliaments should be encouraged and supported to provide disaggregated data and timely reports on their deliberations.

Endnotes

Supplementary material for this chapter is available on LSE Press's Zenodo site (https://zenodo.org/communities/decentralised_governance/). See: *Supplementary material for*: Michael Mbate (2023) 'Can parliamentary sanctions strengthen local political accountability? Evidence from Kenya', Chapter 8 in Jean-Paul Faguet and Sarmistha Pal (eds) *Decentralised Governance: Crafting Effective Democracies Around the World*, London: LSE Press. https://doi.org/10.5281/zenodo.7919826

[1] *Supplementary material for*: Michael Mbate (2023) 'Can parliamentary sanctions strengthen local political accountability? Evidence from Kenya', Chapter 8 in Jean-Paul Faguet and Sarmistha Pal (eds) *Decentralised Governance: Crafting Effective Democracies Around the World*, London: LSE Press. https://doi.org/10.5281/zenodo.7919826

References

Afrobarometer Data, Kenya, Round 6 (2015)
https://www.afrobarometer.org/survey-resource/kenya-round-6-data-2015

Akech, Migai (2011) 'Abuse of Power and Corruption in Kenya: Will the New Constitution Enhance Government Accountability?' *Indiana Journal of Global Legal Studies*, vol.18, no.1, pp.341–94. https://doi.org/10.2979/indjglolegstu.18.1.341

Ayaga, W. (2015) 'Crisis in Parliament as Bribes Rock Committees', *The Standard*.
https://www.standardmedia.co.ke/politics/article/2000155265/crisis-in -parliament-as-bribes-rock-committees

Bachelard, Jerome Y. (2010) 'The Anglo-Leasing Corruption Scandal in Kenya: The Politics of International and Domestic Pressures and Counter-Pressures', *Review of African Political Economy*, vol.37, no.124, pp.187–200. https://doi.org/10.1080/03056244.2010.483903

Besley, Timothy and Case, Anne (1995) 'Incumbent Behavior: Vote-Seeking, Tax Setting, and Yardstick Competition', *American Economic Review*, vol.85, no.1, pp.25–45. http://doi.org/10.3386/w4041

Burgess, Robin; Jedwab, Remi; Miguel, Edward; Morjaria, Ameet; and Miquel, Gerard (2015) 'The Value of Democracy: Evidence from Road Building in Kenya', *American Economic Review*, vol.105, no.6, pp.1817–51. http://doi.org/10.1257/aer.20131031

Coviello, Decio and Gagliarducci, Stefano (2010) 'Building Political Collusion: Evidence from Procurement Auctions', IZA Discussion Paper No.4939. Institute for the Study of Labor. https://dx.doi.org/10.2139/ssrn.1631074

Dauda, Hambali; Suhuyini, Alhassan Sayibu; and Antwi-Boasiako, Joseph (2020) 'Challenges of the Public Accounts Committee of Ghana's Parliament in Ensuring an Efficient Public Financial Management', *The Journal of Legislative Studies*, vol.26, no.4, pp.542–57. https://doi.org/10.1080/13572334.2020.1784527

D'Arcy, Michelle and Cornell, Agnes (2016) 'Devolution and Corruption in Kenya: Everyone's Turn to Eat?' *African Affairs*, vol.155, no.459, pp.246–73. https://doi.org/10.1093/afraf/adw002

De Mendonça, Helder Ferreira and Baca, Adriana Cabrera (2018) 'Relevance of Corruption on the Effect of Public Health Expenditure and Taxation on Economic Growth', *Applied Economics Letters*, vol.25, no.12, pp.876–81. https://doi.org/10.1080/13504851.2017.1374533

De Vos, Pierre (2013) 'Balancing Independence and Accountability: The Role of Chapter 9 Institutions in South Africa's Constitutional Democracy', in Chirwa, Danwood and Nijzink, Lia (eds) *Accountable Government in Africa: Perspectives from Public Law and Political Studies*, Tokyo: UNU, pp.160–77. https://library.oapen.org/bitstream/handle/20.500.12657/25282/1/1004814.pdf#page=177

Fashagba, Joseph (2009) 'Legislative Oversight under the Nigerian Presidential System', *The Journal of Legislative Studies*, vol.15, no.4, pp.439–59. https://doi.org/10.1080/13572330903302497

Finan, Frederico and Mazzocco, Maurizio (2020) 'Electoral Incentives and the Allocation of Public Funds', *Journal of European Economic Association*, vol.19, no.5, pp.2467–512. https://doi.org/10.1093/jeea/jvaa055

Foster, Helen (2015) 'The Effectiveness of the Public Accounts Committee in Northern Ireland', *Public Money and Management*, vol.35, no.6, pp.401–08. https://doi.org/10.1080/09540962.2015.1083684

Gaines, Brian; Goodwin, Mark; Holden Bates, Stephen; and Sin, Gisela (2019) 'The Study of Legislative Committees', *The Journal of Legislative Studies*, vol.25, no.3, pp.331–39. https://doi.org/10.1080/13572334.2019.1662614

Golooba-Mutebi, Frederick (2016) 'Cost of Politics in Uganda', Background paper. London: Westminster Foundation for Democracy.

Hansen, Martin Ejnar (2019) 'Distributing Chairs and Seats in Committees: A Parliamentary Perspective', *Parliamentary Affairs*, vol.72, pp.202–22. https://doi.org/10.1093/pa/gsy008

Harris, J. Andrew and Posner, Daniel N. (2019) '(Under What Conditions) Do Politicians Reward Their Supporters? Evidence from Kenya's Constituencies Development Fund', *American Political Science Review*, vol.107, no.3, pp.397–417. https://doi.org/10.1017/S0003055418000709

Hope, Kempe Ronald (2014) 'Kenya's Corruption Problem: Causes and Consequences', *Commonwealth & Comparative Politics*, vol.52, no.4, pp.493–512. https://doi.org/10.1080/14662043.2014.955981

Holzhacker, Ronald (2005) 'The Power of Opposition Parliamentary Party Groups in European Scrutiny', *The Journal of Legislative Studies*, vol.11, no.3–4, pp.428–45. https://doi.org/10.1080/13572330500273711

Hughes, Tyler and Carlson, Deven (2015) 'Divided Government and Delay in the Legislative Process: Evidence from Important Bills, 1949–2010',

American Politics Research, vol.43, no.5, pp.771–92. https://doi.org/10.1177/1532673X15574594

Jablonski, Ryan S. (2014) 'How Aid Targets Votes: The Impact of Electoral Incentives on Aid Distribution', *World Politics*, vol.66, no.2, pp.293–330. https://doi.org/10.1017/S0043887114000045

Jensen, Christian B.; Kuenzi, Michelle; and Lee, Daniel J. (2020) 'The Effects of Political Parties on Roll-Call Voting in Kenya's Parliament', *The Journal of Legislative Studies*, vol.26, no.4, pp.523–41. https://doi.org/10.1080/13572334.2020.1782077

Keneck-Massil, Joseph; Nomo-Beyala, Clery; and Owoundi, Ferdinand (2021) 'The Corruption and Income Inequality Puzzle: Does Political Power Distribution Matter?' *Economic Modelling*, vol.103, pp.1–32. https://doi.org/10.1016/j.econmod.2021.105610

Keyes, John Mark (2021) 'Parliamentary Scrutiny of the Quality of Legislation in Canada', *The Theory and Practice of Legislation*, vol.9, no.2, pp.203–26. https://doi.org/10.1080/20508840.2021.1904567

Laffont, Jean-Jacques and Tirole, Jean (1991) 'The Politics of Government Decision-Making: A Theory of Regulatory Capture', *The Quarterly Journal of Economics*, vol.106, no.4, pp.1089–127. https://doi.org/10.2307/2937958

Longley, Lawrence and Davidson, Roger H. (1998) 'Parliamentary Committees: Changing Perspectives on Changing Institutions', *The Journal of Legislative Studies*, vol.4, no.1, pp.1–20. https://doi.org/10.1080/13572339808420537

Mai, Hassan (2020) 'The Local Politics of Resource Distribution', in Cheeseman, Nicholas; Kanyinga, Karuti; and Lynch, Gabrielle (eds) *Oxford Handbook of Kenyan Politics*, Oxford University Press, pp.482–96. https://doi.org/10.1093/oxfordhb/9780198815693.001.0001

Matthews, Felicity and Flinders, Matthew (2015) 'The Watchdogs of "Washminster" – Parliamentary Scrutiny of Executive Patronage in the UK', *Commonwealth & Comparative Politics*, vol.53, no.2, pp.153–76. https://doi.org/10.1080/14662043.2015.1013295

Mboya, Tom (2020) 'The Cost of Parliamentary Politics in Kenya', Westminster Foundation for Democracy. https://www.agora-parl.org/sites/default/files/agora-documents/The%20Cost%20of%20Parliamentary%20Politics%20in%20Kenya.pdf

McGee, David G. (2002) *The Overseers: Public Accounts Committees and Public Spending*, London: Pluto Press.

Meriläinen, Jaakko and Tukiainen, Janne (2018) 'Rank Effects in Political Promotions', *Public Choice*, vol.177, pp.87–109. https://doi.org/10.1007/s11127-018-0591-8

Mickler, Tim (2017) 'Committee Autonomy in Parliamentary Systems – Coalition Logic or Congressional Rationales?' *The Journal of Legislative Studies*, vol.23, no.3, pp.367–91. https://doi.org/10.1080/13572334.2017.1359941

Mwangi, Oscar Gakuo (2008) 'Political Corruption, Party Financing and Democracy in Kenya', *The Journal of Modern African Studies*, vol.46, no.2, pp.267–85. https://doi.org/10.1017/S0022278X08003224

Norton, Phillip (ed.) (2020) *The Impact of Legislatures: A Quarter-Century of the Journal of Legislative Studies*, Oxford: Routledge.

Norton, Phillip (2019) 'Post-legislative Scrutiny in the UK Parliament: Adding Value', *The Journal of Legislative Studies*, vol.25, no.3, pp.340–57. https://doi.org/10.1080/13572334.2019.1633778

Nyamori, Robert Ochoki and Nyamori, Bosire (2015) 'Evolution and Effectiveness of the Kenyan Public Accounts Committee', in Hoque, Zahirul (ed.) *Making Governments Accountable: The Role of Public Accounts Committees and National Audit Offices*. Routledge.

Opalo, Ken Ochieng' (2021) 'Leveraging Legislative Power: Distributive Politics and Committee Work in Kenya's National Assembly', *The Journal of Legislative Studies*, vol.28, no.4, pp.513–32. https://doi.org/10.1080/13572334.2021.1935017

Opalo, Ken Ochieng' (2019) *Legislative Development in Africa: Politics and Post-colonial Legacies*, Cambridge: Cambridge University Press.

Osei, Anja (2020) 'Post-conflict Democratization in Sierra Leone: The Role of the Parliament', *Journal of Legislative Studies*. https://doi.org/10.1080/13572334.2020.1809806

Public Expenditure and Financial Accountability (PEFA) (2020) 'Global Financial Report on Public Financial Management', PEFA.

Pelizzo, Riccardo and Kinyondo, Abel (2014) 'Public Accounts Committees in Eastern and Southern Africa: A Comparative Analysis', *Politics and Policy*, vol.42, no.1, pp.77–102. https://dx.doi.org/10.2139/ssrn.2426199

Pelizzo, Riccardo and Stapenhurst, Rick (2008) 'Public Accounts Committee', in Stapenhurst, Rick; Pelizzo, Riccardo; Olson, David; and von Trap, Lisa (eds) *Legislative Oversight and Budgeting: A World Perspective*, Washington DC: The World Bank.

Pelizzo, Riccardo and Stapenhurst, Rick (2014) 'Oversight Effectiveness and Political Will: Some Lessons from West Africa', *The Journal of Legislative Studies*, vol.20, no.2, pp.255–61. https://doi.org/10.1080/13572334.2013.829277

Pukelis, Lukas (2016) 'The Role of Parliamentary Committee Chairs in Coalition Governments: Office and Policy Theses Reconsidered', *East*

European Politics, vol.32, no.2, pp.215–35.
https://doi.org/10.1080/21599165.2016.1154844

Rugene, N. (2009) 'Bribery in Kenya's Parliament', *Daily Nation (Nairobi)*,
16 May.
http://www.nation.co.ke/News/-/1056/599016/-/u6adu9/-/index.html

Stapenhurst, Rick; Jacobs, Kerry; and Olaore, Oladeji (2016) 'Legislative
Oversight in Nigeria: An Empirical Review and Assessment', *The Journal
of Legislative Studies*, vol.22, no.1, pp.1–29.
https://doi.org/10.1080/13572334.2015.1134908

Shaw, Malcolm (1998) 'Parliamentary Committees: A Global Perspective',
The Journal of Legislative Studies, vol.4, no.1, pp.225–51.
https://doi.org/10.1080/13572339808420547

Strøm, Kaare; Müller, Wolfgang; and Smith, Daniel Markham (2010)
'Parliamentary Control of Coalition Governments', *Annual Review of
Political Science*, vol.13, no.5, pp.517–35.
https://doi.org/10.1146/annurev.polisci.10.071105.104340

Strøm, Kaare (1998) 'Parliamentary Committees in European Democracies',
The Journal of Legislative Studies, vol.4, no.1, pp.21–59.
https://doi.org/10.4324/9780203044797

Supreme Auditor (2015) 'Measuring the Impact of Audit', Office of the
Auditor-General Kenya.

Tirole, Jean (1986) 'Hierarchies and Bureaucracies', *Journal of Law,
Economics, and Organization*, vol.11, pp.181–214.
https://doi.org/10.1093/oxfordjournals.jleo.a036907

Transparency International (2014) 'The Impact of Corruption on Growth
and Inequality', Transparency International.
https://www.transparency.org/files/content/corruptionqas/Impact_of
_corruption_on_growth_and_inequality_2014.pdf

Wehner, Joachim (2006) 'Assessing the Power of the Purse: An Index of
Legislative Budget Institutions', *Political Studies*, vol.54, pp.767–85.
https://doi.org/10.1111/j.1467-9248.2006.00628.x

Zubek, Radoslaw (2008) 'Parties, Rules and Government Legislative Control
in Central Europe: The Case of Poland', *Communist and Post-Communist
Studies*, vol.41, pp.147–61.
https://doi.org/10.1016/j.postcomstud.2008.03.004

PART 3
Mechanism design

9. Centralised versus decentralised monitoring in developing countries: a survey of recent research

Farzana Afridi, Amrita Dhillon, Arka Roy Chaudhuri, and Dashleen Kaur

Summary

We consider the effectiveness of centralised and decentralised monitoring using a theoretical framework of factors affecting each approach. Centralised monitoring is more costly, yet more professional. However, the monitors themselves are not directly affected by the activity they are monitoring, so they may have less at stake in policies or services working well. By contrast, in community monitoring local people and civil society have high stakes in improving local outcomes. In the political economy literature, top-down audits have been seen as more effective in certain types of activities (like procurement) where detailed documentation exists, and where corruption can be more clearly defined as compared to mismanagement. Community monitoring has had higher efficacy when collective action problems can be solved, when monitoring teams have a sense of agency, and when the composition of teams is more homogeneous. Community monitors have deeper knowledge of local agents, so that (*ceteris paribus*) this approach should be less costly for the government because monitoring resources can be targeted better. However, both local monitoring and local agents may suffer from problems of elite capture.

How to cite this book chapter:

Afridi, Farzana; Dhillon, Amrita; Chaudhuri, Arka Roy and Kaur, Dashleen (2023) 'Centralised versus decentralised monitoring in developing countries: A survey of recent research', in: Faguet, Jean-Paul and Pal, Sarmistha (eds) *Decentralised Governance: Crafting Effective Democracies Around the World*, London: LSE Press, pp. 235–269. https://doi.org/10.31389/lsepress.dlg.i License: CC BY 4.0

Corruption is a global phenomenon with varying effects, both on the economy and society. It inhibits economic growth (Li, Xu, and Zou 2000; Mauro 1995), affects business operations, employment and investments (Colonnelli and Prem 2022; Shleifer and Vishny 1993; Hanousek and Kochanova 2016) and reduces tax revenue along with the effectiveness of a variety of financial assistance and public programmes (Tanzi and Davoodi 2001). The IMF has recently put governance issues at the forefront of its macroeconomic policies,[1] the 16th SDG has emphasised the importance of effective governance, and the World Bank has recognised that Covid-19 created new opportunities for corruption that will become manifest only later, and released a report on enhancing government transparency (Bajpai and Myers 2020). So, the need for better governance has never been more apparent.

In a seminal paper, Bardhan and Mookherjee (1998) discussed the trade-off between centralisation and decentralisation in public service delivery from the point of view of reducing corruption.[2] A centralised system is prone to officials taking bribes from non-targeted beneficiaries of a targeted public service delivery programme. This is traded off against elite capture, to which decentralised systems are more prone. Their main conclusion is that the comparison is ambiguous in the absence of institutional detail. While centralised governance has had the advantage of performing better at scale, decentralised systems have been better at targeting the intra-community beneficiaries of anti-poverty programmes. They also emphasise the importance of enhancing local democracy and reducing asset inequality in order to prevent elite capture; this change is an essential condition for decentralisation to succeed.

These considerations are reflected in some of the empirical literature: Wade (2000) argued that India's corruption in the context of irrigation was due to the centralised nature of the bureaucracy. On the other hand, Treisman (2000) concluded that corruption is more likely to be a problem in federal governments. A review of 56 studies by Shah, Thompson and Zou (2004) found that decentralisation sometimes improved service delivery and corruption among other benefits, but at other times worsened it, with the pattern holding across a large range of countries. While tackling corruption is central to many decentralisation programmes, the emerging literature on the comparative efficacy of centralised versus decentralised monitoring of corruption remains rather disperse. In this survey we compile the existing literature, develop a theoretical framework for comparing the efficacy of these alternative anti-corruption monitoring strategies, and then review the existing empirical evidence in the light of this theoretical model. This enables us to identify the conditions under which centralised and decentralised monitoring strategies may function better – and our conclusions echo many of the propositions in early theoretical work by Bardhan and Mookherjee (1998).

The remainder of the chapter is organised as follows: Section 9.1 provides a look ahead to the key issues in comparing the two types of monitoring, and some brief signposts to our approach and conclusions. Section 9.2 provides a conceptual framework to understand how different types of audits can help in reducing corruption. Section 9.3 covers third-party audits at central level, and Section 9.4 focuses on community monitoring, In Section 9.5 we look at the literature that combines both top-down and bottom-up monitoring. Our conclusions highlight some open questions.

9.1 Understanding top-down and bottom-up monitoring

In top-down or third-party audits a specifically assigned independent organisation audits the activities of other institutions in the public sector. For example, in India the Comptroller and Auditor General (CAG) is an independent auditing agency responsible for auditing the expenditures and receipts of all central and state government departments and other public sector organisations. In Brazil, a similar function is performed for municipalities by the Comptroller-General of the Union (CGU), including judicial powers to prosecute. An alternative bottom-up approach seeks to allow local communities to collectively monitor the performance of an activity, a programme, a policy, or an organisation in the social welfare sector.

Until recently the data to study the efficacy of such audits in developing countries has not been available to researchers. One of the main constraints in studying corruption has been the measurement of corruption outcomes (Olken and Pande 2012). Some interesting findings have come from a recent literature (for example, Avis, Ferraz, and Finan 2018; Ferraz and Finan 2008; Ferraz and Finan 2011; and others), based on a few selected countries (like Brazil) that have made data available for research. Decentralised monitoring has also been acquiring increasing importance – over the last decade, the World Bank has dedicated about $85 billion towards local participatory developments. There have been some reviews and meta-analyses of community monitoring (for example, Mansuri and Rao 2013; Molina et al. 2016). Yet there is no comprehensive survey of the relationship between the two approaches and the similarities (or otherwise) in the findings. Our main contribution here is to present some selected studies on both types of monitoring, their design, and the similarities in questions asked, as well as their key results. Such a comparative overview of both together can best enable scholars to advance the literature in more useful ways. Papers are selected for the survey mostly on the basis of being able to provide credible causal evidence and our coverage is restricted mainly to developing countries.

We also provide a conceptual framework that highlights the different ways in which we expect top-down audits to differ from bottom-up approaches. Building on the criminal deterrence literature we highlight the importance of the probability of audits (whether top-down or bottom-up), the likelihood of punishment in each case, the type of punishment, and so on in deterring corrupt behaviours. The framework allows us to explain (for instance) why top-down audits are more likely to suffer from problems such as collusion or an inability to target the right types of corruption, while bottom-up monitoring is likely to suffer from collective action problems. We believe this framework helps to reconcile the different ways that empirical work has approached these two types of monitoring. Methodologically, the literature on community monitoring is based mainly on experimental evidence, while the literature on top-down audits is based on observational data. Studies of top-down audits have mostly focused on corruption outcomes (which are hard to measure), while in contrast studies of community monitoring have tended to analyse more outcome measures that are easier to measure. However, the main research questions across both types of study have been similar in addressing how to tackle the moral hazard problem where an agent (government official or politician) has incentives misaligned with citizens' interests.

In terms of our framework, we find that studies on top-down audits typically focus on how the intensity of audits affects outcomes, whether past audits affect corruption outcomes, and which types of activities are more affected, while those on bottom-up monitoring focus on interventions that aim at increasing the transactions costs of corruption by empowering citizen monitoring groups with information on their entitlements.

Looking ahead to our results, they suggest that top-down audits have high efficacy in reducing corruption when legal punishments follow any audit findings. However, this may not translate into better economic outcomes. For some types of public good services, where it is not easy to document wrong-doing (such as health), top-down audits may be counterproductive. On the other hand, for procurement they are more likely to work in reducing corruption when punishment is well-defined. The literature has progressed methodologically on the lines of being able to measure corruption outcomes and using random audits to identify causal effects. The main gap is to extend these studies to other settings for external validity, because this kind of innovative research has largely focused on Brazil and a few other Latin American countries. Extending the research to cover the eventual outcomes of policy may be fruitful, but the links between the intermediate outcomes are equally important to understand the logical chain.

In community monitoring what has worked is not just information by itself but the task being monitored: how complex it is, whether it is a private or public good, what support is given in negotiating with the service providers, whether community monitors feel empowered enough to change things, what punishment is available for being caught, and the composition of community monitoring committees. Focusing as they do on outcomes, an open question for this literature is why the results are mostly negative – very few studies find significant or substantial effects from better community monitoring on final outcomes. The political economy of power relations seems to be a key reason. Since voting is one of the few ways in which communities can hold politicians accountable, linking the success of community monitoring to voting outcomes might be an avenue to explore this issue. Afridi et al. (2021) is one of the few studies on this topic.

Some of the issues that arise in top-down audits also arise in community monitoring such as the effects on corruption not translating into outcomes for similar reasons, variations across the type of service being monitored, and the salience of the punishment available for wrong-doing. However, the collective action problem is unique to community monitoring as well as the lack of empowerment versus the authority and power of the central audit agency. The strength of community monitoring lies in the greater knowledge in the community about the quality of public services they have been provided with. Unempowered community monitors may not be effective and the types of services that are best served by community monitoring include health, education, and public service delivery programmes, rather than procurement, where top-down audits have the edge. Studies that compare the two types of monitoring (Olken 2007) or that combine them (Serra 2011) are rare, but perhaps deserve further attention from scholars.

9.2 Modelling incentives for honest or dishonest behaviour

Consider an agent who chooses an action $a_i \in [0, 1]$, where 0 stands for honesty and 1 for complete dishonesty, in order to create a revenue stream X out of which a proportion β can be skimmed off in corruption (β measures the opportunity for corruption or the transaction costs associated with it). The agent gets paid a fixed wage w for doing their job. The actual amount of revenues lost due to corruption is private information to the agent who holds that job, creating a moral hazard problem. However, with some probability q, audits take place after the corruption has taken place. Audits can be third-party and top-down audits (assumed to be carried out by an independent regulator) or can be bottom-up social audits (or both). Audits have two consequences: they can expose corruption with some probability and, where exposure occurs, they may lead to punishment with some probability. We assume here that only corrupt agents are caught with probability 1, although everyone is monitored – that is, there are no mistakes in the monitoring technology. When corruption is caught, the agent can be punished – via a legally mandated punishment F, which could either be a fine or jail term (there may or may not be limited liability), or the agent can also be removed from the job, for example via elections or dismissal. An alternative punishment for corrupt agents is loss in status, S, caused by reputational loss or a loss of self-image due to its exposure. We assume that punishment occurs with probability m_k, where k can be either a top-down or a social audit.

We can interpret the agent as an official or an elected representative (as much of the empirical literature on audits reviewed here also does). When corruption is revealed via audits, for example, voters can discipline incumbents by throwing out corrupt incumbents. Here f_k is interpreted as the probability of losing the next election and F can be interpreted as the present value of future rents, that is, the opportunity cost of corruption.

$$EU_i(a_i) = (1-q)g(a_i\beta X + w) - q f_k(F+S)a_i \qquad [1]$$

We assume that the function g is sufficiently concave to guarantee an interior solution. The fine and loss of status are increasing linearly in a_i (the action). (See Chalfin and McCrary (2017) for similar functions used in the criminal deterrence literature.)

The timeline is the following. (1) An audit probability q is announced, (2) the agent gets wage w and chooses $\in a_i$ [0, 1], (3) the audit takes place, and (4) payoffs are realised. Implicitly we assume that the agency can commit to a certain q. There may be situations where instead audits respond to changes in a_i (a simultaneous move game).

Solving by backward induction, for the choice of ai, we have:

$$(1-q)g'(a_i,\beta X,w)\beta X = qf_k(F+S) \qquad [2]$$

Since $g'(a_i)$ is decreasing in a_i there is a unique solution a_i^* which is decreasing in q, F, f_k, S, w and increasing in βX (the proportion captured by corruption). The first-order conditions imply $(1 - q)g'(a_i, \beta X, w)\beta X = qf_k(F + S)$, or:

$$\frac{qf_k(F+S)}{g'(a_i,w)\beta X} = \frac{1-q}{q} \qquad [3]$$

Given the concavity of g we can predict that:

a. The lower the transaction costs, the higher the level of the corrupt action.
b. The higher the punishment, the lower the corrupt action.
c. The higher the probability of being monitored, the lower the level of the corrupt action.

This is line with Becker (1968), where increasing the threat of audit is a substitute for higher punishment. Taking a simple example:

$$g = \ln(\beta X + w)$$

So, we have,

$$\frac{\partial a_i^*}{\partial q} = \frac{-1}{q^2 f_k(F+S)}$$

That is, the agent's responsiveness to a change in the probability of audit is lower when q is high and when punishment is high.

This benchmark model can be extended to include the type of the agent. Some agents are intrinsically motivated to be honest ($a_i = 0$), others less so. We assume that only dishonest agents are ever caught (since there are no mistakes in the monitoring technology). If agents are honest then the utility function needs to be modified:

$$U_i(a_i) = g_i(w) - qz_i \qquad [4]$$

where g_i is the level of intrinsic motivation (potentially a function of wages) and z_i is the loss in utility due to being monitored when the agent is honest. We assume that a fraction $1/\gamma$ of the agents are completely honest. While γ is known, the type of any given individual is private information, known only to themselves. Now we discuss what centralised and decentralised monitoring can do to reduce corruption.

First, we consider the choice of a centralised agency, A, who can deduce the $a_i^*(q)$. The agency is assumed to care about minimising corruption. The cost of auditing is linear cq, with $c > 0$. We abstract from issues of collusion or capture, although they are important issues that have not been tackled in the empirical literature. Moreover we have abstracted from the career concerns of audit officers; these may be important but they have not been discussed in the empirical literature. For an official $U_A = B(a_i^*(q)) - cq$, where $B(.)$ measures the social benefits from reducing corruption (such as better public service delivery). Consider what happens if

a. An increase in q occurs. This is costly and depends on the cost parameter c. The cost includes the salaries of administrative staff, the expenses associated with audits and so on. Moreover, since individual types are not known, q cannot be conditioned on type.

b. Punishment parameters vary: $\dfrac{\partial a_i^*}{\partial q}$ may depend on the punishment parameters as well as βX. In our example higher punishment and higher q are substitutes: responsiveness to higher q decreases as punishment increases, and vice versa (as q goes up, so the disincentive effect of greater punishment levels falls off).

Therefore the optimal choice of q (the probability of audits occurring) will depend on all these parameters – in the example the optimal probability depends on the initial level of q, F, f_k (that is, all the factors that affect responsiveness). Although we did not model it, the optimal audit probability can also depend on an individual's risk preferences via their responsiveness of a_i to q.

Now we consider a decentralised choice of q (the probability of audits) – either through community monitoring or social audits. The obvious problem here is the collective action problem – do citizens internalise the social benefits of monitoring when a public good is provided? Typically, community monitoring has been studied for health and education or poverty alleviation programmes – and here, while there are some private benefits from undertaking monitoring, the social benefits are likely larger. Assume there is a community of n citizens who are the main beneficiaries of a public service programme. Assume that the utility of an individual citizen is represented by:

$$U_j(q_j) = V_j(a_i^*(q)) - c_j(q_j, q_{-j}) \qquad [5]$$

Let Q denote the equilibrium level of $q = f(\bar{q})$ that the agent faces as a result of strategic interactions between the citizens. An individual citizen 1 can decide how much effort to spend on monitoring. If others increase their monitoring and the policy benefit delivered is a public good, then citizen 1 may decide to lower their own monitoring (strategic substitutes). Alternatively, if more monitoring by others encourages citizen 1 to monitor as well, that could imply strategic complementarity. Strategic substitutability is more likely for monitoring activities involving pure public goods, for example road-building for a village. Complementarity is more likely for some types of monitoring activities, such as attending weekly meetings to hold officers to account. Cost could be individual or could depend on how many others monitor – for example, if there is intimidation of community auditors by officials or incumbents then the more that other citizens monitor the lower the chances that any individual would be punished for monitoring.

If there is strategic substitutability, then we can expect free riding – leading to a suboptimal Q. Consider a society of $n = 2$ individuals. Suppose only one person is needed to monitor $q = \max(q_1, q_2)$, and costs depend only on each individual's own q_j but private benefits are a proportion α_j to each individual, that is, $V_j = \alpha_j g'(a_i^*)$, then no one contributes if the private marginal benefit $\alpha_j g'(a_i^*)$ is less than the private marginal cost $c_j'(q_j)$ of doing so. This is sub-optimal when aggregate marginal benefits are larger than the social marginal cost (which is also $c_j'(q_j)$).

Strategic complementarity can be modelled by assuming instead that $q = q_1 q_2$. In this case monitoring incentives increase with the monitoring intensity of other citizens. This generates a coordination game: if the individual citizen's beliefs are that others will monitor, then their own incentives to monitor increase: if, for example, q_2 is sufficiently high, then individual 1 would choose $q_1 = 1$, otherwise $q_1 = 0$. So, there will be two pure strategy equilibria: one where both citizens monitor and one where no one does.

In practical terms, community monitoring usually involves delegation to a team. In this case the analysis above applies not to all citizens but just to members of the team. Another important issue is the composition of the monitoring team – if the team is less empowered than the agents whom they are monitoring then 'elite capture' may subvert the process. This is also related to building a sense of agency among the team members.

With decentralised monitoring, local communities have better information on the types of agents. They can target monitoring more efficiently. Then a_i^* can be affected by the following:

a. If monitoring activities are strategic substitutes, then the higher the difference between individual and group payoffs, the lower q.
b If strategic complementarities exist in monitoring, then the higher the beliefs on others' participation q_{-i}, the higher q.

c. $\frac{\partial a_i^*}{\partial q}$ depends on the punishment parameters as well as βX. This is the same as in top-down audits.

d. Targeting monitoring resources towards dishonest agents (who are assumed to be known with a higher probability than in the case with top-down monitoring).

e. The composition of the monitoring team, the degree to which they have 'agency'.

f. Changes in the transaction costs of corruption β. Providing information/awareness of entitlements may decrease β, leading to changes in equilibrium Q.

In the following sections, we organise the literature according to our framework above. Section 9.3 looks at third-party audits and the impact on corruption.

9.3 Centralised monitoring

The conceptual framework presented above suggests that changes in the intensity of monitoring have an effect on agent behaviour, although the effect is via forward-looking agents: they decide their behaviour anticipating q. The literature however has focused on the effect of *past* audits. Theoretically past audits should not have an effect unless there is no commitment on q, or there are selection effects, or there is a difference between the actual and perceived risk of being caught. (See also Malmendier (2021) on how experiences shape reasoning.) There may also be some differences in information between the law enforcers and agents (Apel 2013). There is some analogous work on deterrence in criminal behaviour in the law and economics literature (see the survey by Chalfin and McCrary 2017). Indeed Becker (1968) showed that theoretically increasing the threat of punishment (with full commitment) was more likely to lower crime than increasing the size of the punishment for risk-averse individuals. We explore key issues first in Brazilian studies of municipality audits, then in studies from other countries, and last in studies of individual decision makers.

Brazil – randomised audits

The empirical literature on centralised audits departs from the theory in a number of ways. The theory suggests that varying the announced q can have an effect on corruption. Avis, Ferraz, and Finan (2018) used publicly available audit reports of municipalities from Brazil's anti- corruption audit programme, which started in 2003. It is implemented through the autonomous Controladoria-Geral da União (Office of Comptroller-General, hereafter abbreviated to CGU). CGU randomly choose municipalities every month from a sample of all Brazilian municipalities with fewer than 450,000 inhabitants.

CGU auditors inspect the chosen municipality's accounts and also carry out physical verification of public works and service delivery. The auditors also meet with local officials and members of the community. Based on their findings, a report is prepared, which is presented to higher authorities for action.[3] A summary of the principal findings for the audited municipalities is then also released to the media and posted on the internet (Ferraz and Finan 2008; Ferraz and Finan 2011).[4] The announced q is, therefore, equal across municipalities. The types of punishment include legal action (F in the model), as well as perception of the incumbent mayor by voters ($f_k S$ in the model).

What Avis, Ferraz, and Finan (2018) found, however, was that municipalities that had been audited in the past had corruption levels 8 per cent lower than others. Past audits also affect the behaviour of neighbouring municipalities with local media, who get to know about the results of nearby audits. Corruption levels went down by 7.5 per cent due to an additional neighbour being audited. Having had an audit in the past also increased the chances of legal action being taken against the mayor by 20 per cent. They attribute the lower corruption levels to the higher perceived credibility of associated legal punishment by decision makers who have been audited and the neighbouring municipalities. In the criminal deterrence literature this effect is referred to as specific deterrence, as opposed to general deterrence (Chalfin and McCrary 2017).

The Avis, Ferraz, and Finan (2018) structural model allowed them to run some alternative policy simulations to understand which policies would help to reduce corruption most effectively – in effect asking which of the punishments outlined in the model work best to reduce corruption – increasing audit probabilities (q), improving the exposure of corruption to voters via audit reports (f_k), increasing the legal costs of being caught for corruption (F), and improving the educational/occupational background of candidates running for office (γ). Out of these they found the largest effects for increasing the legal costs of corruption – in line with Becker (1968), if we assume risk aversion among agents as well as increasing q.

Zamboni and Litschig (2018) designed a randomised policy experiment in Brazil to ask the following questions: (i) does a higher probability of getting audited (a higher q) discourage rent extraction by local government officials? And (ii) does the higher audit probability have a differential effect on different sectors – procurement versus health service delivery and targeted cash transfers? According to the framework we proposed, it is more difficult to deter corruption in sectors with high possibilities of extracting rent – in their setting this was procurement. In addition, the efficacy of q is affected by the levels of punishment and the probability of legal sanctions. In Brazil the chances of punishment and the level of punishment were much higher for procurement-related irregularities. This effect should dominate the higher βX in procurement relative to other sectors. So, Zamboni and Litschig (2018) hypothesised that the responsiveness of corruption in procurement to higher audit risk would be greater because punishments for such corruption types is higher in Brazil, involving long jail terms and fines. By contrast, in health service delivery the type of corruption is in the nature of absenteeism from work, and targeted cash transfers, where corruption is highly visible.

The Zamboni and Litschig (2018) experiment was run jointly with the Comptroller-General of the Union (CGU) and involved the randomisation of 120 municipalities into two groups, a high audit risk group, exposed to an audit risk of 25 per cent and a low audit risk group (control group), exposed to an audit risk of 5 per cent. Results show that corruption was affected the most in procurement, especially in those programmes that allowed greater discretion for the officials (opportunities for corruption in our conceptual framework).

In relation to the lower efficacy of audits in the case of service provision, the authors conceded that it was challenging to detect the inconsistencies in service provision (of health or targeted transfers) through a CGU audit. Even if they were detected, punishment involved at most the loss of that official's job. Public complaints were not recorded on paper anywhere, and the officials were able to dispute these complaints. This made it difficult for the auditors to verify which of the competing claims was true.

However, it is much easier to detect irregularities in procurement with audits because local officials were required to document the purchasing process in a detailed manner, and their punishments were relatively severe, including not only job termination but also potential fines and a jail term too. Thus, these findings suggest that increasing the probability of an audit alone is not sufficient to deter rent-taking, and it might prove futile to do so for programmes that are targeted based on easily observable individual or household characteristics (like cash transfer programmes).

Ferraz and Finan (2008) also exploited the randomised timing and public dissemination of the audits conducted in Brazil to investigate whether voters punished politicians who were exposed as corrupt due to audits – that is, they examined how large F was in the context of municipal elections in Brazil. Theoretically, Persson and Tabellini (2002) and Besley and Prat (2006) argue that making more information available to voters should lead to better accountability via re-elections. In order to test this proposition, exposure to information should be exogenous, otherwise (for instance) an observed correlation between high exposure and low re-election could simply be capturing a greater presence of media in places that are also more competitive, or where voters are more aware of local politics, or where voters are more likely to be affected by corruption and therefore put more effort into finding out about it.

They compared the electoral outcomes of mayors eligible for re-election between municipalities audited pre and post the 2004 local elections (covering July 2003 to June 2005).[5] If information on corruption is a salient factor affecting re-election, then there should have been a significant difference between re-election rates in those municipalities that were audited before the election versus those audited after the election. The municipalities where audits took place after the election counted here as a control group – in the sense that audit findings are not able to affect an election held before they are produced, while the treatment group was those that had audits before election. Ferraz and Finan (2008) measured corruption as the number of violations associated with the sum of fraud in procurement, diversion of public funds, and/or over-invoicing. Media sources were measured using the number of locally present radio stations in a municipality. This allowed the authors to test whether the audits had any differential impact across areas with or without a strong presence of local media.

Overall, the authors found that on average the electoral performance of mayors audited before elections was not significantly different from those audited after them. However, once they compared mayors with the same measured corruption levels, they found a 17 per cent reduction in the probability of re-election if the audit was done before the election rather than after. This probability reduced more when corruption was higher. Where audits found no corruption the chances of re-election increased for incumbent mayors audited before elections. These effects were more prominent in municipalities where local radio was present. The evidence is consistent with a narrative where voters have a prior belief about incumbent corruption and then revise it upwards or downwards based on the reports.

Voters may have many different reasons to punish corrupt incumbents. For example, in Brazil, the discretionary funds allocated to municipalities are reduced where mayors have been found to be corrupt. Brollo (2008) used this reduction to show that voters actually punish politicians who are responsible for a reduction in transfers to their municipality, rather than politicians who are exposed as corrupt. Even if voters punish corrupt politicians, it may not follow that politicians reduce corruption as a result.

Ferraz and Finan (2011) also argued that politicians do respond to re-election incentives in local governments in Brazil. They used the political agency framework of Besley (2006) as a conceptual framework. The model is based on voters deciding to re-elect an incumbent, without observing his or her type or actions but based on a signal from voters' own utilities, which are affected by actions of incumbents. The model predicts that mayors who face re-election incentives will be less dishonest than those who do not because corrupt (type) mayors wanting to be re-elected can foster support by behaving like non-corrupt mayors and not indulging in rent-seeking activities. Corrupt mayors thus exploit the information asymmetry with voters. So, mayors who are audited and face re-election should turn out to be less corrupt than those who are audited but do not face re-election. The empirical finding was that municipalities with mayors in their first term had a significantly lower percentage of stolen resources as compared to those with mayors in their second (and hence) last term. Thus, the results on re-election incentives were consistent with the theoretical model.

Their evidence therefore complements Ferraz and Finan (2008), who showed that voters make use of the publicly available information to punish corrupt politicians. Together, the authors say, these results imply that electoral accountability acts as a powerful tool to align politicians' actions with the voters' preferences. In terms of our conceptual framework, the link from audits to information exposure to punishment at the ballot box to incumbents then reducing corruption in response to re-election motives is complete.

Ultimately, the primary purpose of reducing corruption via audits is to improve economic performance. Reducing corruption may come at the cost of a loss in intrinsic motivation for agents who are honest or who are afraid to make mistakes and as a result decide not to take risky decisions. Colonnelli and Prem (2022) evaluated the impact of audits on firm performance and local economic activity. They used the extensive audit data available in Brazil, with a particular focus on government procurement records. The anti-corruption programme in Brazil allowed them to address issues of measurement via audit measured corruption and endogeneity (firm-level activity, economic activity and corruption are simultaneously determined), taken care of by the random audits.

They combined audit reports and the administrative matched employer-employee data (as well as some censuses on retail and service sector firms) on the Brazilian formal sector. This data is used to compare the economic outcomes of randomly audited municipalities (treatment) with either later randomly audited or never-audited municipalities (control). Results suggest that treatment municipalities experience higher levels of economic activity, improved access to finance, and more entrepreneurship as compared to the control ones. These findings imply that the anti-corruption crackdown positively affected the local economy and thus lend empirical support to the 'sand in the wheel' view (reduction in corruption increases economic activity). They complement their results with a firm-level analysis. Like the municipal level analysis, the firm-level analysis is based on a comparison between firms involved in dubious government procurement ('corrupt firms') and similar firms operating in the same sector that are situated in never-audited municipalities (control group). A dynamic difference-in-difference specification is used to show that corrupt firms that are audited perform better than the control group. Their results show that it is precisely those firms that rely on government (procurement) that benefit the most from the anti-corruption crackdown. Overall, the results of the paper consistently support the 'sand in the wheel' argument, that is, corruption acts as an institutional failure, while suggesting costs and distortions to firms dependent on the government as the primary channel through which corruption hinders overall economic growth and firm performance. Moreover, they find no support of a politician selection channel (at local level) from audits but rather a disciplining channel.

In contrast, Lichand, Lopes, and Medeiros (2016) found a negative impact of audits on health outcomes in Brazil. The main idea is that audits and the punishment from audits might lead bureaucrats to take fewer decisions and to reduce procurement. As our model suggests, since audits cannot be targeted to dishonest politicians they may reduce incentives to work among honest agents as well. They analysed the effects of audits both on corruption within the health sector and on downstream outcomes in Brazil's health sector. Their data is on the incidence of corruption in health transfers between 1997 and 2007, captured extensively in the audit reports. They employed a difference-in-difference (pre and post audit, procurement-related transfers vs other transfers) strategy to tease out the causal effects of audits on corruption in procurement-related transfers in the health sector. Moreover, they used the effects of announced audits on neighbouring municipalities to tease out the effects of announcement of audit vs actual audit. If officials reacted to audits in nearby areas, they attributed it to a behavioural response. Results show that both corruption and procurement irregularities within health transfers came down as a result of the audit programme in Brazil. On the other hand, public spending witnessed a decline, as a result of which infrastructure and medication suffered. At the same time, linked to the reduction in corruption, mismanagement rose, especially in problems linked to the stock of medication and quality of health infrastructure. Thus, the programme brought about a reduction in procurement purchases, either because bureaucrats could no longer capture rents or because they were scared of being caught and punished. Consistent with the impact of the programme on bureaucratic performance, a detrimental impact on the health indicators is also seen. A comparison between the indicators directly concerned with municipalities' health spending – like preventable deaths – to those that are not – like the deaths caused by external causes – shows how the audit programme, despite reducing corruption, considerably worsened the quality of health services over the long term. Overall, the paper provides evidence that anti-corruption programmes might have an adverse consequence for social welfare.

Other countries – non-random audits

Bobonis, Cámara Fuertes, and Schwabe (2016) employed similar measures of corruption as Ferraz and Finan (2008; 2011) to answer whether monitoring corrupt activities (audits) induce a *sustained* reduction in corruption. Like Avis, Ferraz, and Finan (2018), their research question was whether past audits help to reduce current corruption. The Bobonis, Cámara Fuertes, and Schwabe study used the timing of municipality audits in Puerto Rico between 1987 and 2005. In Puerto Rico, municipalities are audited by an autonomous audit authority (Office of the Comptroller of Puerto Rico – OCPR) in a pre-specified order that was determined in the 1950s. Once an auditing round is completed, the next one follows the same order. The empirical strategy in this paper exploits the differences among municipalities who are audited before an election (timely audit) and those audited after an election (untimely audit). However, they found the opposite result on the long-run effects of past audits on corruption.

The key reason for this contrast across the two studies is that in Puerto Rico audits occur at predetermined times, as opposed to randomly in Brazil. Prefixed audits are different in the sense that an agent would know exactly when they are due to be audited, $q = 1$ in some years and $q = 0$ in other years. There-fore (out of the fraction y of agents who are not always honest) we should see corruption being low when the audit is due, assuming that there is a credible punishment for it. Bobonis, Cámara Fuertes, and Schwabe considered the punishment as being the exposure of corruption to voters, as a result of which voters would throw out corrupt incumbents. Whether such a disciplining effect lasts longer depends on what we assume about voters' behaviour, term limits, and the time horizons during which incumbents expect to be in power. In their setting, turnover of politicians is high, so that these time horizons are short. In addition, there may be selection effects (see for example, Persson and Tabellini 2002, Ch. 4), where voters use signals of dishonesty to throw out corrupt incumbents: this effect leads to lower corruption over time.

So, the hypothesis is that timely audits lead to sanctioning effects where voters punish incumbents who are shown to be corrupt. Incumbents expect-ing an audit before election will then reduce corruption in response, implying lower irregularities when there are timely audit reports. If audits induce a pos-itive selection of less corrupt politicians, then the lower corruption for munic-ipalities with timely audits would lead to lower corruption in the long run as well. Bobonis, Cámara Fuertes, and Schwabe (2016) measured the short-run impact of timely audits on corruption by regressing irregularities in year t on whether audits were carried out in the two years prior to election. The long-run impact was measured by regressing irregularities four years later on audits in year t. Finally, they tested for the impact of the timeliness of audits reports on re-election rates. They showed that timely audits induce a signifi-cant short-term reduction in municipal corruption levels of approximately 67 per cent, as well as an increase in mayors' re-election rates in audited munici-palities. Yet there were no significant differences in the long-term corruption levels between those municipalities that had timely audits versus those that did not. The authors deduced that selection of politicians happens, but not on honesty – rather, voters seem to reward competence. The combination of sanctioning effects in the short term and selection effects towards competence in the long run can explain their findings.

The issue of punishment for those caught by top-down audits is also taken up in greater detail by Michael Mbate in the chapter in this book on parliamentary sanctions and local accountability (2023, Chapter 8). In their former territories, the British colonisers left a legacy of parliamentary democ-racy along with supreme audit institutions and parliamentary sanctions for those caught by the audit agency. In practice, however, political economy con-cerns (like partisan loyalties) have often led to low punishment by parliamen-tary sanctions.

Studying audit impacts on individual decision makers or units

Kleven et al. (2011) studied the role of audits on tax evasion by looking at individual-level behaviours in an advanced economy, Denmark. Similarly to

Avis, Ferraz, and Finan (2018) and Bobonis, Cámara Fuertes, and Schwabe (2016), this paper provides further evidence of the efficacy of audits. They studied the effects of past audits as well as anticipated audits on tax evasion. Their main contribution is to show that audits affect only corruption in discretionary income – in terms of the model – this suggests that audits have a greater effect when the opportunity for corruption – βX is higher. Thus they echo the results of Zamboni and Litschig (2018). These papers implicitly test the interaction of q with βX and F – while Zamboni and Litschig (2018) considered the interaction of F with q, Kleven et al. (2011) studied the interaction of q with βX.

The authors based their theoretical model on the tax evasion model of Allingham and Sandmo (1972).[6] They designed a field experiment that imposed different audit regimes on randomly chosen taxpayers. Their sample consisted of 40,000 individuals who duly filed income tax. The first stage involved the random selection of half of these taxpayers for unannounced audits of tax returns filed in 2007. The rest of them remained unaudited. The first randomisation exercise allows for the estimation of the impact of past audits on future reported income, which is carried out as a comparison of the two groups in the subsequent year. The second stage of the experiment is based on an arbitrary selection of employees in both audit and no-audit groups for pre-announced audits of tax returns filed in 2008 (letters were sent out to announce the audits in advance). The authors examined the threat as well as the no-threat group to study the impact of the possibility of an audit on the reported income. The experiment resulted in an almost negligible tax evasion rate for income subject to third-party reporting, while the tax evasion rate was substantial for self-reported income. Prior audits and threat-of-audit letters had a significant impact on the tax evasion associated with self-reported income.

In all of the papers considered so far, the audit agency is assumed to be independent (and evidence is provided to show that it is) and non-corruptible. It is still an open question under what conditions audit can make outcomes worse due to bribing of auditors. However, Duflo et al. (2013) did this for a private sector firm – they showed that, when firms pay for their own audits, the conflict of interests results in underestimation of irregularities. Chander and Wilde (1992) explore this question theoretically and show that tax audits can reduce tax evasion when auditors are honest but, when that is not the case, audit design can lead to surprising results. The model allows for collusion between taxpayers and auditors. The audit agency is treated as a separate player who is interested in maximising expected tax revenue net of costs of audit. Taxpayers who are audited pay the additional tax due plus a penalty. Taxpayers will be willing to pay bribes (dishonest evaders) to auditors when the cost of paying tax plus the fine is higher than the expected cost of bribing the auditor and being caught with some probability. Auditors are willing to accept bribes when the private costs to them of being caught are lower than the bribe income. The model shows that dishonest evaders are more likely than honest evaders to evade taxes. Since the returns from evasion increase when tax rates go up, and the returns from bribing also go up, it is likely that higher taxes lead to higher audit and lower revenues for the tax authority. In some cases, the tax agency may prefer to forgo auditing altogether as it is costly and collusion leads to too low tax collections. We do not know of any empirical work on collusion between a governmental audit agency (SAI) and auditees – however, Duflo et al. (2013) is an example of a study where there is collusion between private sector firms and a third-party audit agency.

To summarise, in this section we find that electoral incentives can be a powerful force in reducing corruption via voters' information on politicians' corruption. However, the effects of electoral punishment are short-lived, and weaker than non-electoral (judicial) punishment. Audits have more of a disciplining effect in reducing corruption rather than a selection effect. The effects of audits on corruption vary by the nature of the service being audited – for example, procurement is more responsive to the threat of audit than, say, absenteeism of workers owing to both the rules being defined much more clearly and the punishment being higher. In terms of effects on ultimate outcomes, there is some evidence that audits may not help in improving outcomes due to the problem of the auditees not willing to take the risk of being caught inadvertently. This is especially interesting due to recent interest in outcome-based auditing.[7]

9.4 Community monitoring

Community monitoring is a part of the broader concept of community participation schemes, which Mansuri and Rao (2013) suggested can be looked at as a solution to 'civil society failures' when people who live in geographical proximity to each other are unable to solve collective action problems. In this survey, however, we are more focused on enhancing grassroots participation by enabling the community to monitor, which can sometimes improve upon top-down monitoring in curbing corruption for several reasons. Service or benefit recipients have better information on corruption. They have stronger incentives to watch the service providers in order to avoid any costs generated by corruption. Community monitoring also create higher non-monetary costs (the fear of social disapproval and sanctions, S in the model) faced by the officials (World Bank 2003; World Bank 2007). We first discuss the political economy literature on community monitoring and corruption (which is still quite limited) before moving on to community monitoring and the effect on performance in service delivery.

Banerjee et al. (2018) studied the impact of providing information to targeted beneficiaries in a redistribution programme in Indonesia. We can view the intervention as changing the transaction costs of corruption, βX: an external agency provides information on entitlements so that users can understand where they are being cheated. In a subsidised rice programme, they tested the impact of providing information on whether people were eligible and on the amount of the subsidy they were entitled to. Eligible households received a 26 per cent increase in subsidy despite imperfect implementation. Indeed, the more relevant information they were give (such as co-pay amounts), the better off the households were. Moreover, when the list of eligible households was made publicly available, the benefits received increased further. The study highlights the importance of improving the bargaining position of beneficiaries by giving them more information (or reducing β) and using public sanctions. The main contribution was that here an information-only treatment seemed to work when the public service was easily observed – but such an approach may not work in procurement.

In a similar study by Fiala and Premand (2018), the researchers partnered with the Inspectorate General (IG) of the Ugandan government, an independent arm of the government responsible for fighting corruption, in order to provide training in social accountability and provide information on project performance for a large-scale public development plan. Training covered how to monitor and report mismanagement, while information was also provided on the quality of services across different communities. The study found that the combined effect of both the training and the informational treatment was significantly better than these treatments handled individually. Both types of interventions aimed at increasing the transaction costs of corruption. Moreover, the impact was much higher in the areas which local officials reported as being highly mismanaged or corrupt.

Social audit is a special form of community monitoring that combines elements of top-down audits with elements of community monitoring. Social audits have a long history in India, starting with the MKSS (Mazdoor Kisan Shakti Sangathan), a voluntary organisation in Rajasthan in 1990. Accordingly, we focus first on a few studies based in India, describing the process in some detail to show how it combines elements of information, community participation and top-down audits.

Most studies of social audits focus on Andhra Pradesh (AP), one of the large states in India that has had exceptional performance in conducting social audits. Although the efforts of a majority of states in carrying out social audits have been disappointing, the SSAAT (Society for Social Audit Accountability and Transparency) in Andhra Pradesh successfully institutionalised this process (Aakella and Kidambi 2007; Aiyar and Mehta 2015). This arm of the Department of Rural Development conducted regular social audits of projects in all the districts of AP that formed part of a large employment guarantee programme (whose acronym is MGNREGA) operating in rural areas across India since 2005. The results have shown that, even if they are not specifically focused on corruption, social audits may help to improve performance outcomes.

Singh and Vutukuru (2010) studied the impact of social audits on the size of MGNREGA as well as its payment process. The demand for MGNREGA drives its size, which means that the state has to employ all those who register for the scheme for up to 100 days. It is a wage employment programme, and the guidelines make it clear that workers should receive their wages every week or not later than 15 days after the completion of work. The authors therefore look at timely payments by comparing the percentage of workers who received their payments within 15 days versus those with overdue payments. They also followed up on the change in these proportions after one round of audit, assuming that the impact would be fully reflected in the next year. Fifty-five treatment *mandals* (a type of local government area) were selected based on the timing of the social audit. These *mandals* had a round of social audit in the latter half of 2006–07 (December 2006 to March 2007). This was followed by the selection of control *mandal* for each treatment *mandal*. The control *mandals* were the ones where a social audit was conducted after September 2007, which meant that they had no social audit in 2006–07. The results showed significant improvement in the person-days generated, a key measure of the size of the programme. However, social audits failed to have an impact on the proportion of timely payments. Singh and Vutukuru (2010) suggested that the high demand for employment from MGNREGA put enormous pressure on the delivery system for payments.

Afridi and Iversen (2014) used a much larger sample to study the impact of social audits on employment generation and complaints of irregularities registered under MGNREGA. They found insignificant effects on corruption, which they attributed to the lack of punishment mechanisms. Since these audits were not randomly done, they relied instead on a strategy of analysing changes in irregularities found by the audit teams over successive rounds of audit for the same subdistrict. The original social audit reports (three rounds) from Andhra Pradesh are used for the years 2006–10. The authors narrowed down the sample to 300 gram panchayats (GPs, or village council areas) in eight districts of AP, and research focused on different types of complaints (related to labour, materials, and provision of worksite facilities) and the programme and employment expenditure under the programme.

The dependent variables were the social audit findings for a particular GP, and NREGA performance measures such as the programme expenditure and employment generation in a GP. The independent variable was an audit variable.[8] The regression estimates suggested an insignificant impact of social audits on both employment generation and the total number of irregularities. However, there was a marginal (not significant) decline in the complaints related to the labour-related irregularity, matched by an increase in the material-related irregularities. Although social audits are useful in detecting irregularities, it is hard to say whether they alone can help deter malpractice in any way. A process that ensures follow-up of social audit findings and punishes the transgressors strictly seems to be needed.

Afridi et al. (2021) then used the same setting to ask whether electoral punishment after social audits exposed corruption was a suitable deterrent to corruption. They used data on village elections in 2006 and data on irregularities over the five-year electoral term of incumbent village heads. Similar to the findings of Avis, Ferraz, and Finan (2018), they found that electoral punishment was not a sufficient deterrent. As electoral competition increased, the labour-related irregularities went down somewhat but the material-related irregularities were not responsive. Moreover, when elections were very close, even labour-related irregularities went up with competition.

Molina et al. (2016) conducted a meta-analysis of 15 studies (up until 2013) on a large number of community monitoring interventions (CMI) including information campaigns, citizen scorecards, and social audits. They analysed the effects on corruption outcomes as well as service delivery. On average they found positive effects of CMIs in reducing corruption and improving service delivery, but there was a lot of heterogeneity. The interventions that had the biggest impact seemed to be those that aimed at increasing citizen participation and specifically included tools to monitor politicians (for example, Olken 2007). Other reasons for failure included collective action problems – citizens maybe did not participate due to lack of information about their entitlements (Banerjee et al. 2010), free riding incentives, pessimistic beliefs about the social auditors' incentives, the lack of redress mechanisms (Afridi and Iversen 2014), doubts about the response of service providers or about the beliefs of other citizens to participate. All these factors may have depended on the degree of inequality or ethnic fractionalisation (for example, Björkman and Svensson 2010).

Turning to community monitoring, in their the P2P (Power to the People) study, Björkman and Svensson (2009) analysed the impact of a randomised field experiment conducted in all four regions of Uganda on the quantity and quality of health care provision – quantities being measured by daily patient registers, immunisation cards, and so on. They focused on local community-based monitoring of public health care providers. Fifty public dispensaries and the respective users of health care services in nine districts were randomly assigned into the treatment and control group. Each treatment facility and its community had a unique report card, through which information on the quality of services, comparisons with other health facilities, and so on were disseminated based on the surveys in their areas. A style of local NGO (non-governmental organisation) called a community-based organisation (CBO), promoted village and staff meetings. These meetings were crucial in making each community in charge of establishing ways of monitoring their provider, after a series of initial meetings. Thus, these interventions were ways to improve q (the likelihood of audits) that were determined endogenously. They addressed β via giving better information to the recipients of the service and also helped in training them to solve the collective action problems and create the sense of agency needed to make community monitoring work. The treatment communities became more involved and began monitoring the health unit extensively as a result of the intervention. A year later and significant improvement in the weight of infants, declines in the under-five mortality rate, and higher utilisation of health care services were observed in the treatment groups when compared with the control group. These results imply that changes in the quality and quantity of health care providers could be attributed to the behavioural changes of the staff.

In contrast to these positive effects of community monitoring on providers' behaviour, in Brazil, Zamboni and Litschig (2018) showed that top-down audits did not improve health service delivery because of the lower punishments involved. Björkman Nyqvist et al. (2017) went back into the field to study the long-run impact of the intervention. They presented evidence to show the long-run benefits of the intervention and also that a *crucial part of the intervention was the provision of information on performance.* Perhaps social sanctions work better as punishment mechanisms in the setting of health provision, where exposure is less of an issue relative to awareness about entitlements.

The results of the 'P2P' research have recently been challenged by a larger study in the same setting of the Ugandan health sector (Raffler and Parkerson 2019). They found only modest positive effects from community monitoring on treatment quality and patient satisfaction over 20 months, but no changes in utilisation rates or the health outcomes used in the P2P study. Moreover, they found that the effects of community monitoring were negligible by themselves but did have a significant impact on change when coupled with top-down oversight. This might also plausibly be explained by very different (and improved) baseline measures.

An interesting study that shows how important it is to interpret outcomes with caution is that by Christensen et al. (2021). They looked at West Africa's response to the Ebola crisis. Based on an experiment they had run two years before the outbreak in Sierra Leone, they looked at two treatments aimed at improving the quality of service delivery by health workers – one was community monitoring and the other was status rewards for health workers. They found that before the outbreak service quality improved from the treatments, and that they also led to higher reporting of cases with lower mortality from Ebola.

Banerjee et al. (2007) and Banerjee et al. (2010) focused on educational services in India, conducting a survey in a rural district in Uttar Pradesh. The authors surveyed village education committee (VEC) members,[9] rural households, parents, and teachers, regarding the educational services and their own participation in the delivery of educational outcomes. Their primary survey showed that 30–40 per cent of students between the ages of six and 14 were unable to do basic arithmetic operations, read simple texts, and write a basic sentence correctly. Furthermore, teachers, parents, and VEC members did not seem to be fully aware of the range of the problem. Parents and VEC members were unaware of the essential roles they played within the academic system. The baseline findings of the survey pointed to a significant gap in knowledge regarding the status of education within the villages.

Banerjee et al. (2010) then studied the impact of public action campaigns on local participation in VECs in Uttar Pradesh (UP), one of the most populous and poorest states in India. They analysed whether information and participation in VECs improved the learning outcomes of children in the schools. To do this, the authors designed three interventions and assessed their impact on local participation and whether they can improve school functioning. The interventions all target β via information and training in community monitoring, as well as a task that improves the agency and capability of the citizens. A country-level education NGO called Pratham then evaluated and compared the results of the three interventions, designed to enhance community participation Pratham teams facilitated the village meetings and encouraged discussions as a part of the first intervention. They convinced village administrators to share information about the structure of local service delivery at these meetings. Pratham activists distributed pamphlets post meetings. These pamphlets described the responsibilities of VEC members and the training of individual VEC members.

The second intervention provided the same information as the first one, along with the training of the community members so they could undertake a simple reading test with children. Community members were asked to prepare report cards on the state of enrolment and learning in their village. The village-wide meetings involved the presentation of information from these report cards. The idea of this intervention was to provide citizens with tools to measure learning that could improve participation and effectiveness. The third and final intervention included all elements from the first two but added the recruitment of one or more volunteers per village. They were given a week's training in a pedagogical technique for teaching necessary reading skills developed and implemented by Pratham. The trained volunteers were then responsible for holding reading camps in the villages, with classes daily outside school for two months. This intervention allowed individuals to try and improve learning among children directly.

An evaluation of surveys conducted post interventions showed that none of the three methods led to a significant increase in the involvement by any of the players (the parents, the VEC, or the teacher). They also failed to improve school performance (measured by the attendance of children and teachers' or community participation in schools). It is hard to say why, because the mobilisation did not entirely fail. Almost everybody in the villages turned up for the meetings planned by Pratham. Moreover, the third intervention led to a massive volunteer mobilisation, followed by a great response by the parents outside the school system. The results from the third intervention showed that teaching children how to read is not an impossibly difficult task. In the context of UP, these results imply that providing information on the status of education and the existing institutions of participation alone was not sufficient to promote beneficiary involvement in public schools.

On a positive note, though, the results suggest that information combined with the offer of a right course of action can result in collective action and improve outcomes. There was a greater willingness of individuals to help improve the situation (via volunteer teaching) rather than undertake collective action to reform institutions and systems. The authors suggested that this could be explained by pessimism on the part of community members about being able to influence outcomes. In the one part of the intervention that did not require official functionaries, however, the researchers found positive results.

Following on from this study, Pandey, Goyal, and Sundararaman (2009) ran a community-based information campaign on health and school performance in the form of a cluster randomised control trial (RCT) in 610 villages across three Indian states. They found notable positive impacts on teacher effort, and delivery of entitlements, with less effect on educational outcomes. They reached similar conclusions as Banerjee et al. (2010) about the delivery of final learning outcomes, which is a puzzle since teacher effort went up and one year later they find an increased demand for services in UP.

By contrast, in Andrabi, Das, and Khwaja (2017), providing information via report cards on children's test scores relative to a mean test score across the village had positive effects on parental awareness about private school quality. It also led to positive outcomes on learning as well as reduced prices for private school fees. The research suggested that *comparative* information on children's' test scores within and across schools was useful in encouraging participation and accountability. Afridi et al. (2020) conducted a randomised report card campaign where contiguous village councils in the Indian state of Rajasthan were randomly assigned to either a control group or to one of four treatment groups in which student report cards on curriculum-based tests were provided to schools, to parents, or both. They found no changes in academic performance in public schools, but student performance in private schools improved by one-third of a standard deviation when parents and schools could simultaneously place themselves in the distribution of scores in the neighbouring villages. There was no systematic change in performance for any treatment that involved only schools, or where households were not informed about the relative performance of all schools in the community. They reconciled the divergent findings of Banerjee et al. (2010) and Andrabi, Das, and Khwaja (2017), by suggesting that the design of information campaigns – that is, ensuring common knowledge of relative (rather than absolute) school quality – and provider incentives can both play a critical role in improving learning outcomes. Overall, these results suggest that, when providing information to the recipients of public services, their being able to benchmark performance is key. Again, these types of intervention raise the transaction costs β in officials engaging in corruption or equivalently not putting in full effort.

The next two papers were aimed at improving the beliefs and agency of the community monitors themselves, which can impact collective action. In Ugandan schools, Barr et al. (2012) ran a field experiment to tease out the reasons why scorecards or informational interventions had succeeded in some cases but not in others. They found that treatments encouraging the community to develop their own goals and objectives/plans on monitoring (designing the score cards) were more likely to succeed because they encouraged cooperation (tested using a public goods contribution game) and therefore improved collective action. They concluded that small changes in the design of participatory interventions can have large effects.

Pradhan et al. (2014) undertook an innovative RCT to improve educational outcomes in Indonesia by instituting elections for the school committee members and facilitating deliberations between committee members and the village council (linkage) – all this in addition to the traditional ways of improving community participation such as grants and training. Linkage with the village elected council body meant that the school committee had a greater bargaining power in effecting change. A second treatment was on electing the members in the committee – if instead the school could choose its own members then their monitoring might not be very effective. Thus, in terms of our framework, these interventions aimed at changing the collective action payoffs by (i) changing the composition of the committee and (ii) increasing the probability that action would be taken.

Effects from how the community monitoring teams are composed were studied by Björkman and Svensson (2010). They built on the P2P study to show that ethnically fractionalised communities did much worse than homogenous communities in generating participation and monitoring. This suggests that collective action is affected by the fractionalisation of the team: higher free riding or coordination problems being higher could explain these results. Björkman Nyqvist et al. (2017) conducted a survey of the villages four years and an information treatment and found persistent effects. They concluded that a necessary condition for building participatory community monitoring is to provide both information and the tools to use information to monitor providers (the traditional tools to encourage community participation).

How much do citizens actually participate in social accountability? Despite the hype, participative democracy and community engagement agendas may not be very useful if citizens are not empowered enough to make their views known. There may be many reasons for this. For instance, the bureaucrats responsible for encouraging local accountability are the often the same officials who have the least incentives to do so. Large inequalities in status between different participants can be another constraint. This question was studied by Parthasarthy, Rao, and Palaniswamy (2019) using natural language processing techniques on a corpus of village assembly transcripts from rural India. They found that women were significantly less likely to speak in these meetings, and when they did speak they were much less likely to be heard. When women are local leaders, however, this dynamic changes.

To summarise, the literature has studied two types of interventions in community monitoring: (i) Information treatments where relevant information on public services such as entitlements, score cards on performance, and so on are provided and (ii) training on how to monitor effectively. The results have largely confirmed the problems due to a lack of empowerment, and elite capture, as well as difficulties from free riding. The exact design of the intervention is important. There are few studies that examine how to break the constraints imposed by political economy – that is, issues of elite capture are still first-order.

9.5 Studies comparing top-down versus social audits

The first paper in this section made a clear comparison between the two techniques and compared their final impact on corruption levels in Indonesia. The intervention involved aimed to increase q (the frequency of audits) in top-down audits and to increase β in community monitoring. Olken (2007) conducted randomised field experiments for both top-down and bottom-up monitoring in 600 villages for a year (from September 2003 to September 2004). The timing of the experiment matched the nationwide village-level infrastructure project (construction of roads) in Indonesia, which allows randomly selected villages to undertake projects and who were subsequently audited by the central government audit agency. The probability of audit for treated villages thus went up from 4 per cent to 100 per cent. The villages were informed regarding the audit treatment only when they received the funding for construction and before it began, so that the project funding and design remained exogenous to the experiment.

The first part of the experiment captured the impact of top-down or external monitoring. It produced a significant reduction in missing expenditures. However, the evidence suggested that it was more the threat of audit rather than the audit itself that had the effect, since the audit reports conducted were mainly on procedural issues rather than addressing corruption per se. This is in contrast to the results discussed earlier (such as Bobonis, Cámara Fuertes, and Schwabe (2016) or Avis, Ferraz, and Finan (2018)), where past audits had an effect rather than the threat of audits.

The second part of the experiment was subdivided into two smaller experiments, designed to increase grassroots participation in the monitoring process and analyse the overall impact on corruption. The first subpart of the second experiment aimed to encourage direct participation by sending out invitations to village-level accountability meetings where the project officers would explain and account for how they spent the project funds. The second part added anonymous comment forms, which were distributed alongside the invitations to meetings;[10] the idea here was to allow villagers to convey information about the project without any fear. Of course, Olken noted that, if numbers in a village were small, anonymity might not be perfect even with such forms. Two different forms of distribution of forms were used – one where the village government distributed forms and one where the schools did so.

The second experiment succeeded in gearing up community participation in the monitoring process. However, the change in the attitudes of people in the treatment villages did not translate into a reduction in missing expenditures. What was striking, however, was that treatment areas saw a reduction in missing labour expenditures, but no effect on missing materials expenditures. Olken (2007) speculates that distribution via schools bypasses the local government and also keeps a check on the village elites to ensure that they do not direct the comment forms to their supporters. Thus, for bottom-up monitoring to lower corruption it is important to prevent elite capture and problems of free riding in monitoring.

Another paper by Serra (2011) captures the potential effectiveness of a combined accountability system (because bottom-up monitoring can trigger top-down auditing). A lab experiment about bribery was used to capture the strategic interaction between private citizens and public officials for the provision of a public good under different anti-corruption systems: one with no monitoring but just top-down auditing (external controls in the form of a fine applied with a low probability) and the other using combined monitoring (where citizens could report corrupt officials that would lead to top-down auditing). The game was played by a total of 180 Oxford University students who randomly took up the roles of private citizens and public officials in groups of 15 and filled in a questionnaire after participating in the experiment. In the set-up public officials had a choice of demanding or not demanding a bribe from the private citizens, and, if they chose to demand it, they could also choose to demand any bribe amount they wished. The private citizens also had the option of deciding whether and how much to pay as a bribe. The payoffs generated by a bribe made the briber and the bribee better off but made others in the society worse off. The analysis of data collected from the questionnaires showed that combined monitoring reduced bribe-demanding behaviour by the public officials in the game, which ultimately lowered corruption. In contrast, top-down auditing alone did not significantly reduce the officials' tendency to demand bribes. Serra's suggested explanations include the extra risk of social disapprobation with the bottom-up method, the risk of betrayal by the bribe giver, and erroneously ascribing higher probabilities to being caught. This preliminary evaluation of different policies suggests that a system in which bottom-up monitoring triggers top-down auditing (with some probability) could be efficient in curbing corruption.

Conclusions

Our survey of the literature has presented some of the seminal recent research on monitoring both by third-party audits (top-down) and community monitoring. The main findings from the literature can be summarised as follows. Top-down audits causally reduced corruption in Brazil via electoral accountability – incumbents who were corrupt were less likely to be re-elected and this motivated them to reduce corruption. Past audits reduced corruption not only when the electoral punishment is higher but more so when judicial punishment was used. However, in Puerto Rico, anticipated audits did not significantly reduce corruption – audits seemed to lead to a selection of more competent politicians rather than more honest politicians.

The type of public service also matters. Decision makers in procurement respond more to audits due to the presence of clear rules and regulations in procurement, greater discretion in the use of funds, as well as higher punishment for violators. In contrast, in services where punishment is lower and the financial aspects of irregularities are lower (absenteeism rather than outright theft), audits had less of an effect on corruption. Audits might also have negative effects when they lead to demotivated bureaucrats. In terms of our theoretical framework, the literature has focused mainly on responsiveness to changes in q, and in punishment – both the chances of being punished f_k and the size of punishment F.

The findings on community monitoring are less clear. In India, social audits had positive effects in reducing some types of irregularities, where stakeholders were directly affected. But in terms of performance outcomes the jury is still out. In terms of more broadly defined community participation, the literature has focused mainly on two types of interventions – informational-only treatments and information accompanied by tools to encourage participation. Results suggest that collective action problems are pervasive. Agents who are not empowered did not engage unless they had some control on the final decisions. More fractionalised groups had more severe problems and, even within groups, women were less likely to speak up. Elite capture and intimidation by elites is another important problem. As in top-down audits, successful community monitoring may also lead to worse outcomes when there is too much interference in the working of the service providers. In understanding the heterogeneous effects of community monitoring, policy design seems important – less-complex tasks may respond better to community monitoring. This insight carries over to combinations of top-down and social audits. In terms of our framework, the literature has focused on changes in q (collective action-changing composition, providing incentives, and information on stakes involved), as well as the transaction costs of corruption or low effort β.

A thoughtful review by Hollyer (2012) covers the shortfalls of experimental and quasi-experimental literature on both top-down and bottom-up monitoring. Both top-down and bottom-up anti-corruption interventions have been successful in some instances and failed at some. The author points out that in fact, despite causality being established credibly in many interventions, the causal chains involved are quite long and so it is hard to identify why the intervention worked in some conditions but not in others. Variation in formal and informal institutions may affect the effectiveness of interventions, especially the composition of institutions that regulate the relationship between politicians, bureaucrats, and citizens. The competitiveness of political contestation, the nature of civil service rules, and the independence of oversight institutions are some of the crucial factors. The efficiency of the attempts to combat corruption is contingent on factors that tend to vary across countries, regions, municipalities, and villages. Hollyer (2012) suggested two ways of overcoming the problems faced in measuring the nature of the impact of anti-corruption interventions. One is a design-based approach – theory can be used to supervise experimental designs and case selection to allow for stronger tests of the effects of the treatments. A second mitigating approach involves meta-analysis or aggregation across multiple studies.

Some open questions remain for further research. First, in both top-down and social audits, the gap between finding irregularities/corruption and finding improvements in outcomes (the ultimate goals of audit) is considerable. Not only did studies fail to find effects on outcome variables; sometimes they found them in the wrong direction. Understanding the conditions and processes for which top-down audits work well and those under which social audits work well seems a first-order question. This is especially important as many supreme audit authorities are moving towards a system of outcome-oriented audits. Second, the literature on the efficacy of audits in relation to punishments is sparse, yet this may also be related to what types of processes are more suitable for top-down audits. For community monitoring there is a much greater wealth of information on outcomes, while in top-down audits there are only limited studies, most of which are focused on South America, with the heavy representation of Brazil. This may be due to the fact that it is much easier to get NGOs than supreme audit institutions to collaborate on research. The most promising lines of enquiry here seem to be on the composition and design of audit teams when the aim is to get representation, voice, and impact. As with top-down audits, here too developing an outcome orientation is important.

Some main policy prescriptions also emerge from our survey. Monitoring ultimately aims to improve outcomes and not just lower corruption, though that is an important mediating link. Since top-down audits are costly, it is worthwhile knowing whether they improve citizens' wellbeing. For instance, if audits reduce officials' or policymakers' motivation to take risks with potentially useful but difficult projects, or, if they are difficult to press charges on, citizens' welfare may not be improved. In addition, while activities like procurement lend themselves to audits naturally, the same cannot be said of other public service delivery where community monitoring is more suitable. So top-down audits should be used only in contexts similar to procurement, where the documentation to take legal action exists.

Acknowledgements

This work was funded by DFID's Global Integrity-Anti Corruption Evidence project. We thank the workshop participants, an anonymous referee and especially the editors Sarmistha Pal and J.-P. Faguet for their insightful comments.

Endnotes

[1] https://www.imf.org/en/Publications/Policy-Papers/Issues/2018/04/20
/pp030918-review-of-1997-guidance-note-on-governance

[2] Updated in Mookherjee and Bardhan (2005).

[3] CGU office in Brazil, Brazilian federal accountability office, public prosecutors and municipality legislative branch.

[4] Avis, Ferraz, and Finan (2018) measured corruption as the log of number of irregularities classified as either moderate or severe in audit reports, mismanagement as the number of irregularities registered under administrative and procedural issues, and as an indicator variable whether legal action had ever been taken against a mayor in a municipality. Irregularities associated with mismanagement remain unaffected by the history of audits in a municipality. Interestingly, they do not find much evidence of selection effects: if increased information about elected leaders causes voters to throw out corrupt incumbents, then over time the fraction of corrupt leaders should go down in audited municipalities, but they do not find this.

[5] Mayors in Brazil face a two-term limit, wherein a mayor who gets elected for the first time serves their first term and becomes eligible to stand for re-election. If re-elected, the mayor who is in his/her second term faces a term limit of standing for further elections.

[6] The model by Allingham and Sandmo (the AS model) focuses on studying the choice of a taxpayer who trades off the benefits from tax evasion and the risky costs and fines from detection.

[7] See for example, https://timesofindia.indiatimes.com/india/cag-to-introduce-outcome-based-aud its/articleshow/64482292.cms

[8] The first round of audit is considered as a reference point.

[9] The VECs exist in every village in Uttar Pradesh. They consist of the elected head of village government, the headteacher of the government school, and three parents of students enrolled in government schools in the village.

[10] The comment forms were filled by the villagers and submitted before the village meetings. They were summarised and read out during the meeting.

References

Aakella, Karuna Vakati and Kidambi, Sowmya (2007) 'Challenging Corruption with Social Audits', *Economic and Political Weekly*, vol.42, no.5, pp.345–47. https://www.jstor.org/stable/4419201

Afridi, Farzana; Barooah, Bidisha; and Somanathan, Rohini (2020) 'Improving Learning Outcomes through Information Provision: Experimental Evidence from Indian villages', *Journal of Development Economics*, vol.146, p.102276. https://doi.org/10.1016/j.jdeveco.2018.08.002

Afridi, Farzana; Bhattacharya, Sourav; Dhillon, Amrita; and Solan, Eilon (2021) 'Electoral Competition and Corruption: Theory and Evidence from India', CAGE Working Paper 569.

Afridi, Farzana and Iversen, Vegard (2014) 'Social Audits and MGNREGA Delivery: Lessons from Andhra Pradesh', *India Policy Forum*, vol.10, no.1, pp.297–341. https://dx.doi.org/10.2139/ssrn.2424194

Aiyar, Yamini and Mehta, Soumya Kapoor (2015) 'Spectators or Participants? Effects of Social Audits in Andhra Pradesh', *Economic and Political Weekly*, vol.50, pp.66–71. https://www.jstor.org/stable/24481397

Allingham, Michael G. and Sandmo, Agnar (1972) 'Income Tax Evasion: A Theoretical Analysis', *Journal of Public Economics*, vol.1, no.3–4, pp.323–38. https://doi.org/10.1016/0047-2727(72)90010-2

Andrabi, Tahir; Das, Jishnu; and Khwaja, Asim Iyaz (2017) 'Report Cards: The Impact of Providing School and Child Test Scores on Educational Markets', *American Economic Review*, vol.107, no.6, pp.1535–63. https://doi.org/10.1257/aer.20140774

Apel, Robert (2013) 'Sanctions, Perceptions, and Crime: Implications for Criminal Deterrence', *Journal of Quantitative Criminology*, vol.29, no.1, pp.67–101. https://doi.org/10.1007/s10940-012-9170-1

Avis, Eric; Ferraz, Claudio; and Finan, Frederico (2018) 'Do Government Audits Reduce Corruption? Estimating the Impacts of Exposing Corrupt Politicians', *Journal of Political Economy*, vol.126, no.5, pp.1912–64. https://doi.org/10.1086/699209

Bajpai, Rajni and Myers, C. Bernard (2020) 'Enhancing Government Effectiveness and Transparency: The Fight Against Corruption', World Bank Group. https://policycommons.net/artifacts/1250808/enhancing-government -effectiveness-and-transparency/1811297

Banerjee, Abhijit; Banerji, Rukmini; Duflo, Esther; Glennerster, Rachel; Kenniston, Daniel; Khemani, Stuti; and Shotland, Marc (2007) 'Can Information Campaigns Raise Awareness and Local Participation in Primary Education?' *Economic and Political Weekly*, vol.42, no.15, pp.1365–72. https://www.jstor.org/stable/4419472

Banerjee, Abhijit; Hanna, Rema; Kyle, Jordan; Olken, Benjamin A., and Sumarto, Sudarno (2018) 'Tangible Information and Citizen Empowerment: Identification Cards and Food Subsidy Programs in Indonesia', *Journal of Political Economy*, vol.126, no.2, pp.451–91. https://doi.org/10.1086/696226

Banerjee, Abhijit; Banerji, Rukmini; Duflo, Esther; Glennerster, Rachel; and Khemani, Stuti (2010) 'Pitfalls of Participatory Programs: Evidence from a Randomized Evaluation in Education in India', *American Economic*

Journal: Economic Policy, vol.2, no.1, pp.1–30.
https://doi.org/10.1257/pol.2.1.1

Bardhan, Pranab and Mookherjee, Dilip (1998) 'Expenditure Decentralization and the Delivery of Public Services in Developing Countries', UC Berkeley Working Paper. http://dx.doi.org/10.22004/ag.econ.233623

Barr, Abigail; Mugisha, Frederick; Serneels, Pieter; and Zeitlin, Andrew (2012) 'Information and Collective Action in the Community Monitoring of Schools: Field and Lab Experimental Evidence from Uganda', Unpublished Working Paper.

Becker, Gary S. (1968) 'Crime and Punishment: An Economic Approach', *Journal of Political Economy*, vol.76, no.2, pp.169–217. https://doi.org/10.1086/259394

Besley, Timothy. (2006) *Principled Agents?: The Political Economy of Good Government*, Oxford University Press.

Besley, Timothy and Prat, Andrea (2006) 'Handcuffs for the Grabbing Hand? Media Capture and Government Accountability', *American Economic Review*, vol.96, no.3, pp.720–36. https://doi.org/10.1257/aer.96.3.720

Björkman, Martina and Svensson, Jakob (2009) 'Power to the People: Evidence from a Randomized Field Experiment on Community-Based Monitoring in Uganda', *The Quarterly Journal of Economics*, vol.124, no.2, pp.735–69. https://doi.org/10.1162/qjec.2009.124.2.735

Björkman, Martina and Svensson, Jakob (2010) 'When Is Community-Based Monitoring Effective? Evidence from a Randomized Experiment in Primary Health in Uganda', *Journal of the European Economic Association*, vol.8, no.2–3, pp.571–81. https://doi.org/10.1111/j.1542-4774.2010.tb00527.x

Björkman Nyqvist, Martina; De Walque, Damien; and Svensson, Jakob (2017) 'Experimental Evidence on the Long-Run Impact of Community-Based Monitoring', *American Economic Journal: Applied Economics*, vol.9, no.1, pp.33–69. https://doi.org/10.1257/app.20150027

Bobonis, Gustavo J; Cámara Fuertes, Luis R; and Schwabe, Rainer (2016) 'Monitoring Corruptible Politicians', *American Economic Review*, vol.106, no.8, pp.2371–405. https://doi.org/10.1257/aer.20130874

Brollo, F. (2008) 'Who Is Punishing Corrupt Politicians–Voters or the Central Government? Evidence from the Brazilian Anti-corruption Program', IGIER Working Paper No.336. https://repec.unibocconi.it/igier/igi/wp/2008/336.pdf

Chalfin, Aaron and McCrary, Justin (2017) 'Criminal Deterrence: A Review of the Literature', *Journal of Economic Literature*, vol.55, no.1, pp.5–48. https://doi.org/10.1257/jel.20141147

Chander, Parkash and Wilde, Louis (1992) 'Corruption in Tax Administration', *Journal of Public Economics*, vol.49, no.3, pp.333–49. https://doi.org/10.1016/0047-2727(92)90072-N

Christensen, Darin; Dube, Oeindrila; Haushofer, Johannes; Siddiqi, Bilal; and Voors, Maarten (2021) 'Building Resilient Health Systems: Experimental Evidence from Sierra Leone and the 2014 Ebola Outbreak', *The Quarterly Journal of Economics*, vol.136, no.2, pp.1145–98. https://doi.org/10.1093/qje/qjaa039

Colonnelli, Emanuele and Prem, Mounu (2022) 'Corruption and Firms', *The Review of Economic Studies*, vol.89, no.2, pp.695–732. https://doi.org/10.1093/restud/rdab040

Duflo, Esther; Greenstone, Michael; Pande, Rohini; and Ryan, Nicholas (2013) 'Truth-Telling by Third-Party Auditors and the Response of Polluting Firms: Experimental Evidence from India', *The Quarterly Journal of Economics*, vol.128, no.4, pp.1499–545. https://doi.org/10.1093/qje/qjt024

Ferraz, Claudio and Finan, Frederico (2008) 'Exposing Corrupt Politicians: The Effects of Brazil's Publicly Released Audits on Electoral Outcomes', *The Quarterly Journal of Economics*, vol.123, no.2, pp.703–45. https://doi.org/10.1162/qjec.2008.123.2.703

Ferraz, Claudio and Finan, Frederico (2011) 'Electoral Accountability and Corruption: Evidence from the Audits of Local Governments', *American Economic Review*, vol.101, no.4, pp.1274–311. https://doi.org/10.1257/aer.101.4.1274

Fiala, Nathan and Premand, Patrick (2018) 'Social Accountability and Service Delivery: Experimental Evidence from Uganda', World Bank Policy Research Working Paper No.8449. https://ssrn.com/abstract=3182880

Hanousek, Jan and Kochanova, Anna (2016) 'Bribery Environments and Firm Performance: Evidence from CEE Countries', *European Journal of Political Economy*, vol.43, pp.14–28. https://doi.org/10.1016/j.ejpoleco.2016.02.002

Hollyer, James R. (2012) 'Is It Better to Empower the People or the Authorities? Assessing the Conditional Effects of "Top-Down" and "Bottom-Up" Anticorruption Interventions', in Serra, Danila and Wantchekon, Leonard (eds) *New Advances in Experimental Research on Corruption*, Emerald, pp.247–77. https://doi.org/10.1108/S0193-2306(2012)0000015011

Kleven, Henrik Jacobsen; Knudsen Martin B.; Kreiner, Claus Thustrup; Pedersen, Søren; and Saez, Emmanuel (2011) 'Unwilling or Unable to Cheat? Evidence from a Tax Audit Experiment in Denmark', *Econometrica*, vol.79, no.3, pp.651–92. https://doi.org/10.3982/ECTA9113

Li, Hongy; Xu, Lixin Colin; and Zou, Heng-fu (2000) 'Corruption, Income Distribution, and Growth', *Economics & Politics*, vol.12, no.2, pp.155–82. https://doi.org/10.1111/1468-0343.00073

Lichand, Guilherme; Lopes, Marcus F.; and Medeiros, Marcelo C. (2016) 'Is Corruption Good for Your Health?' Working Paper. https://oconnell.fas.harvard.edu/files/glichand/files/is_corruption_good_for_your_health_-_jan24.pdf

Malmendier, Ulrike (2021) 'Exposure, Experience, and Expertise: Why Personal Histories Matter in Economics', *Journal of the European Economic Association*, vol.19, no.6, pp.2857–94. https://doi.org/10.1093/jeea/jvab045

Mansuri, Ghazala and Rao, Vijayendra (2013) 'Localizing Development: Does Participation Work?' World Bank Policy Research Report, Washington, DC. http://hdl.handle.net/10986/11859

Mauro, Paolo (1995) 'Corruption and Growth', *The Quarterly Journal of Economics*, vol.110, no.3, pp.681–712. https://doi.org/10.2307/2946696

Mbate, Michael (2023) 'Can Parliamentary Sanctions Strengthen Local Political Accountability? Evidence from Kenya', in Faguet, John-Paul and Pal, Sarmistha (eds) *Decentralised Governance: Crafting Effective Democracies Around the World.* London: LSE Press. DOI: XXX

Molina, Ezequiel; Carella, Laura; Pacheco, Ana; Cruces, Guillermo; and Gasparini, Leonardo (2016) 'Community Monitoring Interventions to Curb Corruption and Increase Access and Quality of Service Delivery in Low- and Middle-Income Countries: A Systematic Review', *Campbell Systematic Reviews*, vol.12, no.1, pp.1–204. https://doi.org/10.4073/csr.2016.8

Mookherjee, Dilip and Bardhan, Pranab (2005) 'Decentralization, Corruption and Government Accountability: An Overview', Boston University, Department of Economics Working Papers Series WP2005-023.

Olken, Benjamin A. (2007) 'Monitoring Corruption: Evidence from a Field Experiment in Indonesia', *Journal of Political Economy*, vol.115, no.2, pp.200–49. https://doi.org/10.1086/517935

Olken, Benjamin A. and Pande, R. (2012) 'Corruption in Developing Countries', *Annual Review of Economics*, vol.4, no.1, pp.479–509. https://doi.org/10.1146/annurev-economics-080511-110917

Pandey, Priyanka; Goyal, Sangeeta; and Sundararaman, Venkatesh (2009) 'Community Participation in Public Schools: Impact of Information Campaigns in Three Indian States', *Education Economics*, vol.17, no.3, pp.355–75. https://doi.org/10.1080/09645290903157484

Parthasarthy, Ramya; Rao, Vijayendra; and Palaniswamy, Nethra (2019) 'Deliberative Democracy in an Unequal World: A Text-As-Data Study of South India's Village Assemblies', *American Political Science Review*, vol.113, no.3, pp.623–40. https://doi.org/10.1017/S0003055419000182

Persson, Torsten and Tabellini, Guido (2002) *Political Economics: Explaining Economic Policy*. Cambridge, MA: MIT Press.

Pradhan, Menno; Suryadarma, Daniel; Beatty, Amanda; Wong, Maisy; Gaduh, Arya; Alisjahbana, Armida; and Artha, Rima Prama (2014) 'Improving Educational Quality through Enhancing Community Participation: Results from a Randomized Field Experiment in Indonesia', *American Economic Journal: Applied Economics*, vol.6, no.2, pp.105–26. https://doi.org/10.1257/app.6.2.105

Raffler, Pia; Posner, Daniel; and Parkerson, Doug (2019) 'The Weakness of Bottom-Up Accountability: Experimental Evidence from the Ugandan Health Sector', Unpublished Working Paper.

Serra, Danila (2011) 'Combining Top-Down and Bottom-Up Accountability: Evidence from a Bribery Experiment', *The Journal of Law, Economics, and Organization*, vol.28, no.3, pp.569–87. https://doi.org/10.1093/jleo/ewr010

Shah, Anwar; Thompson, Theresa; and Zou, Heng-fu (2004) 'The Impact of Decentralization on Service Delivery, Corruption, Fiscal Management and Growth in Developing and Emerging Market Economies: A Synthesis of Empirical Evidence', CESifo DICE Report, Ifo Institute – Leibniz Institute for Economic Research at the University of Munich. https://www.econstor.eu/bitstream/10419/166793/1/ifo-dice-report-v02 -y2004-i1-p10-14.pdf

Shleifer, Andrei and Vishny, Robert W. (1993) 'Corruption', *The Quarterly Journal of Economics*, vol.108, no.3, pp.599–617. https://doi.org/10.2307/2118402

Singh, Ritesh and Vutukuru, Vinay (2010) 'Enhancing Accountability in Public Service Delivery through Social Audits: A Case Study of Andhra Pradesh, India', Accountability Initiative, Centre for Policy Research, New Delhi. https://namati.org/resources/enhancing-accountability-in-public-service -delivery-through-social-audits-a-case-study-of-andhra-pradesh-india

Tanzi, Vito and Davoodi, Hamid (2001) 'Corruption, Growth and Public Finances', in Jain, Arvind K. (ed.) *The Political Economy of Corruption*, Routledge, pp.89–110. https://doi.org/10.4324/9780203468388

Treisman, Daniel (2000) 'The Causes of Corruption: A Cross-National Study', *The Journal of Public Economics*, vol.76, no.3, pp.399–457. https://doi.org/10.1016/S0047-2727(99)00092-4

Wade, Robert (2000) 'How Infrastructure Agencies Motivate Staff: Canal Irrogation in India and the Republic of Korea', in Mody, Ashoka (ed.) *Infrastructure Strategies in East Asia: The Untold Story*, the World Bank, pp.109–30.
http://documents.worldbank.org/curated/en/510051468774847688/Infrastructure-strategies-in-East-Asia-the-untold-story

World Bank (2003) 'World Development Report 2004: Making Services Work for Poor People'.
https://openknowledge.worldbank.org/handle/10986/5986

World Bank (2007) 'Strengthening World Bank Group Engagement on Governance and Anticorruption', Washington, DC: World Bank.
http://documents.worldbank.org/curated/en/426381468340863478/Main-Report

Zamboni, Yves and Litschig, Stephan (2018) 'Audit Risk and Rent Extraction: Evidence from a Randomized Evaluation in Brazil', *Journal of Development Economics*, vol.134, pp.133–49.
https://doi.org/10.1016/j.jdeveco.2018.03.008

10. Subnational governance in Ghana: a comparative assessment of data and performance

Daniel Chachu, Michael Danquah, and Rachel M. Gisselquist

Summary

In this chapter, we conceptualise an ideal framework that captures three reinforcing levers for measuring local government performance in sub-Saharan Africa, specifically Ghana, namely policy pronouncement, political processes and internal operations, and policy implementation. Given data limitations we employ a 'next best' approach to apply this framework and measure local government performance by combining a weighted 'quality of reporting' measure with selected available measures on political processes and internal operations, and policy implementation, so as to construct a composite index for local government performance (LGI). We also look at the relationship between our performance indices and other indices of local government performance in Ghana, as well as poverty headcounts. We find that, on average, urban districts perform better than their rural counterparts and also districts located in the southern half of Ghana perform better. Our constructed composite index is positively correlated with indices from Ghana's district league tables. It has a negative relationship with poverty headcount in districts, indicating that districts with lower poverty incidence are more effective and responsive to their citizens. The findings provide a snapshot of institutional performance across Ghana's districts, and offer a more comprehensive basis for considering variations in subnational institutional performance, including the effects of decentralisation than previous studies of Ghana – or indeed African countries more broadly.[1]

How to cite this book chapter:

Chachu, Daniel; Danquah, Michael and Gisselquist, Rachel M. (2023) 'Subnational governance in Ghana: a comparative assessment of data and performance', in: Faguet, Jean-Paul and Pal, Sarmistha (eds) *Decentralised Governance: Crafting Effective Democracies Around the World*, London: LSE Press, pp. 271–299. https://doi.org/10.31389/lsepress.dlg.j License: CC BY 4.0

By bringing government closer to the people, it has often been argued, decentralisation has the potential to make government more effective and responsive, with positive influence not only on accountability and political participation but also on public goods provision and economic outcomes (Bojanic and Collins 2021; del Granado, Martinez-Vazquez, and McNab 2018; Otoo and Danquah 2021). To assess such claims empirically, valid and reliable measures of subnational institutional performance are needed. How effective and responsive are local governments? How do they compare with central governments? What factors (including decentralisation) influence the performance of local governments? Where decentralisation processes have occurred, is there evidence of local governments becoming more effective and responsive as a result? The first of these questions is the focus of this chapter.

There is a substantial body of literature on the quality of local governance[2] (including comparative measurement in multiple contexts). Yet there remain significant gaps with respect to the conceptualisation and measurement of the quality of local governance in non-Western contexts, especially in sub-Saharan Africa (Iddawela, Lee, and Rodríguez-Pose 2021). Here we develop an ideal framework for measuring local government performance in Ghana based on three reinforcing levers – policy pronouncement (the institutional framework or rules), political processes and internal operations, and policy implementation. Adequate data for measuring all three levers for subnational units in Ghana are not available, so we employ a 'next best' approach that combines the weighted quality of reporting measure with selected available measures on political processes and internal operations, and policy implementation to construct a composite index for local government performance. We also look at the relationship between the local government performance indices and other indices of local government performance in Ghana as well as poverty headcounts. Ghana is one of Africa's most stable democracies, and is among the countries in the region where statistical data are more readily available and progressively improving in quality. However, this is less true of subnational institutional data on multisectoral indicators that aid the measurement and understanding of variations in local governance. Given the lack of data on sub-Saharan African countries, many studies on this subject matter including Ghana compare only a few districts; thus, our comparison of all districts speaks directly to gaps in the literature.

Ghana is also an interesting case because local governance and decentralisation have been topics of significant recent public debate, especially prior to the presidential elections held in 2020, when a referendum was proposed for the election of metropolitan, municipal, and district assembly chief executives (MMDCEs). Although the referendum was eventually cancelled, with the president citing a lack of national consensus on the topic, Afrobarometer data suggest that voters favoured the election of MMDCEs (Armah-Attoh and Norviewu 2018).

Multiple definitions of good governance and alternative frameworks are used in the large literature on the subject (Gisselquist 2012; Weiss 2000). A common working definition of 'governance' is as given by the World Bank (2017, p.3): 'the process through which state and nonstate actors interact to design and implement policies within a given set of formal and informal rules that shape and are shaped by power'. This is applicable both at national and subnational levels.

Weiss's (2000) list of key attributes of (good) governance included: universal protection of human rights; non-discriminatory laws; efficient, impartial and rapid judicial processes; transparent public agencies; accountability for decisions by public officials; devolution of resources and decision-making to local levels from the centre; and meaningful participation by citizens in debating public policies and choices. He argued that these go beyond the Western construct of democracy and must be accompanied by the needed resources and situated within the relevant cultural context. In a similar vein, Gisselquist (2012) identified seven core components of good governance as the concept is applied in international development. These include (i) democracy and representation, (ii) human rights, (iii) rule of law, (iv) effective and efficient public management, (v) transparency and accountability, (vi) developmentalist objectives, and (vii) political and economic policies, programmes, and institutions (for example, elections, a legislature, a free press, and secure property rights).

Related terms used in the literature include institutional development and political development. Moore (2001), for instance, emphasised the exercise of legitimate authority over territory and active engagement with citizens from whom legitimate authority is derived and in the interest of whom legitimate authority is exercised as key defining elements for political development. The case for 'good' local governance is often premised on its potential to deliver public goods to heterogeneous groups whose varying needs would have likely been missed by central government. Thus, 'local' suggests some form of federalism, decentralisation, deconcentration, or devolution of power from a central authority to a subcentral or subnational unit. Decentralisation's links to beneficial development outcomes has been extensively discussed (Faguet and Pöschl 2015). Faguet, Fox, and Pöschl (2015) identified four mechanisms through which decentralisation impacts on the performance of a state:

- The ability of a subnational unit to exercise authority over territory and people, thereby maintaining peace and avoiding conflict.
- Policy autonomy and the ability to uphold law.
- Responsiveness and accountable service provision.
- Social learning achieved through citizenship participation.

Ahmad, Devarajan, Khemani, and Shah (2005) argued that the need to improve the quality of service delivery is the principal motivation for the adoption of decentralisation, because, in essence, it is a path to transparency, inclusiveness, accountability, and, ultimately, responsive development. Despite the potential for decentralisation to have such positive impact on accountability and development, more evidence is needed on actual impact. Some studies suggest that, especially in developing countries, impacts in practice often fall short of what citizens expect (Brierley 2020; Yeboah-Assiamah 2016). We begin this chapter by examining the available subnational data for Ghana and then Section 10.2 looks at how our performance concept can be operationalised in the Ghanaian context given data constraints. In Section 10.3, we present our results on measuring local government performance in Ghana. The conclusion includes a discussion of areas for further study.

10.1 Subnational governance research and data in sub-Saharan Africa: the case of Ghana

Although there exists substantial literature on governance in sub-Saharan Africa, analysis is usually at the national level (Iddawela, Lee, and Rodríguez-Pose 2021). In terms of data, there are also an increasing number of living standard measurement surveys (LSMS), demographic and health surveys, censuses, and other databases that capture household-level data across multiple socio-economic (and in some cases governance) indicators. However, multiple-indicator-based data sets for subnational institutional entities are usually lacking. This challenge has implications not only for research but also for the effective monitoring of subnational governance. Many researchers rely on their own primary surveys of selected areas (Brierley 2020; Burgess et al. 2015) and available secondary data (Fumey and Egwaikhide 2018; Otoo and Danquah 2021). Other recent studies have employed satellite data (Dahis and Szerman 2021; Iddawela, Lee, and Rodríguez-Pose 2021) and elections data (Asunka et al. 2017).

For Ghana, various subnational data collection efforts have been undertaken, focusing on regional coordinating councils; metropolitan, municipal and district assemblies (MMDAs); and their sublevel structures. Most of these surveys have been of limited scope, but a few recent attempts have yielded large data sets, although these are not yet publicly available (Dzansi et al. 2018; Williams 2017). Data have also been drawn from community focus groups and household surveys of limited scale (Akudugu 2013; Debrah 2009).

Assessing the decentralisation–development nexus in Ghana

Ghana has a four-level governance structure shown in Figure 10.1 comprising: (i) national-level ministries and their sector agencies; (ii) decentralised structures such as the regional coordinating councils; (iii) MMDAs (also referred to as districts); and (iv) subdistrict structures such as urban, town,

Figure 10.1: Ghana's subnational governance structure

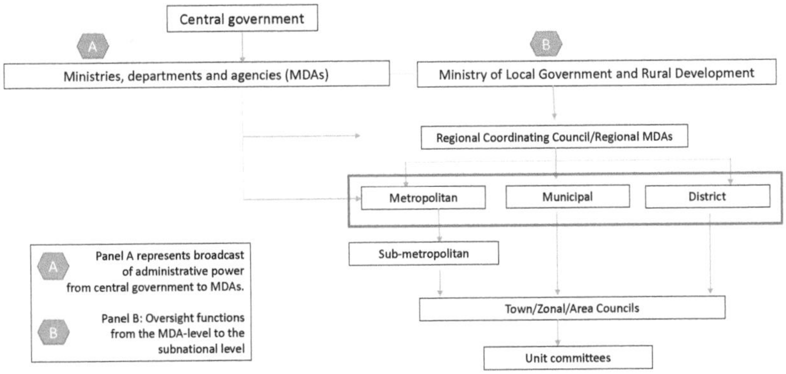

Source: Authors.

and zonal or area councils (Ayee 2013). Local assemblies are at the core of the decentralised structures and have powers to function as political and administrative authorities, as well as development, planning, budget, and rating authorities (Ayee 2013). These structures come under the direct supervision of the Ministry of Local Government and Rural Development, which is in turn subject to cabinet, headed by the president. In addition to being a deliberative and law-making arm of government, the parliament of Ghana also has the authority to hold levels of the subnational governance structure accountable.

During the pre-colonial era, local governance was mainly through traditional rulers and clan heads. The British indirect rule system led to the establishment of selective, formal native authorities through which the country was administered. After independence in 1957, Ghana went through several local government reforms that redefined the role of traditional authorities as heads and appointing authorities. In 1979 a new constitution made the president the appointing authority with support from traditional rulers (see Ahwoi [2010] for a review of Ghana's historical experience). The next important reform was the promulgation of a new local government law in 1988 (PNDC Law 207). It began a new decentralisation policy with the primary aim of bringing development and improved governance to the doorstep of the citizenry (Ayee 2013). A direct product of this was the creation of additional MMDAs. Beginning with 65 MMDAs in 1988, by 2020 the number had increased to 261. The three main sources of revenue for MMDAs are:

- transfers from the central government mainly through the District Assemblies Common Fund (DACF);
- internally generated funds (IGFs), such as licences, rates, fees, and ther charges; and
- donations and grants (for example, development partner support through the District Development Facility).

Except for the large metropolitan assemblies, which rake in more from IGFs, the most important sources of revenues for most MMDAs are decentralised transfers. By law, all expenditure is drawn from a budget approved by the local assembly. Local government expenses range from recurrent items covering staffing remunerations and administrative expenses to capital expenditure on programmes and projects covered in the district development plan.

Analyses of Ghana's decentralisation present a mixed picture of local government performance (Ayee 2008; Osei-Akoto, Darko, William, George, and Adiah 2007), building on diverse methods and frameworks. Our analysis builds upon this rich literature (and see Chachu 2021). For instance, Crook (1994), who was among the first to assess the performance of the newly created districts, focused on performance in terms of output effectiveness, responsiveness and acceptability. Ayee (1996) assessed local government performance against three objectives: participation, effectiveness, and accountability. Using Ho and Keta districts as case studies, he found marginal delivery of public goods despite signs of increased participation. In other work, Ayee (2013) examined the political economy of creating subnational structures. In a study conducted in five districts, Mohammed (2016) considered how decentralisation promotes local participation. Collectively, the research literature on Ghana points both to the promise of decentralisation as well as a variety of factors contributing to its limits, including challenges of central government control over key local functions, limited local capacity, political capture, misplaced priorities, poor coordination, inadequate financing, and increased borrowing by local authorities (Ayee 2013; Ayee 2008).

Civil society organisations (CSOs) have also played a major role in analysis and public debate about local governance and decentralisation in the Ghanaian context. Over several years, the Integrated Social Development Centre (ISODEC) has monitored the disbursement and use of the District Assembly's Common Fund, while the Send Foundation of West Africa tracked the use of Heavily Indebted Poor Countries' (HIPC) funds at the local government level. The Local Governance Network, an umbrella of CSOs, has been engaged in research and policy advocacy on local governance since 2003, including participation in the nationwide subnational institutional performance assessment process under the District Assessment Performance Assessment Tool (DPAT).

With support from UNICEF, CSOs like the Centre for Democracy and Development (CDD) have led the development of the District League Table (DLT).[3] The DLT, developed to promote citizens' awareness and social accountability, is an assessment tool that uses government data to rank all district assemblies on the basis of their social development, covering indicators in education, sanitation, rural water, health, security, and governance. One possible critique of this existing rich literature is that a number of indicators employed in analyses arguably are not valid measures of local government performance because they fall outside the control of local district assemblies. For example, performance in the Basic Education Certificate Examination is used in some analyses but key factors that influence this outcome (such as training and deployment of teachers) are determined by central government and not locally.

10.2 A framework for studying local government performance

In developing our ideal framework, we draw inspiration from Putnam, Leonardi, and Nanetti (1994; hereafter PLN). Although best known for their argument about the role of social capital, their assessment of the quality of institutional performance across Italy's regional governments provides insights for setting up our framework. Core to PLN's assessment of local governance are 'responsiveness' and 'effectiveness'. Responsiveness represents the ability of institutions to demonstrate awareness of public needs, as well as their willingness and ability to engage with citizens towards meeting those needs. Effectiveness speaks to the extent to which those needs are met in a timely and satisfactory manner. The link between social demands and implementation is mediated by political interactions, the workings of government, and policy choices.

Following PLN, we consider three reinforcing levers of local government performance (Figure 10.2). The first is *policy pronouncement (institutional framework)*, or the rules and norms that constrain behaviour and guide interactions at all levels of a subnational polity. For example, does the local government have a set of comprehensive and innovative laws in place? While the concepts of 'comprehensiveness' and 'innovation' may be normative, they speak to how adaptable a local government is to the existing and changing needs of its constituents.

The second lever comprises the *political processes and internal operations* within the subgovernance structure. These include decision-making processes among the arms of the local government, the nature and timing of the local budget cycle and other procedural mechanisms determining how long it takes for meaningful action on local laws and policies. For example, how long does it take for a local government to develop and approve a budget? The constituents of this lever contribute to understanding the extent to which laws and policies can be translated into meaningful action.

The third (and last) lever is *policy implementation*, which encompasses how far local government actions are responsive to the needs of citizens, for example, in delivering an appropriate quantity and quality of public goods. Following PLN, we aim to focus more on *output* measures of local government performance, rather than *outcome* measures (which can be confounded by factors beyond the control of local governments).

Figure 10.2: Conceptual framework for analysing local government performance

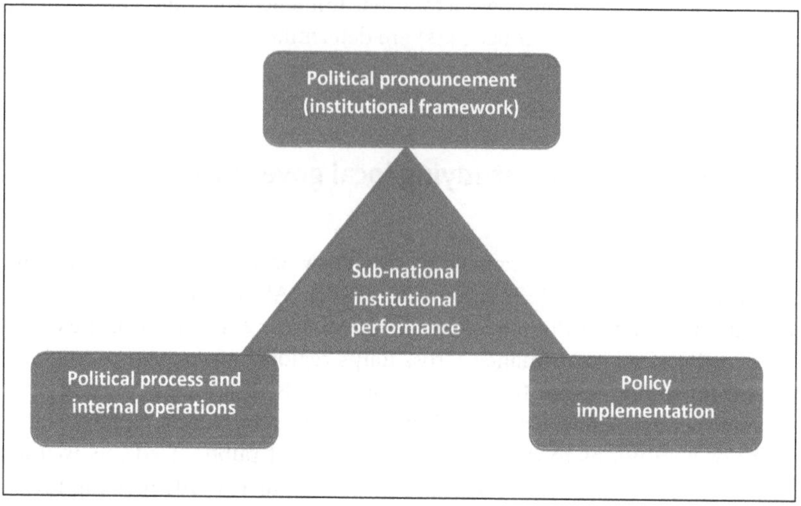

Source: Authors' construct based on PLN (1994).

Subnational institutional performance then is conceptualised as a product of the existing institutional framework, policy processes and internal operations, and policy implementation (Figure 10.2).

Defining the measurement framework – list of indicators and measures

Putnam et al further offer several criteria to consider in the development of these output measures of local government performance:

- Comprehensiveness: the measures reflect the diversity of action and innovation.
- Internal consistency: indicators used to assess institutional performance will be 'multidimensional' but their use should display consistency.
- Reliability: rankings or evaluation outcomes must not change arbitrarily, especially at short intervals.
- Acceptability: measures applied in assessment exercises must not be alien to the constituency, audience or the context of interest.

Guided by PLN's measurement framework, we developed 22 indicators for Ghana based on the country's existing legal and policy framework for national and subnational governance (Republic of Ghana 2014a; Republic of Ghana 2014b), that are summarised in Table 10.1. Our extended list of measures is needed to capture the three levers described in Figure 10.2 and the multidimensional nature of Ghana's local governance, particularly where actual data for some measures may be missing.

Table 10.1: Indicator framework for Ghana

Theme	Indicator	Measures
Policy pronouncement (institutional framework)	Reform legislation	The extent to which a district assembly has comprehensive, coherent and creative by-laws
	Legislative innovation	How soon a model by-law is picked up and passed by a district assembly
Political process and internal operations	Cabinet stability	Number of times a district chief executive is replaced over a period of 8 years
		Number of times the executive committee of the district assembly sits for deliberations within a typical year*
		The average share of district assembly members that participate in district assembly meetings for a particular year/period
	Budget promptness	The average time it takes a district assembly's annual budget to be approved
		The average number of budget/public hearings conducted by a district assembly within a year*
		The ratio of IGFs to total annual District Assembly Common Fund (DACF) disbursement[a]*
	Statistical and information services	The availability of a statistical and information office in a district and the extent to which the office is equipped for its role*
Policy implementation	Daycare centres	Ratio of total number of enrolled children in public kindergartens to the number of public kindergartens*
		Ratio of primary school enrolment to number of public primary schools with permanent structures*
	Family clinics	Number of CHPS compounds in operation per district standardised by the rural population*
	Industrial policy instruments	The number of potential tools of industrial policy deployed in a district in a reference year*
	Agricultural spending capacity	Number of agriculture extension officers per (farmer) population in a reference year
		Total agriculture expenditure standardised by district population in a reference year
		Total agriculture expenditure standardised by farmer population in a reference year*
	Local health unit	Total health expenditure per capita at the district level

(Continued)

Table 10.1: Continued

Theme	Indicator	Measures
	Housing and urban development	Total amount of funds disbursed towards housing and urban development standardised by district population
		Water supply coverage*
	Bureaucratic responsiveness	Number of building permits successfully granted or rejected as a share of total request for a given year*
		Percentage of reported cases on child rights protection (maintenance, custody, paternity and family reconciliation) successfully closed*
		FOAT Performance

Source: Putnam, Leonardi, and Nanetti (1994) and authors' construction.
Notes: [a] Though this measure could also be classified under policy implementation, we leave it here given that it is a critical prerequisite for any policy implementation. The DACF is a central government grant that is transferred to all district assemblies under a parliament-approved disbursement formula (variations largely based on needs and pressure on local government services due to migration). CHPS stands for Community Health and Planning Services. This is a national strategy for providing primary health care to communities. FOAT stands for Functional Operational Assessment Tool. This is an index that captures quality of government operations, service delivery and accountability. It is also now referred to as the District Assessment Performance Assessment Tool (DPAT).
* The starred criteria were incorporated into the measures included in the 'quality of reporting' index – see Section 10.3.

10.3 The Ghana data and data gaps

Moving from the ideal framework presented above to measurement underscores the limits of available data. In building our database on Ghana, we drew on several sources, in particular data compiled by the annual progress reports (APRs) of district assemblies. APRs constitute a key element of the national monitoring and evaluation system as set out in the legislation establishing local governments (Acts 462, 479, and 480). District assemblies are expected to produce and submit APRs to the National Development Planning Commission (NDPC), a state development planning, monitoring, and evaluation agency, through the regional coordinating councils (RCCs).[4] As an accountability tool, APRs are intended to show how resources are generated and utilised for development at the MMDA level in each financial year. In principle these APRs should provide data for all Ghana's districts on most of the measures identified in our framework. But in practice they do not. They are not available for all districts in any one year and even when available they do not provide data on all performance measures. Given this problem of missing data, we complement the information compiled from APRs with additional data for selected districts compiled from other government sources.[5]

MMDAs also report on progress in the implementation of their annual action plans, which are usually drawn from the MMDAs' medium-term development plans. The latter are developed based on the national medium-term development plan with guidance and technical support from the NDPC. Reporting is also provided on key performance indicators defined under the national development policy framework.

At the time of data collation in early 2021, archived online reports covered the period 2015 to 2018. We draw here on 2016 APRs because they provided the most comprehensive coverage when compared to other years. In addition, 2017 and 2018 constituted a transition period following elections in some districts, when new MMDA chief executives were being appointed and confirmed, thus offering an uneven snapshot of government functioning across districts (some of which had accomplished transitions while others did not). Out of 216 MMDAs, 210 had 2016 reports online.[6] We also complemented the data from these APRs with data from other reports (especially 2017) when they covered 2016.

Given the challenges of missing data in fully capturing our ideal framework, we employ a 'next best' strategy in three stages. First, we construct a new measure (quality of reporting), as a preliminary step, to reflect the comprehensiveness of MMDA reporting on key performance indicators. In essence, the measure speaks to the nature of 'missingness' in data relevant for assessing variations in local governance. Additionally, the measure, which describes the extent to which the MMDA fulfils a government reporting requirement at the heart of public accountability, provides an indicator of MMDA statistical and information services, that is one of the three core components of *policy process and internal operations* in our ideal framework.

Second, in the absence of better data, we consider three other alternative performance indicators that are available for most districts. We combine these data with our quality of reporting measure to arrive at a (second-best) measure of local governance for comparative assessment. Third, we assess correlations between our measures and other key indicators of subnational governance and development.

Stage 1: Quality of reporting measure

Comparing the indicators identified in our ideal framework (as set out in Table 10.1) against what is available in the 2016 APRs, we arrive at a list of 14 measures on which at least one district reports (most of which are indicated by a * in Table 10.1). In addition, two measures not included in the table also met our criteria and were included in the LGI alongside the starred items: number of general assembly meetings within a year, and population estimate.

Nearly two-thirds of these measures are in the area of *policy implementation*. In our coding, an MMDA gets a score of 1 for each indicator reported on. The highest score of 10 was recorded in Mfantseman Municipality (Central region), while five districts received scores of zero: Gushiegu (Northern),

Kadjebi (Volta), Kwahu South (Eastern), Nanumba North (Northern), and Wa East (Upper West). Only 16 per cent of MMDAs had a score of 5 or higher, while more than half recorded a score of 2 or below. The picture provided by these scores is broadly consistent with the NDPC's own assessment that about 93 per cent of districts were unable to comply with any of the reporting formats for 2016 (NDPC 2016).

Next, we adopt weights for each indicator to approximate the relative importance of specific sectors as revealed by government spending on social protection and poverty reduction (about 19.4 per cent of total government spending in 2016, mostly done at the ministries, departments, and agencies (MDA) and MMDA levels) (NDPC 2016). In other words, the greater the weight of an indicator, the larger the share of government spending on the sector associated with the indicator. Thus, lack of reporting on indicators covering sectors prioritised by government should be revealing of variations in the level of weakness in statistical and information services across MMDAs. Table 10.2 summarises spending and proposed weights across key sectors and indicators.

As Table 10.2 shows, the education sector receives the largest share of poverty reduction spending (over 45 per cent). Reporting on each of the two education measures is therefore assigned the largest weight of half that (see fourth column). The application of these weights to the reporting scores yields the weighted quality of reporting measure. Table 10.3 and Figure 10.3 show that the majority of MMDAs have very low weighted scores for their quality of

Table 10.2: Sectoral spending of poverty reduction and proposed weights

Key area of poverty reduction expenditure	Spending as a percentage of total poverty reduction spending (%)	Related measure	Weight per measure
Education (basic)	45.55	Kindergarten and, primary school enrolment ratios	45.55 / 2 = 22.775
Health (primary)	19.26	CHPS compounds	19.26
Agriculture	1.86	Agriculture expenditure	1.86
Water (rural)	0.45	Water supply coverage	0.45
Other expenditure (governance, housing, human rights, vocational/ employment skills, roads, electricity, etc.)	32.88	*All other measures*	32.88 / 9 = 3.65

Source: Authors' construct.

Table 10.3: Summary statistics on quality of reporting (weighted) measure

Category	Mean	Median	Standard deviation	Minimum	Maximum	N
All MMDAs	19.54	8.5	19.98	0	77.5	210
Urban MMDAs	20.11	8.5	23.37	0.5	87.5	58
Rural MMDAs	19.31	10.5	18.6	0	87.5	152

Source: Authors' construct.

Figure 10.3: Histogram of quality of reporting score

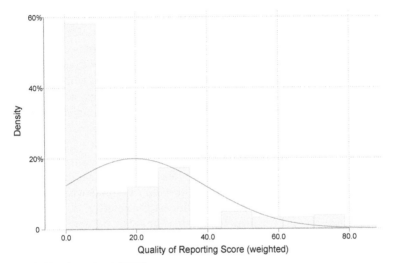

Source: Authors' construct (2022).

reporting. The variation in scores across all districts is also high and skewed to the right, with a standard deviation of approximately 20, a mean of 19.5, and a median of 8.5. The corresponding summary statistics for urban (that is, metropolitan and municipal assemblies only) and rural districts are also presented in Table 10.3.

A full list of district rankings is provided in Table 10.A1 in this chapter's Supplementary Materials.[7] Overall, Mfantseman Municipal, which was first in the unweighted quality of reporting measure, retains the top spot in the weighted rankings. It also scores highly in terms of other reported results. For example, all reported cases on child rights protection were successfully resolved or referred for appropriate redress. About a third of its local revenue sources comes from internally generated funds, suggesting significant local government fiscal capacity relative to other district assemblies, which largely rely on the District Assemblies Common Fund. In the district, 91 per cent of its population has access to safe water sources, a measure at the 95th percentile of the distribution. To some extent, variation in reporting quality can be explained by the variation in capacity of district administration as well as level of economic activities. Poorer performance of districts with respect to quality of reporting may be attributed to lack of staff and resources, among other factors.

Stage 2: Local government performance index (LGI)

Next, in line with pulling together the components of subnational institutional performance shown in Table 10.1, we construct a composite index that combines the weighted quality of reporting measure with measures on education delivery (policy implementation), district assembly financing (policy process and internal operations), and district assembly governance (policy process and internal operations) for the year 2016.[8] The choice of the measures seeks both to optimise the application of our theoretical framework and achieve a comparative assessment of most MMDAs with available data. Although some information on other sectoral measures is available (for example, on policy pronouncement), significant gaps in the data across districts means that their inclusion would effectively reduce the number of MMDAs that can be scored and ranked, and thereby further limit a meaningful comparative assessment across the country. Given the extent of missing data, employing standard methods of data imputation in the construction of our index is not advisable. Thus, we focus on case deletion, an alternative option, taking advantage only of data available. The measures are shown in Table 10.4.

The measure of education delivery addresses the ability of districts to provide sufficient school structures for children in public primary schools. The finance measure gives an indication of a district assembly's capacity to raise revenues within its jurisdiction, relative to decentralised transfers from the central government. The governance indicator is a 'FOAT' score, an index that captures the effectiveness of district assembly operations, service delivery, and accountability.

The FOAT score is normalised to 100, and we normalise the education and finance measures as follows:

$$NormX_{di} = \left(\frac{X_{di} - Min(X)}{Max(X) - Min(X)} \right) * 100$$

where $NormX_{di}$ is the normalised score for variable X in district i, X_{di} is the raw score for variable X in district 'i', $Max(X)$ is the maximum score for variable X, and $Min(X)$ is the minimum score for variable X. The composite index is then derived using the simple average of the three variables in Table 10.4, combined with the weighted score on quality of reporting.

Table 10.5 and Figure 10.4 depict this local government performance index (LGI) for different categories of local authority (the MMDAs). The full list of indices for the MMDAs is available in the online Supplementary Materials

Table 10.4: Measures for constructing the local government performance index (LGI)

Measure	Definition
Education delivery performance	Ratio of public primary school population to public primary schools
District Assembly financing	The ratio of internally generated funds to total annual District Assemblies Common Fund (DACF) disbursement
FOAT	Multi-indicator index measuring effectiveness of district assembly operations, service delivery, and accountability
Quality of reporting	Quality of APRs to capture indicators on MMDA performance in local governance

Table 10.5: Summary statistics on local government performance index (LGI)

Category	Mean	Median	Standard deviation	Minimum	Maximum	N
All MMDAs	36.13	34.35	7.39	23.01	64.76	157
Urban MMDAs	40.2	38.08	8.74	27.44	64.76	46
Rural MMDAs	34.44	32.85	6.03	23.01	55.29	111

Source: Authors' construct (2022).

Table 10.A2.[9] The distribution of the LGI for all 157 MMDAs with data is skewed to the right with a mean value of approximately 36. The minimum and maximum values are approximately 23 and 65, respectively. Table 10.5 and Figure 10.4 further depict summary statistics for other categories of the MMDAs. On average, urban MMDAs perform better than their rural counterparts. A test of difference in mean performance is statistically significantly distinguishable from zero at the 1 per cent level.

Figure 10.4 shows more dispersion in local government performance within urban MMDAs relative to rural MMDAs despite better performance, on average, for the former. Figure 10.5 further depicts that there is a concentration of better performance, on average, not just for urban MMDAs but also for MMDAs located in the southern half of the country. The challenge of missing data covering the index is also more concentrated in the north-eastern part of the country. These variations may be due to the availability and capacity of staff and resources as well as access to critical infrastructure for urban and southern districts compared to those in the rural and northern parts of Ghana.

Table 10.6 lists the top 20 MMDAs, which is mostly made up of urban MMDAs. Not surprisingly, the top three positions are dominated by three large urban metropolitan and municipal assemblies: Kumasi Metropolitan, Accra Metropolitan, and Adentan Municipal. This is largely attributable to the performance of these districts in mobilising IGFs, which expands the fiscal

Figure 10.4: Histogram of local government performance index (LGI) by category

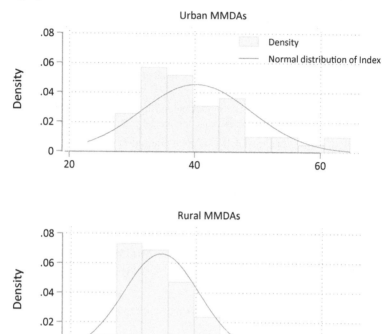

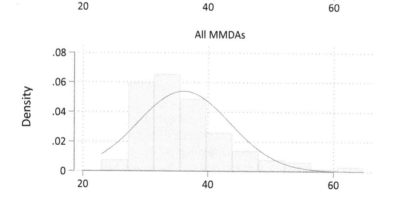

space for spending across priority sectors. Relative to rural districts, these larger MMDAs are less dependent on decentralised transfers from central government, which are often irregular and delayed. A sensitivity analysis that omits the IGF measure produces the result captured in Table 10.7.

Although the results in Table 10.7 still compare with those in Table 10.6, we see a number of rural districts rising further to the top. Besides Pusiga and Jirapa, others like Binduri and Bosomtwe districts occupy a top 10

Figure 10.5: Variations in local government performance index (LGI) across MMDAs for 2016

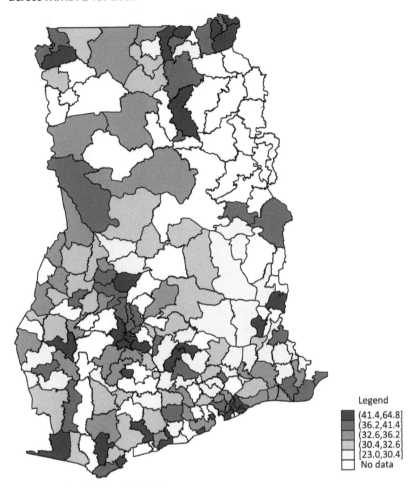

Legend
- ■ (41.4,64.8]
- ■ (36.2,41.4]
- ■ (32.6,36.2]
- ■ (30.4,32.6]
- □ [23.0,30.4]
- □ No data

Source: Authors' construct (2022).

position. This result underscores the combined role of fiscal and administrative capacity in influencing variations in local government performance and merits further examination. These top-performing rural districts may be constrained in their efforts to mobilise domestic revenues owing to several factors including limited economic diversification, a greater dependence on rain-fed agriculture, and a lower population density. Yet they may also be benefitting from an institutional or administrative capacity dividend, a possibility that requires further study.

There might be a concern here that the quality of reporting measure is already captured in the FOAT variable and is therefore redundant in the composite measure. While this is not the case when the correlation coefficient is

Table 10.6: Ranking of LGI for the top 20 localities (MMDAs)

Name of region	Name of district	Total score	Overall rank
Ashanti	Kumasi Metropolitan	64.8	1
Greater Accra	Accra Metropolitan	61.1	2
Greater Accra	Adentan Municipal	60.1	3
Upper East	Pusiga	55.3	4
Upper West	Jirapa	54.9	5
Greater Accra	Tema Metropolitan	54.8	6
Central	Mfantseman Municipal	53.1	7
Greater Accra	La Nkwantanang-Madina Municipal	50.6	8
Greater Accra	Ashaiman Municipal	49.9	9
Greater Accra	Kpone Katamanso	49.8	10
Upper East	Binduri	49.7	11
Ashanti	Bosomtwe	49.0	12
Ashanti	Obuasi Municipal	47.1	13
Upper East	Garu-Tempane	46.5	14
Brong Ahafo	Nkoranza South Municipal	46.5	15
Northern	Savelugu Nanton Municipal	46.1	16
Central	Efutu Municipal	45.2	17
Eastern	Kwahu West Municipal	44.9	18
Volta	Hohoe Municipal	44.8	19
Central	Awutu Senya East Municipal	44.8	20

Source: Authors' construct (2022).

taken into consideration, we conduct additional sensitivity tests that exclude the FOAT score. The results are consistent with the broad patterns already described.

Stage 3: Selected comparisons with other indices

A key comparator for the local government performance index is the District League Table (DLT) for 2016. Although the DLT is explicitly a measure of social development, rather than subnational institutional performance, it similarly aims to track the effectiveness and responsiveness of all MMDAs. Thus, we would expect the two indices to be fairly correlated (even if measured differently). Figure 10.6 shows the correlation between the DLT and our composite index (LGI), suggesting a moderately positive and statistically significant relationship. The names of MMDAs that are abbreviated with the first three letters.

Table 10.7: LGI ranking for top 20 MMDAs, excluding the IGF/DACF indicator

Name of region	Name of district	Total score	Overall rank
Greater Accra	Adentan Municipal	75.3	1
Upper East	Pusiga	73.6	2
Greater Accra	Accra Metropolitan	73.2	3
Upper West	Jirapa	73.1	4
Central	Mfantseman Municipal	70.2	5
Upper East	Binduri	66.2	6
Ashanti	Ejisu-Juaben Municipal	65.4	7
Ashanti	Bosomtwe	64.9	8
Greater Accra	Ashaiman Municipal	64.4	9
Greater Accra	Kpone Katamanso	64.1	10
Greater Accra	La Nkwantanang-Madina Municipal	62.9	11
Upper East	Garu-Tempane	61.8	12
B. Ahafo	Nkoranza South Municipal	61.7	13
Ashanti	Adansi North	61.2	14
Northern	Savelugu Nanton Municipal	61.0	15
Greater Accra	Tema Metropolitan	60.8	16
Central	Awutu Senya	60.5	17
Ashanti	Obuasi Municipal	60.4	18
Central	Efutu Municipal	59.8	19
Central	Cape Coast Metropolitan	59.3	20

Source: Authors' construct (2022).

On the other hand, one would expect a negative relationship between poverty headcount and local government performance. The fitted line in Figure 10.7 confirms a negative relationship in the data; in effect, districts that are more effective and responsive to their citizens are more likely to have lower poverty incidence.

Finally, given that our quality of reporting measure captures an element of subnational institutional performance and is more comprehensive in terms of data coverage across the MMDAs than our LGI, we also compare this measure with variations in poverty across MMDAs using heat maps. In Figure 10.8, the heat map depicts a north–south regional pattern in poverty. The Northern, Upper, and Volta regions are among the most deprived in Ghana, with poverty rates above the national average (Ghana Statistical Service 2018).

Figure 10.6: Comparison between local government performance index (LGI) and District League Table (DLT) 2016

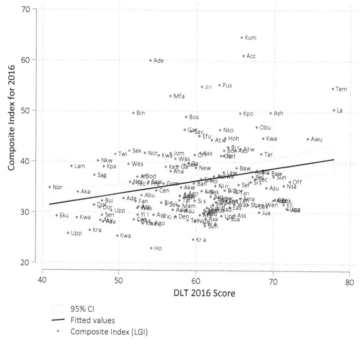

Source: Authors.
Notes: DLT score indicates District League Table.

Notably, these regional poverty patterns appear to be inversely correlated with both the mean and median regional score in the quality of reporting measure. The Northern, Volta, and Central regions obtain the highest regional average scores. In essence, the quality of reporting appears to be better in the more deprived regions of the country. Similar patterns are also evident at the district level, as Figure 10.9 suggests.[10]

This inverse relationship between poverty and the quality of reporting calls for further research. There are a variety of possible explanations. It may be that local government employees in poorer (northern) districts devote more attention to APR reports because these districts rely more heavily on goodwill and resources from the central government. Alternatively, some of these selected districts may in fact be truly 'overperforming' given their levels of poverty in terms of statistical and information services. If this is true, we would expect to see in longitudinal data evidence of such administrative capacity supporting improvements in poverty over time. Or it may be that the relationship is driven by a third factor. For instance, external technical assistance may go more to poorer districts and also facilitate statistical and information services tasks (such as completing APR reports). While we cannot specifically test the

Figure 10.7: Comparison between local government performance index (LGI) and poverty headcount index

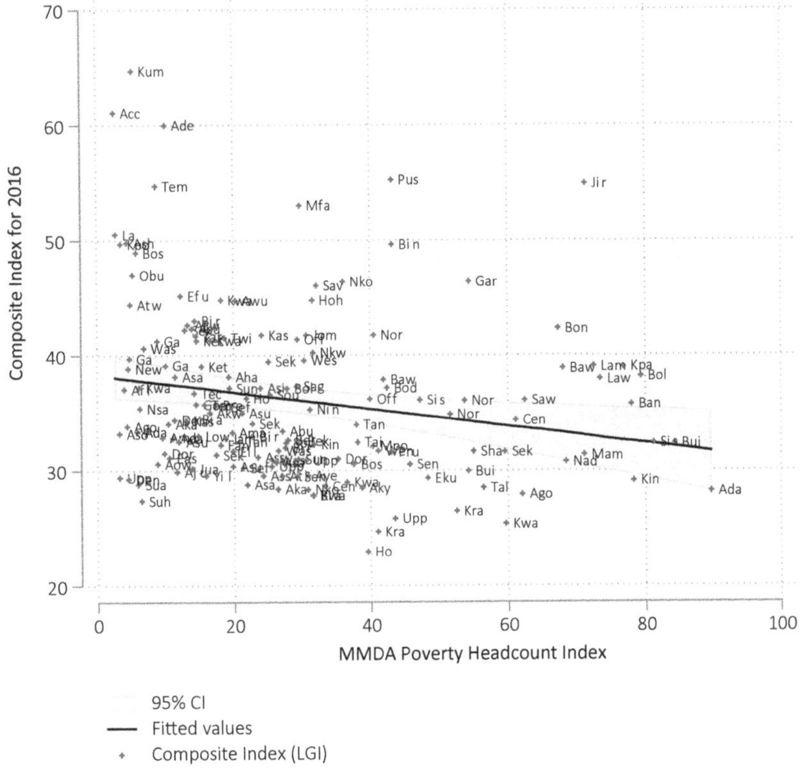

Source: Authors.

validity of these arguments with the data used here, we hope to address them in future research.

Conclusions – further areas of study

After conceptualising good local governance we have explored the available data for Ghana, moving from an 'ideal' set of measures to a streamlined 'next best' set that can be captured with existing data, despite significant limitations. The measures presented here provide a snapshot picture of institutional performance across the vast majority of districts and offer a more comprehensive basis for consideration of variation in subnational institutional performance than other studies of Ghana or other African countries more broadly.[11] Much of the extant literature on subnational institutional performance in African countries has compared two or several districts or regions; few studies draw

Figure 10.8: Regional comparison: quality of reporting measure (mean) and poverty gap

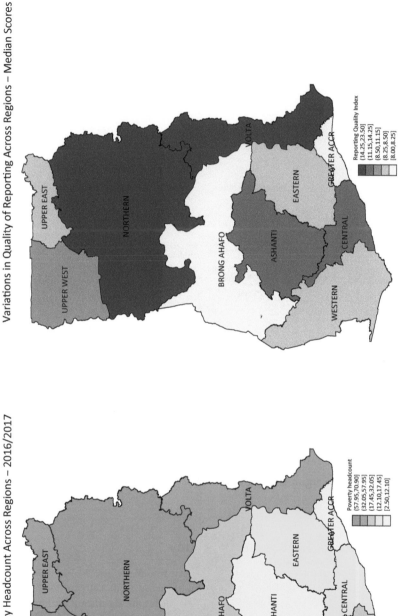

Variations in Quality of Reporting Across Regions – Median Scores

Variations in Poverty Headcount Across Regions – 2016/2017

Source: Authors' construct based on Ghana Statistical Service 2018 (poverty headcount) and District Annual Progress Reports, 2016 (Quality of Reporting Index).

Figure 10.9: MMDAs comparison: poverty headcount and quality of reportin

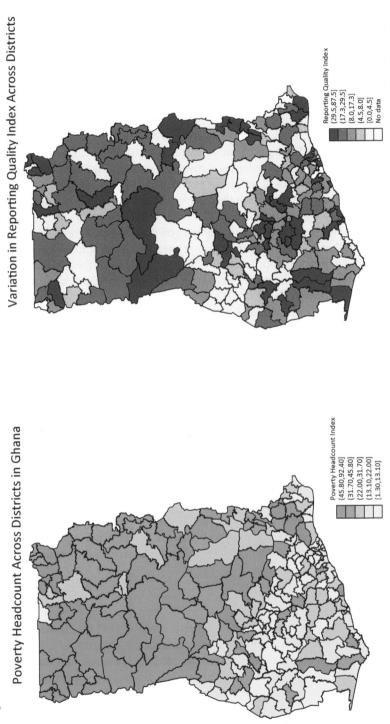

Poverty Headcount Across Districts in Ghana

Variation in Reporting Quality Index Across Districts

Poverty Headcount Index
- [45.80,92.40]
- [31.70,45.80]
- [22.00,31.70]
- [13.10,22.00]
- [1.30,13.10]

Reporting Quality Index
- [29.5,87.5]
- [17.3,29.5]
- [8.0,17.3]
- [4.5,8.0]
- [0.0,4.5]
- No data

Sources: Authors' construct based on Ghana Statistical Service, 2015 (poverty headcount index) and District Annual Progress Reports (Quality of Reporting Index).

on comparison of all districts or all regions in a country (Dahis and Szerman 2021; Iddawela, Lee, and Rodríguez-Pose 2021).

The lack of such comprehensive data for African countries has been a distinct challenge in research, limiting the study of many important research questions. In terms of decentralisation, these data can help us to consider one of the key claims in the literature, that bringing government closer to the people will result in greater public sector efficiency and accountability. While our data alone do not tell us whether local government is more/less efficient and accountable than central government, they shed light on how efficient and accountable local government in fact is across Ghana. On the basis of these data, it is clear that some local governments perform comparatively well and some poorly. Thus, if we expect to realise the promise of decentralisation optimists, we need to research the broader influences on variation in Ghana's local governments' performance.

The literature offers multiple hypotheses on the causes and correlates of such variation, but empirical examination of them has been limited for African countries, notably by data constraints. One key example is the 'diversity debit' hypothesis – that ethnic diversity drives negative public goods outcomes – which is routinely applied to African countries. For instance, Alesina, Baqir, and Easterly (1999) examined this hypothesis drawing on data from US cities, counties, and metropolitan areas, but it has not been possible to replicate such analysis at the subnational level in African countries. Efforts to test this hypothesis in African countries include studies in South Africa (Gibson and Hoffman 2013) and Zambia (Gisselquist, Leiderer, and Niño-Zarazúa 2016), but these draw on a more limited set of budgetary, census, and survey data.

Another key hypothesis to be considered in future work concerns the role of social capital, with roots in Putnam's work – which serves as a starting point in this chapter for our measurement framework (Putnam, Leonardi, and Nanetti 1994). The argument that institutions are shaped by the social contexts in which they operate, in particular the vibrancy of civic community, has been heavily critiqued. Yet it has also been deeply influential in contributing to a large body of subsequent research on the influence of civil society, social capital, trust, and associational life on the quality of governance and economic development (Boix and Posner 1998). Systematic exploration of this hypothesis within an African context is another key direction for future work.

Endnotes

Supplementary material for this chapter is available on LSE Press's Zenodo site (https://zenodo.org/communities/decentralised_governance/). See: *Supplementary material for*: Daniel Chachu, Michael Danquah, and Rachel M. Gisselquist (2023) 'Subnational governance in Ghana: A comparative assessment of data and performance', Chapter 10 in Jean-Paul Faguet and Sarmistha Pal (eds) *Decentralised Governance: Crafting Effective Democracies Around the World*, London: LSE Press. https://doi.org/10.5281/zenodo.7919727

1   This research has been supported by UNU-WIDER and the University of Zurich's 'Equality of Opportunity' Research Priority Program.

2   See Brierley (2020); Burgess et al. (2015); Dahis and Szerman (2021); Gisselquist (2012); Moore (2001); Weiss (2000), among others.

3   Currently mainstreamed into the national monitoring and evaluation system and led by the National Development Planning Commission (NDPC).

4   There have been no stringent penalties to districts that do not prepare and submit their APRs to the NDPC.

5   These include the Ministry of Finance and the Ghana Statistical Service.

6   The remaining six districts were Tamale Metropolitan Assembly, Shama, Nandom, Kpando, Ketu North and Ga South Municipal. Direct follow-ups with the NDPC also did not yield these reports.

7   See Supplementary Material for: Daniel Chachu, Michael Danquah, and Rachel M. Gisselquist (2023) 'Subnational governance in Ghana: A comparative assessment of data and performance', Chapter 10 in Jean-Paul Faguet and Sarmistha Pal (eds) *Decentralised Governance: Crafting Effective Democracies Around the World*, London: LSE Press. https://doi.org/10.5281/zenodo.7919727

8   In this stage, we complement data gathered on education and local resources from the APRs with data from other government sources such as the Ghana Statistical Service.

9   See Supplementary Material. https://doi.org/10.5281/zenodo.7919727

10   Data on poverty and inequality at the MMDA level is drawn from a Ghana Statistical Service Report (2015) that uses the small area methodology to derive MMDA estimates based on the sixth round of the Ghana Living Standards Survey and the 2010 Population Census.

11   See Akudugu (2013); Ayee (2008); Debrah (2009); Osei-Akoto et al. (2007).

References

Ahmad, Junaid; Devarajan, Shantayanan; Khemani, Stuti; and Shah, Shekhar (2005) 'Decentralization and Service Delivery: World Bank Policy Research Working Paper 3603', World Bank.

Ahwoi, Kwamena (2010) *Local Government and Decentralization in Ghana*, Accra: Unimax Macmillan.

Akudugu, Jonas Ayaribilla (2013) 'Inducing Local Government Performance in Ghana: The Case of the District Development Facility', *International Journal of Asian Social Science*, vol.3, no.6, pp.1402–17. https://archive.aessweb.com/index.php/5007/article/view/2502

Alesina, Alberto; Baqir, Reza; and Easterly, William (1999) 'Public Goods and Ethnic Divisions', *The Quarterly Journal of Economics*, vol.114, no.4, pp.1243–84. https://doi.org/10.1162/003355399556269

Armah-Attoh, Daniel and Norviewu, Newton (2018) 'Demand for Transparency, Accountability Drives Call for Electing Local Leaders in Ghana', Afrobarometer Policy Paper, 48, pp.1–22. https://www.afrobarometer.org/wp-content/uploads/migrated/files/publications/Documents%20de%20politiques/ab_r7_policypaperno48_should_ghana_elect_its_mmdces_2.pdf

Asunka, Joseph; Brierley, Sarah; Golden, Miriam; Kramon, Eric; and Ofosu, George (2017) 'Electoral Fraud or Violence: The Effect of Observers on Party Manipulation Strategies', *British Journal of Political Science*, vol.49, no.1, pp.129–51. https://doi.org/10.1017/S0007123416000491

Ayee, Joseph R.A. (1996) 'The Measurement of Decentralization: The Ghanaian Experience, 1988–92', *African Affairs*, vol.95, no.378, pp.31–50. https://doi.org/10.1093/oxfordjournals.afraf.a007712

Ayee, Joseph R.A. (2008) 'The Balance Sheet of Decentralization in Ghana', in Saito, Funmihiko (ed.) *Foundations for Local Governance: Decentralization in Comparative Perspective*, Physica-Verlag HD, pp.233–58. https://doi.org/10.1007/978-3-7908-2006-5_11

Ayee, Joseph R.A. (2013) 'The Political Economy of the Creation of Districts in Ghana', *Journal of Asian and African Studies*, vol.48, no.5, pp.623–45. https://doi.org/10.1177/0021909612464334

Boix, Carles and Posner, Daniel (1998) 'Social Capital: Explaining Its Origins and Effects on Government Performance', *British Journal of Political Science*, vol.28, no.4, pp.686–93. https://www.jstor.org/stable/194054

Bojanic, Antonio N. and Collins, LaPorchia A. (2021) 'Differential Effects of Decentralization on Income Inequality: Evidence from Developed and Developing Countries', *Empirical Economics*, vol.60, no.4, pp.1969–2004. https://doi.org/10.1007/s00181-019-01813-2

Brierley, Sarah (2020) 'Unprincipled Principals: Co-opted Bureaucrats and Corruption in Ghana', *American Journal of Political Science*, vol.64, no.2, pp.209–22. https://doi.org/10.1111/ajps.12495

Burgess, Robin; Jedwab, Remi; Miguel, Edward; Morjaria, Ameet; and Padró I Miquel, Gerard (2015) 'The Value of Democracy: Evidence from Road Building in Kenya', *American Economic Review*, vol.105, no.6, pp.1817–51. https://doi.org/10.1257/aer.20131031

Chachu, Daniel (2021) 'Review of Sub-national Institutional Performance in Ghana', UNU-WIDER Background Note. Helsinki, Finland. https://doi.org/10.35188/UNU-WIDER/WBN/2021-1

Crook, Richard C. (1994) 'Four Years of the Ghana District Assemblies in Operation: Decentralization, Democratization and Administrative Performance', *Public Administration and Development*, vol.14, no.4, pp.339–64. https://doi.org/10.1002/pad.4230140402

Dahis, Richard and Szerman, Christiane (2021) 'Development via Administrative Redistricting: Evidence from Brazil'. https://dx.doi.org/10.2139/ssrn.3125757

Debrah, Emmanuel (2009) 'Assessing the Quality of Accountability in Ghana's District Assemblies, 1993–2008', *African Journal of Political Science and International Relations*, vol.3, no.6, pp.278–87. http://www.academicjournals.org/AJPSIR

del Granado, F. Javier Arze; Martinez-Vazquez, Jorge; and McNab, Robert M. (2018) 'Decentralized Governance, Expenditure Composition, and Preferences for Public Goods', *Public Finance Review*, vol.46, no.3, pp.359–88. https://doi.org/10.1177/1091142116639127

Dzansi, James; Jensen, Anders; Lagakos, David; Otoo, Isaac; Telli, Henry; and Zindam, Cynthia (2018) 'Survey of Local Government Taxation Capacity, 2017', International Growth Centre REF S-33417-GHA-1. https://www.vng-international.nl/sites/default/files/internally _generated_funds_survey_report_final.pdf

Faguet, Jean-Paul; Fox, Ashley M.; and Pöschl, Caroline (2015) 'Decentralizing for a Deeper, More Supple Democracy', *Journal of Democracy*, vol.26, no.4, pp.60–74. http://doi.org/10.1353/jod.2015.0059

Faguet, Jean-Paul and Pöschl, Caroline (eds) (2015) *Is Decentralization Good for Development?: Perspectives from Academics and Policy Makers*, Oxford University Press, USA.

Fumey, Abel and Egwaikhide, Festus O. (2018) 'Political Economy of Intergovernmental Fiscal Transfers: The Rural-Urban Dynamics in Ghana', *African Development Review*, vol.30, no.1, pp.33–44. https://doi.org/10.1111/1467-8268.12310

Ghana Statistical Service. (2018) 'Ghana Living Standards Survey Round 7 (GLSS 7): Poverty Trends in Ghana 2005–2017'. https://www2.statsghana.gov.gh/docfiles/publications/GLSS7/Poverty% 20Profile%20Report_2005%20-%202017.pdf

Gibson, Clark C. and Hoffman, Barak D. (2013) 'Coalitions not Conflicts: Ethnicity, Political Institutions, and Expenditure in Africa', *Comparative Politics*, vol.45, no.3, pp.273–90. https://doi.org/10.5129/001041512X13815255434852

Gisselquist, Rachel M. (2012) 'Good Governance as a Concept, and Why This Matters for Development Policy', No.2012/30, WIDER Working Paper. http://hdl.handle.net/10419/81039

Gisselquist, Rachel M.; Leiderer, Stefan; and Nino-Zarazua, Miguel (2016) 'Ethnic Heterogeneity and Public Goods Provision in Zambia: Evidence of a Subnational "Diversity Dividend"', *World Development*, vol.78, pp.308–23. https://doi.org/10.1016/j.worlddev.2015.10.018

Iddawela, Yohan; Lee, Neil; and Rodríguez-Pose, Andres (2021) 'Quality of Sub-national Government and Regional Development in Africa', *The Journal of Development Studies*, vol.57, no.8, pp.1282–302. https://doi.org/10.1080/00220388.2021.1873286

Ministry of Local Government and Rural Development. (2010) *Government of Ghana: Functional & Organizational Assessment Tool (FOAT).* http://www.mlgrd.gov.gh

Mohammed, Abdulai Kuyini (2016) 'Decentralization and Participation: Theory and Ghana's Evidence', *Japanese Journal of Political Science*, vol.17, no.2, pp.232–55. https://doi.org/10.1017/S1468109916000050

Moore, Mick (2001) 'Political Underdevelopment: What causes "bad governance"', *Public Management Review*, vol.3, no.3, pp.385–418. https://doi.org/10.1080/14616670110050020

Osei-Akoto, Isaac; Osie, Robert Darko; Adiah, Adayi-Nwoza George; and Quarmine, William (2007) 'Public Spending at the District Level in Ghana', Africa Portal. https://www.africaportal.org/publications/public-spending-at-the-district-level-in-ghana

Otoo, Isaac and Danquah, Michael (2021) 'Fiscal Decentralization and Efficiency of Public Services Delivery by Local Governments in Ghana', WIDER Working Paper 2021/88. Helsinki: UNU-WIDER. https://doi.org/10.35188/UNU-WIDER/2021/028-3

Putnam, Robert D.; Leonardi, Robert; and Nanetti, Raffaella Y. (1994) *Making Democracy Work: Civic Traditions in Modern Italy*, Princeton University Press.

Republic of Ghana (2014a) 'Coordinated Programme of Economic and Social Development Policies 2014–2020: An Agenda for Transformation'. https://www.cabri-sbo.org/uploads/bia/ghana_2014_planning_external_national_plan_author_region_english_.pdf

Republic of Ghana (2014b) 'Medium-Term National Devepment Policy Framework 2014–2017', in *Ghana Shared Growth and Development Agenda*. https://ndpc.gov.gh/media/Ghana_Shared_Growth_and_Development_Agenda_GSGDA_II_2014-2017.pdf

Republic of Ghana (2015) 'Results for 2015 Annual Performance Evaluation of RCCs & MMDAs', vol.6, no.i. https://lgs.gov.gh/results-for-2015-annual-performance-evaluation-of-rccs-mmdas

Unicef/CDD (2014) 'Ghana's District League Table 2014: Ghana's District League Table 2014'.
https://citifmonline.com/wp-content/uploads/2015/11/District-League
-Table-report-Edit-NEW-R31.pdf

Unicef/CDD (2015) 'Ghana's District League Table 2015-Strengthening Social Accountability for National Development'.
https://www.cddgh.org/wp-content/uploads/2019/01/2015_DISTRICT_
LEAGUE_TABLE_REPORT.pdf

Unicef/CDD (2016) 'District League Table 2016 What Is the District League. December, 1–8'.
https://cddgh.org/wp-content/uploads/2019/01/2016_DISTRICT_
LEAUGE_TABLE_REPORT.pdf

Unicef/CDD. (2017) 'Ghana's District League Table 2017: Towards Equitable and Sustainable Development: A Call for Central Government to Review Resource Allocation to Districts'.
https://citifmonline.com/wp-content/uploads/2017/11/DLT-REPORT
-UNICEF-FINAL-2017-Website.pdf

Unicef/CDD (2019) '2018/2019 District League Table II with New Perspectives and Modified Methodology', 72.
https://www.unicef.org/ghana/media/2131/file/2018-2019-The-District
-League-Table-II.pdf

Williams, Martin J. (2017) 'The Political Economy of Unfinished Development Projects: Corruption, Clientelism, or Collective Choice?' *American Political Science Review*, vol.111, no.4, pp.705–23.
https://doi.org/10.1017/S0003055417000351

World Bank (2017). 'World Development Report 2017: Governance and the Law', The World Bank. https://doi.org/10.1596/978-1-4648-0950-7

Yeboah-Assiamah, Emmanuel (2016) 'Power to the People! How Far Has the Power Gone to the People? A Qualitative Assessment of Decentralization Practice in Ghana', *Journal of Asian and African Studies*, vol.51, no.6, pp.683–99. https://doi.org/10.1177/0021909614555349

11. Birth registration, child rights, and local governance in Bangladesh

Abu S. Shonchoy and Zaki Wahhaj

Summary

Historically, the practice of registering births with government authorities has been rare in developing countries, often limited to major urban centres. The absence of systematic birth records can be a serious impediment for implementing government policies related to children such as school enrolment requirements for children of primary school age or restrictions on minimum age of marriage. Recent initiatives to create digital birth records in a number of countries has the potential to address this issue and enhance the capacity of local government authorities to implement state policies. In Bangladesh, there has been increased provision of birth registration at local, government-run digital centres linked to a national database, and having a birth certificate has been made a requirement for receiving various government services including school enrolment and marriage registration. Using first-hand survey data on households with adolescent girls from a rural district in one of the poorest regions in Bangladesh, we document the knowledge, understanding, and behavioural response in relation to these policies at the household level. We also document the phenomenon of invalid birth certificates and provide suggestive evidence that it is due to limited local administrative capacity to register births.

Article 7 of the United Nations Convention of the Rights of the Child mandates that every 'child shall be registered immediately after birth'.[1] Although the convention has been ratified by most countries around the world, universal birth registration remains far from reality in many of them. About

How to cite this book chapter:

Shonchoy, Abu S. and Wahhaj, Zaki (2023) 'Birth registration, child rights, and local governance in Bangladesh', in: Faguet, Jean-Paul and Pal, Sarmistha (eds) *Decentralised Governance: Crafting Effective Democracies Around the World*, London: LSE Press, pp. 301–333. https://doi.org/10.31389/lsepress.dlg.k
License: CC BY 4.0

two-thirds of children under five are registered but the registration rate varies from over 90 per cent in industrialised countries to less than 50 per cent in sub-Saharan Africa and South Asia (UNICEF 2013). Birth registration rates also vary widely within countries, with higher registration rates in major cities compared to rural areas, and for babies born in hospitals compared to those born at home (UNICEF 1998). Without a well-functioning birth registration system, a modern state cannot ensure that key services (access to health care, education, and social welfare programmes) and legal protection (against early marriage, child labour, military service, child trafficking) extend to all children born within it. Given the immense potential social benefits of birth registration and other forms of vital registration, the World Bank and World Health Organization developed a 10-year Global Vital Registration Scaling Up Plan in 2014, with the goal of registering all births, deaths, marriages, and other vital events by 2030.[2]

Presently, survey data on birth registration of children is available for a wide range of countries, allowing comparison of birth registration rates across countries and regions and monitoring progress over time. However, it is important to recognise that governance issues may manifest themselves not just in the form of incomplete coverage but also reporting errors, the circulation of fake documents, and inconsistencies between archival records and digital databases.[3] These types of problems may not be picked up through self-reported birth registration data or even spot checks on birth certificates carried out by enumerators.

To document this issue in a systematic manner, we conducted a household survey in rural Bangladesh that includes not only self-reported data on birth registration but also validity checks on birth certificates for a specific demographic group: unmarried adolescent girls. Birth registration status of adolescent girls is particularly important because of the high rate of underage marriage (that is, marriage below the legal minimum age) among women in Bangladesh and the legal protection provided, at least in theory, by birth registration documents.

In our sample households could produce birth registration records for about 80 per cent of the girls. Survey enumerators verified, for each birth certificate, whether it had a digital record in the national birth registration database on the basis of the birth certificate number. The exercise revealed that just 54 per cent of the girls had a valid birth certificate. Controlling for individual and household characteristics, we found some significant differences in birth certification among adolescent girls across unions, that is, the level of the local authority responsible for registering births and issuing birth certificates.[4] But differences across unions explained a much larger fraction of the variation in *validated* birth certificates, suggesting that the issue of invalid certificates has been a problem stemming from governance issues at the level of the local authority. In line with this evidence, focus-group discussions with local stakeholders revealed concerns about capacity constraints and corruption at the local level, as well as birth registration targets set by the central authority that are not aligned with local institutional capacity.

Our study contributes to a growing academic literature on birth registration in LMICs (Ebbers and Smits 2022; Mohanty and Gebremedhin 2018; UNICEF 2013; UNICEF 2015; World Bank 2016). A strand in this literature focuses on demand-side and supply-side factors that limit birth registration. An important finding from the existing body of work is that both parental/household-level characteristics and local/contextual factors are important determinants of birth registration. A second strand in the literature, which we review in Section 11.3, evaluates the efficacy of recent innovations in registration systems, often involving the use of new information technologies to develop and transmit digital birth records. This strand in the literature highlights that, in the absence of comprehensive local capacity-building and mobilisation, these types of interventions ultimately may not realise their objective of improving birth registration rates in the long run. Our findings are also related to an emerging literature providing rigorous empirical evidence on the role of active monitoring and verification through decentralised local governance, especially emerging e-governance platforms (Banerjee et al. 2020; Muralidharan, Niehaus, and Sukhtankar 2016; Muralidharan, Niehaus, and Sukhtankar 2020).

Our work contributes to the existing literature by documenting, and investigating the determinants of, invalid birth certificates. We argue that individual and household characteristics and limitations in local capacity in registering births may translate not only into low birth registration rates but also the reliability of existing birth records; the latter metric is missing from existing micro-level data on birth registration rates that are widely used in this literature.

The remainder of this chapter is organised as follows. We first provide a conceptual discussion of factors that may undermine birth registration process in the presence of weak governance. We next give an overview of birth registration systems in LMICs and recent interventions to improve birth registration rates in Section 11.2, with a focus on innovations aimed at improving local institutional capacity. Section 11.3 describes the regulations and institutions underpinning the existing birth registration system in Bangladesh. We use data from our purposefully designed household survey to present descriptive statistics on birth registration rates in rural Bangladesh and highlight the issue of invalid birth registrations. In Section 11.4, we use a regression framework to investigate the determinants of birth certification as well as valid registration among unmarried adolescent girls and discuss whether differences in birth registration at the local level could be due to administrative capacity. The conclusions discuss the implications of our analysis.

11.1 Birth registration systems and sources of weakness

Policymakers and international development agencies have long recognised that an effective system for documenting births is critical for national governments to ensure that access to essential services and legal protection against various sorts of harm reach all children. Among advanced economies, most births are registered successfully within the recommended time period. By contrast, birth registration has not been a priory in the majority of low- and middle-income countries (LMICs), albeit with a few exceptions. Lack of resources is the most important reason for the absence of an effective birth registration system in many LMICs.

In LMICs there are vast differences in the birth registration facilities in urban and rural areas. However, there may be significant variation at the local level too because of political factors, cultural norms, and the knowledge, understanding, and priorities of parents. But there are other reasons why birth registration systems may be weak. Parents may not sufficiently value the services and protection provided by the state, or they may lack an understanding of the link between them and birth registration. Hence they may not take the appropriate steps to get registered. Perhaps just as importantly, they may not make political demands to ensure that the registration process is hassle-free and inexpensive. A recent review of the literature highlights both supply-side (legal barriers, poor infrastructure, limited resources) and demand-side factors (lack of sufficient perceived benefits net of costs) as factors contributing to low birth registration rates in LMICs (World Bank 2016).

It may also be that the legal protection provided by the state upon the registration of a child conflicts with traditional norms, or with the economic reality of the households in which the children are born. A case in point is the traditional practice of marriage among adolescent girls soon after they reach puberty, which often contradicts the legal minimum age of marriage within the country. In these instances, parents may be reluctant to register their children or, at any rate, may circumvent the process (for example, by misreporting a girl's birth date) so that they are able to continue with traditional practices.

Local governance typically plays an important role in the birth registration system, either by actively collecting information on births or by providing services that allow parents to register their children, issuing certificates, and so on. So, variation in the quality of local governance may lead to variations in the efficacy of birth registration systems across locality and thus contribute to inequitable access to government services and legal protection for children born in different parts of country.

A number of LMICs have long-standing civil registration systems. For example, in Botswana, a civil registration system was established at its independence, in 1966. At its inception, the registration of births and deaths was compulsory in towns and major villages only. But the registration of vital events became mandatory nationally in 1998. In 2003 Botswana's civil registration system was automated following the establishment of the Department of Civil and National Registration (Republic of Botswana and World Bank 2015). In the case of the Philippines, the registration of all vital events (births, deaths, and so on) was made mandatory in 1930 through the Civil Registry Act. But public awareness and compliance was low due to the general lack of understanding of the process, high costs, and cultural and language barriers

(Celeste and Caelian 2021). On the other hand, low per-capita-income countries – such as Armenia, Azerbaijan, China, Honduras, Kyrgyzstan, Mongolia, Sri Lanka, and Tajikistan – have managed to register at least 90 per cent of births (UNICEF 1998). Overall, birth registration in LMICs is characterised by low compliance. In Africa, one in seven registered children in school do not have a birth certificate (UNICEF 2013). However, there exists major variability across regions and countries. For example, about 50 per cent of school-registered children possess birth certificates in eastern and southern Africa, while the corresponding number is 88 per cent in west and central Africa.

In recent years, a number of studies have investigated to what extent demand-side and supply-side factors limit birth registration. The existing research reveals that both parental/household-level characteristics and local/contextual factors have been important determinants of birth registration. For example, using data from the India Human Development Survey-II, Mohanty and Gebremedhin (2018) found that the maternal autonomy and control over resources were important determinants of birth registration, but the marginal effects of maternal autonomy also varied across districts in India. Using data from the Demographic and Health Surveys for 34 countries in sub-Saharan Africa, Ebbers and Smits (2022) found that household poverty, lack of education, absence of the father, restricted autonomy of women, and belonging to a traditional religion affected registration negatively, but so did local factors such as lack of professional care during pregnancy, delivery, and early life and lack of local health care facilities. In a mixed-methods study of birth registration in south-eastern Kenya, Pelowski et al. (2015) highlighted a different issue. A quantitative survey in the region designed to better understand the current state of registration and parental understanding and attitudes revealed high levels of awareness and low barriers to birth registration – yet over 50 per cent of children in the sample were unregistered. Based on responses by parents during focus-group discussions, the authors concluded that:

> a series of small annoyances [that is, non-monetary transaction costs], coupled with the lack of immediate incentive, … add up to a deliberate decision by a parent that it is *not worth the trouble* of seeking registration. (p.898)

They argued that this phenomenon may be present in other developing countries too.

In order to improve compliance with birth registration system, LMICs have introduced late fees, fines, and even judicial procedures. Such negative mechanisms could incentivise parents to complete birth registration on time. However, they could also create a burden for economically, socially, and geographically marginalised families (UNICEF 2013). Moreover, in some countries, existing laws make it more difficult to register children born out of wedlock or when the father is absent. Hanmer and Elefante (2015) gave a number of examples along these lines. In Egypt, the mother can register the birth of a child only if she provides proof of marriage. In Iran, both parents must appear before a civil registrar to register their child if their marriage has not been registered.

11.2 Interventions to improve birth registration in LMICs

In recent years, a variety of interventions have been introduced in LMICs to improve birth registration processes. They often include the use of digital technologies to transmit birth registration information from rural communities to local or regional administrative offices, and/or improving human resources available at the local government level for collecting and recording the information. We examine a number of examples from the literature, with a focus on innovations aimed at improving local institutional capacity, to illustrate both the range of solutions considered, as well as their potential pitfalls.

In Malawi, the government introduced a national registration system in 2007. This involved the use of paper-based village registers to record births and deaths as well as the number of people living in each village. The registers were maintained by the village head-persons, who were also responsible for obtaining and recording the required information for village members (Gadabu et al. 2014; Gadabu et al. 2018; Singogo et al. 2013). Although the system allowed the recording of births and deaths, it was impossible to collate and analyse the data from villages in a timely way due to poor infrastructure, limited human resources, and a poor transportation network. Paper registers were also easily damaged through manual handling or being eaten by termites.

In March 2013, a pilot project involving the use of electronic village registers (EVRs) was launched in a single Malawi village in an area without electricity and modern amenities (Gadabu et al. 2014). The EVRs were used to transmit data through wireless connections from the village head through a series of intermediaries to the District Commissioner. The EVR was designed to overcome challenges typical of rural communities in low-income countries: lack of electricity supply, low literacy levels, and lack of IT skills. In particular, the EVR set-up included a touchscreen computer to overcome the lack of IT skills, a solar panel to overcome the problem of lack of electricity supply, and a user interface in the local language to overcome the language barrier to using standard digital technologies. Based on the success of the pilot, the project was scaled up in 2016 to 83 other villages, with modifications to improve its user-friendliness and robustness (Gadabu et al. 2018).

Because of the low frequency of births and deaths at the village level, a village head in charge of an EVR typically interacted with the system just once every two to three months, which meant that operators had a low level of familiarity with the system, potentially leading to reporting errors. There were also cases of double registrations due to attempts to correct data entry errors, as well as under-reporting of births and deaths. Compared to the low frequency of use, the EVR system also had a relatively high cost, at US$2,430 per village (Gadabu et al. 2018).

Tanzania's civil registration (CR) system is managed by the government's Registration, Insolvency and Trusteeship Agency (RITA) within the Ministry of Justice and Constitutional Affairs. The system is operated through district civil registrars (DCRs) and village executive officers (VEOs), who maintain in ledgers a record of births and deaths reported by households. Obtaining a birth registration certificate typically involves a series of visits by a relative to the VEO and the district civil registrar's office over the course of several weeks (Kabadi, Mwanyika, and de Savigny 2013). The system's lack of simplicity, coupled with lack of commitment from VEOs to regularly visit villages and households as required, is a potential reason why so few births were reported and registered.

The Swiss Tropical and Public Health Institute and the Ifakara Health Institute implemented a project in Tanzania between September 2012 and March 2013 to explore the potential of adding a mobile phone step to the CR system. The project, called 'Monitoring of Vital Events through the Use of Technology', or MOVE-IT, had its pilot in a rural setting and was developed to add a SMS technology process to the existing CR process. It aimed at improving the functioning of the CR system by enabling the village executive officers to electronically transfer the details of births and deaths to the district civil registrar through a cloud-based SMS platform. This would enable DCRs to effectively monitor households' compliance with the legally required reporting of births for registration and certification. It was expected that this would improve the rate of coverage of the CR system and lead to timely registration of births and deaths. The MOVE-IT project raised the rate of birth notifications by an impressive 86 per cent by the end of the intervention period. The change in the number of birth certificates issued was, however, less impressive, rising by just 9 per cent by the end of the intervention (Kabadi, Mwanyika, and de Savigny 2013).

The use of Tanzanian government civil servants as VEOs created conflicts between their routine jobs and CR duties, leading to few visits to households and villages to follow up on birth events. Some VEOs preferred not to pay visits to villages but required parents of newborns to make trips to their offices for the registration of births. This situation affected the reporting of births as well as the rate of registrations. Second, getting contractual agreements from mobile network providers to enable VEOs to use their mobile phones for reporting events was problematic, adding to the inefficiency of the system and lowering the impact of the MOVE-IT project. In terms of coverage, some villages could not participate in the project due to a lack of mobile phone network coverage (Kabadi, Mwanyika, and de Savigny 2013).

Birth registration in Ghana is a legal requirement under the Registration of Births and Deaths Act (1965). The country is divided into 170 registration districts, each with at least one registration office. These offices are usually within the premises of or near public health facilities. Despite this legal framework, the registration of births in Ghana was plagued by a shortage of registration offices and a lack of trained personnel, and this problem was particularly severe in rural areas. In most cases, the distance to the nearest registration office added substantial indirect costs (such as time away from work and travel expenses) to the monetary cost of registering a child. Public awareness of the benefits of child registration seemed generally low (Fagernäs and Odame 2013).

To address some of these challenges, Plan International and UNICEF collaborated with the Ghana Births and Deaths Registry to launch a birth registration campaign between 2004 and 2005. The campaign aimed at extending the legal period for free registration of infants, incorporating birth registration in child health promotion weeks, training community health workers on how to register births quickly, using community registration volunteers, and registering children during celebrations (Fagernäs and Odame 2013). Over the campaign period, the registration of births increased substantially as birth registration services became easily accessible and the need to travel long distances to a registration centre was removed. While only 44 per cent of children younger than five years were registered in 2003, the rate had increased to 71 per cent by 2008. However, a full coverage of birth registration has yet to be achieved amid slowing progress.

A second initiative to boost the progress of birth registration in Ghana was the implementation of a low-cost 'real-time' vital registration system launched in 2006 in the Bonsaaso Millennium Village in the Ashanti Region. It integrated 'real-time' vital registration with a verbal autopsy system within an open-source electronic medical record to improve the coverage of maternal child health services. The project involved training community health workers (CHWs) to deliver health information and services to households, gather data on vital events (births and deaths), and transfer the information to the OpenMRS (a medical record system) using introspective data entry (Ohemeng-Dapaah et al. 2010).

The project led to a rise in the number of health facilities established, reducing the travelling distance for households. The number of professional health workers trained in the project area also rose, including skilled birth attendants and CHWs, and led to a shift in births from home delivery to delivery at health clinics. Thus, births became more visible and were registered more promptly (Ohemeng-Dapaah et al. 2010). The project was largely successful because birth registrations seemed accurate and easy to implement. It is worth noting here that a high level of community mobilisation as well as an awareness and appreciation of the work of the CHWs was essential to its success.

In Liberia, after the second civil war (1999–2003), birth registration was reinstated as part of the government's post-reconstruction and development efforts. It was recognised that every child had a right to be registered and efforts were made by the government to ensure that the country had a well-functioning and sustainable CR system. The process of birth registration was centrally managed by the Ministry of Health and Social Welfare (MoHSW) from offices in the capital city, Monrovia (Virhiä et al. 2010). This centrally controlled process proved very inefficient because most of the citizens found it difficult to travel to the capital city to register a child's birth. As a result, only about 5 per cent of children under the age of five were registered in 2007 (Toivanen et al. 2011).

The government eventually embarked on a decentralisation of the birth registration process. This involved the establishment of health districts across the country, appointing county registrars (CRs), district health officers (DHOs), and general town chiefs (GTCs) to provide birth registration services at their respective levels of jurisdiction. The process of registering a birth now began with a visit by the DHO to the village or community to collect already-filled registration forms from the GTCs. These were forwarded as was by the DHOs to the county registrar's office and then to the national office of the MoHSW in Monrovia for processing. Birth certificates would then be printed at the central level and sent back to households through the DHOs and local chiefs. Although easy to implement, this paper-based decentralisation had several drawbacks including the possible loss of information through the manual handling of forms, the difficulty of interpreting handwritten information among third parties, and the need to transfer information from paper-based forms to a digital database. These issues often created huge pressure on the central office personnel, leading to long delays in the registration process (Virhiä et al. 2010).

A mobile birth registration (MBR) project was launched in 2009 as part of the Liberian government's Crisis Management Initiative, to complement the manual registration process (Virhiä et al. 2010; Toivanen et al. 2011). The MBR was designed to facilitate the collection of birth registration data in rural communities, minimise the need for households to travel long distances to provide registration information, and reduce the issuing time for birth certificates. The project utilised the Nokia Data Gathering (NDG) solution in gathering information on births from households. This was then transmitted to the central birth registration database. At the same time, county registrars could download files to their electronic devices and print corresponding birth certificates for households within their respective counties. The pilot scheme, launched in a single county, achieved its goal of making birth registration services easily accessible to rural households in its area, which then informed the government's plans to scale up the mobile birth registration project to all the counties in the country.

The discussion above illustrates how interventions in LMICs aimed at decentralising birth registration have had mixed results. In instances where the decentralisation process has been accompanied by comprehensive capacity-building and mobilisation at the local level (for example, in Ghana and Liberia) the results have been impressive. But there have also been cases where local authorities lacked the capacity to adopt the innovations introduced (as in Malawi and Tanzania), so that the interventions ultimately did not realise their objective of improving birth registration rates in the long run. Yet, in addition to local administrative capacity, the existing literature also highlights a range of factors that lead to low registration in LMICs including lack of public awareness of the process; the distance to and difficulty in accessing registration offices; the monetary cost of registration; the limited autonomy of mothers and often the absence of the father; and parents perceiving only small benefits from registration.

11.3 Birth registration in Bangladesh's rural areas

The authority responsible for birth registration in Bangladesh is the LGD, Local Government Division (and its associate agencies), while oversight of the process is done by the Civil Registration and Vital Statistics (CRVS) sec-retariat under the government's Cabinet Division (PLAN-Bangladesh and EATL 2020). The LGD's registration activities are governed by the 'Birth and Death Registration Act 2004' and operated by the Registrar General Office under LGD. LGDs operate in each of the eight divisions in Bangladesh, cov-ering all 64 districts of the country. At the district level, birth registration is predominantly done by the union parishad (UP), the lowest tier of local government administration in Bangladesh – except for urban areas and cit-ies where the birth registration is done by the municipality or the city cor-poration, respectively. The UP is headed by an elected representative who works under the subdistrict administration, known as 'upazila parishad'. As part of the 'Digital Bangladesh' mandate introduced in 2008, the Bangladesh government established union digital centres (UDCs) in almost all the UPs in Bangladesh, operated under a public–private partnership model, combining a government facility and a local entrepreneur as a service delivery agent. UDCs are equipped with computers and internet connections, facilitating one-stop service delivery for various services, including birth certification digitisation.

According to the current law (Birth and Death Registration Act 2004), it is mandatory to register birth for anyone born in the country irrespective of race, religion, or nationality. The rule specifies that the birth registration of newborns should be completed within 45 days of birth (UNICEF2015). If the registration is completed within two years of birth, there are no fees associated with this process. However, registration after two years entails paying various fees based on the fee structure depicted in Table 11.1. (The detailed application and verification processes are described in Table A1 and Figure A1 in this chapter's Supplementary Materials.[5])

According to the 2004 Birth and Death Registration Act, a birth certifi-cate is required documentation for enrolment in the government primary schools, registering marriages, and obtaining passports and national ID cards. Although a birth certificate is, officially, a document required for admission into schools, the rule may not be universally enforced. Hence the compliance rate is imperfect, especially in rural areas (see below). The 2004 Birth and Death Registration Act came into force in 2006 and, over the next five years, the birth registration rate for children under five increased sharply from 12 to 31 per cent (UNICEF 2013). However, the registration rate declined thereafter, reaching 20 per cent in 2014 before increasing again to

Table 11.1: The fee structure for birth registrations in Bangladesh

Date when registered	Union parishad and municipality	City corporation
Within 2 years of birth	None	None
For every year, after 2 years of occurrences	5	10
For duplicate copies of Birth Certificates	25	25
For the correction of any clerical mistake	10	10

Source: UNICEF (2015).
Note: Figures are for Bangladesh Taka (BDT) charged. BDT 94 = US$ 1 (as of 5 July 2022).

25 per cent in 2017–18 (NIPORT 2020). There is significant regional variation in registration rates, from 17 per cent in Rajshahi Division to 34 per cent in Sylhet Division.

Focusing down specifically on rural Bangladesh, we next provide evidence on birth registration patterns based on a purposefully designed survey conducted in 2020 called the Gaibandha Birth Registration and Helplines Survey. Survey data on birth registration of children is presently available for a wide range of countries. In particular, the MICS (Multiple Indicator Cluster Surveys) have collected birth registration data since 1999 and the DHSs (Demographic and Health Surveys) have collected birth registration data since 1993. What makes the present survey in rural Bangladesh distinctive is that it includes not only self-reported data on birth registration but also independent checks on birth certificates against the national birth registration database for a particular demographic group, namely unmarried adolescent girls, for whom certificates numbers were recorded during the survey.

Our survey and descriptive statistics

The study sample for the 2020 Gaibandha Birth Registration and Helplines Survey was drawn from 240 communities (specifically subunits of villages called '*paras*') in the district of Gaibandha in northern Bangladesh.[6] The communities are spread across five unions that are broadly similar in terms of population and geographic size as reported in Table 11.2.

The process of identifying sample households was as follows. In late 2019, for each village included in the study, the research team requested community elders to identify households within the village with unmarried girls in the age group 13 to 17 years. This exercise produced an initial listing of 2,498 households with unmarried adolescent girls in the 240 communities. The rationale for this sampling strategy is that the data collection was linked to a subsequent invention aimed at reducing the incidence of female early marriage in the study communities.

A household survey was conducted in the listed households between February and March 2020, which provided two key types of information. First,

Table 11.2: The areas, populations and households in the five unions used for the study sample

	Union				
	Gojaria	Kanchipara	Udakhali	Uria	Vorotkhali
Area (in acre)	7,120	6,610	5,170	5,840	3,520
Population	19,320	27,070	25,300	17,060	23,290
Number of households	4,890	6,950	6,380	4,290	5,840

Note: Taken from Bangladesh Population Census 2011. Numbers rounded to nearest 10.

the household head reported on the birth registration status of each member of the household. Second, for unmarried adolescent girls in the household, the enumeration team verified whether the girl had a birth certificate, and subsequently checked whether the certificate with that number had a digital record in the national birth registration database. The survey also included questions aimed at testing knowledge and understanding of the birth registration process among the mothers of unmarried adolescent girls.

In addition to the quantitative survey, we conducted qualitative interviews and focus-group discussions with local stakeholders to understand the local administrative capacity. We also conducted semi-structured interviews with the UDC private sector entrepreneur responsible for birth registration in each of the five unions covered in the survey and collected the information that they follow during birth registration and digitisation of existing birth records. We checked the IT and other equipment available for birth registration work within the office, and the interviewer also noted observations on the available equipment and office set-up. We report on the additional findings gathered in this way after reporting the findings from the quantitative analysis.

Table 11.3 presents summary statistics on the characteristics of the survey households. On average, households had 4.9 to 5 members and about 79 per cent of them owned land. The household head averaged 45 years with 3.15 years of education, and about 11 per cent of household heads were women. These characteristics make the sample households typical of rural households in Bangladesh.[7] However, due to our focus and sampling strategy, the households had more than twice as many girls as boys (on average 1.6 girls and 0.7 boys below age 18). The marriage rate was about 1.8 per cent among adolescent girls aged 13–17 years, much lower than the national average.[8] Nevertheless, the survey data can provide important insights about birth registration patterns in rural Bangladesh and their determinants.

Birth registration status and knowledge

Table 11.4 presents summary statistics for *each household member* recorded in our survey. The third row of the table shows that household heads reported

Table 11.3: Characteristics of households in our survey

Variable	Count	Mean	SD	Range	Median
Age (years) of household head	2449	44.5	9.32	14–95	44
Household annual income (000 BDT)	2494	117.3	117.4	0–4000	96
Household size		4.898	1.327	1–12	5
Number of boys in household		0.709	0.719	0–4	1
Number of girls in household		1.557	0.749	0–5	1
Number of girls married before age 18	2499	0.018	0.140	0–2	0
% girls married before 18		0.944	7.671	0–100	0
Household owns any land		0.792	0.406	0–1	1
Female household head		0.115	0.319	0–1	0
Education level of head:					
Never been to school		0.312	0.464	0–1	0
Class 1–10		0.379	0.485	0–1	0
Pre-sch/adult education	2449	0.194	0.395	0–1	0
High school/college		0.096	0.295	0–1	0
Degree/higher education		0.019	0.136	0–1	0

Source: 2020 Gaibandha Birth Registration and Helplines Survey and authors' calculations. See Section 11.3 for further details about the survey.
Note: In 51 households, no member present is designated as the head. SD: Standard deviation. The range shows minimum to maximum. Categorical variables were coded either 0 or 1.

birth registration had been done for 67 per cent of the household members. But there was significant variation in birth registration by demographic group. Figure 11.1 shows the birth registration rate by sex and age for children up to age 18. For children aged 24 months or younger, the number was 58 per cent for boys and 45 per cent for girls. The registration rate increased to about 60 per cent for children aged three to six years, with girls in this age nearly catching up but still lagging behind boys. For children aged seven to 12 years, the number was 85 per cent for boys and three points higher for girls. This suggests that a significant proportion of birth registration takes place at when a child enters school. Within the same age group, only one in 100 have never been to school, implying that more than one in eight boys and girls aged seven to 12 had enrolled in school without a birth certificate. So, there is still imperfect compliance with the legal requirement that a birth certificate is shown when a child is enrolled in school. Household heads reported that birth registration had been done for 95 per cent of adolescent girls aged 13 to 17 years.

Table 11.4: Summary statistics on household members

Variable	Mean	SD	Median	Range
Age (years)	26.30	17.42	19	0–120
Female member	0.60	0.49	1	0–1
Birth registration	0.67	0.47	1	0–1
Education classification:				
Never been to school	0.205	0.404	0	0–1
Class 1–10	0.581	0.493	1	0–1
Pre-sch/adult education	0.113	0.317	0	0–1
High school/college	0.086	0.281	0	0–1
Degree/higher degree	0.014	0.119	0	0–1
Occupation type:				
No occupation	0.749	0.434	1	0–1
Wage labourer	0.117	0.321	0	0–1
Self-employed	0.033	0.179	0	0–1
Trader	0.033	0.178	0	0–1
Salaried	0.025	0.155	0	0–1
Other	0.044	0.206	0	0–1
Marital status:				
Unmarried	0.517	0.50	1	0–1
Married	0.441	0.497	0	0–1
Widowed	0.038	0.191	0	0–1
Divorced	0.002	0.049	0	0–1
Separated	0.001	0.037	0	0–1

Source: 2020 Gaibandha Birth Registration and Helplines survey and authors' calculations.
Note: SD: Standard deviation. The range shows minimum to maximum. Categorical variables were coded either 0 or 1.

However, information from the validity checks on the birth certificates of adolescent girls paints a somewhat different picture. Table 11.5 presents summary statistics for the 2,643 unmarried adolescent girls aged 13–17 included in the households in our survey. In contrast to the figure provided by the household head, a birth certificate could be produced for only about four-fifths of the girls.[9] Only 58 per cent of adolescent girls had a birth certificate that passed the research team's validity check, that is, a certificate with a digital record in the national birth registration database.[10]

We found some variation by union in the proportion of adolescent girls for whom a birth certificate could be produced, ranging from 85 per cent

Figure 11.1: The birth registration of children in our sample, by sex and age

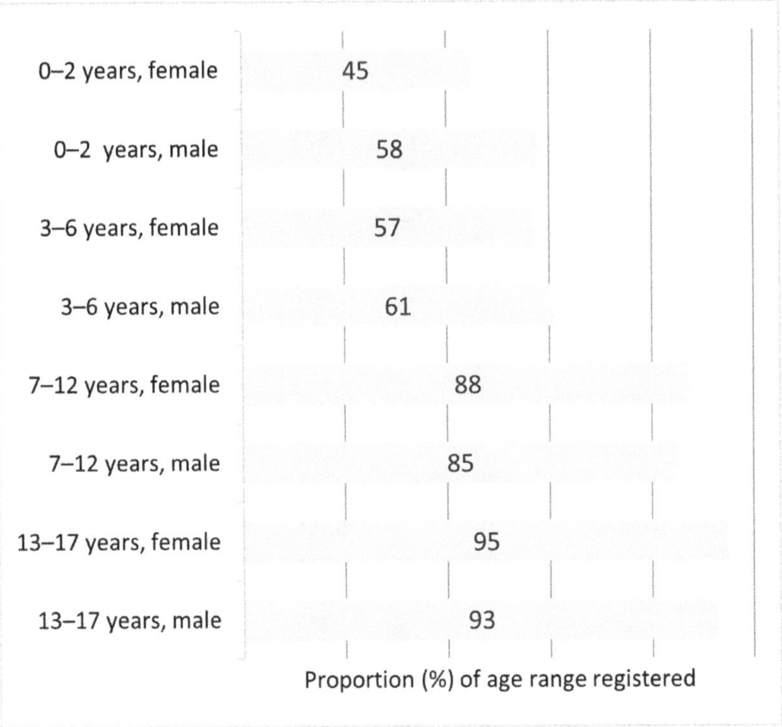

Age/Sex	Proportion (%)
0–2 years, female	45
0–2 years, male	58
3–6 years, female	57
3–6 years, male	61
7–12 years, female	88
7–12 years, male	85
13–17 years, female	95
13–17 years, male	93

Proportion (%) of age range registered

Source: 2020 Gaibandha Birth Registration and Helplines survey and authors' calculations.

in Vorotkhali union to 74 per cent in Uria union. But the differences in *validated* birth certificates across unions are more pronounced, ranging from two-thirds in Gojaria union to under two-fifths in Udakhali union. The differences in our two measures of birth registration across the 240 communities in the sample are even more striking: there are four communities where *all* adolescent girls have validated birth certificates and several where *none* of them do. Figure 11.2 shows a scatterplot by community of the proportion of adolescent girls for whom birth certificates could be shown and validated – with wide variation in both measures across the communities.[11]

In Table 11.6 we present summary statistics on an adult household member's knowledge about birth registration. These questions were intended for the mother of the adolescent girls in the household but, in cases where the mother was unavailable (about 16 per cent of cases), the question was asked of the father. Almost all respondents had heard about birth registration (99 per cent), knew where to go to register a child (94 per cent), and that a child could be registered once only (92 per cent). But less than half knew that the registration had to be done within 45 days of birth, and less than a quarter

Table 11.5: Summary statistics for adolescent girls in the survey

Variable	Count	Mean	SD	Range	Median
Age of girl	2643	15.1	1.19	13–17	15
Girl enrolled in school/college	2624	0.96	0.20	0–1	1
Girl current grade	2514	8.25	1.79	1–13	8
Girl birth registration status	2620	0.96	0.19	0	1
Showed birth certificate	2620	0.79	0.40	0	1
Validated birth certificate	2643	0.54	0.50	0	1
Father's age	2223	45.1	8.17	17–95	45
Mother's age	2511	36.7	6.59	18–70	35
Father's education:					
No education		0.318	0.466	0–1	0
Incomplete primary		0.305	0.461	0–1	0
Primary education	2223	0.103	0.305	0–1	0
Incomplete secondary		0.121	0.326	0–1	0
Secondary/higher		0.152	0.360	0–1	0
Mother's education:					
No education		0.261	0.439	0–1	0
Incomplete primary		0.356	0.479	0–1	0
Primary education	2511	0.114	0.318	0–1	0
Incomplete secondary		0.180	0.384	0–1	0
Secondary/higher		0.089	0.285	0–1	0

Source: 2020 Gaibandha Birth Registration and Helplines Survey and authors' calculations.
Note: SD Standard deviation. The range shows minimum to maximum. Categorical variables were coded either 0 or 1.

could mention a correct way of checking the validity of a birth certificate. On average, the respondents could mention about 2.9 reasons for, or advantages of, registering a child, with the number of reasons provided ranging from 0 to 7.

We find some improvement in knowledge about birth registration by the level of education. Figure 11.3 shows the values of two of the knowledge variables by level of education, for adult female respondents only. The proportion who were able to mention at least one correct method for checking for birth registration validity increased with respondents' level of education, from about 15 per cent among women with no education to about one-third for women in the sample who have completed secondary or higher education. Knowledge about when to register a child showed an increase with secondary education or above. We did not find a relation for the other knowledge variables (numbers not shown here).

Figure 11.2: The proportion (%) of validated birth certificates in communities by the proportion (%) showing a certificate

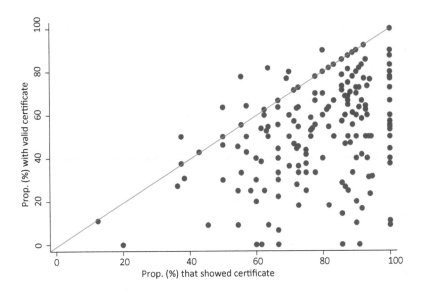

Source: 2020 Gaibandha Birth Registration and Helplines Survey and authors' calculations.

11.4 Determinants of birth registration among adolescent girls

To better understand the factors behind the invalid birth certificates discussed in the previous section, we explore the determinants of birth registration status of adolescent girls in our survey sample within a regression framework. Specifically, we estimate linear probability models of the following form:

$$BHS_{ihvu} = \alpha + X'_{ihvu}\beta + Z'_{hvu}\gamma + N'_{vu}\eta + \epsilon_{ihvu} \qquad [1]$$

where BHS_{ihvu} is a binary variable indicating the birth registration status of person i in household h, community v, union u; X_{ihvu} is a vector of individual characteristics; Z_{hvu} is a vector of household characteristics; N_{vu} is a vector of gender norms measured at the community level and ϵ_{ihvu} is the error term. Finally, α, β, γ and η are vectors of parameters to be estimated. In a second specification, we add fixed effects at the level of the union as follows:

$$BHS_{ihvu} = \alpha + X'_{ihvu}\beta + Z'_{hvu}\gamma + N'_{vu}\eta + d'_u\delta + \epsilon_{ihvu} \qquad [2]$$

where d_u is a vector of union dummies in registering births and issuing certificates. As each union falls under the jurisdiction of a different UDC that registers births and issues certificates, sizeable union-level fixed effects may

Table 11.6: Summary statistics on adult knowledge

	Count	Mean	SD	Range	Median
Age in years	2485	38.2	9.086	13–90	35
Female respondent		0.844	0.363	0–1	1
No education		0.260	0.439	0–1	0
Incomplete primary		0.344	0.475	0–1	0
Primary education	2485	0.115	0.319	0–1	0
Incomplete secondary		0.171	0.377	0–1	0
Secondary/higher		0.110	0.313	0–1	0
Head		0.251	0.434	0–1	0
Spouse	2485	0.697	0.460	0–1	1
Other relation to head		0.052	0.223	0–1	0
Heard about birth registration		0.992	0.087	0–1	1
Knows when to do birth registration		0.433	0.496	0–1	0
Knows where to do birth registration	2497	0.937	0.243	0–1	1
Knows # times birth registration can be done		0.922	0.269	0–1	1
Knows how to check validity		0.237	0.425	0–1	0
# Advantages of birth registration are mentioned		2.92	1.05	0–1	3

Source: 2020 Gaibandha Birth Registration and Helplines Survey and authors' calculations. Note: SD: Standard deviation. The range shows minimum to maximum. Categorical variables were coded either 0 or 1.

indicate variation in local administrative capacity in registering births and issuing certificates. In a third specification, we replace the union fixed effects with community fixed effects (and drop the community-level gender norms) as follows:

$$BHS_{ihvu} = \alpha + X'_{ihvu}\beta + Z'_{hvu}\gamma + c'_{vu}\delta + \epsilon_{ihvu} \qquad [3]$$

where c_{vu} is a vector of community dummies. Although all communities within the same union are covered by the same UDC, there may be significant differences between them because of local transmission of information and attitudes, and imitation of good or bad practices across neighbours. There may also be systematic variation across communities in terms of wealth and occupational composition of households, as well as attitudes towards child marriage and female schooling. Sizeable community-level fixed effects would indicate that at least some of these factors are important determinants of birth registration.

Table 11.7 reports on estimates of Equations [1] to [3] using the availability of *any birth certificate* as the dependent variable. The explanatory variables

Figure 11.3: Knowledge of birth registration versus education

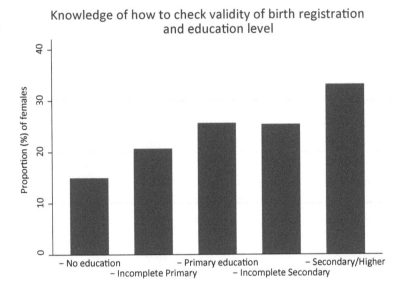

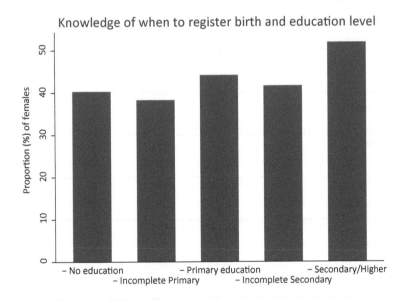

Source: 2020 Gaibandha Birth Registration and Helplines survey and authors' calculations.

Table 11.7: Determinants of any birth certificate for unmarried girls in the household

Explanatory variables	Dependent variable = Any birth certificate					
	Model 1		Model 2		Model 3	
Age of girl	−0.006	(0.008)	−0.007	(0.008)	−0.008	(0.008)
# Siblings	0.006	(0.017)	0.013	(0.016)	0.013	(0.018)
Birth order	−0.004	(0.013)	−0.005	(0.014)	−0.008	(0.015)
Household size	−0.008	(0.010)	−0.011	(0.010)	−0.012	(0.011)
Log of household income	0.019	(0.016)	0.011	(0.015)	0.008	(0.016)
Female h'head	0.020	(0.030)	0.012	(0.030)	−0.006	(0.036)
Household owns land	−0.001	(0.022)	−0.001	(0.023)	−0.003	(0.027)
Muslim	−0.038	(0.042)	−0.042	(0.043)	−0.002	(0.043)
H'head education = 1, incomplete primary	−0.002	(0.028)	−0.007	(0.027)	−0.017	(0.030)
H'head education = 2, primary education	0.062**	(0.031)	0.065**	(0.031)	0.048	(0.033)
H'head education = 3, incomplete secondary	−0.023	(0.035)	−0.024	(0.034)	−0.021	(0.037)
H'head education = 4, secondary/higher	−0.010	(0.035)	−0.011	(0.035)	−0.021	(0.037)
Mother's education = 1, incomplete primary	−0.004	(0.027)	−0.001	(0.027)	0.016	(0.030)
Mother's education = 2, primary education	0.007	(0.037)	0.005	(0.037)	0.000	(0.039)
Mother's education = 3, incomplete secondary	0.002	(0.033)	−0.008	(0.033)	0.000	(0.036)
Mother's education = 4, secondary/higher	−0.096**	(0.044)	−0.104**	(0.043)	0.078* –	(0.047)
Age (yrs) of h'head	−0.002	(0.001)	−0.001	(0.001)	−0.001	(0.002)
Mother's age	−0.002	(0.002)	−0.002	(0.001)	−0.003	(0.002)
Heard about birth reg	−0.065	(0.131)	−0.027	(0.127)	−0.009	(0.130)
Knows when to do birth reg	−0.009	(0.020)	−0.004	(0.020)	0.000	(0.023)
Knows where to do birth reg	0.018	(0.049)	−0.014	(0.049)	0.021	(0.054)
Knows # times birth reg can be done	0.063	(0.039)	0.064	(0.040)	0.038	(0.044)
Knows how to check validity	−0.026	(0.023)	−0.016	(0.024)	−0.010	(0.028)
# Advantages of birth reg mentioned	0.016*	(0.010)	0.014	(0.010)	0.017	(0.012)

(Continued)

Table 11.7: Continued

Explanatory variables	Dependent variable = Any birth certificate				
	Model 1		Model 2		Model 3
Norm – man should be sole decision maker	−0.132***	(0.046)	−0.136***	(0.042)	
Norm – woman should not work outside	0.008	(0.040)	0.020	(0.038)	
Norm – woman should not work outside 2	0.047	(0.030)	0.059**	(0.028)	
Norm – household work for all	−0.083	(0.062)	−0.077	(0.058)	
Norm – woman should give income to man	0.075*	(0.039)	0.053	(0.035)	
Norm – Woman to ask permission to work	0.107*	(0.059)	0.091	(0.059)	
Norm – Girls to marry before 18	−0.072*	(0.040)	−0.074*	(0.038)	
Norm – Girls only schools	0.013	(0.032)	−0.008	(0.030)	
Norm – Girls should finish secondary school	0.029	(0.070)	0.069	(0.066)	
Norm – Boys should finish secondary school	−0.040	(0.055)	−0.080	(0.054)	
Norm – Sec school more important for boys	−0.100***	(0.031)	−0.077***	(0.028)	
Norm – Boy more desirable as successor	0.035	(0.024)	0.027	(0.024)	
Union = 2, Kanchipara			0.035	(0.030)	
Union = 3, Udakhali			−0.002	(0.030)	
Union = 4, Uria			−0.111***	(0.040)	
Union = 5, Vorotkhali			0.081***	(0.030)	
Observations	2,440		2,440		2,440
R-squared	0.040		0.058		0.171
Union FE			Yes		
Community FE					Yes

Source: 2020 Gaibandha Birth Registration and Helplines Survey and authors' calculations. Notes: Standard errors are in parentheses and italics. ***p < 0.01, **p < 0.05, *p < 0.1. The abbreviation h'head means head of household. Errors are clustered at the community level. The dependent variable indicates whether the adolescent girl has any type of birth registration whether valid or invalid. The sample includes all unmarried adolescent girls in the study area. In the third column the reference union is Gojaria.

include the age of the girl, household demographic characteristics, education level of the mother and the household head, the mother's knowledge about birth registration, and 12 distinct measures of community gender norms. We interpret the estimated coefficients not as causal effects but as indicating the predictive ability of a range of predetermined characteristics.

Before discussing the results, it is also worth noting that, because the sample includes *unmarried* adolescent girls only, the estimated coefficients may be affected by selection bias. In particular, if certain socio-economic characteristics reduce risk of early marriage as well as positively affect birth certification, this will lead to a downward bias in our point estimates. For this reason, in the following discussion we focus primarily on the community-level and union-level variables: as community and union-level factors are less likely to affect marriage timing than household and individual-level factors.

Of the explanatory variables, the only one that 'affects' the probability of having a birth certificate across all three specifications is the mother's level of education. In fact, other things equal, if the mother has secondary or higher education, the girl is about 8 to 10 percentage points *less likely* to have a birth certificate than one whose mother has never attended school. We also find that three of the gender norm variables have predictive power regarding the presence of a birth certificate in both specifications that they are included: the proportion of respondents in the community who agree with the statements that 'A man should be the sole decision maker', 'Girls should marry before 18', and 'Secondary school education is more important for a boy than for a girl'. Increased agreement with any of these statements within the community decreases the probability that a girl has a birth certificate.

The individual, household, and community characteristics explain just 4 per cent of the variation in birth certificates among adolescent girls, as indicated by the R-square in column 1 of Table 11.7. The inclusion of union fixed effects in column 2 improves the R-square only slightly to 0.058. The estimated coefficients for the union dummies indicate some variation in the birth certification rate across unions: in Uria, the rate is about 11 percentage points lower than in the reference union (Gojaria) and about 19 percentage points lower than in Vorotkhali. The inclusion of community fixed effects improves the R-square to 0.171. Thus, a significantly larger part of the variation in birth certification is explained by differences across communities (that, within union boundaries, are served by the same local authority) rather than at the union level.

Table 11.8 reports on estimates of Equations [1] to [3] using the availability of a *valid* birth certificate as the dependent variable. The explanatory variables are identical to those in Table 11.7. Again, we find that the only explanatory variable that 'affects' the probability of having a valid birth certificate across all three specifications is the mother's level of education, but in a perhaps surprising way (see below): an adolescent girl whose mother has secondary or higher education is about 10–12 percentage points *less likely* to have a birth certificate than one whose mother has never attended school. Unlike the case

Table 11.8: Determinants of valid birth certificate for unmarried girls in the household

Explanatory variables	Dependent variable = Valid birth record certificate					
	Model 1		Model 2		Model 3	
Age of girl	−0.007	(0.009)	−0.003	(0.009)	−0.003	(0.009)
# Siblings	0.012	(0.019)	0.002	(0.018)	0.000	(0.019)
Birth order	−0.000	(0.016)	0.010	(0.016)	0.005	(0.017)
Household size	−0.007	(0.012)	−0.004	(0.012)	−0.005	(0.013)
Log of household income	−0.001	(0.017)	0.004	(0.017)	0.011	(0.018)
Female household head	−0.032	(0.039)	−0.004	(0.038)	0.019	(0.041)
Household owns land	−0.035	(0.029)	−0.012	(0.028)	−0.029	(0.031)
Muslim	−0.052	(0.052)	−0.048	(0.047)	−0.035	(0.050)
Household head education = 1, incomplete primary	−0.003	(0.032)	−0.012	(0.031)	−0.029	(0.033)
H'head education = 2, primary education	0.029	(0.041)	0.020	(0.038)	0.018	(0.040)
H'head education = 3, incomplete secondary	0.004	(0.040)	−0.002	(0.040)	−0.005	(0.041)
H'head education = 4, secondary/higher	−0.008	(0.046)	−0.010	(0.044)	−0.020	(0.044)
Mother's education = 1, incomplete primary	−0.005	(0.030)	−0.002	(0.030)	−0.003	(0.031)
Mother's education = 2, primary education	−0.007	(0.043)	−0.005	(0.041)	−0.009	(0.043)
Mother's education = 3, Incomplete secondary	−0.046	(0.041)	−0.036	(0.039)	−0.030	(0.040)
Mother's education = 4, secondary/higher	−0.110**	(0.050)	−0.103**	(0.049)	−0.121**	(0.051)
Age (yrs) of h'head	0.001	(0.002)	0.000	(0.002)	0.001	(0.002)
Mother's age	−0.003	(0.002)	−0.004**	(0.002)	−0.004*	(0.002)
Heard about birth reg	−0.178	(0.146)	−0.140	(0.141)	−0.162	(0.146)
Knows when to do birth reg	0.003	(0.023)	−0.008	(0.022)	−0.000	(0.023)
Knows where to do birth reg	0.034	(0.052)	0.001	(0.050)	0.017	(0.056)
Knows # times birth reg can be done	0.057	(0.046)	0.066	(0.046)	0.040	(0.047)
Knows how to check validity	0.001	(0.028)	−0.011	(0.028)	0.026	(0.031)

(Continued)

Table 11.8: Continued

Explanatory variables	Dependent variable = Valid birth record certificate					
	Model 1		Model 2		Model 3	
# advantages of birth reg mentioned	0.014	(0.011)	0.014	(0.011)	0.017	(0.013)
Norm – Man should be sole decision maker	−0.042	(0.064)	−0.030	(0.057)		
Norm – Woman should not work outside	−0.021	(0.058)	−0.022	(0.052)		
Norm – Woman should not work outside 2	−0.031	(0.041)	−0.027	(0.038)		
Norm – Household work for all	−0.081	(0.095)	−0.051	(0.083)		
Norm – Woman should give income to man	0.050	(0.054)	0.068	(0.048)		
Norm – Woman to ask permission to work	0.134	(0.090)	0.075	(0.080)		
Norm – Girls to marry before 18	0.008	(0.053)	−0.019	(0.049)		
Norm – Girls only schools	0.011	(0.047)	0.037	(0.041)		
Norm – Girls should finish secondary school	0.081	(0.114)	0.011	(0.104)		
Norm – Boys should finish sec school	−0.046	(0.100)	0.010	(0.088)		
Norm – Sec school more imp. for boys	−0.028	(0.047)	−0.063	(0.043)		
Norm – Boy more desirable as successor	−0.042	(0.038)	−0.038	(0.035)		
Union = 2, Kanchipara			−0.017	(0.038)		
Union = 3, Udakhali			−0.284***	(0.043)		
Union = 4, Uria			−0.082*	(0.046)		
Union = 5, Vorotkhali			−0.222***	(0.038)		
Observations	2,440		2,440		2,440	
R-squared	0.020		0.070		0.221	
Union fixed effect			Yes			
Community fixed effect					Yes	

Notes: Standard errors in parentheses. ***$p < 0.01$, **$p < 0.05$, *$p < 0.1$. Errors are clustered at the community level. The dependent variable indicates whether or not the adolescent girl has a birth certificate identified as 'valid' by enumerator. The sample includes all unmarried adolescent girls in the study area. In the third column the reference union is Gojaria.

of any birth certification, none of the gender norm variables consistently predicts valid birth certification.

The individual, household, and community characteristics explain just 2 per cent of the variation in valid birth certificates among adolescent girls. The inclusion of union fixed effects improves the R-square substantially to 0.07. And we obtained larger differences in the rates of valid birth certification across unions compared to the case of any birth certification discussed above. In the Udakhali and Vorotkhali unions, the rates were 28 and 22 percentage points, respectively, lower than in the reference union, Gojaria. In another union, Uria, the valid birth certification rate is also lower than in the reference union by eight percentage points. The inclusion of community fixed effects improves the R-square further to 0.22.

The persistently negative coefficient in Tables 11.7 and 11.8 for the dummy variable corresponding to the attainment of secondary or higher education by mothers merits further comment. At first sight, the pattern is puzzling since women with secondary education appear to have better knowledge about birth registration (Figure 10.3). But recall that the sample used for the regression analysis includes only *unmarried* daughters. Mothers with less education are more likely to have *married* adolescent girls (confirmed in our data), who are, thus, absent from the sample. If married adolescent girls have a lower birth registration rate (which we cannot confirm on the basis of our data as reliable birth certification data was collected for unmarried adolescent girls only but is a plausible hypothesis), this would inflate, within the sample, the birth registration rate for girls whose mothers have less education compared to girls whose mothers have completed secondary education.[12]

Conclusions

Using the estimates in column 3 of Tables 11.7 and 11.8, we can calculate the predicted probability of having any birth certificate and a validated birth certificate by community. Figure 11.4 shows the distribution of these predicted probabilities across communities using sample mean values of all other covariates in the respective models. Both distributions are single-peaked and, as expected, the mode of the distribution of the predicted probabilities of validated birth certificate was lower than that for any birth certificate. More strikingly, we observed a much wider spread in predicted probabilities across communities in the case of validated birth certificates. This pattern was also reflected in the predicted probabilities calculated at the level of the union shown in Table 11.9.

These patterns raise the question whether the differences in valid birth certification among adolescent girls across unions could be attributed to local institutional capacity to register births and maintain birth records. In focus-group discussions on birth registration with local stakeholders, participants highlighted a number of governance issues leading to low compliance:

Figure 11.4: Predicted birth registration probability for adolescent girls by community

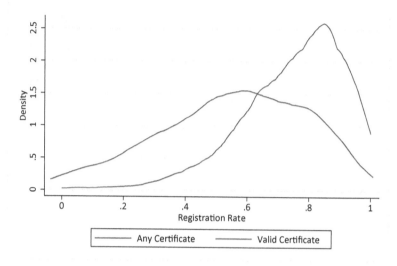

Notes: The probability density function is used to specify the probability of the variable falling within a particular range of values, as opposed to taking on any one value. It need not fall in the range 0–1. The probability is given by the area under the curve.

Table 11.9: Predicted probabilities for a birth registration certification (BRC) of adolescent girls in our sample across unions

Union	Valid birth certificate	Any birth certificate
Gojaria	0.683	0.749
Kanchipara	0.665	0.785
Udakhali	0.399	0.747
Uria	0.601	0.638
Vorotkhali	0.461	0.831

Source: 2020 Gaibandha Birth Registration and Helplines Survey and authors' calculations. Notes: The table shows the predicted birth registration probabilities for adolescent girls by union based on the estimates in column 2, Tables 11.7 and 11.8. Sample mean values are used for all other covariates.

- lack of education and awareness within the local union parishad leadership,
- lack of experience among the union digital centre (UDC) staff in registering births,
- corruption and nepotism leading to lack of appropriate equipment for registering births in the UDC, and

- unqualified persons being assigned to the UDC, and unrealistic targets set by the Bangladeshi government to process birth registrations within a set time frame without sufficient investment in capacity-building.

The semi-structured interviews with the five UDC private sector entrepreneurs also revealed a lot of variation in their technical and management capacity, in terms of educational qualifications, IT training, training on digitisation of birth registration records, and practices in terms of documentation, security, file management, and archiving records.[13]

In the absence of systematic large-scale data on local institutional capacity, it is difficult to verify to what extent the issue of invalid birth certificates is due to local institutional capacity. However, we highlight here some suggestive evidence in line with this hypothesis. There are large differences in the *overall* self-reported birth registration rates (more precisely, as reported by the household head) across the five unions covered in our survey: the percentage rates were 86 in Gojaria, 77 in Uria, 66 in Vorotkhali, 65 in Udakhali, and 52 in Kanchipara. Given that these unions are broadly similar in terms of their demographic composition, and that there is little reason to expect systematic differences in reporting errors across unions, these numbers can be interpreted as rough indicators of local institutional capacity relating to the creation and maintenance of birth registration records.[14]

The variation in birth registration rates across unions suggests that there are large differences in local institutional capacity. Moreover, the ordering of the unions in terms of their overall birth registration rates is similar to the ordering implied by the predicted valid birth registration probabilities in Table 11.9 – albeit with the exception of the Kanchipara union. This pattern suggests that variations may be due to differences in local institutional capacity. More precisely, the differences in the technical and management capacity of UDC entrepreneurs observed through the semi-structured interviews (in terms of IT training, training on digitisation of birth registration records, and the adoption of practices for documentation, security, file management, and archiving records) are plausibly responsible for at least part of the variation in validated birth registration certificates across unions.

In theory, decentralisation should improve efficiency in governmental activities that require reliable local information. Well-known examples are real estate and property tax collection (since tax assessment requires property valuation), which can be done far more accurately at the local level rather than by a central administration. Similarly, conducting vital registration (including birth registration and the digitisation of birth records) at the lowest administrative level allows the use of localised information support and lowers transaction costs. Although decentralisation should make these processes more cost-effective, weaker administrative capacity due to supply-side issues (such as corruption, nepotism, inadequate infrastructural support, and inexperienced service providers) could dilute decentralised efforts of providing birth registrations locally. Such problems can make the compliance standard of such activities questionable, with potentially important consequences on public policy responses in other vital areas.

We have explored this issue in a setting where valid birth registration could potentially help to reduce the incidences of female early marriage. Bangladesh has one of the highest rates of female early marriage in the world. The latest figures indicate that about 59 per cent of women marry before reaching the age of 18 (Amin et al. 2019). The practice is strictly prohibited by the Child Marriage Restraint Act 2017. But law enforcement agencies require a valid documentation of age to take necessary action against the practice, while the current birth registration rate in Bangladesh is far from universal. Although there are demand driven issues – for example, lack of awareness on the importance of the birth registration by rural parents (many of them are low-educated and often illiterate) – we provide suggestive evidence of substantial supply-side constraints.

Evaluating the birth registration issues of a rural district in Bangladesh, we documented that nearly one-third of the sample did not have their birth registered at the time of the survey, with a sizeable gender gap for children aged 0–24 months (58 per cent of boys were registered compared to 45 per cent of girls). For girls aged 13–17 years (an age group that is highly susceptible to female early marriage), the household was able to show the birth registration document in 80 per cent of cases. However, the research team's validity check against records in the national database revealed that, of the birth registration documents produced by the households during the survey, 46 per cent were, in fact, invalid.

The survey also revealed that, while most rural households have basic knowledge about birth registration, fewer than half knew the deadline for completing the registration without incurring a registration fee, and less than a quarter knew how to check the validity of a birth certificate. What is more striking is the local-level variation in compliance rates. Our estimates indicate that there are statistically significant discrepancies in the local government's ability to produce valid birth certificates, ranging from 39 per cent to 67 per cent across five local authorities within a single district in Bangladesh. Relatedly, using data drawn from semi-structured individuals with the entrepreneurs responsible for birth registration at the union-level, we find large differences in terms of educational qualifications, IT training, training on digitisation of birth registration records, and practices (data security, file management, archival procedures) across the UDCs. And differences across unions explain a much larger fraction of the variation in *validated* birth certificates than the presence of any certificate. We argue that the issue of invalid certificates is a problem stemming from limited administrative capacity at the level of the local authority.

We conclude with two policy implications of our findings. The differences in qualifications, resources, and processes across union digital centres were evident from our engagements with UDC entrepreneurs. So, the provision of up-to-date training (and refresher courses) and equipment would help to improve the quality of birth registration process in rural Bangladesh. Birth certificate validity checks along the lines conducted for this study can easily be replicated by schools, and can help identify unions with high rates of invalid certificates, and thus the UDCs that could benefit from such training and investments. Although the institutional set-up for birth registration differs across countries, this two-pronged strategy may also help improve birth registration rates and the reliability of birth registration records in other developing countries. In turn, digitisation of birth registration records (and allocating resources and training to ensure that the birth registration system is effective) can significantly improve state capacity to deliver a range of public services to citizens, similar to the effects of biometrically authenticated payment infrastructures obtained by Muralidharan, Niehaus, and Sukhtankar (2016).

Acknowledgements

This chapter is based on research undertaken for a project titled 'Enduring more agency and community surveillance support to reduce child marriage in Bangladesh', conducted with the financial support of Grand Challenges Canada and the Government of Canada, through Global Affairs Canada (GAC) (Grant Number: R-ST-POC-1909-28916). We would like to thank MOMODa Foundation for their invaluable partnership and support in this project, the editors and reviewers for their feedback on earlier versions of the chapter, and to Aniema Atorudibo, Josephine Brett and H.M. Masudur Rahman for their excellent research assistance.

Endnotes

Supplementary material for this chapter is available on LSE Press's Zenodo site (https://zenodo.org/communities/decentralised_governance/). See: *Supplementary material for*: Abu S. Shonchoy and Zaki Wahhaj (2023) 'Birth registration, child rights, and local governance in Bangladesh', in Jean-Paul Faguet and Sarmistha Pal (eds) *Decentralised Governance: Crafting Effective Democracies Around the World*, London: LSE Press. https://doi.org/10.5281/zenodo.7920630

[1] The Convention, which was signed in 1989 and became effective in 1990, is an international human rights treaty that sets out the civil, political, economic, social, and cultural rights of children. States that have ratified the Convention are bound to it by international law. As of present, it has been ratified by all United Nations members except the United States. Source: https://www.Unicef.org.uk/what-we-do/un-convention-child-rights

[2] The full scaling-up plan is available here: https://www.worldbank.org/en/topic/health/publication/global-civil-registration-vital-statistics-scaling-up-investment

[3] For example, in February 2022, a BBC Bangla news article reported that several million individuals in Bangladesh who had previously registered their births would need to reregister online as their previous birth registration records had 'disappeared' from the system during a process of digitising birth records. See: https://www.bbc.com/bengali/news-60262339

[4] A 'union' is the lowest tier of the local government administration in Bangladesh.

[5] Supplementary material for: Abu S. Shonchoy and Zaki Wahhaj (2023) 'Birth registration, child rights, and local governance in Bangladesh', in Jean-Paul Faguet and Sarmistha Pal (eds) *Decentralised Governance: Crafting Effective Democracies Around the World*, London: LSE Press. https://doi.org/10.5281/zenodo.7920630

[6] Although the *para* has no administrative significance, the subdivision of villages into *paras* is widely practised in rural Bangladesh and residents tend to self-identify with the *paras* in which their homesteads are situated (White 1992).

[7] In the latest available Bangladesh Household Income and Expenditures Survey (2016–17), the average rural household size is 4.11 and the proportion of rural households that are headed by a woman is 11% (BBS 2017).

[8] Figures provided in the Bangladesh Demographic and Health Survey 2017–18 Final Report indicate a marriage rate of 43.1% among women aged 15–19 years, with 12.4% married by age (NIPORT and ICF 2020).

[9] The primary reasons that respondents gave for being unable to show the birth certificate were that the certificate was lost (36%), misplaced (38%), or kept at the girl's school (23%).

[10] There are two main reasons why there may be no digital record of the certificate in the national database. This may happen if the certificate is fake – that is, produced by someone other than the proper authorities – or if it was issued by the proper authorities but mistakes were made in the registration process.

[11] Note that in a small number of communities the proportion for whom birth certificate could be shown was lower than the proportion with validated birth certificates. This may be because the two checks were conducted on different days and some respondents could not show a birth certificate for the adolescent girl during the interview in spite of having a valid one.

[12] Consistent with this reasoning, the birth registration rate for adolescent girls in the sample whose mothers have completed secondary education is 9–10 per centage points lower than those whose mothers have less

education. This pattern holds both for any birth certificate and for validated birth certificates.

[13] As these interviews involved just five individuals, we do not provide
further details on the responses to avoid disclosing personal information.

[14] Although the self-reported birth registration data is based on the
household survey, recall from section 10.3 that it is based on a different
question and procedures to that used to check for valid birth registration.

References

Amin, Sajeda; Asadullah, Niaz; Hossain, Sara; and Wahhaj, Zaki (2019) 'Is
the Law Enough to End Child Marriage?' Technical report, LSE International Development blog.
https://blogs.lse.ac.uk/internationaldevelopment/2019/11/08/is-the-law
-enough-to-end-child-marriage

Banerjee, Abhijit; Duflo, Esther; Imbert, Clement; Mathew, Santhosh; and
Pande, Rohini (2020) 'E-governance, Accountability, and Leakage in
Public Programs: Experimental Evidence from a Financial Management
Reform in India', *American Economic Journal: Applied Economics*, vol.12,
no.4, pp.39–72. https://doi.org/10.1257/app.20180302

Bangladesh Bureau of Statistics (BBS) (2017) 'Preliminary Report on Household Income and Expenditures Survey 2016', Technical report, Bangladesh Bureau of Statistics, Dhaka.
https://catalog.ihsn.org/index.php/catalog/7399/related-materials

Celeste, Jeremy G. and Caelian, Merlita V. (2021) 'Civil Registration Awareness, Compliance, Purpose, and Challenges among Municipal Residents
in the Philippines', *Philippine Social Science Journal*, vol.4, pp.104–14.
https://doi.org/10.52006/main.v4i2.332

Ebbers, Anne Lieke and Smits, Jeroen (2022) 'Household and Context-Level
Determinants of Birth Registration in Sub-Saharan Africa', *PloS One*,
vol.17, no.4, e0265882. https://doi.org/10.1371/journal.pone.0265882

Fagernäs, Sonja; and Odame, Joyce (2013) 'Birth Registration and Access to
Health Care: An Assessment of Ghana's Campaign Success', *Bulletin of
the World Health Organization*, vol.91, pp.459–64.
http://dx.doi.org/10.2471/BLT.12.111351

Gadabu, O.; Ben-Smith, A.; Douglas, G.; Chirwa-Nasasara, K.; Manjomo,
R.; Harries, A.; Dambula, I.; Kangʼoma, S.; Chiumia, T.; and Chinsinga,
F. (2018) 'Scaling Up Electronic Village Registers for Measuring Vital
Statistics in Rural Villages in Malawi', *Public Health Action*, vol.8, no.2,
pp.79–84. https://doi.org/10.5588/pha.17.0116

Gadabu, O.; Manjomo, R.; Mwakilama, S.; Douglas, G.; Harries, A.; Moyo, C.; Makonokaya, L.; Kang'oma, S.; Chitedze, P.; and Chinsinga, F. (2014) 'An Electronic Register for Vital Registration in a Rural Village with No Electricity in Malawi', *Public Health Action*, vol.4, no.3, pp.145–49. https://doi.org/10.5588/pha.14.0015

Hanmer, Lucia and Elefante, Marina (2015) 'The Role of Identification in Ending Child Marriage', Washington, DC: World Bank. https://openknowledge.worldbank.org/handle/10986/25184

Kabadi, Gregory; Mwanyika, Henry; and de Savigny, Don (2013) 'Innovations in Monitoring Vital Events: Mobile Phone SMS Support to Improve Coverage of Birth and Death Registration: A Scalable Solution', *The Lancet*, vol.381, no.2, p.S69. https://doi.org/10.1016/S0140-6736(13)61323-9

Mohanty, Itismita and Gebremedhin, Tesfaye Alemayehu (2018) 'Maternal Autonomy and Birth Registration in India: Who Gets Counted?' *PloS One*, vol.13, no.3, e0194095. https://doi.org/10.1371/journal.pone.0194095

Muralidharan, Karthik; Niehaus, Paul; and Sukhtankar, Sandip (2016) 'Building State Capacity: Evidence from Biometric Smartcards in India', *American Economic Review*, vol.106, no.10, pp.2895–929. https://doi.org/10.3386/w19999

Muralidharan, Karthik; Niehaus, Paul; and Sukhtankar, Sandip (2020) 'Identity Verification Standards in Welfare Programs: Experimental Evidence from India', Technical report, National Bureau of Economic Research. https://doi.org/10.3386/w26744

NIPORT (2020) 'Bangladesh Demographic and Health Survey 2017–18', Dhaka and Maryland.

NIPORT and ICF (2020) 'Bangladesh Demographic and Health Survey 2017–18', Final report, NIPORT and ICF, Dhaka, Bangladesh, and Maryland, USA. https://www.dhsprogram.com/publications/publication-fr344-dhs-final-reports.cfm?cssearch=609736_1

Ohemeng-Dapaah, Seth; Pronyk, Paul; Akosa, Eric; Nemser, Benneth; and Kanter, Andrew S. (2010) 'Combining Vital Events Registration, Verbal Autopsy and Electronic Medical Records in Rural Ghana for Improved Health Services Delivery', in *MEDINFO 2010*, IOS Press, pp.416–20.

Pelowski, Matthew; Wamai, Richard G; Wangombe, Joseph; Nyakundi, Hellen; Oduwo, Geofrey O.; Ngugi, Benjamin K.; and Ogembo, Javier G. 2015) 'Why Don't You Register Your Child? A Study of Attitudes and Factors Affecting Birth Registration in Kenya, and Policy Suggestions',

The Journal of Development Studies, vol.51, no.7, pp.881–904.
https://doi.org/10.1080/00220388.2015.1010156

PLAN-Bangladesh and EATL (2020) 'Digital Birth Registration in Bangladesh. Technical Analysis Study: Strengthening CRVS in Bangladesh through the Appropriate Use of Digital Technologies'.
https://plan-international.org/uploads/sites/72/2021/12/digital_birth_registration_in_bangladesh_technical_analysis_final_draft.pdf

Republic of Botswana and World Bank (2015) 'Integration of Civil Registration and Vital Statistics and Identity Management Systems: Botswana Success Story', Technical report, Washington DC: World Bank.
https://doi.org/10.1596/28079

Singogo, E.; Kanike, E., Van Lettow, M., Cataldo, F., Zachariah, R., Bissell, K.; and Harries, A. (2013) 'Village Registers for Vital Registration in Rural Malawi', *Tropical Medicine and International Health*, vol.18, no.8, pp.1021–24. https://doi.org/10.1111/tmi.12132

Toivanen, Hannes; Hyvönen, Jukka; Wevelsiep, Mathias; and Metsäniemi, Mika (2011) 'Mobile Birth Registration in Liberia: CMI Project Mid-term Review', VTT Technical Research Centre of Finland.

UNICEF (1998) 'UNICEF on Deficient Birth Registration in Developing Countries', *Population and Development Review*, vol.24, pp.659–64.
https://doi.org/10.2307/2808179

UNICEF (2013) 'Every Child's Birth Right: Inequities and Trends in Birth Registration', Final report, New York: UNICEF.
https://data.unicef.org/resources/every-childs-birth-right-inequities-and-trends-in-birth-registration

UNICEF (2015) 'Birth Registration: A Comparative Report Prepared for UNICEF', Final report, New York: UNICEF.

Virhiä, Tuulia; Roberts, Gama; Itälä, Timo; and Varpilah, Tornorlah (2010) 'Mobile Solution for Birth Registration in Liberia: A Case Study of Using ICT in State Building', 2010 Ninth International Conference on Mobile Business and 2010 Ninth Global Mobility Roundtable (ICMB-GMR), IEEE, Athens, Greece, pp.448–52.
https://doi.org/10.1109/ICMB-GMR.2010.29

White, Sarah C. (1992) *Arguing with the Crocodile: Gender and Class in Bangladesh*, London: Zed Books.

World Bank (2016) 'Incentives for Improving Birth Registration Coverage: A Review of the Literature', Technical report, Washington, DC: World Bank. https://openknowledge.worldbank.org/handle/10986/31827

12. Administrative decentralisation and its impacts on educational expenditure and student outcomes: evidence from Colombia

Valentina Chegwin, Isabela Munevar, and Fabio Sánchez

Summary

A substantial decentralisation reform occurred in Colombia school education in 2001. The government established an arbitrary rule that granted municipalities with a population greater than 100,000 almost complete autonomy to provide education services (certification). Going beyond some mechanisms identified in previous policy evaluations (such as a higher proportion of higher-quality teachers) we analysed how reform affected the investment of local resources in education and the distribution of the total budget in key areas of the school system. Certified municipalities experienced an increase in education expenditure, after discounting teachers' payroll, because of increased efficiency in the management of total resources, both locally raised and central government transfers. This allowed higher expenditures in school infrastructure, education quality, and other education-related programmes, all key components of education policy. In addition, after 2002 the competitiveness of public schools increased in certified municipalities, compared to non-certified areas. Achieving better student outcomes was primarily explained by changes in the allocation of resources in certified municipalities that resulted in increased efficiency after gaining autonomy. Lastly, certification enhances competitiveness of public schools as against private ones.

How to cite this book chapter:

Chegwin, Valentina; Munevar, Isabela and Sánchez, Fabio (2023) 'Administrative decentralisation and its impacts on educational expenditure and student outcomes: evidence from Colombia', in: Faguet, Jean-Paul and Pal, Sarmistha (eds) *Decentralised Governance: Crafting Effective Democracies Around the World*, London: LSE Press, pp. 335–369. https://doi.org/10.31389/lsepress.dlg.l
License: CC BY 4.0

Since the 1980s Colombia has undergone a progressive process of administrative and political decentralisation that allowed the enactment of the election of mayors in 1986 and of governors in the early 1990s (Falleti 2005; Falleti 2010). As a consequence of the 1991 constitution, resources transferred from the central government to departments and municipalities began to grow rapidly in the early 1990s. But, later in the decade, the nation's fiscal situation became critical, which triggered a set of reforms in 2001 aimed at reducing the public deficit. Among them was a decentralisation reform that limited the growth of resources transferred from the central government to subnational governments and altered the distribution of transfers across municipalities. A set of municipalities became officially decentralised, which meant that they received higher transfers from the central government and greater responsibilities in the delivery of public services.

One of the core laws of the reform (Law 715/2001) shifted the management of public education to either municipalities or departments. Starting in 2002, municipalities with 100,000 or more inhabitants became 'certified in education', which conferred on them the responsibility for supervising, planning, and delivering public education in their territories. Their duties included managing central government transfers, teacher hiring and transfers, and other education-related programmes to improve both school student enrolment rates and education quality. Municipalities with fewer than 100,000 inhabitants were not certified, and their public education activities remained a departmental-level responsibility. Becoming certified meant transitioning from receiving and managing a lower amount of transfers, and being subject to departmental supervision, to having greater managerial and financial autonomy. By contrast, non-certified municipalities gave up their already-limited powers to their respective department (Bonet, Pérez, and Ayala 2014; Brutti 2020).

We first describe the educational decentralisation process in Colombia, including some background on the pre-reform scenario and the technical implications of the reform in the public delivery of education across municipalities in the country. We next expand the slim existing literature on the reform's impact (for example, Elacqua et al. (2021) and Pritchett (2014); see also the Annex to this chapter) by exploring some previously untapped channels that account for part of the improved student outcomes. Elacqua et al. (2021) found positive impacts of decentralisation on academic achievement and enrolment, but only explored a few of the underlying mechanisms such as improved teacher hiring and increased tax collection, which only account for a small part of the observed changes (see Annex, Table 12D). Our research builds upon their findings by identifying the ways in which decentralisation contributes to these improvements, specifically in relation to municipal educational spending. We also delve deeper into the effects on school enrolment by comparing the increase in public primary and secondary school enrolment to that of private schools, indicating a heightened competitiveness in the public education system.

We find that, beyond improving student outcomes, allotting autonomy to local governments strengthened the competitiveness of the public school system vs private institutions. This study adds to the existing literature by filling in the gap in understanding how decentralisation leads to improved educational outcomes and contributes to the ongoing debate on the most effective ways to improve education delivery. Our results suggest that the mechanisms associated with these improvements primarily relate to efficiency gains in the management and allocation of resources in newly autonomous certified municipalities. Our results thus contribute to the existing literature by addressing the gap in understanding the relationship between decentralisation and improved educational outcomes, thus adding to the ongoing discourse on the most effective methods to improve education.

12.1 Decentralisation in Colombia

In the mid-1980s, Colombia initiated a process of gradual decentralisation that started with political decentralisation in 1986 with the election of mayors of the 1,121 municipalities and continued in 1991 with the election of the governors of the country's 32 departments (each spanning many municipalities) by popular vote. Prior to these changes, mayors were appointed by governors and the governors by the president (Cortés 2010). In 1993, with the enactment of Law 60, the process of administrative decentralisation deepened and both municipalities and departments assumed greater responsibilities in the delivery of education, health, and potable water and sewage (Faguet and Sanchez 2009; Faguet and Sanchez 2014). This reform was accompanied by a significant increase in central government transfers to departments (known as the Situado Fiscal) and municipalities (the Municipal Share). Law 60 specified that municipalities were to oversee the management of preschool, primary, and secondary education services. In addition, municipalities should allocate resources to finance school construction and education programmes and projects and oversee and evaluate the delivery of educational services. The responsibilities of departments included the same roles as the municipalities, which entailed a great deal of coordination between the two levels of government. In addition, departments were also put in charge of the hiring, training, and ranking of teachers, as well as their assignment across municipalities. Teacher payrolls were to be paid by departments, financed with central government transfers to them (Bonet, Pérez, and Ayala 2014; Borjas and Acosta 2000).

The absence of a clear delineation of the responsibilities of each level of government generated an overlapping of functions that blurred lines of accountability. For example, prior to the 2001 reform, teachers were in fact paid by both departments and municipalities. Estimates by Borjas and Acosta (2000) indicated that the department payrolls covered 85–90 per cent of all public school teachers. Municipalities hired and paid the remaining 10–15 per cent, and in addition assigned teachers across schools within their jurisdiction. In many cases the entities put in charge of certain educational services did not have enough resources and legal authority to fulfil their responsibilities. For example, municipalities had a key role in the management of public schools, but they had very limited authority to appoint or dismiss staff (Borjas and Acosta 2000). In practice, during the 1990s and until 2002, departments performed the chief role in the administrative decentralisation of education. They also received a higher percentage of the central government transfers earmarked for education.

The 2001 Decentralisation Reform of Education

However, by the late 1990s, the structure of administrative decentralisation and central government transfers associated with it had become fiscally unsustainable, given its increasing cost. The Colombian economic and fiscal crisis of 1999 sparked a reform of the system of central government transfers to subnational entities. However, the reform required a set of constitutional and legal changes and involved a great deal of political and technical discussions. Law 715 was enacted in 2001, and since then, with some modifications, it has been the main regulatory framework of Colombia's administrative decentralisation. The reform limited the annual growth of central government transfers and tried to fix the shortcomings of Law 60 regulations, mainly by simplifying the overlapping responsibilities between departments and municipalities (Bonet, Perez, and Ayala 2014; Brutti 2020).

Under Law 715, administrative decentralisation and the supervision, planning, and delivery of education began to be managed by certified territorial entities (Entidades Territoriales Certificadas – ETCs), which could be either departments (at regional level) or municipalities (at local level). The departments managed most of the supervision, planning, and delivery roles for the non-certified municipalities within their jurisdiction. The law established that certification would be granted to all municipalities with more than 100,000 inhabitants at the end of 2002, of which there were 46. In addition, after 2003, municipalities not initially certified in 2002 were allowed to become so if an evaluation by their supervising regional department found that they had the technical, administrative, and financial capacity to manage the provision of education despite having fewer than 100,000 inhabitants (Ministerio de Educación Nacional 2005). Seventeen more municipalities became certified through this process.

As for teachers, Law 715 established that certified entities had the legal authority to hire principals and teachers, although owing to resource constraints the Ministry of Education imposed restrictions on the number that could be hired. These limits were implemented to avoid the disorderly increase in teacher payrolls characteristic of the 1990s (Congreso de Colombia 2000; Duarte 2001). Before 2002, the hiring of teachers and principals by the departments occurred after a determination of eligibility based on the credentials of the applicants (degrees, experience) and interviews.

Once teachers were deemed eligible, the educational authority assigned the new teachers to the department's schools based on the number of available vacancies (Brutti and Sanchez 2022; Ome 2013). This credential-based system was replaced in 2002 by an exam-based system under which the candidate applied to become a teacher in a specific certified entity. Candidates were required to pass the subject exam with a minimum score (60/100) and, once that requirement was met, the candidate would take a psychometric test, meet credential requirements, and be interviewed. Eligible new teachers then chose schools among the available vacancies. Certified entities placed applicants into vacancies based on the rankings of eligible teachers.

Once staff were in the system, the educational authority of each certified entity had the legal authority to reassign teachers within the entity. Departments assigned teachers across multiple non-certified municipalities in their area, according to the teachers' ranking and preference across these jurisdictions. More advantaged and high-performing schools were often chosen first by the highest-scoring teachers, so the low-performing teachers were often assigned to underachieving, isolated, and disadvantaged schools. Certified entities could also hire temporary teachers if they deemed it necessary. A high percentage of these teachers either did not undergo the eligibility process or did not pass the mandatory exams.

Certified entities tended to have no restrictions either on the use of their diverse sources of funding (for example, their own local taxes, debt, or dividends from public companies) or on how they distributed resources to programmes or interventions aimed at improving educational outcomes. Likewise, non-certified municipalities could add their own resources for the educational inputs they considered important. Such inputs could cover (i) furniture, texts, libraries, didactic, and audiovisual materials; (ii) improvement of school management; (iii) construction, maintenance, and adaptation of infrastructure; (iv) public services and operation; (v) improvement of working conditions of teachers; and (vi) non-teaching staff. Certified entities could attract teachers to schools in their jurisdiction by improving working conditions and giving incentives to high-performing candidates. These municipalities could also allocate resources for school transportation and school meal programmes (Ministerio de Educación Nacional 2002).

The structure of the central government transfers for education

Between 1993 and 2022 the distribution of transfers to subnational entities in Colombia operated under two legal and regulatory frameworks. Under Law 60 of 1993, 60 per cent of total transfers to departments (Situado Fiscal) had to be allocated to education and 20 per cent to health. In addition, 30 per cent of central government transfers to all municipalities (Participación Municipal) were earmarked for education and the rest to other social services and local running costs. The distribution of transfers across municipalities depended upon population, poverty rates, and many other variables.

Under Law 715 in 2001, coming after the economic and fiscal crisis of the late 1990s, central government transfers – known as the General System of Revenue Sharing (Sistema General de Participaciones) – were set to finance the provision of social services in general, and public education in particular, according to the responsibilities assigned under decentralisation. The structure of central government transfers to subnational entities expressed in Law 60 was radically changed. Law 715 introduced a new set of rules to distribute monies paid under the General System of Revenue Sharing (SGP). The total amount of transfers would grow at a fixed annual rate of 2 per cent and fund the provision of education, health, and water and sanitation services. Up to 2022, the legislation stated that 58.5 per cent of the SGP total must be allocated to education, and 90 per cent of that 58.5 per cent (or just under 53 per cent of the total) was to be distributed across 'certified' entities depending on the total number of students and their regional costs, as well as on national objectives for enrolment growth. These funds covered personnel costs (teachers and administrative staff) and could also be used to contract private schools when places for students in public schools were in short supply. The remaining 10 per cent of central government transfers for education were distributed across municipalities and allocated to quality improvement (for example, school transportation, school meals, utilities, minor school construction, school computers, and teacher training) (Alvarez et al. 2018).

Figure 12.1 presents the evolution of per capita central government transfers to departments and municipalities using the Law 715 classification of 'certified' and 'not-certified' entities for the period 1994–2015. It is immediately apparent how profoundly the 2001 reform altered the distribution of central government transfers (Figure 12.1a). In the 1996–2002 period, the large municipalities (certified in 2002) received the same per capita transfers for education as those that would become non-certified. However, in 2003 per capita transfers for non-certified municipalities abruptly declined, while transfers for certified municipalities and departments sharply increased (Figure 12.1b).

Still, despite the fall in transfers from the central government to non-certified municipalities, overall transfers and transfers for education spending were much higher for non-certified municipalities, as they depended on their transfers from the central government in addition to the departments' transfers. This change entailed that certified municipalities did acquire more independence in the administration of their resources, but that the change did not mean an increase in total transfers received beyond the resources available for non-certified municipalities. This detail is crucial when thinking about the impacts of decentralisation because any effects caused by the 2021 reform can be interpreted as an effect of gained autonomy at the local level, and not as a consequence of an increase in the absolute value of the transfers received.

To help readers' appreciation of these differences between certified and non-certified municipalities, the Annex to this chapter (especially Tables 12A, 12B, and 12C and their accompanying text) give additional background infor-

Figure 12.1: Central government transfers before and after the administrative decentralisation reform

a. Total central government transfers per capita

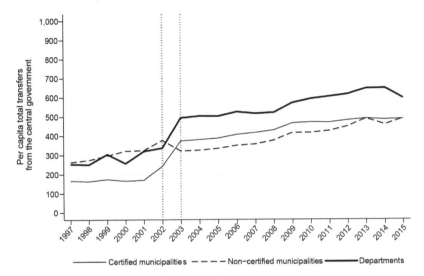

b. Transfers for education per capita

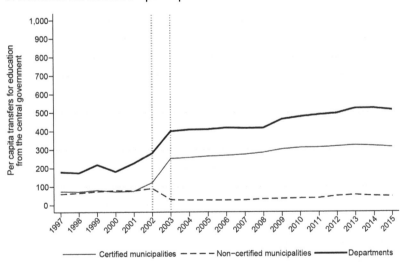

Source: National Planning Department. Author's calculations.
Note: Per capita educational transfers in thousands of Colombian 2018 pesos.

mation on the differences between the two authorities in terms of their social characteristics, their inputs into education and their school students' performance on various test scores.

The second part of the Annex also looks at previous work in this field, describing the findings of Elacqua et al. (2021), who evaluated the impact of administrative decentralisation on educational outcomes, including student enrolment and student achievement, and on the contractual and educational characteristics of teachers. Their results suggest that the decentralisation process in Colombia substantially altered the way in which local governments assigned and executed their resources. While certified municipalities had the mandate to plan, manage, and deliver the provision of education and seem to have successfully improved enrolment, quality, and equity in their school systems, departments had a similar mandate (and received higher per capita transfers from the central government to deliver education in the non-certified municipalities), but showed lower educational outcomes. The reform had positive and significant effects on enrolment and student performance and Elacqua et al. (2021) attributed these effects to a greater percentage of teachers with higher education and improved fiscal efforts in certified territories.

Figure 12.2: Total transfers (from both central government and departments) to municipalities before and after the administrative decentralisation reform

a. Total transfers from both central government and departments per capita

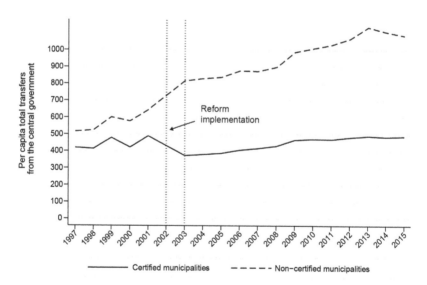

Source: Elacqua, Munevar, Sanchez, and Santos (2021).
Note: Per capita transfers in thousands of Colombian pesos as at 2018. (For this figure, 500,000 COP = US$105 US approximately per capita; and COP 1,000,000 = US$208 approx, per capita.) Until 2002 all municipalities received central governments' transfers both directly and indirectly through departmental spending. Since 2003, certified municipalities have received only direct transfers from the central government, while non-certified municipalities receive central government transfers both directly and indirectly through departmental spending.

(Continued)

Figure 12.2: Continued

b. Transfers for education from both central government and departments (in thousands of Colombian pesos)

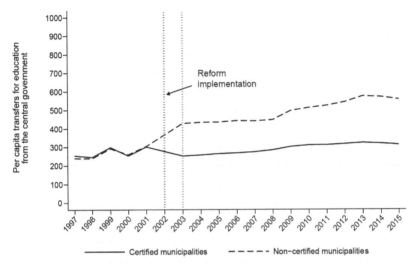

Note: Per capita educational transfers in thousands of Colombian 2018 pesos. Until 2002 all municipalities received central governments' transfers for education both directly and indirectly through departmental spending in education. Since 2003 certified municipalities have received only direct transfers for education from the central government, while non-certified municipalities receive central government transfers for education both directly and indirectly through departmental spending in education.

It seems plausible to assume that by creating greater municipal autonomy certification prompted significant efficiency gains, by lowering transaction costs due to more and better information, more transparent negotiation processes, and rapid adjustment to correct errors (Pritchett 2014; Pritchett and Pande 2006). Local governments in certified municipalities might have gained the power to use their resources in a way that served the needs of their particular populations, while the freedom to better tailor their budgets might have enhanced the efficiency of the resources spent. Improved teacher hiring seems likely to be only part of the story, and other pieces of the puzzle (both mechanisms and longer-term outcomes) may explain the superior path observed in certified municipalities years after the reform's implementation of the reform.

12.2 Analysing the efficiency effects of decentralisation on outcomes

We next focus on breaking down the 'efficiency' hypothesis – namely, the proposition that part of the effects of the reform came from a 'better' or more efficient use of both central government transfers and own local resources in

Figure 12.3: How the ramifications of certification operated after the 2001 decentralisation reform – outcomes and mechanisms

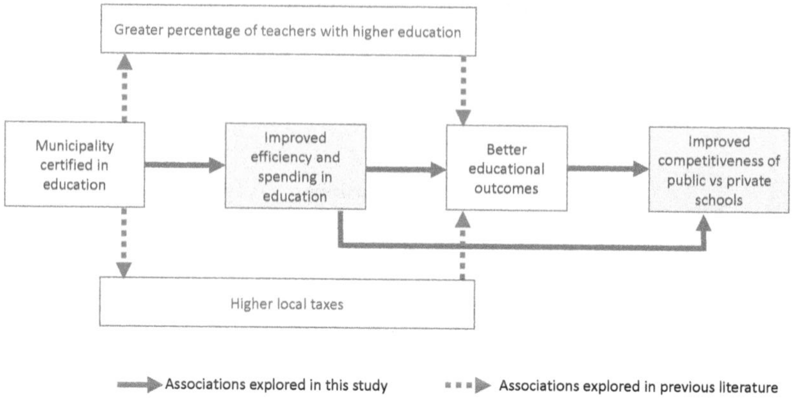

Source: Authors' creation.

certified municipalities. More specifically, we explored the effect of the reform on (i) the amount of local resources that certified municipalities spent on education, and (ii) the way local governments assigned and spent their resources. We found that while these municipalities were able to spend more in important educational programmes, they did not require additional fiscal efforts to do so. We then analysed the mediating effect of increased efficiency and improved allocation of resources on student outcomes, and we discuss below how all these existing channels translated into a stronger public school system.

We propose that being certified (understood as the ability to assign and manage education resources autonomously) produced efficiency gains because decision makers gained more access to information about local educational needs and a stronger capacity to allocate resources effectively (see Figure 12.3). Additionally, this gained autonomy might have allowed certified entities to redistribute and invest their available resources (both locally raised and central government transfers) across key areas of the education system in a way that increased the productivity of the resources spent and more accurately served the needs of their municipalities. We also hypothesise that both an improved education system and the more efficient use of resources triggered more permanent, or structural, transformations in the way that local communities related to their public school system, promoting parental demand and higher student enrolment in local public schools.

To evaluate the effects and mechanisms of the decentralisation reform, we used four different sources of data: (i) the population census of 1993 which forecasted 2001 municipal population sizes, used to determine which municipalities became certified; (ii) a panel database, constructed by the Center of Economic Studies of Los Andes University, that contains data from different public sources and contains diverse geographic, demographic, and socio-economic characteristics for the 1,121 Colombian municipalities; (iii) the Territorial Administrative Report – Formato Unico Territorial (FUT) – which contains detailed reported annual expenditures in each municipality, including itemised expenditures in education; and (iv) a database from the National Bureau of Statistics (Departamento Administrativo Nacional de Estadística, DANE), with information on the numbers of students by level of education (preschool, primary, and secondary) in all Colombian public and private schools since 1996.

To evaluate the effects of the decentralisation reform, we exploited the quasi-experimental treatment of the 'certified' municipalities using a variant of differences-in-differences (DD) models that controlled for municipality and year fixed effects, and for department-year interactions, to account for any educational policies and interventions in non-certified municipalities that could be carried out by the departmental authorities. Because certification in 2002 was arbitrarily assigned based on a population size cut-off, municipalities could not 'choose' to be certified. Given the impossibility of self-selection, as well as the existence of parallel trends in the pre-reform period (which can be observed in Figures 12.8 and our Annex Figures 12.A and 12.B), we justify the use of a DD model to estimate the effects of the reform on our outcomes.

The difference-in-differences model we estimated was the following:

$$Y_{m,t} = \beta_m M_m + \beta_t T_t + \beta_3 Certified_m * post2002_t + \beta_{dt} Departmentx Year + u_{mt} \quad [1]$$

where $Y_{m,t}$ represents the outcomes of study – local and itemised expenditures in education and share of public vs private student enrolment. Our key explanatory variable is the interaction between the two $Certified_m * post2003_t$. $Certified$ is a dummy that takes a value 1 when a municipality was certified after 2003; Post2002 is a dummy that takes a value 1 in the years after 2002; it is zero for pre-2002 years. We also include M_m to account for the time-invariant municipal fixed effects, year fixed effects T_t and department-level time-varying unobserved factors Department × Year; the latter control for any annual shocks and educational departmental policies that may affect educational spending at a local level. Ceteris paribus, our coefficient of interest is β_3, which captures the effect of a municipality being certified after 2002 on $Y_{m,t}$ compared to those not being certified. Note, however, that the control group of non-certified municipalities did not remain unchanged after 2002; these became centralised after 2002. As such, it is difficult for us to capture the pure effect of decentralisation. We can thus estimate only the differential effects of becoming decentralised in education compared to being centralised after 2002. The estimated treatment effects as captured by $Certified_m * post2002_t$ can still be biased because of the unobserved municipality-level time-varying characteristics, for example whether it is allied with the departmental government or not, that determines that a municipality may receive additional direct investments from it; as such we need to be cautious about interpreting these estimates.

We also test the robustness of Equation [1] using the standard differ-ence-in-difference equation specification as follows:

$$Y_{m,t} = \beta_1 Certified_m + \beta_2 post2002_t + \beta_3 Certified_m * post2002_t$$
$$+ \beta_m M_m + \beta_{dt} Departmentx Year + u_{m,t} \qquad [2]$$

How more autonomy in public education affected subnational education expenditures

We theorise that certified municipalities gained the autonomy to prioritise and assign education resources in a way that better responded to the needs of the communities they serve, while non-certified municipalities remained subject to the decisions and mandates of their government at the department level. Previous literature has identified an increase in local taxes post-reform, yet we argue that an increase in per capita local taxes does not necessarily translate into higher local resources spent on education. More autonomous management of education-related resources could promote education goals within local governments policy agenda without necessarily requiring addi-tional fiscal efforts for education, if resources are efficiently used. With equal or even reduced resources, certified municipalities might be able to attain equal or better results, generating increased productivity per peso spent. So, testing for efficiency gains consists of exploring whether local governments assigned their locally raised resources to education-related expenses before and after the reform.

To explore whether the reform affected the total amount of local resources spent in education, and the way municipalities assigned resources across the different components of education policy, we first analysed the percent-age of local resources assigned to education, and then we looked at trends in expenditure by item across certified and non-certified municipalities. The information on total and itemised expenditures was obtained from the FUTs, annual administrative reports giving disaggregated information on which services municipalities spend their resources on. For this exercise, we homo-genised all education-related expenses by municipality, since 1994. By creat-ing this standardised panel, we were able to do year-to-year and expenditures comparisons across municipalities. To our knowledge, we are the first study to clean and standardise this administrative data in a way that allows across time and territorial analysis. To study changes in particular expenses before and after the reform, between certified and non-certified municipalities we looked at: (i) per capita spending in school infrastructure; (ii) per capita spending in teacher salaries; (iii) per capita spending in education quality; and (iv) per capita spending in other education programmes. School infrastructure, teacher quality, investments aimed at improving education quality, and other education-related programmes are all key components of education pol-icy and have been linked to improved school performance and educational

Table 12.1: School expenditures by category

Category	Expenses
Infrastructure	• School infrastructure related studies, designs, and consulting services • School space improvements and interventions • Constructions • Extensions, adaptations, and improvements of educational infrastructure • Maintenance of educational infrastructure • Payment of public services • Improvements and provision of teaching materials and resources for learning • Improvement of accessibility conditions • Institutional endowment • Leasing of properties intended for the provision of education-related services
Other education-related programmes	• School feeding programmes • School transportation • Other education-related school programmes
Education quality	• Training for teachers and teaching managers • Design and implementation of quality improvement plans • Institutional modernisation • Implementation of information systems • Connectivity

outcomes (Belmonte et al. 2020; Cuesta, Glewwe, and Krause 2016; Goldhaber and Brewer 1996; Wang and Fawzi 2020).

To explore differences in the management of total resources spent across municipalities, we looked at the total expenditure in key education items and the distribution across these categories. Specifically, we grouped reported school expenditures into three main categories: infrastructure investments, investments in other education-related programmes, and investments to improve education quality. These are summarised in Table 12.1.

One of the corollaries of Law 715 was that certified municipalities would receive greater transfers, mainly designated to hiring teachers and managing their school assignments. Complemented by the municipalities' own resources, these transfers raised the total resources for education in certified municipalities. And after 2002, local governments could manage these resources freely, as long as they complied with the teacher requirements of their respective school systems. Figure 12.4a shows how the expenditure on teacher salaries increased in certified municipalities but decreased in non-certified areas as this responsibility was transferred to departmental governments. Clearly, certified municipalities managed significantly more resources after the reform than non-certified municipalities did. But, since resources were primarily destined for teacher salaries, it did not necessarily imply higher per capita education expenditure in these municipalities. Elacqua et al. (2021) inferred that higher transfers could boost fiscal efforts in decentralised territories to increase the share of local resources allocated to education. Contrary to their beliefs, we test for increases in locally raised resources allocated to education and argue that, instead of a boost in available additional resources, autonomy gained by certified municipalities allowed them to assign their resources in a more efficient manner. The latter would translate bigger gains by per capita peso spent, without the need to assign more local resources to education policy. This is explained below.

Figure 12.4b shows the assignment of locally collected resources to education in both certified and non-certified municipalities. After 2002, the total amount of per capita local resources spent on education at first fell sharply in certified municipalities, but almost immediately increased again. It then fluctuated but remained somewhat below the resources spent in non-certified municipalities in the years that followed. This could not be attributed to increased fiscal efforts for education in certified municipalities. Instead, the performance of the education system was highly dependent on the way the certified municipalities managed the central government transfers and the assignment of all resources to the different items of their education agendas.

Figure 12.4: Distribution of per capita expenditures in certified and non-certified municipalities, in thousands of Colombian pesos

a. Per capita expenditures on teachers' salaries

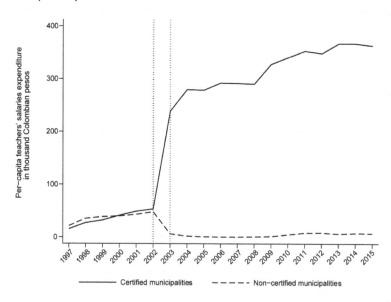

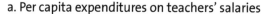

(*Continued*)

Figure 12.4: Continued

b. Per capita education expenditure from local resources

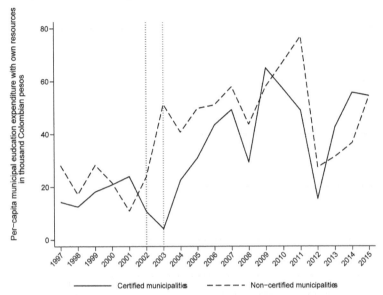

Source: Authors' calculation. FUT database from the Colombian National Planning Department (1997–2015).
Note: Panel a shows per capita transfers for teacher salaries in thousands of Colombian 2018 pesos.
Panel b depicts average municipal per capita expenditure with local resources (that is, total expenditure minus transfers from the central government). Municipal education expenditure was reported in thousands by the municipalities and was then divided by the municipal population and transformed to 2018 Colombian pesos. Data from 2010 was not included due to missing information.

Figure 12.5 shows that before 2003 non-certified municipalities (serving smaller populations than certified authorities) spent substantially more per capita resources in school infrastructure, education-related programmes, and education quality investments. After 2003, the gaps in all three of these expenditures were significantly reduced given the growth in certified municipalities' spending, especially in infrastructure and other programmes.

The expansion of total resources in certified municipalities cannot be attributed to the expansion of *locally raised* resources for education, since Figure 12.4b shows that certified municipalities spent less than non-certified municipalities. The central government transfers that the certified entities received after 2002 responded to projected teacher costs in those territories. If these municipalities became more efficient in hiring and assigning teachers, then they freed up resources for other types of educational spending. By contrast, efficiencies in the use of teacher salaries were not possible for non-certified municipalities because they lacked financial autonomy.

Figure 12.5: Trends in per capita education-related expenses in certified and non-certified municipalities, in thousands of Colombian pesos

a. School infrastructure

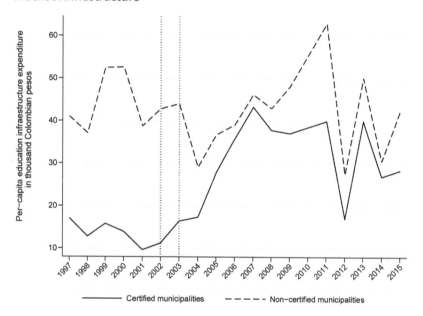

b. Other education-related programmes

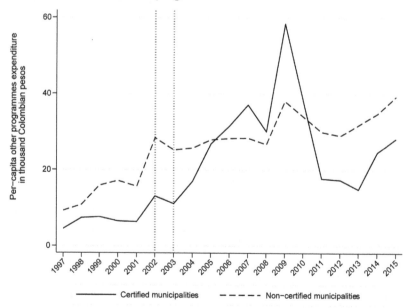

(*Continued*)

Figure 12.5: Continued

c. Education quality

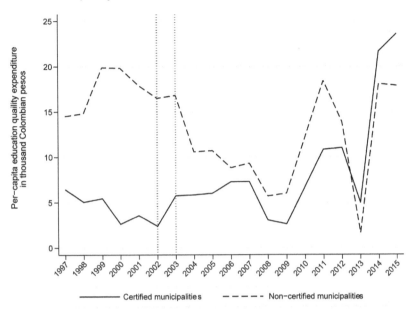

Source: FUT database from the Colombian National Planning Department (1997–2015).
Note: Expenditure in the different education components was reported in thousands
by the municipalities and then divided by the municipal population and transformed to
2018 Colombian pesos. Data from 2010 was not included due to missing information.

Hence, if non-certified municipalities wished to expand spending in
educational programmes, they needed to make a greater fiscal effort than certified municipalities.

For both types of municipality, Figure 12.6 shows the total per capita
expenditure in education after subtracting teacher salaries. Consistent with
our hypothesis, we observed an increase in total resources available in certified municipalities that cannot be explained by an expansion in local
resources. In non-certified municipalities, the resources maintained the trend
observed before the reform, while the growth in certified municipalities suggests that the lower teachers' payroll per capita allowed for some resources to
be allocated to other education expenditures. Put together, the trends in itemised expenditures and total expenditures after teacher salaries suggest that the
reform did promote changes in the way certified municipalities assigned their
education resources.

Since our preliminary analysis pointed towards efficiency gains arising from
increased autonomy after certification, we further tested our hypothesis using
a difference-in-difference model as per Equation [1]. All per capita outcome
variables had a logarithmic transformation for ease of interpretation. Table 12.2
shows the coefficient estimate of Certified×Post2002 as per Equation [1].

Figure 12.6: Per capita total expenditure in education net of teacher salaries, in thousands of Colombian pesos

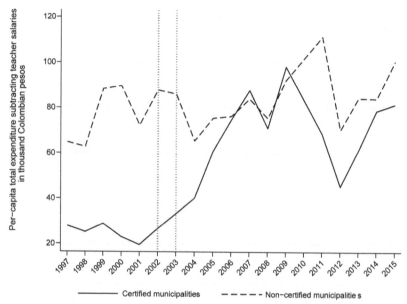

Source: Authors' creation. FUT database from the Colombian National Planning Department. 1997–2015.
Note: This figure depicts the total average municipal per capita expenditure after subtracting teachers' salaries. Municipal education expenditure was reported in thousands by the municipalities and was then divided by the municipal population and deflated to 2018 Colombian pesos. Data from 2010 was not included due to missing information.

The estimated coefficients of the key interaction term Certified×Post2002 in Table 12.2 show that the proportion of own resources spent in education as well as per capita expenditure with own resources fell in newly autonomous certified municipalities after 2002 relative to newly centralised non-certified municipalities. In contrast, per capita expenditure net of teacher salaries, increased for school infrastructure, education quality, and other programmes in certified (relative to non-certified) municipalities after 2002, indicating a reallocation of total expenditure into productive education items that help boosting student performance. We get similar results using the alternative specification Equation [2] as summarised in the Annex, Tables 12E and 12F. Taken together, certified municipalities were able to reallocate resources from teacher payroll to other educational expenses according to student needs, in this case for school infrastructure, and other quality expenses, after gaining autonomy after 2002. That budget flexibility is not possible for centralised non-certified municipalities that do not have the autonomy to assign their educational resources. Quality and infrastructure investments are likely to respond, and be tailored to, the specific needs of the schools and their members, and have been found to boost educational outcomes and enrolment

Table 12.2: Average effects of certification in education on measures of municipal education expenditure

	Dependent variable (in natural log)		
	Proportion of own resources in total expenditure	Per capita expenditure with own resources	Per capita total expenditure minus teacher salaries
Certified×Post2002	−0.385*** (0.014)	−0.457*** (0.112)	0.637*** (0.061)
N	18,289	18,555	18,555

	Dependent variable		
	Per capita infrastructure expenditure	Per capita quality expenditure	Per capita expenditure in other programmes
Certified×Post2002	0.713*** (0.068)	0.715*** (0.072)	0.301*** (0.067)
N	18,555	18,555	18,555

Source: Colombian National Planning Department. Authors' calculations.
Note: The table shows the estimated coefficient of certified×Post2002 using difference-in-difference Equation [1]. In all models the number of years = 18; the number of municipalities = 1070; and fixed effects are included for Year; Municipality; and Department × Year. Robust standard errors in italics and parentheses. ***$p < 0.01$, **$p < 0.05$, *$p < 0.1$.

by improving learning conditions (Belmonte et al. 2020; Cuesta, Glewwe, and Krause 2016).

In the Annex to this chapter, Figures 12.A and 12.B show the estimated coefficients of year–certification interactions to our estimations: per capita education expenditure from locally raised resources, per capita total education expenditure net of teacher salary, and per capita education expenditure on key accounts, respectively. Since the resource allocation scheme was the same for all municipalities before the reform, we should not observe significant differences in these expenditure items between certified and non-certified municipalities prior to 2003. The pre-reform coefficients in both sets of figures confirm no significant pre-existing differences in various per capita education expenditure items between non-certified and certified municipalities, which in turn validate the existence of parallel trends before the enactments of the reform. This is essential for the consistency of the difference-in-difference estimates shown in Table 12.2.

Furthermore, these figures show the long-term effects of the 2002 reform. Although the effect of per capita expenditure remained close to zero in the years following the reform, per capita education expenditure after deducting teacher salaries remained positive and significant for at least a decade after the certified municipalities gained financial autonomy over the management of their resources. In addition to the higher expenditures in key items of municipal education policy shown in Table 12.1, Figure 12.B shows that these indicators remained above the pre-reform levels in certified municipalities way past 2003.

Decentralisation and enrolment in public and private schools

Investments in school infrastructure, and resources destined to education-related programmes and education quality, have all been associated with improved student outcomes (Hong and Zimmer 2016; Wall et al. 2022). So, increases in these investments boost factors that the previous literature has associated with positive effects on student performance and enrolment. Accordingly, we hypothesised that more structural, or long-term gains would be likely to occur as an improved public school system eventually attracted parents who before would have opted to enrol their children in private school. If so, then the enrolment composition of the public and private school systems should change in certified municipalities.

To assess the effects of the decentralisation process on the composition of public vs private student enrolment, we used data from the C-600 database of the National Bureau of Statistics, which contains information on the number of students by level of education (preschool, primary, and secondary) in all Colombian schools, by year, both private and public. We calculated a two-way fixed effect model leveraging on the variation in the proportion of enrolment in public schools as a percentage of total enrolment, before and after the 2001 reform and between certified and non-certified municipalities.

Figure 12.7 shows percentage shares of public enrolment in total enrolment, in certified and non-certified municipalities, before and after the decentralisation reform. The proportion of public enrolment in certified municipalities was increasing before 2001, although rates were significantly below the rates of non-certified municipalities for both primary and secondary schools. After 2002, the growth of public enrolment in certified municipalities started accelerating, reducing the gap with non-certified municipalities. Public enrolment at the primary stage increased sharply in certified municipalities after 2002, but then fell away again compared to non-certified areas, reopening a large gap in Figure 12.7a. However, at the secondary stage Figure 12.7b shows that the immediate post-reform improvement in the share of public schools in certified municipalities was sustained in subsequent years.

Table 12.3 shows the coefficients of a difference-in-difference model that regresses municipal certification on primary and secondary public enrolment rates using Equation [1]. Each estimated coefficient is positive and statistically significant, indicating that certified (relative to non-certified) municipalities experienced significantly higher share of public enrolment after 2002. We obtain similar estimates when using Equation [2] as summarised in Annex Table 12G. Figure 12.8 further shows that certification had a positive effect on annual public enrolment in primary schools (panel a) and also a positive

Figure 12.7: Trends in the proportion public enrolment, as a proportion of total enrolment, in certified and non-certified municipalities

a. Primary enrolment

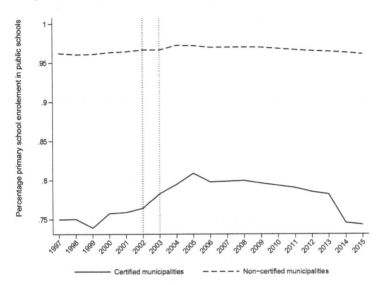

b. Secondary enrolment

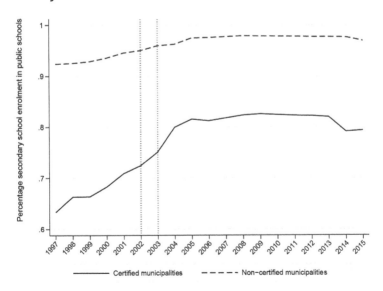

Source: The National Administrative Department of Statistics. Authors' calculations.
Note: This depicts the average percentage enrolment in primary and secondary school, of the total municipality enrolment from 1997 to 2015. Information from 2007 was omitted due to misreporting.

effect on public secondary enrolment (panel b), compared to non-certified municipalities, lending support to our view of the increased competitiveness of public schools.

Did increased expenditure (from increased efficiency in the use and allocation of resources) mediate the effect of certification on student performance and share of public enrolment? Table 12.4 shows the results of a regression of six different per capita municipal expenditure measures on high-school exit exam test scores and municipal enrolment rates, controlling for year, municipal, and departmental fixed effects. The exercise aimed to investigate whether the differential way in which certified municipalities spent their resources did

Table 12.3: Average effects of certification in education on proportion of public enrolment

	Dependent variable					
	Change in share of public enrolment		Change in share of primary public enrolment		Change in share of secondary public enrolment	
Certified×Post2002	0.055***	(0.003)	0.027***	(0.003)	0.090***	(0.004)
N	20,214		20,214		20,119	

Figure 12.8: The effect of certification on the proportion of public primary and secondary enrolment

a. Primary enrolment

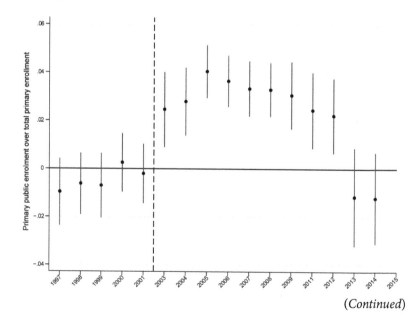

(*Continued*)

Figure 12.8: Continued

b. Secondary enrolment

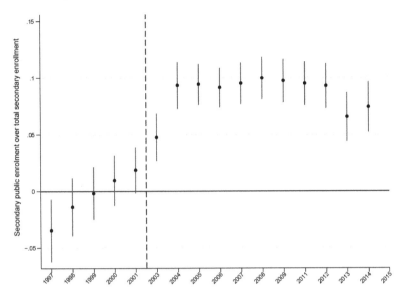

Source: The National Administrative Department of Statistics. Authors' calculations.
Note: These graphs show the estimated coefficients of a difference-in-difference estimation that regresses the public education participation of total enrolment on municipal
certification for each year from 1997 to 2015. Dots represent estimated coefficients and
the lines their corresponding confidence intervals. Municipal investment had a logarithmic transformation for the ease of interpretation.

explain part of the improvements in student academic performance and public enrolment rates in certified municipalities.

We found that per capita measures of total expenditure net of teachers' salaries, plus infrastructure and quality expenditure were strongly correlated with
both student performance and enrolment rates. An increase in total per capita expenditure in other education programmes did not show any significant
impact on academic performance but it did affect enrolment rates in both
primary and secondary schools. The results in Table 12.4 serve as evidence
to validate the view that flexibilities in expenditure decisions and efficiencies
in the use of resources in certified municipalities have been strong drivers of
the improvements in local education systems in certified municipalities compared to non-certified municipalities after 2002.

Conclusions

Our study capitalised on the major educational decentralisation reform that
occurred in Colombia in 2001, where the government established an arbitrary rule that granted municipalities with a population greater than 100,000

Table 12.4: Associations between local expenditures, student outcomes, and public enrolment rates

Explanatory variables	Dependent variable			
	SABER 11 scores		Share of public enrolment	
Per capita total expenditure subtracting teacher salaries	0.049***	(0.018)	0.014***	(0.002)
Per capita expenditure in school infrastructure	0.028**	(0.012)	0.007***	(0.001)
Per capita expenditure in school quality	0.034***	(0.010)	0.004***	(0.001)
Per capita expenditure in other education programmes	−0.008	(0.014)	0.012***	(0.002)
N	18,321		18,554	
# Municipalities	1,068		1,070	

Explanatory variables	Share of public primary enrolment		Share of public secondary enrolment	
Per capita total expenditure subtracting teacher salaries	0.014***	(0.003)	0.009***	(0.002)
Per capita expenditure in school infrastructure	0.008***	(0.002)	0.004***	(0.001)
Per capita expenditure in school quality	0.005***	(0.001)	0.001	(0.001)
Per capita expenditure in other education programmes	0.009***	(0.002)	0.011***	(0.001)
N	18,554		18,554	
# Municipalities	1,070			

Source: Authors' calculations. Colombian National Planning Department, the National Administrative Department of Statistics.
Note: This table regresses high-school exit exam test scores and municipal enrolment rates on six different per capita municipal expenditure measures controlling for year, municipal and departmental fixed effects. Robust standard errors are shown in italics and parentheses. ***$p < 0.01$, **$p < 0.05$, *$p < 0.1$.
In all models: the number of years = 18; and fixed effects were applied for Year, Municipality, and Department × Year.

almost complete autonomy to provide education services (certification). Our four main findings are:

- Certified municipalities experienced efficiency gains that increased the productivity of educational expenditures. Why? We observe that after the reform:

- o Per-student transfers are lower in certified municipalities than in non-certified.
- o Per capita spending with locally raised resources is also lower in certified municipalities than in non-certified.
- o Certified municipalities have both higher student enrolment (Elacqua et al. 2021) and a higher share of public enrolment.
- Newly autonomous certified municipalities were able to increase their per capita expenditure (net of teachers' salaries) in key areas of education, such as infrastructure and other education-related programmes.
- Improvements made in efficiency and student outcomes increased the attractiveness of public versus private schools, thus increasing the share of total students enrolled in public institutions.

Our results suggest that the higher education expenditures did not come from increased fiscal efforts allotted to education but from efficiency gains enjoyed by certified municipalities in their use of available resources after gaining autonomy. As such, our work goes beyond Elacqua et al. (2021) and provides evidence on the mechanisms through which decentralisation improves educational outcomes, specifically through increased efficiency and better allocation of resources.

Annex: Background information on the characteristics and behaviours of certified and non-certified municipalities

We first outline some key differences between certified and non-certified areas and their schools systems, and then briefly consider previous work on the educational decentralisation reforms.

Social characteristics and school education inputs and performance

Given the fixed size rule of 100,000 people applied in 2002 for municipalities to become certified, they were on average larger than non-certified areas. Consistent with this size difference, Table 12A shows that certified municipalities were also on average more developed, as measured by the Municipality Development Index. They had lower levels of poverty, as measured by the Unsatisfied Basic Need Index. And on average certified municipalities were less unequal, as measured by the municipal Land GINI.

Table 12B shows some pre-reform differences on local education expenditures, broken down by development/poverty indicators between the two types of municipalities. Overall, non-certified municipalities sustained higher per capita investments in infrastructure, education quality, and other education programmes, compared to those municipalities that would become certified. Additionally, the share of enrolled students in public versus private schools was higher in non-certified municipalities.

Table 12A: Pre-reform development, poverty, and inequality in certified and non-certified municipalities, 2001

Index (2001 mean scores)	Certified (N = 45)	Non-certified (N = 986)	Estimated difference and (standard error)	
Municipal development Index	51.42	34.89	12.641***	(1.813)
Unsatisfied Basic Needs (UBN)	30.82	53.26	−18.790***	(3.532)
Land GINI	0.436	0.459	−0.009	(0.007)

Source: National Planning Department, CEDE municipal PANEL, and the National Administrative Department of Statistics (DANE). Authors' calculations.
Notes: The first two columns report 2001 mean of each variable for certified and non-certified municipalities.
The last column reports the estimated difference for each variable between certified and non-certified municipalities that results from an OLS regression that controls for the 2001 municipal population. Robust standard errors in italics and parentheses. ***$p < 0.01$, **$p < 0.05$, *$p < 0.1$.

Table 12B: Pre-reform local expenditures in education and public versus private school enrolment in certified and non-certified municipalities, 2001

Indicator	Certified (N = 45)	Non-certified (N = 986)	Difference and (standard error)	
Per capita infrastructure investment (log mean)	1.412	2.456	−0.479**	(0.194)
Per capita education quality investment (log mean)	0.772	1.699	−0.490**	(0.196)
Per capita investment in other education programmes (log mean)	0.947	1.496	−0.403**	(0.205)
Public school participation in local enrolment (mean)	0.709	0.955	−0.215***	(0.014)

Source: as per Table 12A.
Note: The first two columns report 2001 mean of each variable for certified and non-certified municipalities. The last column reports the estimated difference for each variable between certified and non-certified municipalities that results from an OLS regression that controls for the 2001 municipal population. Robust standard errors in italics and parentheses. *** $p<0.01$, **$p < 0.05$, *$p < 0.1$.

Regarding student outcomes, Table 12C shows that in 2001 students in municipalities that would become certified performed better than did students in non-certified municipalities, as measured by the SABER 11 standardised test (the Saber test is further described below). While in non-certified municipalities the enrolment rates in public primary schools were above that of certified municipalities, the rate of enrolment in public secondary schools was

Table 12C: Pre-reform student performance, enrolment, rural–urban ratios, and student–teacher ratios in certified and non-certified municipalities, 2001

Indicator	Certified (N = 45)	Non-certified (N = 986)	Difference and (standard errors)	
SABER 11 Math Score	49.80	48.79	0.817**	(0.377)
SABER 11 Total Score	49.50	47.25	1.768***	(0.587)
Public primary school enrolment rates	0.854	1.186	−0.254***	(0.052)
Public secondary school enrolment rates	0.417	0.388	0.047	(0.030)
Rural–urban student ratio	0.137	0.516	−0.304***	(0.041)
Student–teacher ratio	27.77	22.10	3.920***	(0.886)

Sources: as per Table A.1.
Note: The first two columns report the 2001 mean of each variable for certified and non-certified municipalities. The last column reports the estimated difference for each variable between certified and non-certified municipalities that results from an OLS regression that controls for the 2001 municipal population. Robust standard errors in parentheses. ***$p < 0.01$, **$p < 0.05$, *$p < 0.1$.

higher in the certified areas. Lastly, the ratio of rural to urban students was higher in non-certified municipalities, while the student–teacher ratio was higher in certified municipalities.

Previous work on how Colombia's reform changed education outcomes

What were the effects of the 2001 decentralisation reform on student and education system outcomes? And what mechanisms lie behind these effects? Colombia's 2001 decentralisation reform provides a unique research opportunity because it arbitrarily granted almost total administrative autonomy to one set of municipalities while almost totally reducing the autonomy of other municipalities, with no changes in political or fiscal decentralisation. This 'natural experiment' allowed the study of whether administrative decentralisation at the municipal level on local outcomes could translate into higher efficiency and performance in a quasi-experimental setting.

Elacqua et al. (2021) evaluated the impact of administrative decentralisation on educational outcomes, including student enrolment and student achievement, and on the contractual and educational characteristics of teachers. The 2001 reform affected the management of public education, including the appointment and allocation of teachers across schools, handling of programmes to reduce dropout rates and increase enrolment, distribution of financial resources to local schools, and evaluation of principals, among other tasks. It also affected the distribution of the central government transfers between municipalities and departments related to the delivery of public education but did not alter decentralisation in fiscal or political matters. Central government transfers for education were equal per capita in Colombian pesos for the municipalities that would be certified in 2001 and those that would not (see Figures 12.1 and 12.2 above). After 2002, certified municipalities gained more autonomy and received larger per capita transfers; non-certified municipalities lost autonomy and received smaller per capita transfers; and departments acquired stronger administrative powers over non-certified municipalities. This also meant that non-certified municipalities got larger per capita transfers than certified municipalities after adding direct transfers and indirect transfers received through departmental expenditure on the non-certified municipalities. This particular set-up provides an opportunity to evaluate the casual effects of administrative decentralisation in the territories that gained autonomy.

Elacqua et al. (2021) evaluated the effect of the 2001 decentralisation reform on the educational outcomes over which 'certified' municipalities had the autonomy to focus their efforts: student enrolment, teacher quality, and student achievement. Their difference-in-differences and regression discontinuity results showed that municipalities that became autonomous

Table 12D: Summary of the effects of municipal administrative decentralisation on education indicators and local taxes

Outcome	Measure	Coefficient	Interpretation
Academic performance	Exit-high-school Exam (standardised)	0.060***	Students in certified municipalities increased the Saber 11 test scores by 0.6 standard deviations
Enrolment	Enrolment in public schools (log)	0.087***	The growth in the number of enrolled students in certified municipalities in public schools was 10% higher
Teacher quality	Proportion of teachers with higher education	0.021***	The quality of teachers in certified municipalities (measured as the proportion with a college degree) was 2% higher
	Proportion of teachers with permanent contracts	0.041***	The proportion of teachers with permanent contracts was 4% higher in certified municipalities
Fiscal effort	Local taxes	0.044***	In certified municipalities, the growth of per capita local taxes was 4% higher

Source: Elacqua et al. (2021).
Note: Coefficients in column 3 were all estimated using a DD method.

in the delivery of public education after 2001 increased student enrolment, recruited a higher proportion of teachers with higher levels of education, and had students with higher achievement scores on standardised tests. Table 12D gives a summary of their main results.

Using a mediation analysis, Elacqua et al. (2021) found that a significant part of their findings (about 30 per cent of student performance) was explained by higher-quality teachers being hired in the newly decentralised municipalities. They also concluded that local taxes explained about 7 per cent of the difference in student performance and about 15 per cent of the boost they observed in student enrolment there. Still, the results also showed that these researchers' proposed mechanisms only explained a part of the improvements in education outcomes in certified municipalities, and that unknown channels accounted for 65 to 90 per cent of these effects.

Robustness check: Results from estimating Equation [2]

Table 12E

	Dependent variable		
	Proportion of own resources in total expenditure	Per capita expenditure with own resources	Per capita total expenditure minus teacher salaries
Certified×Post2002	−0.404*** (0.012)	−0.523*** (0.107)	0.683*** (0.061)
N	18,592	18,592	18,592

Table 12F

	Dependent variable		
	Per capita infrastructure expenditure	Per capita quality expenditure	Per capita expenditure in other programmes
Certified×Post2002	0.77*** (0.065)	0.864*** (0.072)	0.27*** (0.072)
N	18,592	18,592	18,592

Table 12G

	Dependent variable		
	Change in share of public enrolment	Change in share of primary public enrolment	Change in share of secondary public enrolment
Certified×Post2002	0.057*** (0.003)	0.027*** (0.003)	0.095*** (0.004)
N	20,271	20,271	20,176

Figure 12.A: Yearly effects of certification on per capita education expenditure from locally raised resources and total per capita education expenditure (net of teacher salaries)

a. Per capita expenditure in education from locally raised resources

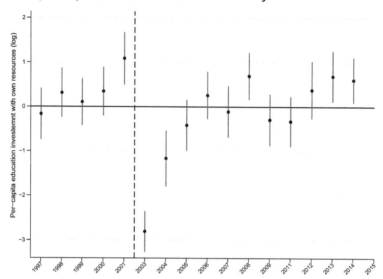

b. Per capita total expenditure in education deducting teacher salaries

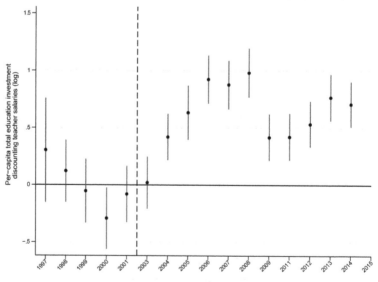

Source: Authors' calculations. Colombian National Planning Department.
Note: These graphs show the estimated coefficients of a difference-in-difference estimation that regresses the municipal per capita investment in each item on municipal certification for each year from 1997 to 2015. Dots represent estimated coefficients and the lines their corresponding confidence intervals. Municipal investment had a logarithmic transformation for the ease of interpretation.

Figure 12.B: The yearly effects of certification on per capita education expenditure on key accounts

a. School infrastructure

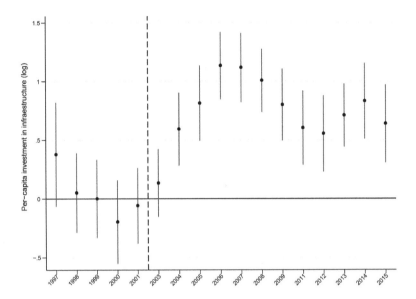

b. Other education-related programmes

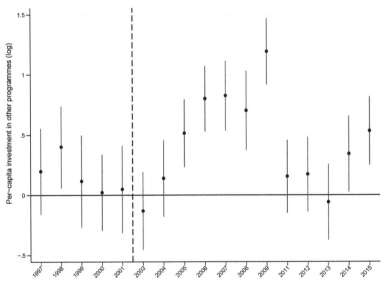

(*Continued*)

Figure 12.B: Continued

c. Education quality

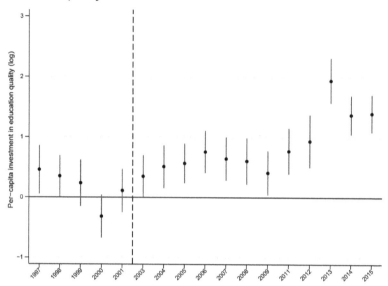

Source: Colombian National Planning Department. Author's calculations.
Note: These graphs show the estimated coefficients of a difference-in-difference
estimation that regresses the municipal per capita investment in each item on municipal
certification for each year from 1997 to 2015. Dots represent estimated coefficients
and the lines their corresponding confidence intervals. Municipal investment had a
logarithmic transformation for the ease of interpretation.

References

Alvarez, Horacio; Elacqua, Gregory; Piñeros, Luis; Rivera, Maria Camila;
and Santos, Humberto (2018) '¿Cómo mejorar la eficiencia y la equidad
de la inversión educativa en Colombia ante un panorama fiscal restric-
tivo?: Diagnóstico y propuestas' ['How to Improve the Efficiency and
Equity of Educational Investment in Colombia in a Restrictive Fiscal Scenario? Diagnosis and Proposals'], Nota Técnica Banco Interamericano de
Desarrollo No IDB-TN-1510. http://dx.doi.org/10.18235/0001327

Belmonte, Alessandro; Bove, Vincenzo; D'Inverno, Giovanna; and Modica,
Marco (2020) 'School Infrastructure Spending and Educational
Outcomes: Evidence from the 2012 Earthquake in Northern Italy',
Economics of Education Review, vol.75, p.101951.
http://dx.doi.org/10.1016/j.econedurev.2019.101951

Bonet, Jaime; Pérez, Javier; and Ayala, Jhorland (2014) 'Contexto histórico
y evolución del SGP en Colombia', Documentos de Trabajo sobre

Economía Regional No 205.
http://dx.doi.org/10.13140/RG.2.2.10598.01606

Borjas, George J. and Acosta, Olga Lucia (2000) 'Education Reform in
Colombia', Documentos de Trabajo (Working Papers Fedesarrollo No.19.
https://www.repository.fedesarrollo.org.co/handle/11445/820

Brutti, Zelda (2020) 'Cities Drifting Apart: Heterogeneous Outcomes of
Decentralizing Public Education', *IZA Journal of Labor Economics*, vol.9,
no.1. https://doi.org/10.2478/izajole-2020-0003

Brutti, Zelda and Sánchez, Fabio (2022) 'Turning around Teacher Quality
in Latin America: Renewed Confidence and Lessons from Colombia',
Economic Analysis and Policy, vol.73, pp.62–93.
https://doi.org/10.1016/j.eap.2021.10.008

Cortes, Darwin (2010) 'Do More Decentralized Local Governments Do
Better? An Evaluation of the 2001 Decentralization Reform in Colombia',
Universidad del Rosario Faculty of Economics Working Paper No.84.
http://dx.doi.org/10.2139/ssrn.1703543

Congreso de Colombia (2000). *Exposición de motivos 715 de 2001 Nivel
Nacional*. Congreso de Colombia, Gaceta del Congreso 294 de 2000.

Cuesta, Ana; Glewwe, Paul; and Krause, Brooke (2016) 'School Infrastructure and Educational Outcomes: A Literature Review, with Special
Reference to Latin America', *Economía*, vol.17, no.1, pp.95–130.
https://www.muse.jhu.edu/article/634033

Duarte, Jesus (2001) 'Política y educación: Tentaciones particularistas en la
educación latinoamericana', in Martinic, Sergio and Pardo, Marcela (eds)
Economía política de las reformas educativas en América Latina. Santiago
de Chile: Centro de Investigación y Desarrollo de la Educación.
https://www.thedialogue.org/wp-content/uploads/2016/04/2001
-Economia-Politica-de-las-Reformas-Educativas-en-America-Latina.pdf

Elacqua, Gregory; Munevar, Isabela; Sánchez, Fabio; and Santos, Hum-
berto (2021) 'The Impact of Decentralized Decision-Making on Student
Outcomes and Teacher Quality: Evidence from Colombia', *World
Development*, vol.141, p.105378. http://dx.doi.org/10.18235/0001822

Faguet, Jean-Paul and Sánchez, Fabio (2008) 'Decentralization's Effects on
Educational Outcomes in Bolivia and Colombia', *World Development*,
vol.36, no.7, pp.1294–316.
https://doi.org/10.1016/j.worlddev.2007.06.021

Faguet, Jean-Paul and Sánchez, Fabio (2014) 'Decentralization and Access to
Social Services in Colombia', *Public Choice*, vol.160, no.1–2, pp.227–49.
https://doi.org/10.1007/s11127-013-0077-7

Falleti, Tulia (2005) 'A Sequential Theory of Decentralization: Latin American Cases in Comparative Perspective', *American Political Science Review*, vol.99, no.3, pp.327–46. https://doi.org/10.1017/S0003055405051695

Falleti, Tulia (2010) *Decentralization and Sub National Politics in Latin America*, New York: Cambridge University Press. https://doi.org/10.1017/CBO9780511777813

Goldhaber, Dan D. and Brewer, Dominic J. (1996) 'Evaluating the Effect of Teacher Degree Level on Educational Performance', *Developments in School Finance*, U.S. Department of Education. https://eric.ed.gov/?id=ED406400

Hong, Kai and Zimmeron R. (2016) 'Does Investing in School Capital Infrastructure Improve Student Achievement?'. *Economics of Education Review*, vol.53, pp.143–58. https://doi.org/10.1016/j.econedurev.2016.05.007

Ministerio de Educación Nacional. (2002) 'Directivas Ministerial No.13 de 2002', https://www.mineducacion.gov.co/normatividad/1753/w3-article-86203 .html

Ministerio de Educación Nacional (2005) 'Guía No.9 Certificación de Municipios Menores de Cien Mil Habitantes' ['Guide No.9 Certification of Municipalities with Less than One Hundred Thousand Inhabitants']. https://www.mineducacion.gov.co/1759/articles-81012_archivo_pdf.pdf

Ome, Alejandro (2013) 'El Estatuto de profesionalización docente: Una primera evaluación' ['The Statute of Teacher Professionalization: A First Evaluation'], Cuadernos de Fedesarrollo No.43. Retrieved from https://www.repository.fedesarrollo.org.co/handle/11445/156

Pritchett, Lant (2014) 'The Risks to Education Systems from Design Mismatch and Global Isomorphism: Concepts, with Examples from India', WIDER Working Paper 2014/039. https://doi.org/10.35188/UNU-WIDER/2014/760-8

Pritchett, Lant and Pande, Varad (2006) 'Making Primary Education Work for India's Rural Poor: A Proposal for Effective Decentralization (English)', Social Development Papers No.95. South Asia series Washington, DC: World Bank Group. http://documents.worldbank.org/curated/en/748351468042304557 /Making-primary-education-work-for-Indias-rural-poor-a-proposal -for-effective-decentralization

Wall, Caitlin; Tolar-Peterson, Terezie; Reeder, Nicole; Roberts, Marina; Reynolds, Abby; and Rico Mendez, Gina (2022) 'The Impact of School Meal Programs on Educational Outcomes in African Schoolchildren: A Systematic Review', *International Journal of Environmental Research and Public Health*, vol.19, no.6, 3666. https://doi.org/10.3390/ijerph19063666

Wang, Dongqing and Fawzi, Wafaie W. (2020) 'Impacts of School Feeding on Educational and Health Outcomes of School-Age Children and Adolescents in Low- and Middle-Income Countries: Protocol for a Systematic Review and Meta-analysis', *Syst Rev*, vol.9, p.55. https://doi.org/10.1186/s13643-020-01317-6

Milton Keynes UK
Ingram Content Group UK Ltd.
UKHW022036270923
429511UK00009B/48